Celebrity Translation in British Theatre

BLOOMSBURY ADVANCES IN TRANSLATION SERIES

Series Editor
Jeremy Munday, Centre for Translation Studies, University of Leeds, UK

Bloomsbury Advances in Translation publishes cutting-edge research in the fields of translation studies. This field has grown in importance in the modern, globalized world, with international translation between languages a daily occurrence. Research into the practices, processes and theory of translation is essential and this series aims to showcase the best in international academic and professional output.

A full list of titles in the series can be found at:

www.bloomsbury.com/series/bloomsbury-advances-in-translation

Related titles in the series include

Collaborative Translation
Edited by Anthony Cordingley and Céline Frigau Manning

Community Translation
Mustapha Taibi and Uldis Ozolins

Intercultural Crisis Communication
Edited by Federico M. Federici and Christophe Declercq

Music, Text and Translation
Edited by Helen Julia Minors

Retranslation
Sharon Deane-Cox

Sociologies of Poetry Translation
Edited by Jacob Blakesley

Telling the Story of Translation
Judith Woodsworth

Translating For Singing
Ronnie Apter and Mark Herman

Translating in Town
Edited by Lieven D'hulst and Kaisa Koskinen

Translation, Adaptation and Transformation
Edited by Laurence Raw

Celebrity Translation in British Theatre

Relevance and Reception, Voice and Visibility

Robert Stock

BLOOMSBURY ACADEMIC
LONDON • NEW YORK • OXFORD • NEW DELHI • SYDNEY

BLOOMSBURY ACADEMIC
Bloomsbury Publishing Plc
50 Bedford Square, London, WC1B 3DP, UK
1385 Broadway, New York, NY 10018, USA
29 Earlsfort Terrace, Dublin 2, Ireland

BLOOMSBURY, BLOOMSBURY ACADEMIC and the Diana logo are trademarks of
Bloomsbury Publishing Plc

First published in Great Britain 2020
This paperback edition published in 2022

Copyright © Robert Stock, 2020

Robert Stock has asserted his right under the Copyright, Designs and
Patents Act, 1988, to be identified as Author of this work.

For legal purposes the Acknowledgements on p. x constitute an extension
of this copyright page.

Cover design: Ben Anslow

All rights reserved. No part of this publication may be reproduced or transmitted
in any form or by any means, electronic or mechanical, including photocopying,
recording, or any information storage or retrieval system, without prior
permission in writing from the publishers.

Bloomsbury Publishing Plc does not have any control over, or responsibility for,
any third-party websites referred to or in this book. All internet addresses given
in this book were correct at the time of going to press. The author and publisher
regret any inconvenience caused if addresses have changed or sites have
ceased to exist, but can accept no responsibility for any such changes.

A catalogue record for this book is available from the British Library.

A catalog record for this book is available from the Library of Congress.

Library of Congress Control Number: 2020940864

ISBN: HB: 978-1-3500-9784-1
PB: 978-1-3501-9913-2
ePDF: 978-1-3500-9785-8
eBook: 978-1-3500-9786-5

Series: Bloomsbury Advances in Translation

Typeset by Deanta Global Publishing Services, Chennai, India

To find out more about our authors and books visit www.bloomsbury.com and
sign up for our newsletters.

For Andrew

Celebrity status ... confers on the person a certain discursive power: within society, the celebrity is a voice above others, a voice that is channeled into the media systems as being legitimately significant.
(Marshall 1997: x)

Contents

List of figures		viii
Acknowledgements		x
Copyright acknowledgements		xi
1	Setting the scene	1
2	Celebrity translation in a theoretical context	11
3	Celebrity translation and relevance theory	31
4	Mark Ravenhill's version of Bertolt Brecht's *Leben des Galilei*	51
5	Roger McGough's version of Molière's *Tartuffe*	85
6	Simon Stephens's version of Henrik Ibsen's *Et dukkehjem*	117
7	From the theoretical to the empirical	161
8	Going forward	181
Notes		199
Select bibliography		202
References		203
Index		219

Figures

4.1	Visualization of layers of interpretation	64
4.2	Potential explicatures and implicatures derived from Brecht's source text (Scene 9)	65
4.3	Visualization of layers of interpretation (Scene 9)	65
4.4	Potential explicatures and implicatures derived from Brecht's source text (Scene 6)	68
4.5	Potential explicatures and implicatures derived from Ravenhill's translation (Scene 5)	68
4.6	First example of the conscious voice	69
4.7	Potential explicatures and implicatures derived from Brecht's source text (Scene 13)	72
4.8	Potential explicatures and implicatures derived from Ravenhill's translation (Scene 13)	74
4.9	Second example of the conscious voice	74
4.10	Potential explicatures and implicatures derived from Brecht's source text (Scene 1)	77
4.11	Potential explicatures and implicatures derived from Ravenhill's source text (Scene 1)	78
4.12	First example of the unconscious voice	79
4.13	Potential explicatures and implicatures derived from Brecht's source text (Scene 14)	81
4.14	Potential explicatures and implicatures derived from Ravenhill's translation (Scene 13)	81
4.15	Second example of the unconscious voice	82
5.1	Potential encyclopaedic entries attached to concept BLATHERSKITE*	93
5.2	Potential encyclopaedic entries attached to concept EROS*	98
5.3	Potential encyclopaedic entries attached to concept BEE*	99
5.4	Potential encyclopaedic entries attached to concept WRETCH/RETCH*	101
5.5	Potential encyclopaedic entries attached to concept CHEST*	102
5.6	Potential encyclopaedic entries attached to concept PRIORY*	104
5.7	Potential encyclopaedic entries attached to concept SWITCH FROM VERSE TO PROSE*	107
5.8	Potential encyclopaedic entries attached to concept ENJAMBMENT*	109
5.9	Potential encyclopaedic entries attached to concept DORINE'S SOCIOLECT*	111
5.10	Potential encyclopaedic entries attached to concept REPEATED EXOTICIZATION*	115
6.1	Chain of weak implicatures implying Englishness	133
6.2	Chain of weak implicatures implying Stephens's sympathies for Nora	135

6.3	Chain of weak implicatures implying emotionally damaged characters	147
6.4	Chain of weak implicatures implying drunkenness	151
6.5	Chain of weak implicatures implying a search for home	154
7.1	Frequency of words appearing in reviews and blogs	167
8.1	Pillars that construct voice	186

Acknowledgements

I would most of all like to express my huge gratitude to my former PhD supervisors, Professor Jean Boase-Beier and Dr Chantal Wright, for their unfailing support throughout the writing of this book. I could not have embarked on this journey without the initial inspiration that they provided or completed it without their constant encouragement. I feel fortunate to now count them among my friends.

Thanks are also due to my celebrity translators, Mark Ravenhill, Roger McGough and Simon Stephens, for their interest in my project and their patience with my questions. This book would not have existed without them. I am also hugely grateful for the assistance provided by literal translators Deborah Gearing and Charlotte Barslund, who generously gave their time and allowed me a unique insight into their role in the celebrity translation process. I am delighted that I have been able to help them and other literal translators become more visible. Equally, I am grateful for the valuable input provided by those who helped to market the plays that feature in my case studies – particularly Richard Leigh at Birmingham Rep, Dominic Beaumont at Liverpool Everyman and Playhouse, and Lucy Gilham at the Young Vic.

I would like to acknowledge the huge number of translation, stylistics and theatre studies scholars who have helped me during the writing of this book, either by responding to my often persistent requests for information and advice with grace and enthusiasm, letting me pick their estimable brains or simply giving me a word of praise or two when I needed it most. There are too many of you to list here – which conveniently means I don't have to apologize to anyone I may have forgotten. Such a large group of encouraging well-wishers only serves to remind us of both the challenges and the rewards of multidisciplinary works such as this one – and of the need to continue championing such work if we are to encourage greater collaboration between scholars, and between the academy and the commercial world.

I must also thank my commissioning editor, Andrew Wardell, as well as Becky Holland, Lianna Iwanikiw and the rest of the team at Bloomsbury for their encouragement from the outset, for calmly responding to my never-ending queries and for smoothing the process from initial draft to completed manuscript. I have thoroughly enjoyed the process, and hope this is just the start of my career as an author.

Final thanks go to my husband, Andrew – for believing in me throughout the writing of this book and beyond, particularly when I didn't dare to believe in myself. I promise there will be no more mountains to climb now – or at least not until the next book.

Copyright acknowledgements

The author and publisher are grateful to the copyright holders of the following material for permission to reprint extracts:

Bertolt-Brecht-Erben/Suhrkamp Verlag, Berlin, for extracts from *Leben des Galilei* by Bertolt Brecht (copyright © 1963).

Bertolt-Brecht-Erben, Berlin, for extracts from *A Life of Galileo* by Mark Ravenhill (copyright © 2013).

Bloomsbury Methuen Drama, London, for extracts from *Tartuffe* by Roger McGough (copyright © 2008) and *A Doll's House* by Simon Stephens (copyright © 2012).

Peters Fraser & Dunlop, London, on behalf of Roger McGough for 'Prayer to Saint Grobianus' reproduced from *Collected Poems* by Roger McGough (copyright © 1994).

Full details of all works can be found in the References.

1

Setting the scene

What is celebrity translation?

In the UK, the translation of theatre is often a two-tier process. Celebrity playwrights or poets (i.e. playwrights or poets who are already well known in their own right) are frequently commissioned to adapt a play using either previously published translations or adaptations, or a specially commissioned literal translation. Such a process appears to date back to a shift in British theatrical practice in the 1960s, when there was a move away from relying on supposedly definitive translations of canonical works to commissioning a fresh translation for each new production (Hampton 2011: 174). In spite of being such a well-established modus operandi, however, the particular role of the celebrity translator in the theatre continues to raise many unanswered questions for translation scholars about how we evaluate theatre translation and how useful existing theories of translation are in describing and reflecting the specific issues relating to the translation of play texts.

The particular aim of this book is to explore the extent to which celebrity translators inject some of their own voice into their translations – either intentionally, because this is part of the brief from the commissioner of the work, or unconsciously, because of the way in which their own experience, style, values, agenda, personality and so on combine to define and perpetuate their status as well-known playwrights. This issue echoes ideas that have emerged in the field of cognitive poetics (and particularly in relevance theory), which explore the effects that a text has on the cognitive state of the reader in the light of the contextual background of the text, its author and its receivers (see Sperber and Wilson 1995; Carston 2002a; Boase-Beier 2015, 2020 and Clark 2013).

Little scholarly attention has so far been paid to the phenomenon of celebrity translation in the theatre, either in theatre studies or in translation studies. A number of scholars (including Bassnett 1991; Perteghella 2004a; Anderman 2005; Marinetti 2013b and Brodie 2018) have explored the issue of two-stage translation in the theatre. But contributions to the literature so far tend to focus on the translation process itself and how this fits with the other artistic processes involved in staging a production. As yet, it appears that no one has investigated in detail the precise role of the celebrity translator in terms of either the influence of celebrity on text *production* or, more importantly, the influence of celebrity on *reception* of that text by the audience. This is the research gap that I intend to fill with this book.

The aspect of celebrity translation in the theatre that fascinates me most is the extent to which well-known translators of play texts inevitably bring with them (1) an identifiable and possibly even *ownable* personal style that will be recognized by spectators who are already familiar (either directly or indirectly) with the celebrity's previous work in and beyond the theatre, and (2) a well-established public profile, which may lead to spectators accessing a variety of contextual assumptions about what the celebrity is attempting to communicate in his or her translation, again on the basis of the spectator's understanding of the celebrity's existing work and persona. So the questions I will be exploring in the following chapters are as follows:

1. To what extent do celebrity translators inject some of their own voice into their translations, either intentionally or unconsciously, because of the way in which their own experience, style, values and so on inevitably permeate their work as a translator?
2. How does the synergy between the source-text playwright's voice and the celebrity translator's voice affect reception of the translated text by audiences?
3. To what extent might celebrity translators attract a different audience to translated drama from unknown translators?
4. Which external (extratextual) influences might impact on the inferences that spectators draw from a performance of a play translated by a celebrity translator (e.g. theatre critics' reviews, theatre bloggers and social media posts)?

I will be analysing the published versions of three play texts translated into English: *A Life of Galileo* by Bertolt Brecht, adapted by playwright Mark Ravenhill (2013a); *Tartuffe* by Molière, adapted by poet Roger McGough (2008); and *A Doll's House* by Henrik Ibsen, adapted by playwright Simon Stephens (2012). In each case, I will compare selected excerpts from the source and the target texts with a view to demonstrating the extent to which spectators may infer dimensions of the celebrity translator's authorial voice from their respective translations. The theoretical framework that I will use in each of my case studies is relevance theory. I will explore in turn the effects of the explicatures and implicatures, the encyclopaedic entries, and the chains of weak implicatures that spectators may access from the play text, citing specific examples from the published versions of those texts. My aim will be to show how spectators' existing cognitive contexts and associations with the celebrity translator might influence the way in which they interpret that celebrity translator's text, and thereby the extent to which they infer some of that celebrity's familiar authorial voice. I will also explore the findings from quantitative and qualitative analysis of material from a variety of external sources (reviews, blogs and social media posts). This is intended to validate the conclusions drawn from my textual analysis and support my overall argument about how audiences may infer the celebrity translator's voice.

Implicit in my exploration of these issues is an attempt to justify, and indeed celebrate, the role of celebrity translators in the British theatrical system. By adding a new perspective on the *performability* and *performativity* debate that pervades much of scholars' thinking about theatre translation (e.g. Bigliazzi, Kofler and Ambrosi 2013; Marinetti 2013b and Brodie 2018), I intend not only to defend the practice of two-tier translation from a theoretical perspective (and thereby to defend the role of the literal translator as well), but also to demonstrate the benefits that this practice brings to the UK theatre market, not least in terms of potentially attracting new audiences to translated theatre, and ideally even broadening the repertoire of play texts that are translated.

This book is also designed to challenge some of the existing ideas within translation studies regarding the visibility of the translator, and more generally to add to our growing understanding of the role played by the receiver's cognitive context in the analysis of translation and the relationship between source and target texts. In particular, I will seek to foreground the role that the audience plays in the theatre translation process and highlight how audiences themselves can act as champions of translated theatre in the UK. I trust that my work will be of interest not only to translation scholars but also to the theatrical community. By showcasing and championing the cause of celebrity translators and their role in raising the profile of plays in translation in the UK, I hope I will also be able to have some influence on attitudes to the commissioning, funding, staging and marketing of translated play texts going forward.

Defining *celebrity translator*

The term 'celebrity' appears to be used increasingly often in contemporary culture to describe anyone in the public eye, however fleetingly – from a member of the royal family to a member of the general public who appears in a reality television show, or from the winner of a talent contest to the winner of a Nobel prize. As celebrity studies scholar Sean Redmond notes, 'In academic terms, the term "celebrity" is used to define a person whose name, image, lifestyle and opinions carry cultural and economic worth' (2014: 5). And as celebrity culture becomes ever more pervasive, and celebrity studies becomes more widely established as an academic discipline, this relative balance of cultural and economic worth is increasingly called into question.

The very notion of celebrity, after all, is predicated on the fundamental logic of consumerism and commercial value (see Marshall 1997 and Turner 2013). Modern-day celebrity culture has spawned an entire industry of press titles, television programmes and social media channels. And it clearly has a considerable impact on the wider economy, whether in terms of the fees that celebrities can command for their work, the price that audiences are prepared to pay to gain access to that work, or the sums that celebrities will spend to maintain or enhance their cultural capital. Celebrities have thereby become commodities that agencies in any given culture can buy, sell, invest in and ultimately divest of in the same way as any other tradable good – what celebrity scholar Graeme Turner describes as 'a very powerful form of legitimation for capitalism's models of exchange and value' (2013: 28).

From the consumer's point of view, on the other hand, sociologist Ellis Cashmore suggests that 'celebrities perform important functions in a mature capitalist economy in which consumer demand is paramount. ... They are parts of an industrial process that maintains our spending levels while keeping us pleasantly occupied' (2006: 264). Media scholar P. David Marshall, meanwhile, sees celebrities as playing a more fundamental role for their admirers, representing 'subject positions that audiences can adopt or adapt in the formation of social identities' (1997: 65). Reflecting on why contemporary society should so often be in thrall to celebrity status, Redmond similarly suggests that 'celebrity matters because it exists so centrally to the way we communicate and are understood to communicate with one another in the modern world. Celebrity culture involves the transmission of power relations, is connected to identity formation and notions of shared belonging' (2014: 3).

Marshall even goes so far as to suggest that all of us in the wider populace who work in the knowledge economy or who engage in social media effectively have a public as well as a private persona. As such, he calls for further investigation of what he terms 'persona studies' – a field of study that allows us to explore 'contradictions of construction and agency throughout the culture and to see how, through various forces of change and transformation which include changes in work, transformation of our forms of social connection and networking via new technologies, and consequent new affective clusters and micropublics, we are witnessing and charting a new constitution of public identity' (2014: 166).

I'm interested in exploring how the issues surrounding the construct of celebrity influence the process and reception of the translation of plays. How might the public persona, that is, either the version of the self that an individual creates or the version of that individual that the audience constructs (which may or may not coincide), influence the way in which we receive his or her translations? And how might the cultural representations that celebrities believe that we hold of them influence the way in which they carry out the process of translation? What influences might other agents in the theatrical system exert on the translator as part of this network of power relations, and how might this affect the reception of translation?

I should point out before I go any further that I will be using the term *celebrity* throughout this book as a shorthand descriptor for those translators who will be known to the audience of their translations for other things, such as their own plays or poetry, or their more general public profile. In no way am I implying that these well-known translators are therefore part of modern-day mainstream celebrity culture, with all the negative connotations that this implies in terms of obsessive interest on the part of the media, and image manipulation and the craving of fame and a celebrity lifestyle on the part of the translators (see de Botton 2014: n.p.).

There are, of course, countless examples of source-text authors of fiction and non-fiction who are celebrities in their own right, whether by virtue of their literary success (e.g. authors such as J. K. Rowling or Stephen King who regularly top bestseller lists), their concomitant media profile (e.g. celebrity chefs such as Jamie Oliver or Nigella Lawson who turn television series into successful books) or simply their literary longevity (e.g. William Shakespeare or Charles Dickens). Examples of *translators* of such authors (or indeed of any authors) who are well-known figures in their own right are, however, more difficult to identify, at least in English-speaking markets. Only in Japan does there appear to be a strong culture of celebrity translators of fiction – an aftereffect of the respect that translators earned for their role in introducing foreign literature into Japanese culture during the country's cultural modernization (see Hadley and Akashi 2015).

The phenomenon of the celebrity translator might already be well established in the field of poetry translation in the Anglophone world. Seamus Heaney, for example, was already a well-known Irish poet, playwright, academic and occasional translator before gaining widespread international acclaim for his 1999 translation of *Beowulf*. British poet Ted Hughes also published translations of poetry, and co-founded the journal *Modern Poetry in Translation*. Contemporary Anglophone poets who also translate other poets include Fleur Adcock, Simon Armitage and Michael Hoffmann. But it is in the *theatre* that celebrity translators are most widely known, to the extent that they have become a regular feature of the British theatrical system.

It now appears to be a readily accepted practice to commission new translations of canonical foreign plays by well-known playwrights each time a new production is staged. In part, this appears to be at the request of directors, who, according to playwright and translator Christopher Hampton, 'are now firmly wedded to the idea of renewing the franchise every time' (2011: 176). To give just a couple of examples, up to the time of writing in 2020 there had been three new British productions of Anton Chekhov's *The Seagull* since 2014 alone, two in London and one in Chichester. These were translated by playwrights Anya Reiss (2014), David Hare (2015) and Simon Stephens (2017). Meanwhile, in the autumn of 2013, there were two different productions of Henrik Ibsen's *Ghosts* being performed in the Greater London area at the same time, one translated by director Richard Eyre at the Almeida Theatre in Islington and the other translated by director Stephen Unwin at the Rose Theatre in Kingston upon Thames. And over and above any influence that directors might have, it would be naïve not to acknowledge producers' and theatres' motivations for wishing to work with a celebrity translator, which may in many cases be commercially as well as artistically driven.

More importantly for the purposes of this book, celebrity translators themselves also have their personal motivations for producing their own adaptations from scratch, usually from a specially commissioned literal translation. On top of any pragmatic reasons for seeking to do this (e.g. copyright issues), working from a supposedly *neutral* translation (i.e. one that has not already been optimized for performance by an experienced playwright) clearly gives celebrity translators the artistic freedom to create their own 'original' work in their own voice without being constrained or overly influenced by another playwright's work – or at least, in principle. As Hampton points out, 'There is a proliferation of versions of most plays around and the fatal thing would be to look at anyone else's, because then you start to think: that's rather good. So it's best not to look at them at all' (2011: 177).

Such continual reimagining of canonical plays does, of course, raise the question as to whether celebrity translations are often actually translations at all, or whether they are more like new plays that are inspired by the original work. In turn, we could ask ourselves whether celebrity translators really are translators, or whether their role is more one of an editor whose job as professional writers is essentially about 'tidying up' a literal translation or previous translations in order to optimize appeal among audiences. Such questions are compounded by the lack of consistency in terminology that translators and directors choose to use. For example, when asked why the front cover of his version of Luigi Pirandello's *The Rules of the Game* claimed that it was 'translated and adapted by' him, playwright David Hare responded, 'I didn't use those descriptions. They stuck them on. It really made me quite queasy when they said "translation" because I said "I don't speak Italian, how can you say I translated it?" I asked them if they could credit the person who did the literal translation but they told me I was better known' (cited in Johnston 1996: 143).

In reality, translations of play texts exist along a broad spectrum. At one end of that spectrum, there are examples of works that closely mirror the source texts in terms of content and style, such as Christopher Hampton's translations of French playwright Yasmina Reza's plays *Art* (1996), *Life x 3* (2001) and *God of Carnage* (2008), whose success suggests that British audiences can indeed respond positively to contemporary French drama in translation (albeit in a domesticated form) if given the chance (see Chapter 8 for more thoughts on this). At the other extreme, we can find examples of theatrical adaptations that are only loosely based on a work originally written in another language, such as Mark Ravenhill's *Candide* (2013), which claims merely to have been 'inspired by' Voltaire's novella.

At first glance, the very nature of celebrity translation might imply that celebrity translators would choose (or be encouraged) to work more at the inspirational end of this spectrum, preferring the opportunity to give free rein to their creativity and express their own voice rather than being forced to work within the confines of another writer's content and style. At the same time, the fact that many (although by no means all) celebrity translators are monolingual[1] might indicate that they have a different level of respect for the source text and the source-text culture than those who are able to read and engage directly with the text that they are translating without the aid of a literal translation. This could potentially lead to a more self-indulgent reworking of the source text that is less constrained by a linguistic empathy with the culture within which it was written.

In fact, there are examples of celebrity theatre translations across this entire spectrum if we assess them purely at a textual level. But the existence of such a wide variety of approaches appears to have less to do with well-known playwrights' different levels of respect for other playwrights' work and more to do with the theatrical system in which celebrity translators operate, that is, the demands placed on these translators to meet the expectations of the director, the production company, the theatre itself and indeed in some cases the trustees of the source-text playwright's estate.

Such issues will be discussed in more detail in later sections of this chapter, which explore how literary and cultural theories (in translation studies and beyond) can help us to understand the phenomenon of celebrity translation. Before then, however, I would like to clarify what exactly I mean when I use the term *voice*.

Defining *voice*

Given how central the issue of *voice* is to my book, I would like at this point to reflect on exactly what I mean by the term. This appears useful not least because voice is a concept that is understood in a variety of different ways by language and literature scholars, whether they be translation scholars or scholars in fields such as cognitive linguistics or literary studies.

Voice is defined by narratologist Gerald Prince as 'the set of signs characterizing the narrator and, more generally, the narrating instance, and governing the relations between narrating and narrative text as well as between narrating and narrated' (1998: 102). Similarly, stylistician Katie Wales suggests that 'voice is popularly used in literary criticism and stylistics … to describe "one who speaks" in a narrative, whether the implied author or character or both' (2011: 347). Both of these definitions, however, emphasize *who* in the text is talking to the reader (or, in the case of my research, the spectator), rather than necessarily *how* he or she is talking to them. And it's the *how* that I am much more concerned with when I talk about the celebrity translator's voice. How does the celebrity translator convey some of his or her own distinctive style, and how is this distinctive style heard by the receiver of the celebrity translator's text? In any case, a focus on *who* is speaking in the context of theatre texts is potentially likely to lead to some confusion with the physical voice of the playwright's characters and the actors playing those characters.

Translator and theatre scholar Richard Aczel's definition of voice as 'an umbrella term for the field of questions relating to the speech acts of the narrator, ranging from narrative situation to narrative idiom' (2005: 634) appears to come closer to addressing the *how*, given the way that he introduces the notion of *idiom* to describe an author's or a character's idiosyncratic way of expressing himself or herself. At the same time, though, his definition appears to me to be so unspecific as to be unlikely to help my own exploration of voice, at least without defining what this field of questions might comprise, and where those speech acts occur.

Given that none of these existing definitions of voice entirely encapsulates exactly how I am seeking to discuss voice in this book, I would like at this point to step back from how voice is *defined* and look more generally at how the term is *used in practice* by language and literary scholars, whether this is concretely laid out in definition form or not. One of the first things that becomes apparent is the frequent confusion surrounding the distinction between *voice* and *point of view* (the latter described by Prince as the *means* by which the narrative conveys what is being seen or perceived – 1998: 102), and between *voice* and *style* (which could be said to comprise the qualitative dimensions of voice in a text, such as register, idiom, tone and so on, that the receiver of that text infers). Such confusion is hardly surprising given the way in which the term *voice* is commonly used even among language and literary scholars to refer both to the perspective from which an author, a narrator or a character is talking – which according to the definitions above might be subsumed under *voice* as well as *point of view* – *and* to the way in which that author, narrator or character is talking – which might be described as his or her *style*, but could also encompass aspects of *voice* or *point of view* as well.

The conflation of *voice* and *style* would appear to be typical of the way in which *narrative voice* is generally viewed among stylisticians and translation theorists. So, when critics refer to an author's voice, they are usually talking about the style of that author's writing (say, his or her use of a particular vocabulary, syntax, type of dialogue, etc.) rather than the narrator's voice. This equates to stylistician Mick Short's first proposed type of *authorial style*, namely, 'a way of writing which recognisably belongs to a particular writer, [that] distinguishes one author's writing from that of others, and is felt to be recognisable across a range of texts written by the same writer' (1996: 327). And it's authorial style in *this* sense that most easily enables us to infer an author's voice – and to recognize it as a familiar voice if we are already aware of that author.

Among translation theorists, meanwhile, there is also a generally held view that the author's voice and the translator's voice are two entirely distinct entities. As translation scholars Jean Boase-Beier and Michael Holman note, the act of translation inevitably involves 'a compromise between faithfulness and freedom, between the need to be true to one's own and the author's voice' (1998: 10). As a result, the words or lines that the reader or the spectator receives in the target language are unquestionably those of the translator rather than the source-text author, irrespective of whether the receiver actively recognizes the act of translation or not. But if we accept the translation scholar's view that the author and the translator are inevitably present in the text, then we must also acknowledge that receivers of that text are potentially able to infer both the author's and the translator's voice in that text as well (see Hermans 1996). The fact that a celebrity translator's style, or voice, is more easily recognizable than that of, say, a translator whose work is barely credited is not to say that unknown translators have no style or voice of their own. Rather, it's simply a reflection of the fact that the celebrity translator's voice is more easily *definable* by virtue of its familiarity. But what exactly should receivers be familiar with in order to be able to hear these two voices and the relative balance between them?

Voice in the sense in which I will be using the term in this book, then, is about more than just the celebrity translator's particular lexical, grammatical or syntactic tics, important though these might be in helping us to infer that celebrity's voice. A celebrity translator's voice may also be inferred more generally from that celebrity's behaviour, demeanour, attitudes, personality, life history, world view and so on – in other words, all those factors and influences that go towards making him or her a celebrity in the first place. This echoes Short's second type of authorial style, which he terms *fingerprinting* (1996: 329) and which is echoed in translation scholar Mona Baker's notion of style as 'a kind of thumb-print that is expressed in a range of linguistic – as well as non-linguistic – features' (Baker 2000: 245). For Short and Baker, then, 'style can be perceived in any consistent writing, literary or otherwise, or, indeed, in *any consistent behaviour*, linguistic or otherwise' (Short 1996: 329, author's italics). *Voice* is therefore not simply a given quality that is present in a text, but rather a construct built by the receiver who interprets that text. This reflects the reader-response view of how texts are interpreted, namely, that receivers create their own, possibly unique, construction of a text, which is the only construction that gives that text its true existence (see Fish 1980 and Tyson 2015).

With this in mind, then, I would like at this point to propose the following definition of voice for the purposes of this book.

> *The summation of all the associations that a receiver attaches to an author (whether of a source text or a translated text), either on the basis of the specific text or utterance that the receiver is interpreting at the time, or as a consequence of any previous experience with that author (either actual or perceived) arising from textual or non-textual interaction.*

Of course, any discussion of voice in the context of translation in the theatre begs questions about the influence of the *actors' voices* on reception of a translation in performance. This adds another layer of complexity to the construct of the celebrity translator's voice, since this is inevitably bound up with the audience's associations with the actors whose actual, human voices are delivering the celebrity translator's text. To give an example from the first case study explored in this book, Mark Ravenhill's adaptation of Bertolt Brecht's *A Life of Galileo*, Galileo was played (both in the original Royal Shakespeare Company production and the production that subsequently toured England) by Ian McDiarmid, who will most likely have been known to many spectators primarily from playing Darth Sidious and Emperor Palpatine in many of the *Star Wars* films. This will arguably have had a significant influence on these spectators' interpretations of Ravenhill's work, to say nothing of their possible motivations for attending performances of that work in the first place. The role of the actor's voice in influencing reception of translated dramatic texts, particularly the interrelation between celebrity actors and celebrity translators, is clearly an area that is ripe for research, but one that is beyond the scope of this book.

For translation scholars, meanwhile, discussion of voice in this context also raises the question of what happens to the voice of the *literal translator* if the celebrity translator has made use of a literal translation to create his or her own work. The role of the literal translator in the creation of the celebrity translator's text is often overlooked, both artistically and financially. But the literal translator's text must inevitably inform the point of view held by the celebrity translator, if not the celebrity translator's style. Just as the source-text author is inevitably present in the translated text, then so too, surely, is the literal translator. This adds an additional dimension to the blend of voices inferred by spectators, even if they are only unconsciously hearing the literal translator's voice. This issue will become clearer when I directly compare a celebrity translation with its corresponding literal translation in Chapter 4.

2

Celebrity translation in a theoretical context

Celebrity translation and theories of translation

Why look at theories of translation anyway?

In this section, I'm interested in exploring whether theories of translation can offer an insight into the phenomenon of celebrity translation, and whether they can help to explain some of the translation strategies adopted by celebrity translators. This isn't intended to be an in-depth exploration of translation studies and its theories per se, but rather an overview of the kinds of ideas that can help us to explain the practice and process of celebrity translation in the British theatre – and hopefully one that readers who are not themselves language scholars will also engage with.

Jean Boase-Beier offers the following view of the usefulness of translation theories. 'Because … theories are partial, descriptive and represent different ways of seeing, they should enable us to free ourselves from naïve conceptions of what translation is. And because they are explanatory they become part of the way we approach the world in a very practical sense' (2010: 27). It's probably unrealistic to assume that any of the celebrity translators explored in this book are themselves aware of translation theories to any large extent or have actively applied them to their work. But where these translators have worked from a literal translation by a professional translator, there is a greater case for speculating whether this direct translation *was* influenced by translation theory. Indeed, the very act of taking on a commission to produce a literal translation surely already presupposes at least some understanding of concepts such as *equivalence* and *faithfulness* to the source text (used here and throughout this book in the sense of *equivalent* or *faithful* to the meaning of the source text, however we might choose to define *meaning* in practice – see Chapter 3). After all, these concepts are inherent in the very notion of *literal translation*.

In the following, I will explore celebrity translation from the perspective of three distinct areas addressed in various theories of translation that appear particularly pertinent to my argument in this book (systems and norms, skopos, and the interrelated issues of domestication, foreignization and visibility) before looking outside translation studies to see what we can learn from theories in other fields.

Systems and norms

Translation scholar Itamar Even-Zohar first discussed the position of translated literature within the literary polysystem in the 1970s. *Polysystem* in this context is used to refer to 'the stratified conglomerate of interconnected elements, which changes and mutates as these elements interact with each other' (Shuttleworth and Cowie 2014: 127). Even-Zohar argues that literature in translation should be seen as a system in its own right with the same sort of 'cultural and verbal network of relations' (2004: 199) between texts as that which exists between indigenous texts in a culture's literary system. He goes on to suggest that translated texts correlate with one another to create their own sub-system in at least two ways – in the way that the target literary culture *selects* the source texts to be translated and in the way that those selected source texts then *adopt certain norms and behaviours* as a result of their relations with the other co-systems of the target culture's literary system (2004: 200).

This first notion of how the target culture selects texts for translation is worth looking at in the context of celebrity translation in the British theatre. That's because it can potentially help us to understand why certain foreign-language play texts are translated with almost predictable regularity, while others appear to be overlooked or even ignored. In this respect, theatre translation scholar Cristina Marinetti notes, somewhat depressingly, that 'the percentage of translations commissioned and produced by British theatres is minimal compared to other countries, even in the most established and publicly funded theatres' (2013a: 29). She also cites data (originally quoted by Bradley 2011: 191–2) to show that of the 250 plays produced by the National Theatre in London between 1995 and 2006, only 41, or 16.4 per cent were translations. More importantly, the plays selected for translation appear to come from an extremely narrow repertoire.

> While Greek, Russian, German, Norwegian and French plays appear at first sight to be well represented, different productions of Oresteia and Oedipus count for over 70% of the Greek plays, the Russian titles are mostly Chekhov, the German Brecht and the Norwegian Ibsen, the French contribution is made up entirely of Marivaux and Molière, while the Swedish and Italian correspond to Strindberg and Eduardo respectively. So not only do mainstream British theatres not invest in translations, but when they do they do not go for new or lesser known authors, they retranslate the classics. (Marinetti 2013a: 30)

Such statistics would appear to confirm Even-Zohar's claim that translated literature has 'a repertoire of its own' (2004: 200), and Lefevere's assertion that sub-systems in the target culture determine which texts will be translated and which ones will not (1992: 14). In the case of the National Theatre, the decision would appear to be primarily driven by economics. As playwright, dramaturg and translator Jack Bradley points out, 'If a show does not take off, then the theatre may find itself staring at a sizeable period of pre-announced performances for which it cannot give away the tickets. … There is a perpetual tension between the temptation to be conservative and the wish to be daring. The question is which impulse wins out' (2011: 190). This question is also an extremely relevant one to consider in the study of celebrity translators, as these translators' work is also subject to the same tension between financial security and risk, and between artistic conservatism and audacity. Bradley's statement is a reminder of the pressure that celebrity translators are placed under, either implicitly or explicitly, to justify their involvement in the creative process (and, of course, their fee) by delivering a profitable production to the theatres that commission their translations. So it would be naïve to assume that such pressure does not, to some extent at least, influence the translation process.

Even-Zohar's second notion of how translated texts create their own sub-systems in the target literary culture by adopting certain norms and behaviours is also interesting to explore in the context of celebrity translation in the theatre. This is because it raises the issue as to what the norms and behaviours in the theatrical system actually are that encourage the use of celebrity translators, and what it is about the UK theatrical system that means that the culture of celebrity translation is much more widespread in this market than in other parts of Europe.

Theatre translation scholar Sirkku Aaltonen argues that a theatrical system is 'a living organism coexisting in a symbiotic relationship with other social and cultural systems', and that translators working within these systems in a particular time and place 'do not act as independent individuals' but rather behave as members of 'a specific culture and society, working for a particular stage at a certain point in time' (2000: 5). With this in mind, it is useful to consider celebrity translation from the perspective of the translation norms originally identified by translation scholar Gideon Toury in the 1970s. That is because these norms can help us to start to understand why celebrity translators exist in the first place and what their role is within the target literary system. Toury's concept of preliminary norms (2004: 209) encompasses norms that could be said to define a definite *translation policy*, and norms related to the *directness* of translation. These issues echo actual behaviour by agents within the theatrical system that govern when and under what circumstances a celebrity translator might be involved in a production. As a result, they can offer us a useful starting point for evaluating the role of the celebrity translator and the external influences on his or her translations.

The gatekeeper of translation in the theatre is typically the literary department, which will be responsible for commissioning translations (either literal translations or indirect translations by a celebrity translator). The translation policy in any given literary department might involve (either explicitly or implicitly) favouring specific translators or particular translation styles. In any event, such preferences will in turn be influenced by the policy of the theatre's artistic director at the time. For example, the Royal Court Theatre in London is renowned not only for foregrounding work by unknown foreign playwrights but also for preferring more direct translations of source texts as a starting point for the development of the target text. Its website points to a very specific translation policy and view on the *directness* of translation.

> All plays submitted to the international department are read in the original language by a team of appointed readers. The department then commissions translations of plays selected for further development. The department has pioneered the use of

theatre practitioners as translators and the integral involvement of the translator in the play development and rehearsal process. Many of the translations are eventually published. (Royal Court Theatre 2014: n.p.)

This compares with a much stricter division of roles at the National Theatre in London, where translation policy is much more about foregrounding the celebrity translator. As Laura Gribble, translator for the National Theatre, explained in a panel discussion on translation at the theatre in 2003,

> The way we try to do it here at the National is that the translator who does the first translation, and who knows the language, does as accurate a translation as possible without worrying too much about making it work as a stage play. The person who then does the stage version would ideally work quite closely with the person who did the literal. (National Theatre 2014: n.p.)

Such a policy is in turn reflected in the National Theatre's practice of always commissioning a new translation of a play text each time it stages a foreign-language play. This is a demonstration of the mediating role of translation that Toury refers to in his discussion of preliminary norms (1995: 82), and of the directness (or lack of directness) of the translation. So, in the case of the National Theatre, we can see that translation is not only indirect in the sense that there is a literal translation acting as mediator between the source text and the ultimate target text (i.e. the document itself acts as mediator). It's also indirect in the sense that each new translation of the same source text plays a different mediating role for each of the agents in the theatrical process, whether it be the director expecting to work with a script that inspires a fresh look at an already familiar play, or the audience hoping for a new and distinctive theatrical experience.

Toury's preliminary norms, then, offer a potentially useful way of theorizing the process of theatre translation, in the sense that they help us to understand both the relationships between the different agents in the process (including the audience) and the 'in-between' role of the literal translation and the literal translator. But while this might be intriguing in itself as a way of studying celebrity translators, I am actually more interested in the way in which the celebrity translator's *voice* is inferred and interpreted by the audience, rather than simply the way in which the celebrity translator and his or her text fit into the theatrical system. With this in mind, then, we need to look to theories that can help to explain the factors that contribute to the *audience's reception* of celebrity translation.

Skopos

The notion of *skopos* (Greek for *aim* or *purpose*) in translation was first discussed in the 1970s by translation scholar Hans J. Vermeer (1970, 1978) and later developed by Vermeer and fellow scholar Katharina Reiß (Reiß and Vermeer 1984). According to skopos theory, 'the aim of any translational action, and the mode in which it is to be realized, are negotiated with the client who commissions the action' (Vermeer

2004: 227). At a practical level, then, skopos theory addresses the issue of the status of the source text, and subsequently of the target text, and the need for translators to be aware of this during the act of translating. It puts forward the idea that it is the *purpose* of the translation that will determine the way in which a text is translated so as to 'produce a functionally adequate result' (Reiß and Vermeer 1984: 119) and a degree of 'intertextual coherence' between target and source text (Vermeer 2004: 229).

This idea does, of course, raise the question as to how we identify and define the status of a text and the purpose of its translation. This is surely particularly difficult in the case of literary texts, where the notions of status and purpose might easily vary between translations, individuals, timeframes and cultures, to the extent that the concept of intertextual coherence becomes a somewhat vague and hypothetical goal. Having said this, skopos theory does introduce two important ideas that are of particular importance to the discussion of celebrity translators.

The first of these is the translation commission, or *Auftrag*, defined by Vermeer as 'the instruction, given by oneself or by someone else, to carry out a given action' (2004: 235). According to Vermeer, the commission should specify the goal of the translation and the conditions under which the intended goal should be obtained – and here, he is thinking primarily about practical issues such as deadlines and fees. In the context of celebrity translation, the concept of *Auftrag* inherently also encompasses the instructions given to the celebrity translator by the commissioner (who could be any one of a number of agents in the theatrical system, from the director or the producer to the head of a theatre's literary department) about the aim of the new theatrical work. Such instructions may well often indicate the expected fit with the theatre's artistic vision and goals, the assumed target audience for this work and the degree of 'originality' (however that might be defined) that the director or theatre company is hoping for compared with previous translations of the same work.

Implicit in these instructions is the degree to which celebrity translators are *expected* to inject some of their own voice into their work. And as this notion of the distinctive voice of the celebrity translator is a central theme of this book, skopos theory potentially provides a highly useful framework within which to describe and assess both the role of the celebrity translator (and indeed of the literal translator) and the relationship between the source and the target texts. Most importantly, by overtly acknowledging the possibility that the same text can be translated in different ways depending on the skopos of the translation (Vermeer 2004: 234), skopos theory effectively justifies both the retranslation and the *revoicing* of canonical play texts in a way that more equivalence-focused translation concepts would typically fail to do.

The second issue raised by skopos theory that is particularly relevant to my argument is that of the relative importance and influence of the different participants in the translation process. In response to the objection that assigning a specific skopos to a text (particularly a literary text) or a particular audience to a text restricts the ways in which it can be interpreted, Vermeer points out that translations realize something different depending on their assumed purpose or assumed audience – not something more or something less – and that the skopos of a text can itself be 'to preserve the breadth of interpretation of the source text' (2004: 232) among particular types of addressee.

This not only raises interesting questions about the various ways in which different audiences will respond to the same text. It also helps us to contextualize the role of the literal translator in the theatre translation process, that is, the linguist who is commissioned to provide a supposedly neutral version of the source text, from which the monolingual celebrity translator then crafts his or her version of the text for performance. The fact that literal translators are all too aware of how their translations will be used means that they have a very clear skopos – in fact, arguably a clearer one than either the source-text playwright or the celebrity translator, who can never be totally sure what the effect of their texts will be either on audiences or on the commissioners of their texts (see Perteghella 2004b). As Vermeer points out, 'The point [when translating] is that one must know what one is doing, and what the consequences of such action are' (2004: 229). What's more, skopos theory also offers us another potential explanation (alongside the explanation that, say, sociologists might offer in the light of systems theory, see Tyulenev 2013) for why certain foreign-language plays are presented in translation on the British stage and others are not, and why certain plays are constantly retranslated and others are not. As theatre translation scholar David Johnston points out, the concept of catering to audience demands is reminiscent of skopos – 'an indication of a subservience of translation to the imperatives of commercial production' (2013: 375).

Such questions (or, for some agents in the theatrical system, concerns) about the importance of considering the audience in any discussion of the aim or purpose of translation are a constant theme throughout this book. At this point, however, it will hopefully already be clear that any consideration of the celebrity translator's *aim* or *purpose* in producing his or her translation, and indeed any evaluation of the *way* in which that translator produces his or her translation, must surely inevitably be accompanied by an exploration of the audience's likely response. That's because without any such exploration there can be no real value in commissioning a celebrity to produce the translation in the first place. After all, as already seen in Chapter 1, it's not just the notion of a theatrical performance that depends on the existence of an audience – the very construct of celebrity depends on there being an audience as well.

Visibility, domestication and foreignization

Translation scholar Lawrence Venuti is perhaps best known in translation studies circles for advocating greater visibility of translation as a process and a product, and for lamenting the fact that translation and thereby translators are largely invisible in British and American literary cultures (see 1998, 2008 and 2013a). He believes that this invisibility is a consequence both of the translator's focus on fluency and readability when translating a text, and of the way in which translated texts are most often read by readers in those target cultures. Venuti's notion of the 'illusion of transparency' (2008: 1) is certainly pertinent to the arguments of this book in that it foregrounds the role of the receiver of the translation text and the effect that translation will have on that receiver. At the same time, it would appear that Venuti's concept of translator visibility is somewhat different from the concept of visibility in the context of the celebrity translator, and that the two notions should not be evaluated in the same light.

Venuti applauds translator visibility because it forcibly reminds readers that they are reading a translation, and because it challenges their lack of receptiveness to 'the foreign' (2008: 12). At the same time, however, we should surely also applaud the visibility of celebrity translators in the British theatre because of the way in which such visibility encourages new audiences to access translated drama – by enhancing the profile of a theatrical work that might otherwise be overlooked, or by showcasing a new perspective on an already familiar work. Put another way, while Venuti's general preference for a more visible (i.e. anti-assimilationist) translation strategy might foreground the *foreignness* of the target text due to that text's lack of fluency or smoothness (while also acknowledging that fluency may be acceptable if it helps to 'smuggle in' texts to a resistant target culture, see Venuti 2008: 228), I would foreground the very *visibility* of the target text as a means of raising public awareness of a translated play text.

This different perspective on the notion of visibility is further complicated by the fact that, as already noted, play texts are often first translated by a literal translator, whose work is then used as the foundation from which the celebrity translator crafts his or her version for the stage. These literal translators are invariably almost entirely invisible as agencies in the translation process, and their translations are normally invisible too, except to the celebrity translator and maybe the theatre's literary department. Perversely, this is in spite of the fact that the literal translator's adopted translation strategy (which is determined by the brief that he or she is given to produce a *word-for-word* translation that preserves the linguistic meaning of the source text in its entirety) leads to texts that are very visibly translations. Here, however, it is important to note that *this* visibility is grounded in a literal approach to the translation of the source text. The visibility that Venuti advocates, on the other hand, is grounded more in what could be described as a foreignizing *patchwork of different Englishes* – an approach that is actually independent of the source text in many respects.

On top of this, Venuti tends to see invisibility as largely going hand in hand with *domesticating* translation strategies. Here, he defines *domestication* as translating in a fluent style that will minimize the foreignness of the target text and thereby lead to an 'ethnocentric reduction of the foreign text to dominant cultural values' in the target-text culture (2008: 68). *Foreignization*, on the other hand, is considered by Venuti to be 'an ethnodeviant pressure on those values to register the linguistic and cultural differences of the foreign text' (2008).

The phenomenon of celebrity translation also offers an interesting perspective on this domestication-versus-foreignization paradigm since the notion of celebrity is inevitably rooted in the premise of cultural closeness – or in other words, the very opposite of foreignness. That's because celebrity is itself a cultural construct – after all, celebrities can only exist within a given culture, whether that culture is local, national, international or global (see Turner 2013). And the issue of cultural closeness, even if not necessarily always expressed in terms of domestication or foreignization, has long been a salient topic in the area of theatre translation, not least because the practice of acculturation is arguably a feature of almost all translated play texts to one extent or another. Theatre translation scholar Gunilla Anderman notes, for example, that 'this process [of acculturation] may not be total but simply take the form of neutralisation through toning down what is deemed to be too "foreign", a practice extending as far back in history as the Romans' (2005: 25). In fact, I would propose that celebrity translation is actually often an example of *total acculturation* in the sense that the celebrity translator is by definition a product of the audience's own culture, and as such his or her translation will be a product of that culture too. Following this argument, celebrity translators are likely to be visible precisely *because* they follow a highly personalizing or assimilationist strategy, which may then often manifest itself as a domesticating strategy if those celebrities are closely associated with particular elements of their own domestic culture. Such elements might comprise, say, a distinctive type of humour or the use of a particular dialect.

Overall, then, the phenomenon of celebrity translation in the theatre would appear to add a new perspective on Venuti's ideas about translator visibility, domestication and foreignization, and on the relative importance of aesthetics and power in translation. The notion of an *invisible celebrity* is something of a paradox, and the notion of a visible translator and simultaneously a strongly acculturating (i.e. domesticating) tendency, which is at the heart of celebrity translation, would seem to challenge the idea that visibility tends to go hand in hand with foreignization. So, while the concept of translator visibility (or invisibility) might provide us with a means of labelling a translation strategy (indeed, see Chapter 3 for some interesting examples of this in Roger McGough's translation of Molière), it's perhaps less able to explain how audiences *respond to* celebrity translation. For such an explanation, it would appear useful to look beyond translation studies, as will become clear later in this chapter.

Contribution of theatre translation scholars

Theatre translation as a cultural product

Theatre translation and adaptation has already received widespread scholarly attention, both among translation studies scholars and, more recently, among scholars in the emerging field of adaptation studies (notably Hutcheon 2006 and Krebs 2014). Over this time, translations of play texts have been variously explored in the context of literary studies, phonetics, semiotics, theatre studies, theatre anthropology and cultural studies as well as translation studies, although, importantly, not yet in the field of celebrity studies (see Marshall 1997; Rojek 2001 and Turner 2013).

Interest in theatre translation has particularly grown since the start of the twenty-first century, both in its own right and in parallel with the growth of translation studies and (more latterly) adaptation studies as distinct academic disciplines. Already, published works devoted exclusively to theatre translation include Aaltonen 2000, Upton 2000, Coelsch-Foisner and Klein 2004, Zatlin 2005, Baines, Marinetti and Perteghella 2011, Bigliazzi, Kofler and Ambrosi 2013, Laera 2014, and Brodie 2018, to name just a selection. Yet in most cases, the focus of attention still appears to be as much on drawing specific conclusions from particularly interesting examples of theatre translation as on developing valid theories of or models for such translation. For example, eleven of the twelve chapters in Upton and eleven of the sixteen chapters in Bigliazzi, Kofler and Ambrosi were devoted to case studies. Indeed, the increasing emphasis on a multidisciplinary approach to theatre translation studies appears to be encouraging an even greater focus on the *practice* of theatre translation and a move away from previous attempts to theorize theatre translation as a cultural product.

But it's actually some of these very ideas about theatre translation as a cultural product that I am most interested in. That is why I would now like to give readers a brief overview of the contributions by theatre translation scholars that *are* relevant to my study of celebrity translation. This is not meant to be a comprehensive history of theatre translation studies (for that I would refer readers to Mary Snell-Hornby's chapter on theatre and opera translation in Piotr Kuhiwczak and Karin Littau's *A Companion to Translation Studies*, 2007). Rather, it's intended as a short examination of ideas about the production and reception of play texts that support my argument for a more sympathetic view towards the phenomenon of celebrity translation in British theatre.

Theatre translation and performance

Perhaps the first emerging translation concept that ignited international debate among theatre translators, and indeed dramatists, was the notion of *deconstruction*. This was advanced in particular by French philosopher Jacques Derrida, whose theories about Western concepts of language coincided with a number of new translations of classical drama from the mid-1960s onwards and with a growing interest in performance studies and alternative expressions of theatre. Of particular note in this respect are the innovative adaptations of Shakespeare by non-European playwrights such as Martinican playwright Aimé Césaire in 1969 and the subsequent radical deconstructions and reframings of canonical texts by New York-based Wooster Group under the direction of Elizabeth LeCompte that began in the 1970s. For theatre scholars, deconstructive analysis was seen as a way of opening a play text up to new possibilities of interpretation and seeing each of the various *texts* at work (the script, the setting, the characters, the performances and so on) as fluid rather than fixed.

While the theory of deconstruction did not deal specifically with plays or productions, its influence opened up a new perspective on theatre translation that was less constrained by the source text and encouraged a more active consumption of translated work than would previously have been considered acceptable (see Snell-Hornby 1984; Bassnett 1985 and Pavis 1989). This is clearly of vital importance to my study of celebrity translators since it recognizes the value of thinking beyond the written text itself and looking more broadly at text as performance, and the different ways in which different spectators might receive a text.

In his theory of *verbo-corps* (1989: 36, translated by Loren Kruger as *language-body*), theatre scholar Patrice Pavis suggests that 'real drama translation takes place on the level of the *mise en scène* as a whole' and that theatre translation should be seen as 'an appropriation of one text by another' (1989: 41). Pavis thereby reframes the aim of theatre translation in the light of reception theory, stating that 'theatre translation is never where one expects it to be: not in words, but in gesture, not in the letter, but in the spirit of a culture, ineffable but omnipresent' (1989: 42). This shift in focus paves the way for my application of relevance theory to theatre translations by celebrities in that it foregrounds the importance of the surrounding culture when evaluating such translations (see Chapter 3).

Pavis's ideas about the extratextual dimensions of theatre translation are echoed in many of the contributions made by theatre translation scholar Susan Bassnett, whose work since the late 1970s onwards has tended to foreground the performance dimension of theatre translation. Bassnett claims that the theatre translator's central consideration must be 'the performance aspect of the text and its relationship with the audience' (1980: 132), and that any notion of theatre that does not see written text and performance as indissolubly linked will 'inevitably lead to discrimination against anyone who appears to offend against the purity of the written text' (1980: 121). Bassnett's focus on the audience is certainly highly relevant to my arguments in this book. But at the same time it does not help to explain why celebrity translators are commissioned more in the theatre than in any other text genre – unless, that is, we assume that sensitivity to the needs of performance is a more elusive skill among theatre translators than, say, writing in an engaging way is among translators of other genres of literature.

Theatre translation and performability

In 1985, Bassnett was the first theoretician to talk about how theatre text is *time bound* in a way that distinguishes it from prose or poetry (89). This is because naturalist dialogue inevitably belongs to a certain time in terms of speech rhythm, syntax and colloquialisms. This, Bassnett believes, explains why there is a special need for 'the continued retranslation or updating of theatre texts, where patterns of speech are in a continuous process of change' (1985: 89). Bassnett also appears to be the first scholar to draw attention to the practice in British theatre of two-stage translation, that is, the commissioning of literal translations that are 'then handed over to a well-known (and most often monolingual) playwright with an established reputation so that larger audiences will be attracted into the theatre' (1991: 101) – evidence, as she sees it, that 'the history of theatre translation into English is inextricably bound up with economics' (1991: 102). In Bassnett's view, the notion of *performability* is simply 'an alternative explanation of a more respectable kind' (102) as to why plays need to be translated by playwrights rather than translators, because only a playwright will be capable of writing the fluent speech rhythms that are required for the target text to be easily performed on stage.

It might at first sight appear disingenuous of Bassnett to single out the theatre as being particularly susceptible to financial considerations – consider, for example, the number of authors of fiction who fail to get their books published because their work is unlikely to find a profitable market. And while the relative lack of public subsidy for the performing arts does make theatres particularly sensitive to commercial failure (see Bradley's comments cited in the previous section of this chapter), the same is surely also true of the publishing industry, which benefits even less from the public purse. Having said this, there must be something specific about the social, cultural and economic factors at play in the theatre that means that celebrity translators exist in this genre when they do not in other genres. In the case of publishing, for example, the British public's appetite (or perhaps more correctly, British publishers' perceptions of the public's appetite) for translation is even less strong than the appetite for translated plays (amounting to less than 5 per cent of all poetry, fiction and drama published in the UK and Ireland in the first decade of the twenty-first century according to Donahaye 2012: 28). This would undoubtedly make the commissioning of a celebrity author financially untenable except perhaps in the case of translated authors who have achieved bestseller status, such as some of the Scandinavian crime authors. I suspect that the answer lies in the performative nature of drama, which lends itself much more readily to constant reinvention than translated fiction does. In such a scenario, the celebrity translator offers producers a useful way of helping a production to stand out from other recent (or in some cases, concurrent) productions of the same play – and in doing so, raises the bar for future productions and sets a challenge for the next celebrity translator in the chain.

In any event, it would appear to be the case that if everyone in the theatrical system agreed with Bassnett, we would have no celebrity translators in the theatre – and that's something that I strongly believe would not necessarily be to the theatre's advantage. I would also take issue with Bassnett's implication that the practice of two-stage translation inherently belittles the role that translators play in the process of theatre translation and adaptation, and that performability is an excuse for the lack of acknowledgement of the translator's craft. As she pointedly remarks, 'Translation is, and always has been, a question of power relationships, and the translator has all too often been placed in a position of economic, aesthetic and intellectual inferiority' (1991: 101). True though this might be in many cases, it fails to acknowledge the positive benefits that celebrity translators can bring to the theatrical system – not least the fact that they potentially bring new audiences to translated plays and thereby raise public awareness of and interest in theatre in translation.

As an aside, it is interesting to note that Bassnett's defensiveness about the lowly status of translators appears to have softened somewhat by the time of her 1998 article 'Still Trapped in the Labyrinth: Further Reflections on Translation and Theatre', in which she revisits the particular challenges of theatre translation and revises some of her previous views. Most significantly, she now suggests that the translator should concentrate on the text itself rather than any deep structures and coded subtexts, thereby altering her previous contention that theatre translators should be aware of the structural features of a play text that make it performable (1998: 107).

Johnston, meanwhile, offers an alternative view of the different approaches to theatre translation, and one that draws attention to the very issue of performability that Bassnett dismisses as elusive. He reminds us of the distinction between an academic, or literary, approach to a play text, and a more purely theatrical approach – 'the first one is legitimately concerned with the play at the level of its constituent semantic units, the level of detail, while the other, although not abandoning word-based analysis, is much more concerned with the play in terms of dramatic impact' (1996: 7). Johnston's distinction clearly mirrors the two-stage translation process on which the entire celebrity translation culture is founded – it is the literal translator's role to provide the scholarly translation and the celebrity translator's role to provide the performable translation. At the same time, we should not assume that Johnston's distinction is intended to imply that the notion of an academic view on dramatic impact is inherently contradictory. Indeed, this book's analysis of the celebrity translation phenomenon from a theoretical perspective will, I hope, prove that theories of communication can indeed help us to understand the dramatic impact of a text, both on the page and in performance.

Theatre translation and ideology

In 2000, translator-trainer Eva Espasa carried out a thorough analysis of the concept of performability that aimed to bridge the gulf between theatre practice and translation theory (2000: 49–62). Most significantly for the purpose of the study of celebrity translation, Espasa argues that performability is not only an issue at a textual or performance level. It's also 'determined by the theatrical ideology of the [theatre] company, and is related to questions of status' (2000:49). This reference to ideology echoes translation scholar Maria Tymoczko's concept of the positionality of the translator (2003). Here, Tymoczko takes issue with the notion of the translator's neutrality, stating that 'the ideology of a translation resides not simply in the text translated, but in the voicing and stance of the translator, and in its relevance to the receiving audience' (2003: 183). She believes that the translator's cultural and ideological position has a more important influence on his or her translations than the temporal or spatial location that the translator speaks from, and thereby rejects the idea of translators operating in an *in between* space in terms of their engagement with the texts that they are translating. Such a view echoes Hermans's view of the translator's voice, which suggests that 'perhaps translation is … best cast as a mimetic representation animated by the translator's vision and to a significant extent under the translator's control' (2007: 75). This surely reminds us of the relative status of the celebrity translator compared with the literal translator within the theatrical system, with only the well-known playwright deemed to have the expertise to produce a performable translation for the stage.

In this respect, it's interesting to note that, while Espasa agrees with Bassnett about the lowly status of translators themselves in the sense that 'the more visibility is granted to a well-known playwright, the more invisible the figure of the translator remains' (58), she disagrees over the issue of cooperative, or collaborative translation. Here, she cites translator and poet Burton Raffel's view (in the context of poetry translation) that collaborative translation is only rarely between equals (1988: 129). Indeed, Raffel's view is echoed by translation scholar Francis Jones, who notes how 'translating, editing and publishing processes depend on the motives, life stories and personae of their main actors … on whether these actors happen to meet, and on how they interact' (2011: 24). So, whereas Bassnett appears to see the mediation of a complex chain of participants as an obstacle to translation, Espasa sees the process of negotiation as an *explanatory* factor of performability, and argues for putting theatre ideology and power negotiation at the heart of performability. This book will support and add further weight to Espasa's view as a way of justifying and even celebrating the phenomenon of celebrity translation in the theatre.

Sirku Aaltonen (2000) offers a methodological framework for studying translation that builds on polysystem theory. Arguing that theatre translation, like all translation, is always an *egotistically* motivated activity, she follows Venuti's line of thought about translation being fundamentally ethnocentric (1998: 11) and suggests that 'in theatre translation, the Foreign is not the primary inspiration in the decision to turn to other cultures. Instead the interest is motivated by the perception of the benefits for the Self of such exchange' (2000: 49). By extension, she believes that 'the choice of suitable texts is always based on the needs of the target system and the compatibility of the discourse of the source text with that of the target culture' (2000). Following the same argument, the choice of a celebrity translator (and, indeed, the decision to adopt the practice of celebrity translation in the first place) will surely also be based on the needs of the target system at a particular time (e.g. the need for either a familiar voice or a more challenging voice depending on the prevailing artistic and social climate), and on the compatibility of the discourse of the celebrity translator's text with that of the target culture (e.g. the extent to which the celebrity translator enhances accessibility of and identification with the text).

Aaltonen's argument raises some interesting questions about the ideological implications of celebrity translation and its influence on British theatre. What is it about the UK theatrical system (and possibly more widely about UK society in general) that means that there is often this perceived need to produce and market foreign plays through the medium of well-known domestic playwrights? Is it symptomatic of a degree of cultural insularity whereby audiences are only willing to open up to the 'foreign' if it's wrapped in the comfort blanket of a familiar name? Or is it more the case that British theatrical producers themselves perceive a constant need to reinvent or refresh classic works in order to attract audiences to translated theatre? Exploring such questions would probably fill an entire book in itself, so here I will mainly restrict my analysis to consideration of how audiences *respond* to celebrity translation rather than allow myself to get sidetracked by the ethics of such translation. In my final chapter, however, I will raise a number of questions of my own about what celebrity translation means for the reception of translated theatre in the UK. And my conclusions will ultimately put a more positive slant on the ideological implications of celebrity translation than some translation theorists might wish to concede.

Theatre translation and cultural encounters

The second decade of the twenty-first century saw much greater emphasis among scholars of literature on reception of texts by the reader (or spectator in this case). This shift not only built on general developments since the turn of the century in stylistics, linguistics and literary theory (see Stockwell 2002, 2013; Wilson and Sperber 2012, and Tsur 2008, to name but a few). It also reflected the move away from the notion of fixed *authorial* meaning to more flexible *readerly* meaning (see among others Boase-Beier 2011 and Stockwell 2013). Against this background, it's not surprising that theatre translation studies has also started to pay much more attention to the reception of play texts and to question the notion of whose play it really is – is it the source-text playwright's, the translator's, the director's or perhaps even the audience's?

For example, theatre translation scholar Geraldine Brodie has expanded on the ideas promoted by Aaltonen about the needs of the target system and offers the view that 'the translator's negotiation of culture may be influenced by many external factors, not limited to a relationship with the original text but also affected by the theatrical translation policy, the expectation of the audience and the marketing and funding requirements' (2012: 78). Here, Brodie sets the scene for my own exploration of the role of the celebrity translator by linking issues that emerge from translation theories (such as translator visibility and the domestication-versus-foreignization paradigm) to practical issues surrounding the staging of translated drama in the British theatrical system (such as why certain plays are constantly retranslated), and consideration of which translation approach is more likely to fulfil the commercial objectives of a theatrical production (see also Brodie 2018).

Marinetti, meanwhile, offers a new perspective on the models proposed by Pavis and Aaltonen that emphasizes the distinct roles played by all the players in the theatrical system (including actors, directors, designers, technicians, etc.) in contributing to the creation of a theatre text (2013a). She argues that Pavis's articulation of the 'language-body' (1989: 30) and Aaltonen's metaphor of 'time-sharing' (2000: 9) imply 'a separation of the "linguistic" from the "dramaturgical" and the "performative"' (2013a: 29). This, she feels, assumes that interpretation of play texts occurs in discrete phases, whereas ideally the creative potential of cultural encounters and engagement with the culture of the source text should be foregrounded throughout the creative process of staging performance (2013a: 29). Such a view clearly echoes the view advanced in modern linguistics that there is no separation between the text and the performance of that text (see McIntyre 2006: 11). On the other hand, of course, the practice of celebrity translation is in many ways the antithesis of Marinetti's ideal view of the translation process. That's because in celebrity translation, the celebrity translator is often foregrounded much more than the source-text playwright – and the target-text culture in some cases overshadows or maybe even completely obliterates the source-text culture. Meanwhile, the creator of the literal translation is frequently marginalized completely.

A final contribution to theatre translation studies that is worth mentioning here because of its relevance to my examination of celebrity translation is that of Roger Baines, Manuela Perteghella and Cristina Marinetti in 2011. These scholars offer a new perspective on the subject again by attempting to 'explore and theorize the relationship between written text and performance starting from actual creative practice' (2011: 2). They argue that translation scholars have up until this point shied away from exploring the practices that underpin translation for the stage and have focused more on how translated plays function as cultural products (see also Aaltonen 2000 and Anderman 2005). My exploration of the celebrity translator in the theatre is designed to answer Baines', Perteghella's and Marinetti's call for 'more work on the interface between translation and performance practice' (2011: 7) by offering insights into how the cultural phenomenon of celebrity translation might actually serve to *foreground* the process of theatre translation, and thereby potentially lead to greater public interest in plays in translation.

To sum up, then, it's hopefully not unfair to conclude that scholars' exploration of theatre translation, while extensive (and constantly expanding), has until very recently often failed to address sufficiently the perspective of perhaps the most important agent in the theatrical system – namely, that of the audience. I say this not only to reinforce the point I have already made (and probably laboured) that without an audience there can be no theatre. And while Brodie has clearly paved the way for a more spectator-led exploration of translation in the theatre, there is still in my view a need to specifically examine the notion of readerly meaning (or in this case *spectatorly* meaning, if such a word were to exist) in the context of theatrical performance – in other words, building on the idea that each spectator creates his or her own meaning of a text in performance and exploring how this may or may not fit with our existing notions of how audiences respond to theatre in translation.

To achieve this, I believe we need to look beyond theories of translation and the ways in which such theories have been used to describe the processes involved in theatre translation. But beforehand, let's briefly have a look at some of the ideas emerging in a different but closely related field of literary studies.

Contribution of adaptation scholars

The second decade of the twenty-first century saw the emergence of *adaptation studies* as a fledgling discipline located within literary studies, with inevitably some crossover with translation studies. This is in spite of long-held views by at least some theatre translation scholars that the distinction between a translation and an adaptation is an artificial one in the case of play texts. Bassnett, for one, claimed back in 1985 that 'the distinction between a "version" of a source language text and an "adaptation" of that text seems to me to be a complete red herring. It is time the misleading use of these terms were set aside' (93). More recently, Johnston offers the view that adaptation has traditionally been perceived in the theatre as a lesser art form: '"straightforward" translation and adaptation/new version come to represent opposite poles of fidelity; rightful inheritor, upright and true, and bastard child, wickedly lively and devil-may-care' (1996: 8).

This debate appears to have continued ever since, although more recently it would seem to be increasingly influenced by the arguments put forward by scholars focusing specifically on adaptations. Here, a groundbreaking work was published in 2006 by literary theory scholar Linda Hutcheon, *A Theory of Adaptation*. Here (and in the second edition with O'Flynn in 2013), Hutcheon explores the very notion of adaptation as a cultural phenomenon rather than the specific processes involved in adapting one work into another. She also addresses the audience's engagement with adaptations (2013: 113–40) and draws a valuable distinction between knowing and unknowing audiences – that is, audiences that are aware that they are reading, watching or in some other way interacting with an adaptation versus those that are not. Hutcheon's distinction chimes with some of the distinctions I will be making later in this book. And even though her arguments are not specifically directed at translation or adaptation in the theatre, her diatribe against what she calls 'the unproductive nature of both that negative evaluation of popular cultural adaptations as derivative and secondary and that morally loaded rhetoric of fidelity and infidelity used in comparing adaptations to "source" texts' (2013: 31) is certainly one that resonates with the arguments I put forward in this book about celebrity translation – not least because it reminds us of the futility of thinking in terms of equivalence when comparing a celebrity's translation with the original playwright's text.

In the context of intralingual adaptation, Hutcheon even dismisses the notion of a source text outright since she sees adaptations themselves as original texts – a view that scholars such as Katja Krebs (2012) and Laurence Raw (2012) would also appear to share. This raises a fascinating question about celebrity translations as well. Should we consider their translations as new source texts that become integral to that celebrity's existing oeuvre in the same way as their other work, or should they still be considered a particular subset of that other work? There's surely a valid case for agreeing to the former from a creative point of view. But at the same time, we must also acknowledge that there are practical issues such as copyright and unwelcome public cries of plagiarism that might make this a more hypothetical than realistic stance. It's also fascinating to note how Hutcheon focuses more on *modes of engagement* than on the comparison of two specific media. She describes these modes of engagement as 'telling', 'showing' and 'interacting with stories' (2013: 22–7), and concludes that by thinking beyond media we can focus more on the contexts of creation and reception of adaptation, which are 'material, public and economic as much as they are cultural, personal and aesthetic' (2013: 28). From a translation scholar's perspective, the parallel conclusion is that by thinking beyond simple comparison of texts, we can focus more on the contexts within which celebrity translations are created and received – contexts that are also governed as much by material, public and economic factors as they are by cultural, personal and aesthetic factors.

An alternative perspective on adaptation specifically in the context of translation for the theatre is offered by Anderman (2005), who suggests that adapters can actually have an advantage over translators because they are more removed from, and therefore less hidebound by, the source text:

> An adapter … is often able, through sheer lack of knowledge of the language in which a play has been written and the culture in which it originates, to assess objectively the aspects of 'otherness' in the work of a foreign playwright and the extent to which this needs adjusting for English audiences. Sometimes this is a more difficult task for the linguist, who is more inclined to consider it a matter of conscience to ensure that the specific cultural details of the original are all acknowledged in the translation. (320)

This is an interesting argument, and one that in principle could possibly help to explain the licence that celebrity translators might feel that they have to depart from the source text – even if in practice celebrity translators' egos and an implicit brief from the commissioner of the translation to inject some of their own voice might be at least as important. Where I tend to disagree with Anderman, however, is in her assertion that 'to safeguard the authenticity of the original is as crucial as the need to make the play in translation more accessible to the audience' (2005: 320). This would suggest that the source-text playwright's voice is the *only* one that should be heard if the integrity of the work and the intended theatrical effects are to be guaranteed. Such a view would surely appear to reduce the role of the translator, whether a celebrity or not, to that of an impartial mediator. This not only sidelines the translator's role completely given the presence of other more proactively involved agents in the theatrical system (the director, for example), who will undoubtedly expect to have an influence on the final production. It also appears to confound much of contemporary thinking in translation studies, which maintains that a translator can never be truly neutral. Recalling Tymozcko again, 'the ideology of a translation resides not simply in the text translated, but in the voicing and stance of the translator, and in the relevance to the receiving audience' (2003: 183). This is to say nothing of the fact that if we dismiss theatre adaptations that are less than totally authentic to the source text, we risk excluding 'a large and important part of translation work in the theatre' (Aaltonen 2000: 4).

Perteghella, finally, analyses adaptations for the theatre in the context of '"culturality" – linked to the adaptor's own cultural background, target audiences and culture, and perceptions of both source and target culture – and … "subjectivity" – linked to the personal aesthetics and idiolect of the translator and his or her personal reading of the source language play' (2008: 62). She suggests that it's this interplay of culturality and subjectivity that can help us to 'understand adaptation as a marked recontextualization of the play, often through the process of intraculturalism and transculturalism, the latter observed in the universalizing of plays from the past, and the former in the translocation of the source language play into contained, specific cultural contexts' (2008: 62).

But while this interplay of culturality and subjectivity is an interesting one, and indeed one reflected in the selection of play texts analysed in this book, it doesn't necessarily get us any closer to defining the difference between translation and adaptation in the theatre beyond reminding us that there is a scale of different approaches that translators can take based on the closeness to or distance from the source text that they wish to reflect. Yet even a play text that is ostensibly far removed from the source text might still justifiably be called a translation rather than an adaptation if it generates an equivalent emotional response among the audience. This then implies that the distinction between translation and adaptation from an interlingual point of view is at best an arbitrary one and at worst a highly misleading one. As already pointed out, it's for this very reason that I will refer throughout this book to 'translators' rather than 'adaptors' when I analyse each celebrity translation.

Brecht's contribution

A study of how theatre audiences make inferences about translation must inevitably explore at least some of the ideas that have been put forward about the reception of texts in performance. So it's essential before going any further to acknowledge the ideas of Bertolt Brecht in this regard. Both as a playwright and a theoretician, Brecht's thinking has had a profound impact both on theatre practice and on critical response to performance. His ideas are rooted in the belief that the theatre should play an overt role in reflecting and shaping political ideology in society. This has clear ramifications for his perception of the role of the audience. As theatre scholar Susan Bennett (not to be confused with theatre translation scholar Susan Bassnett) points out, 'Brecht's theory and practice raise the issue of the ideological status of the theatre and of the political undertaking, either implicit or explicit, of an audience' (1997: 22). This meant not only 'engaging with reality' as a way of making contact with audiences (Brecht 1964: 236) but also interacting with audiences so that spectators are forced to question the relationship between what is happening on their stage and their own social reality.

In practical terms, Brecht was one of the pioneers of *episches Theater* (epic theatre), a form of drama popularized in Germany during the 1920s and 1930s that combined

1. theatrical devices such as narrative descriptions (via the use of choruses or projections onto the back of the stage),
2. a style of acting involving what Brecht termed *gestus* (the simultaneous depiction of an action and an attitude towards that action, as portrayed either in the way in which a character interacts with other characters on stage or via an overt act of narration), and
3. *fabel* (the sequence of portrayals of *gestus* that go together to create the dramatic or theatrical narrative of a play).

The use of such techniques either individually or in combination with one another typically gives rise to the concept of *Verfremdung* that Brecht first proposed in his 1935 essay *Verfremdungseffekte in der chinesischen Schauspielkunst* (translated as *Alienation Effects in Chinese Acting* in Brecht 1974). This concept since became one of the key features of his particular kind of dramaturgy.

Scholars have long debated the most appropriate way of translating *Verfremdung* or *Verfremdungseffekte* (the effects of *Verfremdung*) into English. Essentially a term coined by Brecht as a point of distinction from the regular German term *Entfremdung* (most often translated as *alienation*), translations of *Verfremdung* have included *defamiliarization, distancing* and *estrangement* as well as *alienation*. According to Brecht scholar Anthony Squiers, 'Brecht's use of the term *Verfremdung* and not *Entfremdung* indicates that the moving away or distancing he sought through (*Verfremdungseffekte*) was a distancing of familiar conceptualization not … a distancing of the audience from the play's performance and its content' (2014: 58).

Brecht's methods forced a re-evaluation not only of the relationship between the performance and the audience, but also more generally of how theatre scholars should study theatre audiences (Bennett 1997: 30). Most importantly, Brecht's ideas challenged the traditional top-down concept of the playwright communicating to the audience (via the actors on the stage) as a one-way process, and highlighted the centrality of audiences themselves in the creation, performance and interpretation of drama. Essentially, then, Brecht proposes that the theatrical experience is the consequence of the extent to which the cultural and the political ideologies of the various players involved (the playwright, the performers and the audience) coincide or collide with one another. For a language scholar, it's clear that this has important implications for where the meaning of a play text in performance is located and how that meaning is inferred by the receiver. In the case of a translated play, and in particular one translated by a celebrity translator, the potential for divergent ideologies among the players involved in the dramatic process is amplified, and questions as to how audiences infer meaning from a play text in performance become even more complex. These are just some of the questions that I will explore in my following three case studies.

Thinking beyond theories of translation and adaptation

Exploring the phenomenon of celebrity translation from the perspective of existing theories of translation and adaptation might in some ways help us to theorize the role of celebrity translators within the wider theatrical system. But such theories are ultimately of only limited use in explaining how celebrity translations are produced by their translators and received by their audiences. While concepts such as visibility and performability can help us to start contextualizing the question of why some play texts might benefit from the involvement of a celebrity translator, the artificial distinction between *translation* and *adaptation* often gets in the way of any useful discussion of the phenomenon of celebrity translation and the benefits that it can bring to the theatrical system.

For what it's worth, I certainly have my own hypotheses as to why theories of translation appear unable in themselves to help explain the phenomenon of celebrity translation. First, the *collaborative* nature of translation in the theatre (and, increasingly, of much prose and poetry translation in the UK as well) offers little fit with the way in which translation theories that raise issues such as the translator's skopos or visibility presuppose both a single translator responsible for producing a translation (who can therefore post-rationalize his or her own translation choices) and a single reader at any one time. This collaborative process implies that we might need to look beyond the traditional confines of translation theory and explore ideas emerging from theories in other disciplines for a more useful evaluative framework.

Second, theories of translation often appear to work on the premise of a *fixed relationship* between the translator, the target text and the reader of that text. Consider, for example, the concepts of equivalence and polysystems or the distinction between domestication and foreignization, all of which essentially originate in the notion of fixed relationships between meanings, systems and cultures. But in the theatre the concept of the text is a more fluid one because it's so dependent on performance. As a consequence, the notion of the translator's *ownership* of the text is very different from a situation in which the text exists in an unchanging written form (even if written texts still arguably produce different effects on the reader each time they are read, and almost certainly each time they are read aloud). This uncertain and constantly evolving relationship between the play text, its authors and its receivers inevitably makes it difficult to theorize about the process of translation since that translation exists in so many representations at the same time.

What's more, theories of translation have traditionally tended to focus more on the *text* itself rather than on the *reception* of that text by its receivers. While this perspective might now have changed somewhat with the application to translation of models such as reader-response theories for how human beings process discourse, it often remains the case that the receivers of translated texts are still not taken into consideration sufficiently when translation scholars analyse those texts. In the case of play texts, such a reluctance to consider the audience would appear to be particularly remiss, given how the audience is vital to the process of imbuing a play with meaning and how spectators are effectively active consumers of that work rather than merely passive recipients (see Bennett 1997; Tulloch 2005; McConochie 2008, to name but a few).

Given the dynamic, shared experience of play-text reception, audience reception is arguably an even more important consideration in the analysis of play-text translation than it is in the analysis of the translation of any other literary genre. Even an exploration of the written, published versions of translated play texts (such as I will be conducting in the following chapters) cannot ignore the way in which those texts will be received when performed in public. Moreover, acknowledgement of celebrity status and communal assimilation of celebrity culture also imply that the concept of celebrity translation can only exist in the minds of an audience. That's because, as already pointed out several times in this chapter, without an audience there can surely be no celebrities, or indeed any theatre performances either. Contrast this with creators of literature in general (whether source-text writers or translators), who might depend on an audience for their livelihood, but not for their very existence.

Ultimately, then, I would argue that we need to look beyond translation and adaptation studies (or theatre studies) and to explore theories and models developed in other areas of language and behavioural studies if we are seeking to explain the phenomenon of celebrity translation from a theoretical perspective. So I would now like to explore relevance theory, a theory that has emerged from the field of cognitive poetics (i.e. the study of literary effect based on cognitive rather than non-cognitive linguistics) and explain why I believe it offers a more useful perspective from which to explore celebrity translation in general, and audience reception of celebrity translation in particular.

3

Celebrity translation and relevance theory

Celebrity translation and cognitive poetics

If we want to explore the issue of how celebrity translations of play texts are received by theatre audiences, we have to turn to cognitive theories of language. Cognitive linguistics developed from the 1980s onwards as a result of the emerging interest in the interplay between writer, text, reader and context (see Leech 1983 and Taylor and Toolan 1984). It was a reaction to formalist linguistics, which still remains the basis for much of translation theory with its emphasis on the propositional meaning of a text rather than its function or communicative context.

Now an established discipline in its own right, cognitive linguistics continues to be influenced by other cognitive sciences such as cognitive psychology and cognitive neuroscience. Indeed, cognitive linguistic theories have become so sophisticated that they are already able to make testable predictions about how the brain processes language – see Gonzalez-Marquez et al. 2007 and Geeraerts and Cuyckens 2010 for some particularly useful contributions in this respect. What's more, new fields of study under the umbrella of cognitive linguistics have become established in their own right. Cognitive semantics, for example, explores the relation between language and cognitive structures such as perceptions or image schemas, and suggests that we use language to express cognitive ideas based on our shared experiences (see Albertazzi 2000 and Hampe 2005). Cognitive pragmatics, meanwhile, explores the cognitive aspects of the construal of meaning in context. Such aspects might include social and situational factors (see Fauconnier and Turner 2002; Bara 2010; Schmid 2012). And finally cognitive poetics applies the principles of cognitive linguistics to the study of literary effects (see Stockwell 2002 and Tsur 2008).

It's this latter discipline of cognitive poetics that is of most relevance to my arguments in this book. This is not only because play texts are obviously literary texts – hence the relevance of *poetics*. It's also because I am seeking to demonstrate that the contextual associations with celebrity translators mean that spectators will also take into account a combination of contextual, mental and emotional factors when experiencing a play text over and above those factors that are purely textual – hence the relevance of *cognitive*. Of course, it could be argued that this is the case when engaging with any literary text, whether translated or not, since no text exists completely in isolation. And even if the receiver of that text has no knowledge of the author, he or she will still construct a representation in their minds of that author from their interpretation of the text –

what Jean Boase-Beier terms the *implied author* (2004: 279). But what is particularly interesting in the context of celebrity translation is the fact that there are potentially *two implied authors* – the source-text playwright and the celebrity translator. Receivers' respective associations with each of these authors may coincide – but they may also conflict. Either way, it's the potential breadth of cognitive effects that make such texts particularly fascinating to analyse.

I should stress here that my interest in exploring celebrity translation through the prism of theories derived from cognitive approaches to language in no way implies that I am arguing that audiences will always respond in the *same* or even a *similar* way to a play text at a cognitive level. Each spectator will experience the text with different contextual assumptions about both the source-text author and the celebrity translator, and therefore potentially arrive at a different interpretation of that text, and maybe even a different interpretation if they then see the performance a second time – this is what linguistics scholar Dan McIntyre refers to as the 'ontological status of dramatic performances' (2006:12). What I *am* proposing, however, is that there is scope for some common themes across spectators in terms of contextual assumptions due to the likelihood of shared experiences in the past (e.g. previous experience of the celebrity translator's own theatrical work), exposure to the same external stimuli (e.g. recently published reviews of the particular play in question) and, not least, the growing evidence that all human brains process communication in a broadly similar way (see Evans 2011: 71).

In this respect, my starting point for my analysis echoes David Johnston's view that 'a cognitive approach to spectator experience will certainly serve to remind us of individual uniqueness of response, reinforcing the warning that we should be careful in ascribing apparently univocal responses to audiences, [but] if certain plays – classics, good plays – retain their appeal across time and space, then there is also the strong likelihood of some broad commonality' (2013: 381). In other words, it appears justifiable to think in terms of the experience of watching a play as a unifying experience for the audience, but this is not the same as implying some kind of universal response, which would amount to a naïve interpretation of the role of the translator as cultural mediator.

I will now explain why I have decided to apply one particular cognitive theory, *relevance theory*, to my investigation of celebrity translation.

What is relevance theory?

Relevance theory is an approach to understanding communication based on a general view of cognition. It was fully elaborated for the first time by Dan Sperber and Deirdre Wilson in their 1986 book *Relevance: Communication and Cognition*, and subsequently updated in the second edition of this book in 1995 (which is the version I will be citing here). It offers a valuable framework within which to consider celebrity translation in that it enables us to consider the effects that the celebrity's translated text will have on the receivers of that text at a cognitive level, both in relation to the text itself (e.g. the way in which receivers might react to humour or irony) and in relation to, for example, all the wider associations, thoughts, images that receivers call to mind when they think of that celebrity (e.g. his or her type of humour, political viewpoint, propensity to challenge audiences and so on, or the relationship between the text in question and previous works by that celebrity writer) – in other words, the very factors that go towards making that person a celebrity in the first place.

In relevance theory, such facts, associations, thoughts, images and so on are referred to as *cognitive effects* (Sperber and Wilson 1995: 108–17), that is, effects that either strengthen or contradict assumptions about how communication is to be processed. At a very basic level, all relevant utterances convey cognitive effects as they will inevitably alter the receiver's assumptions that have already been determined by previous acts of comprehension. The important fact in relation to celebrity translation is that these previous acts of comprehension will be much richer and broader in scope than would be the case if those utterances had been made by a non-celebrity translator. This is because the receiver will have a much more clearly defined contextual framework in relation to a celebrity translator (i.e. a much greater and more multidimensional set of contextual associations) than he or she would have in relation to an unknown translator. What this means, then, is that the celebrity translator is potentially both a *real* and an *inferred* author, whereas the unknown translator can arguably only ever be an inferred author.

Relevance in the context of relevance theory is used to describe the prerequisite for *positive cognitive effects*. As Sperber and Wilson explain, 'for an input to be relevant, its processing must lead to cognitive gains', and a positive cognitive effect is 'a cognitive effect that contributes positively to the fulfilment of cognitive functions or goals' (1995: 265). This does not necessarily mean that positive cognitive effects are about *increasing* the amount of knowledge processed by the receiver – they could, for example, lead the receiver to question or discard any previously acquired knowledge. Nor does it mean that such inputs are then processed as *the truth*. Indeed, Wilson and Sperber have insisted that 'verbal communication is governed not by expectations of truthfulness but by expectations of relevance' (2002: 583). Relevance theory similarly dispenses with the view held by Paul Grice that pragmatic interpretation can only be possible if we presuppose that the agent (i.e. the person communicating to us) is rational since it makes no assumptions about the rationality or otherwise of communication.

This foregrounding of relevance over truth or rationality has important consequences for the application of relevance theory to translation. That's because it immediately implies that the role of the translator is not to replicate the truth or rationality of the source-text author's text. Rather, the translator's job is to ensure that the translation has the same *positive cognitive effects* on the receiver of the target text as the source text had on readers of that text – or in other words that the translation brings about the same changes in the reader's beliefs as the source text did in its reader's beliefs (see Sperber and Wilson 1995: 265). Not only does such a focus on the receiver confound many of the more formalist theories of translation that concentrate either on the relationship between the source and target text (e.g. Toury 1980) or on the decoding abilities of the receivers of the translated text (e.g. Nida 1964). It also raises interesting questions about translator visibility in the sense that it implies that visibility is not just about *textual* visibility – that is, whether a text is visibly translated or whether it reads like a text originally written in the target culture and in the target language. Rather, it's also (and in fact more) about *contextual* visibility – that is, whether the voice of the translator is recognized in the translation because of all the receiver's prior associations with that translator.

Relevance theory makes two generalizations about the way in which human beings communicate with one another. These generalizations are now known as the *principles of relevance*. One of these is about human cognition in general, and the other is about ostensive-inferential communication, that is, making manifest to an audience (in an act of ostensive communication) an intention to make manifest a basic level of communication, which the audience then processes as an inference (Sperber and Wilson 1995: 54). These two principles are as follows:

1. Human cognition tends to be geared to the maximization of relevance.
2. Every act of ostensive communication communicates a presumption of its own optimal relevance. (Sperber and Wilson 1995: 260)

The first of these principles essentially says that 'our cognitive system in general tends to allocate attention and processing resources so as to produce as many cognitive effects as possible for as little effort as possible' (Clark 2011: 130). The second, meanwhile, says that each ostensive stimulus is (a) relevant enough for it to be worth the addressee's effort to process it and (b) the most relevant one compatible with the communicator's abilities and preferences (Sperber and Wilson 1995: 270).

What this means in terms of an exchange of communication between two people, then, is that the communicator makes manifest by the very act of communicating that his or her utterance is worth processing by the receiver (even if the receiver then decides that it is not actually worth the effort). It also means that the communicator will communicate in a way that best fits with his or her available knowledge and needs at the time – such as, say, the need to be polite, or the need to withhold certain facts from the addressee. In terms of how the addressee processes that communication, relevance theory offers a way of predicting how the addressee will interpret the communicator's communicative intention called the *relevance-guided comprehension heuristic*. This states, first, that addressees will follow a path of least effort in deriving cognitive effects and test interpretations (such as disambiguations, reference resolutions and implicatures) in order of accessibility. Secondly, it states that addressees will stop once their expectations of relevance are satisfied (Wilson and Sperber 2004: 613–14).

This notion of stopping the search for interpretations once expectations of relevance have been satisfied might appear at first glance somewhat counterintuitive in the context of literary texts. After all, literary texts by definition create more effects the more the receiver thinks about such texts (or at least, should ideally do so). This conundrum has led to the specific development of *relevance theory for literature*, which talks about *maximum* rather than *optimal* relevance (MacKenzie 2002: 31). The implication here is that receivers will seek to find *as many cognitive effects as possible* in a literary text (say, by re-reading that text, discussing it with others, reflecting on it for extended periods of time and so on) rather than opting for the easiest or most readily accessible interpretation that nevertheless satisfies their need for relevance.

Indeed, as pragmatics scholar Adrian Pilkington suggests, literary texts may achieve stylistic (i.e. here cognitive) effects 'by creating special kinds of processing difficulties for the addressee' (1996: 158). The same is clearly true of play texts that might seek to challenge, provoke and disarm audiences. The key issue here is that such effort continues to be worthwhile in that it leads to a rewarding outcome, namely, an alternative interpretation or the dismissal of a previous interpretation. In other words, it continues to deliver positive cognitive effects. For the remainder of this book, then, I will talk of maximizing rather than optimizing relevance – and for the sake of brevity will refer simply to relevance theory even though what I'm actually talking about is relevance theory for literature. I will also demonstrate how expectations of relevance can lead to a *variety* of interpretations of the celebrity translator's target text (either across audiences or within the minds of individual spectators), even if one single interpretation might in itself satisfy the expectation of relevance.

Of course, this notion of an ongoing search for interpretations in order to maximize relevance takes place in parallel with spectators' search for clues that will help them to identify the context in which the celebrity translator intended them to interpret his or her text. This context may or may not overlap with the context intended by the source-text playwright, or the audience's representation of that playwright (the *implied playwright*). The identification of this context will help the spectator to arrive at an interpretation of the celebrity translator's intention, but this is not the same as saying that this interpretation will be the one that the translator had in mind. After all, the spectator may well overlook what the translator had in mind, or conversely identify a meaning that the translator had not ever imagined (see Furlong 2007: 336). So in the following chapters when I suggest how spectators may interpret particular lines from a celebrity translation, I'm not implying that these interpretations are what the translator *actually* intended, but merely that they *might* be what some or all spectators interpret that intention to be. And it doesn't matter whether that interpretation is correct or not – whatever the notion of a 'correct' interpretation really means in the context of literary texts.

I will come back to the issues of meaning and intention in the context of relevance theory in more detail later in this chapter. In the meantime, however, what is it about relevance theory that makes it a particularly useful theoretical framework within which to explore celebrity translation in the theatre?

Relevance theory and the study of celebrity translation

The application of relevance theory to translation has already been discussed by translation scholars Ernst-August Gutt (2000) and Jean Boase-Beier (2004, 2006, and 2011 and 2020), and its application to the reception of play texts was explored by linguistics and literature scholar Anne Furlong in 2014. But so far relevance theory hasn't been explored specifically within the context of the *translation of play texts*. While literary scholar Alain Wolf has looked at inferential meaning in theatre translation (2011: 87–104), this was more in the context of Grice's theory of conversational implicature than specifically in relation to relevance theory – and as seen in the previous section, the basic assumptions that Grice's theory makes about inferences are fundamentally different from those made in relevance theory. Over and above the scope that undoubtedly still exists for further research into how relevance theory can be applied to translation in general, there are some key dimensions of the theory that I would like to highlight here because they appear to me to be particularly useful to my exploration of celebrity translation.

The first of these dimensions is the focus in relevance theory on a receiver's interpretation of a text, and the distinction that it makes between explicit and implicit communication – or what relevance theory calls a text's explicatures and implicatures (see Chapter 4 for more discussion of these). This is obviously an important distinction when considering any poetic texts since such texts depend on interpretation for their poetic effects. It essentially corresponds to the difference between what the author says and the way in which he or she says it – which, as an aside, also corresponds at a very broad level to the distinction between a semantic and a pragmatic approach to language and communication (see Blakemore 1992; Carston 2002a and Clark 2013, to name but a few). In the case of translated poetic texts, relevance theory offers us the opportunity to compare the likely interpretations of the source text and the target text and thereby determine whether these texts have had similar cognitive effects on their respective receivers. In the case of celebrity translators, this will not only involve looking at the typical *stylistic devices* used in that celebrity's own work and how these potentially influence reception of their translations if these are assumed to also contain some of those devices. It will also involve exploring how all the *contextual associations* surrounding that celebrity (and not just those associations triggered by the text itself) potentially influence a spectator's interpretation of that utterance. In other words, relevance theory provides us with a useful framework for exploring the extent to which spectators may infer some of that celebrity translator's *voice*, as defined in Chapter 1.

The second dimension to relevance theory that is useful in this study of celebrity translation in the theatre is the way in which the theory describes *spontaneous* rather than post-rationalized communication, and is concerned exclusively with individual responses to a stimulus. The issue of spontaneity is essential when exploring translation for the theatre since, unlike other forms of literary text, the receiver is not able to re-read parts of the text as a way of absorbing a piece of communication before moving onto the next segment in the stimulus.

The issue of individual responses is a more difficult one to reconcile in the context of the theatre since responses are inevitably governed not only by an individual spectator's own cognitive processes but also by that spectator's response to other spectators' responses – for example, laughing or gasping at the same time as other audience members laugh or gasp. Moreover, in the context of a play text by a well-known author, there will inevitably be a degree of *shared cognitive effects* when experiencing a text in a shared physical environment. If that text is a translation by a celebrity translator, the potential for shared cognitive effects becomes even greater as audiences will most likely already have at least some shared contextual associations with that celebrity.

In the following chapters, then, when I discuss spectators' likely interpretations of a celebrity translator's text, what I'm seeking to imply is that each individual spectator will derive his or her unique interpretation of that text, but that such interpretations will most likely also be guided contextual effects, including those derived from *shared assumptions* about the text and its authors and about other spectators' responses. This relates to what philosophers would call the *common aesthetic effect* whereby members of a culture derive a common sense of the value of a work of art because of the process of enculturation, that is, the process of learning from others about what constitutes worthwhile culture and what does not (see Williams 1977; Bourdieu 1984 and Eagleton 1990, to name but a few).

The third dimension of relevance theory that is particularly interesting in the context of a study of celebrity translation is the notion of *contextual effects*. That's because this notion represents an extremely useful way of thinking about the associations that celebrities inevitably bring with them by virtue of being well known, and about how these associations merge (or sometimes maybe don't merge) with spectators' associations with the original playwright. Importantly, there is a distinction to be drawn here between *contextual effects* and *cognitive effects*. Contextual effects are abstract effects that can be logically inferred in the context of certain assumptions, whereas cognitive effects are effects that receivers infer and that change their beliefs (Sperber and Wilson 1995: 265). Cognitive effects, therefore, may be the same as contextual effects, but they may also be different.

In principle, the concept of contextual effects echoes André Lefevere's notion of refractions, which he used to explain how the context of literary works is created and the ways in which this context influences reception of those works.

> A writer's work gains exposure and achieves influence mainly through 'misunderstandings and misconceptions' or, to use a more neutral term, refractions. Writers and their work are always understood and conceived against a certain background, or, if you will, are refracted through a certain spectrum, just as their work itself can refract previous works through a certain spectrum. (2004: 240)

While the concept of viewing writers and their work through a refracted spectrum is an attractive metaphor and one whose notion of an altered perspective fits with the idea of contextual effects, my concern is that it implies a rather fixed, or at least predictable, relationship between the author and the receivers of his or her texts – as if the cultural connotations that cause the refraction create a predetermined distortion of reality and form a barrier between the author and his or her audience. It also assumes that source and target texts are in some way objects that have a constant relationship with each other irrespective of the ways in which those texts become constantly changing entities in the minds of their receivers.

A metaphor that I find much more engaging as a way of thinking about the contextual effects that are triggered by celebrity translation is Patrice Pavis's concept of translation from one language and culture to another language and culture as an *hourglass*. Pavis imagines how the flow of grains of sand through the neck of the hourglass is subject to a number of filters imposed by the culture receiving the foreign import. These filters represent a blend of intrinsic and extrinsic stimuli, including artistic, sociological and anthropological factors such as the perspective of the translator, the choice of theatrical form and the dramatic means by which the foreign culture is performed in the target culture. According to Pavis, if the hourglass functions as a mill, it will blend all the elements of the source culture, thereby destroying its specificity and leading to output that has not only lost its original shape but also failed to mould itself in a way that meets the target culture's expectations. But if, on the other hand, the hourglass operates more like a funnel, it will 'indiscriminately absorb the initial substance without reshaping it through the series of filters or leaving any trace of the original matter' (Pavis 1992: 5).

This model of filters is an interesting way of thinking about the different ways in which spectators in the theatre will interpret external stimuli. It reminds us that the reception of such stimuli is influenced by factors far beyond those represented by the playwright and the play text itself, or in the case of celebrity translation by the source-text playwright, the source text, the celebrity translator and the celebrity's target text. The contextual effects produced by the actors (who may themselves often be celebrities), the staging of the production, other audience members, the physical space that is the actual theatre and many more additional factors will also play a crucial role in determining how a play text is interpreted in practice.

Many of these factors fall more within the realm of performance studies, and are therefore beyond the scope of this book. My focus as a translation scholar is on those factors that relate most directly to the text, namely, the contextual effects created by the source text versus the translation, and by the source-text playwright versus the celebrity translator. Even from this narrower perspective, however, the concept of *cognitive filters* is a useful way of theorizing the factors that influence the ways in which we respond to an external stimulus. What's more, conceptualizing the grains of sand that pass through these cognitive filters as the different *cognitive stimuli* that spectators perceive while experiencing the translated play text is a useful way of thinking about the different contextual effects that these filters can have on an audience's reception of a celebrity translation, since it reminds us that such stimuli are constantly changing in terms of salience, priority and relationship with one another.

Whereas Pavis's visualization of the hourglass might appear to suggest that cognitive filters work in some kind of sequential way, proponents of relevance theory would argue such filters are actually applied in a more random way – and in a way that will undoubtedly also change over time as experience and new contextual effects reshape the way in which we interpret the world around us. This is in much the same way that, say, filters can be placed over a camera lens in different combinations to achieve different photographic effects. Spectators watching a performance of a play are likely to revise and reprioritize their cognitive filters both during and after the performance, to the extent that they might interpret the play in a completely different way if they see it a second time or after discussing it with others.

To better explain what I mean here, let's apply this notion of cognitive filters to an example of celebrity translation – say, playwright Tom Stoppard's translation of *The Cherry Orchard* by Anton Chekhov, which was first performed and published in 2009. There are many cognitive filters that might influence the way in which spectators view or readers read this text. If, for example, audiences are particularly familiar with Chekhov, they are likely to apply any number of filters, depending on their breadth and depth of knowledge about Chekhov as a writer. These might include any or all of the following:

1. Chekhov was a Russian writer;
2. *The Cherry Orchard* was the last play that Chekhov wrote;
3. *The Cherry Orchard* contains elements of both comedy and tragedy;
4. the overall theme of *The Cherry Orchard* is the effect that social change has on people;
5. *The Cherry Orchard* shows the effects of reforms that took place in Russia in the second half of the nineteenth century, such as the emancipation of serfs in 1861;
6. Chekhov is now felt to be one of the first exponents of early modernism in the theatre;
7. the Marxist interpretation of *The Cherry Orchard* is not accepted by all scholars of Chekhov; and so on and so forth.

In many cases, it would be reasonable to assume that the number of filters that spectators apply and the intensity of such filters correlates exactly with their previous knowledge of Chekhov and his plays. Of course, this is a somewhat hypothetical view. But at the same time it appears wholly logical to accept that the more spectators know about the playwright who wrote the original-language text that they are watching in translation, the more cognitive filters they are likely to apply to their interpretation of that play. Put another way, the more levels that cognitive stimuli have to pass through in a spectator's cultural hourglass, the more the grains of sand in that hourglass will blend with one another to create a constant flow of cognitive effects during the performance itself and for some time afterwards.

If, on the other hand, spectators are more familiar with Stoppard rather than Chekhov, their cognitive filters might include any number or any combination of the following:

1. Tom Stoppard is a British playwright;
2. Tom Stoppard was born in what was at the time Czechoslovakia;
3. Tom Stoppard does not understand any Russian;
4. Tom Stoppard has translated lots of plays;
5. Tom Stoppard has addressed lots of philosophical concepts in his own work;
6. Tom Stoppard has campaigned against political interference in the British press;
7. Tom Stoppard had an affair with Felicity Kendal while married to Miriam Stoppard; and so on and so forth.

Again, logic says that the more spectators know about Stoppard, both as a playwright and as a public figure, the more cognitive filters they are likely to apply to their interpretation of his translation. They might, for example, look for a particular type of humour, or subconsciously listen out for references to a society's right to enjoy freedom of expression, or expect a certain attitude towards women, or any combination of these. Returning to our hourglass analogy, we can visualize grains of sand of a different colour from those representing the cognitive stimuli derived from associations with Chekhov, with a blend of grains of sand of different colours passing through each spectator's differing cognitive filters while watching and thinking about the play.

Another important issue to bear in mind here is that it's not only the *number* of cognitive stimuli that spectators perceive or the number of cognitive filters that spectators apply that determines their interpretation of the play. Their interpretation is also determined by the *intensity* of those stimuli, the *order* in which those filters are applied, and the consequent way in which such stimuli *blend together*. The analogy here might be, for example, that particularly salient cognitive stimuli are represented by especially smooth grains of sand that pass through the cognitive filters of the hourglass more quickly than rougher grains, which are more difficult cognitive stimuli for spectators to process through their filters – an idea that echoes the notion referred to above that literary texts are often made intentionally difficult to interpret (see Pilkington 1996: 158).

As an example, a spectator with only vague knowledge of Chekhov or Stoppard as authors might have read the review of the play in the *Guardian* that talked about Stoppard's 'quip-filled, pun-fuelled' script (Hickling 2010: n.p.) and decided to go to see the play expecting it to be a hilarious comedy. That spectator would then have a very different set of cognitive filters from neighbouring spectators who are more knowledgeable about the source-text or target-text authors, leading to a very different interpretation of the play. This might, for example, become apparent if he or she laughs at different points in the play from other spectators.

This notion of the hourglass does, of course, in some ways echo Gilles Fauconnier and Mark Turner's work on conceptual blending (2002), which can be applied to describe the way in which spectators in the theatre blend in and out of the performance. And even if this notion of blending is coming from a different perspective from my metaphor of different cognitive stimuli blending together and passing through filters in different ways, there are still parallels in both concepts in the sense that both explore the mental process of thematizing and prioritizing external stimuli in order to arrive at a rewarding interpretation that satisfies the search for relevance. But while both relevance theory and conceptual blending theory might be based on quite similar views of cognition, and in particular share the idea that receivers of communication need to make sense of communication in a way that feels rewarding, they are clearly very different in the sense that the former is a theory of communication whereas the latter is a more technical theory of a particular aspect of thought. For the purposes of this book, it's the *emotional* reward (i.e. the pleasure gained from the intellectual stimulation that a play provides) rather than the *physiological* reward (i.e. the likely release of chemicals in the brain) that I'm more interested in. As a result, I will restrict my cognitive–theoretical discussion to relevance theory from now on in this book.

At this point, it's worth stressing that the concept of contextual associations, and indeed the application of relevance theory in general, presupposes that (1) we are able to deduce (or at least, we can attempt to deduce) what either the source-text playwright or the celebrity translator *intended* to communicate in their text; and (2) we are able to deduce (or at least, we can attempt to deduce) how audiences will interpret these intentions, that is, what *meaning* they will attribute to the text. The issues surrounding the way in which relevance theory supposes that we are bound to try and deduce intentions and meaning, and the corresponding caveats that apply to my subsequent analysis of different celebrity translations, will now be discussed in the following sections of this chapter.

Relevance theory and intention

The issue of the source-text author's intention when writing his or her text is one that has long vexed scholars of literature, and by extension, scholars of translation. It's also one that is of particular importance to this study of celebrity translation in British theatre given my hypothesis that celebrity translators may often *intentionally* inject some of their own voice into their translations. That is because any attempt to test such a hypothesis will inevitably involve an analysis of where, how and why such an intention arose.

Literary theorists William K. Wimsatt and Monroe C. Beardsley believed that, in the case of poetry at least, authorial intent is irrelevant to the study of an author's work because there is no way of reconstructing his or her intention at the time of writing – and because the work is in any case a production that becomes separated from its moment of creation (1954: 4). According to their *intentional fallacy*, interpretation is only possible based on what a text actually says, rather than what the author intended it to say. Importantly, this view has often been misinterpreted as implying that authorial intentions do not exist at all. Yet in fact what the two theorists were actually saying was that it's highly unlikely that readers will ever reliably know what the author's intention was. Wimsatt and Beardsley were proponents of what came to be known as *new criticism*, which held that literary works (specifically poems) were autonomous organic structures in their own right, and could not therefore be legitimately analysed in the light of the writer's cultural or biographical context. This is the movement that paved the way for the *death of the author* argument proposed by post-structuralist critic Roland Barthes (1977: 142–8), which claims that any reading or criticism of literature that relies on dissecting any aspects of the author's identity (such as his or her political views, religion, ethnicity, sexuality and so on) inevitably imposes a limit on how that work can be interpreted.

Such ideas not surprisingly provoked much controversy among scholars. Stanley Fish, for example, argued that readers will always try 'to discern and therefore to realize … an author's intention' (1980: 161) as a way of arriving at their own interpretation of a text. This is not to say that there's a right way of interpreting a text – or in other words only one allowable interpretation. Rather, the implication is that readers will seek to arrive at a communal interpretation – one that may still not ever be the one that the author intended, but one that does at least offer the receiver the emotional security of belonging to a 'community' (1980: 161) of readers who agree with one another. This is essentially the logic behind reading reviews of plays before going to see them, and of seeking to experience the performance of a play text with a community of spectators, who can potentially provide immediate validation of an interpretation – for example, by all laughing or all gasping at the same point in the performance.

Literary theorists Steve Knapp and Walter Benn Michaels, meanwhile, put forward the view that there's no such thing as *intentionless* meaning. They argue that any interpretation of literature inevitably involves determining the original intention of the author of that work. That's because there can be 'no possibility of language prior to and independent of intention' (1985: 19). In their view, 'what a text means and what its author intends it to mean are identical' (1985: 19). What this view seems to overlook, however, is that meaning is not the same as authorially intended meaning. If the two were the same, that would imply that writing would never fail to mean what it was intended to mean, which is clearly an absurd argument.

Thinking about the issue of intention purely from a common sense perspective, it's surely hard not to disagree with philosopher François Recanati when he says that 'when someone acts, whether linguistically or otherwise, there is a reason why she does what she does. To provide an interpretation for that action is to find that reason, that is, to ascribe the agent a particular intention in terms of which we can make sense of the action' (2000: 106). This view does perhaps rely too much on Grice's view of pragmatic interpretation, which assumes that humans behave in a wholly rational way when they communicate – for example, by seeking to tell the truth. Nevertheless, it reminds us that there must surely always be an intention behind every act of communication, whether that intention is rational or emotional, conscious or subconscious, and capable or not of being articulated and shared. This idea in turn echoes the concept of the Johari Window that was developed by psychologists Joseph Luft and Harry Ingham in the 1950s as a tool for mapping individuals' awareness of their own personalities (see Luft and Ingham 1963). They put forward the notion that our understanding of others' personalities, attitudes, values and so on can be divided into open (those known to ourselves and to others), hidden (those known to ourselves but not to others), blind (those known to others but not to ourselves) and unknown (those known neither to ourselves nor to others) associations and beliefs.

So what does relevance theory add to the debate around the recoverability of authorial intentions? Relevance theory maintains that texts are always intentional. That is because the theory views texts as first and foremost acts of communication (even if they may also be objects or phenomena with their own existence), which by definition implies a communicative intention. Indeed, it's this notion of the fundamental intention behind every act of communication that underpins the theory's concept of *explicatures* and *implicatures*. Here, the idea of explicit and implicit communication automatically implies that a text (in the sense of being an act of communication) contains elements that the reader can assume, with different levels of confidence, that the author intended to be recovered. As such, texts are 'not treated as objects in the world, to be processed in a context entirely determined by the reader. ... The text provides evidence not just for the interpretation, but for the context which produces that interpretation' (Furlong 2007: 337).

In the context of literary texts (although the same principles apply to all acts of communication), relevance theory suggests that a text can only be successful if the receiver of that text is able to recognize the interpretation that its author intended. Unlike Grice's theory of communication, which assumed that communicators act in a rational way, relevance theory makes no claims about the truthfulness, accuracy or appropriateness of that text. Authors are therefore seen as communicating to provide evidence for a set of assumptions (propositions, ideas, feelings, opinions, prejudices and so on that may or may not be truthful, accurate or appropriate). And it's up to receivers to accept whether these assumptions are true or not, and to then change their view of the world accordingly. The emphasis is therefore on the reader's interpretive capacity in deducing the author's communicative intentions. In relevance theory, then, as Furlong explains, 'there is always an intending author, there is always some responsibility on the reader's part for the construction of the interpretation, and there is always an intended interpretation' (2003: 335). In this respect, relevance theory echoes some of the views held by those 'individualist' reader-response theorists (such as Fish 1980) who maintain that it's the individual receivers, or individual 'interpretive communities' (Fish 1980: 172), who are ultimately in control of deriving the meaning of literary texts.

From the point of view of translation, the implication here is that translators need to understand the author's intentions if they are to be able to produce a target text that allows its receivers to infer the same intention as the source text inferred. In the terms used in relevance theory, the translator ideally needs to replicate the *cognitive state* of the source-text author (either the real or the inferred author). The notion of cognitive state includes authors' *intentions* (i.e. their communicative intentions), their philosophy, attitudes, ideas and specific opinion on the subject that they are writing about.

In my view, though, this appears to be a somewhat hypothetical demand on translators. This is not because the source-text author's cognitive state is a theoretical and often irrecoverable construct. Far from it, in the case of well-known authors of canonical works, the level of biographical information available to the translator would in many cases make it relatively straightforward to at least attempt to replicate the author's cognitive state to some extent, even if that translator did not necessarily share all of that author's attitudes, ideas, opinions and so on. Rather, it's more because the translator may very plausibly have quite different communicative intentions from the source-text author with regard to his or her own target text. Translators' communicative intentions may, for example, be influenced by personal, ideological or commercial factors that bear no resemblance to the factors that influenced the source-text author's intentions – for example, the desire to create a text that will successfully meet the needs of a different culture, audience and publishing context from that of the source text and its author, or the limitations imposed on the translator's freedom of expression by other agents in the publishing system such as rightsholders.

Perhaps most importantly in the context of this study of celebrity translators, the translator's cognitive state will almost by definition include those factors that go to make up the profile of those celebrities – factors such as their assumptions about the public's reception of that work, or about their image in the eyes of the public, fans of their work, critics, publishers and so on. By extension, their translations will inevitably be assessed against the context of a spectator's existing understanding of that celebrity's actual or assumed status, values and beliefs as well as by their understanding of the text itself – that is to say, in the context of the spectator's own cognitive state, which will include all the spectator's personal opinions about the celebrity. In other words, the celebrity translator is inferred by the spectator to fit the spectator's own context (see MacKenzie 2002: 45).

There's clearly potential here for widely varying interpretations of communicative intentions depending on whether an individual spectator is more familiar with the source-text author or with the celebrity translator – that is, whether their cognitive state is dominated more by associations with or opinions about one or the other, or indeed both equally. Similarly, there's also potential for widespread *misinterpretation* of communicative intentions if spectators mistakenly infer a communicative intention that was not actually intended by the celebrity translator – something which might plausibly happen if, say, the associations with the celebrity's political viewpoint are particularly strong, leading to an utterance being interpreted as having a political message when this was not in fact the case. Of course, here it's vital to recognize that how the translator, celebrity or not, intended his or her work to be interpreted is ultimately less important from a relevance-theoretic perspective than how the audience, or audiences, actually do interpret it (see the following section on relevance theory and meaning).

Perhaps somewhat controversially in the eyes of some language scholars, let's start, then, by thinking in terms of the celebrity translator's *motivations* for translating a text in the first place before seeking to uncover his or her communicative intentions. Why is this useful? Well, it's because these motivations will help to shape that celebrity's communicative intentions. So, for example, it may well be interesting to consider the circumstances surrounding the commissioning of a translation and to explore the likely expectations imposed either directly or indirectly by the commissioning body as a way of understanding the context within which the celebrity translator's authorial intentions were moulded. Likewise, any comparison of the target text and the source text will necessitate a similar exploration of the source-text playwright's motivations for creating his or her text, and a subsequent comparison with the motivations of the celebrity translator. Here, it's quite likely that plausible communicative intentions may well coincide even with different motivations. That's because any specific motivations (such as, say, the source-text playwright's desire to tackle a new genre of theatre or the celebrity translator's desire to give a new slant on a canonical work) will still give rise to a range of potential communicative intentions and therefore a range of interpretations.

This concept of the translator's motivations mirrors a number of translation-theoretical ideas around text interpretation, such as Reiß and Vermeer's notion of text type (1984: 196), Peter Newmark's concept of the intention of the text (1988: 12) and even Friedrich Schleiermacher's views on the author's individuality (1977: 166). Most significantly from the point of view of my subsequent text analysis, however, it echoes Fish's concept of the 'informed reader' (1980: 48). So, as well as being assumed to have both a degree of linguistic competence (i.e. he or she can understand the meaning of the text) and literary competence (which we can take in the following analysis to mean a level of experience in interpreting theatrical texts), the receiver of a celebrity translation can be assumed to also have a level of prior understanding of that celebrity in terms of his or her previous work, values, beliefs, personality and so on. And while the precise level of understanding will obviously vary between translators and between spectators, there will nonetheless in almost all cases be a level of *complicity* between the audience and the celebrity translator (and indeed between the audience and the source-text playwright) that will determine the audience's response to the celebrity's translation. This will become clearer in the subsequent chapters when I explore three different examples of celebrity translation and arguably three different levels of complicity between the different agencies involved.

Relevance theory and meaning

In relevance theory, and indeed in other theories of communication, the issue of meaning is inextricably related to the issue of communicative intention. But while for translation scholars the question of meaning involves opening what translator and literature scholar David Bellos describes as 'a philosophical can of worms' (2011: 67), the relevance-theoretic account of meaning is a relatively straightforward one.

As pointed out in the previous section, relevance theory attaches more importance to the way in which communication is *interpreted* than to the author's actual communicative intentions. This certainly makes sense in the context of literary texts, where the notion of a definitive interpretation is a rather meaningless one. What this means, then, is that relevance theory assumes that *intended* and *interpreted* meanings are one and the same. That's because the receiver's inferential recognition of the author's intention is what creates the link between an utterance in a text and the intention behind it. As a result, 'the author is inferred by the reader to fit the latter's own context' (Boase-Beier 2020: 48). Ultimately, then, there can be no such thing as misinterpretation of a literary text according to relevance theory. Moreover, unlike other theories of language and translation, relevance theory 'would not bemoan the impossibility of locating definite meaning, but would celebrate it' (Boase-Beier 2020: 56).

As an extension of this notion that intended and interpreted meanings are one and the same thing, relevance theory can also provide us with a systematic account of how receivers decide on the meaning of texts, offering 'an insight into the process of interpretation which allows readers and theorists to argue fruitfully about their interpretations, and to understand the bases of their conclusions' (Furlong 2007: 328). This has important implications for translation of all kinds, not just celebrity translation. Without going so far as to support Gutt's controversial assertion that relevance theory obviates the need for any special theories of translation (see Malmkjær 1992: 298–309), I would certainly repeat here the view I expressed earlier that relevance theory can at least provide a framework for further discussion about meaning from the perspective of the receiver – which is something that more text-focused theories of translation typically fail to achieve.

Having established that we can assume in the context of relevance theory that the issue of the interpretation of meaning resides with the receiver rather than the author or the text itself, it's interesting at this point to explore how translation scholars view this perspective in terms of the role that it ascribes to the translator. As seen in the previous section, the role of the translator from a relevance-theoretical perspective is to replicate the meaning of the source text by replicating the *cognitive state* of the source-text author – an author who may be either real or inferred. This involves replicating not only the source-text author's communicative intentions but also his or her view of the world and specific opinions on the subject about which he or she is communicating. If translators are to recreate this meaning in translation, then, they need to take account not only of the actual *content* of the text (in terms of the propositions that it expresses) but also of the set of weak implicatures that can be derived by inference from the text. As Boase-Beier points out, 'The fact that they are weak means that the translator, like any reader, takes responsibility for creating meanings which she or he assumes are intended by the inferred author. The element of responsibility lies in that assumption, and it is this that translators may be held to account for, not the supposed views of the inferred author' (2004: 282).

This raises some important issues that are specific to this study of the celebrity translator. First, even in the case of canonical works of drama, we can't necessarily work on the premise that the source-text playwright is actually *real*, in spite of the fact that the audience may well have an established set of contextual assumptions about him or her. Even though source-text playwrights may well be celebrities in their own right (in terms of public awareness and the information, critiques, opinions, debates about their oeuvre and biography that might be accessible to audiences), this doesn't necessarily make them real in the sense that there's a definitive representation of who they are (or were) and what they stand for – consider, for example, the many misrepresentations or misunderstandings that often surround creative figures from any sector of the arts. The same arguments apply to the celebrity translators themselves. Even though they are *real* in that they are more likely to still alive than the playwrights whose canonical plays they are translating (at least if their celebrity translations are recent works), their public personas are arguably no more real than those of authors who lived many years ago. In fact, it could be argued that, in the age of the mass media and the internet, they are actually *less* real than authors who existed in an era when public profiles were more easily managed (at least at the time).

Second, we should consider the issue of *truth* in relation to celebrity translation. I'm using the term *truth* here not to mean an accurate depiction of reality, but rather in the sense of what it is in the text that delivers cognitive gains to its receivers. According to relevance theory, this is much more than the actual propositional content of that text, and encompasses all those explicit and implicit meanings that are derived from the author's communicative intentions – in other words everything that audiences infer from the author's communicative style, or, in the context of a play text, the playwright's *voice*. Boase-Beier argues that 'we are more likely, as readers, to attribute responsibility for the truth to the original writer' than to the translator (2004: 227). This is because truth is typically seen as residing with the source-text author rather than the translator. In other words, translators are generally assumed to provide us with a representation of what someone else (the source-text author) meant rather than what they mean themselves.

But in the case of celebrity translators, though, we could potentially argue that what they say may indeed be something to whose truth they do actually subscribe. That's because their name is more obviously attached to their text than an unknown translator's would be, and because their truth will often reside in the familiar voice that they add to their translation. As a result, spectators will be rewarded with cognitive gains whenever they hear some of the celebrity translator's own voice in the text – and whether that voice was actually intended to be heard or not. Celebrity translators are therefore in a sense the messenger as well as the message, and are more likely to be held accountable for that message by audiences and critics than they would be if they had no public profile. In the case of an unknown translator, on the other hand, the truth of the text is more likely either to be ascribed solely to the source-text playwright or to exist in 'the in-between' (Tymoczko 2003: 181–201), that is, ascribed to neither the source-text author nor the translator. It's this distinctive *power balance* (or *salience balance*) between the source-text playwright and the celebrity translator that lies at the heart of my arguments in this book. Relevance theory's explanation of the factors that combine to create the source-text playwright's and the celebrity translators' respective voices therefore provides a highly useful framework for analysis from a translation scholar's perspective.

Third, the fact that celebrity theatre translation is often indirect translation (i.e. the celebrity playwright works on the basis of a literal translation produced by another translator) raises some interesting questions about how meaning is conveyed between what are essentially three different texts and three different authors. Here, Gutt's relevance-theoretic distinction between direct and indirect translation potentially provides a useful way of theorizing the relationship between these different texts and authors (2000: 136), even if his terms *direct* and *indirect* translation are somewhat confusingly the opposite of those used in practice in the theatrical system. According to Gutt's distinction, the role of the literal translator can be described as one that involves 'interlingual interpretive use' (2000) – in other words, precise in terms of content only, or what Gutt terms *indirect translation*. The celebrity translator's role, on the other hand, is to provide 'communicative clues' that reflect not only the information contained in the source text but also its stylistic features (2000: 135) – or what Gutt terms *direct translation* because of the correspondence between this and direct quotation.

Finally, relevance theory also helps to shed new light on more text-oriented or culturally focused perspectives on meaning in the translation of theatre texts. David Johnston, for example, argues the following.

> Meaning is retroactive, and while texts from the someplace- or sometime-else clearly contain possibilities for meaning that may be lost to us, the translation of other texts into our present contexts, without permitting those current contexts to deracinate the cultural concerns and linguistic shapes of those texts, helps us to discern the ways in which our perspective may illuminate or awaken other possibilities in what may appear only to have a remote or disconnected connection with us. (2013: 382)

Appropriate though this view may be from the perspective of, say Tymoczko's views on the positionality of the translator (2003: 183), the implication in the above that meaning is somehow fixed in a particular time or culture would appear to contradict almost all of the thinking in translation studies from Nida onwards. On the other hand, the cognitive approach to language on which relevance theory is based enables us to assess meaning from the perspective of the mind's cognitive abilities (such as, say, the ability to suspend our notions of time and place in the theatre) rather than seeing language as a 'wholly distinct encapsulated module of the mind' (Evans 2011: 71).

Relevance theory as an analytical framework

As already seen, the concept of celebrity translation in the theatre can only ever exist in the minds of an audience, since without audiences there can be not only no theatre but also no celebrities. It follows from this, then, that any analysis of celebrity translation in the theatre must inevitably focus on the audience's assumptions about the celebrity translator's text, and on the audience's knowledge (or at least their assumptions) about that celebrity's motivations for translating the text in the first place – and about that celebrity's communicative intentions when translating the text. In this sense, then, my analysis of celebrity translation will inherently challenge Wimsatt and Beardsley's argument that it would be fallacious to base a critical judgement about the meaning of a text on any external evidence of the author's intentions (1954: 10). On the contrary, receivers of a text translated by a celebrity will *undoubtedly* rely on such external evidence (i.e. their contextual assumptions about the celebrity and his or her motivations and intentions) when assessing that translation, because otherwise, almost by definition, that translator would not warrant the *celebrity* label in the first place.

With its focus on cognitive effects on the audience and its core tenet that intended and interpreted meaning are one and the same thing, relevance theory clearly provides us with an extremely useful interpretive framework for my subsequent analyses of celebrity translations of play texts. This is not to suggest that relevance theory in itself can bring about a whole new reading of a literary work. Rather, it's to recognize the usefulness of the theory in shedding new light on the process of the reception of communication, on the criteria for interpretation of texts and, perhaps most importantly from my perspective, on the role of *intention* in literary texts (see Furlong 2007: 334).

I should stress here that my interpretations of what both the source-text playwrights and the celebrity translators intended are not supposed to be understood as definitive interpretations – after all, the notion of definitive meaning is as alien to relevance theory as it is to most other theories of language, literature or translation. Nor am I aiming to derive implicatures that are a direct reflection of those envisaged by either the source-text playwright or the celebrity translator since, again, relevance theory makes no claims about being able to do this – not least because it's highly unlikely that either of these authors will be wholly aware of all the potential implicatures that audiences will infer from their respective texts anyway. Instead, all relevance theory claims is that the authors will simply give their audiences (including translation scholars) *sufficient evidence* to be able to construct the context that will provide the interpretation that they intended, or at least foresaw. In this respect, we should remember that cognitive approaches to language such as relevance theory investigate 'how the various aspects of linguistic knowledge emerge from a common set of human cognitive abilities upon which they draw' (Evans 2011: 71). In other words, such approaches are based on our current understanding of how the brain uses its resources, how it reuses existing structures for new purposes, and how similarly different people's brains work. In this sense, then, we can justifiably argue on the basis of relevance theory that spectators with similar contextual associations *are likely to* respond to an external stimulus in a similar way.

In the following chapters I will analyse three different play texts translated by celebrity translators. In each case, I will show how an evaluation of everything that we know or can infer about the source-text playwright's and celebrity translator's motivations (and, where appropriate, the literal translator's motivations) for producing their respective texts can help us to understand those authors' communicative intentions.

In the case of the source-text playwrights and celebrity translators, it's essential to remember that, by virtue of being well-known authors, they are not only widely written about (by scholars, literary critics, journalists and bloggers), but to a greater or lesser extent have themselves also widely written or talked about their own perceptions of their motivations and intentions in media interviews, at public events or in published diaries. Of course, such comments may or may not coincide with the actual motivations and intentions at the time of producing the translations – they may, for example, be revised in the light of public and critical response to their work. But as will be clear from the earlier discussion of relevance theory and intention, the 'accuracy' of an author's perceptions of his or her motivations and intentions is not an issue here. What's more important is how they are inferred by audiences and how such inferences help to either reinforce or call into question the existing contextual associations that spectators have with those authors and their work.

I will also explore spectators' potential inferences from specific textual examples from each of the translated play texts in order to show how each celebrity translator might be perceived as injecting some of his own voice into his work. And while all three case studies follow broadly the same format, I will draw in each on a slightly different dimension of relevance theory to support my arguments. My ultimate aims are to show the different ways in which audiences may hear a celebrity translator's voice when attending a performance of that translator's work, and thereby to defend the practice of celebrity translation in British theatre as a way of enhancing the accessibility and appeal of translated theatre in the UK.

4

Mark Ravenhill's version of Bertolt Brecht's *Leben des Galilei*

Introduction

Bertolt Brecht's *Leben des Galilei* (written in various iterations between 1938 and Brecht's death in 1956) dramatizes the later life of Pisan scientist and astronomer Galileo Galilei (1564–1642). In the play, Galileo has evidence that the earth revolves around the sun rather than the other way around – the opposite of the view that was accepted at the time, not least by the Catholic Church. Torn between his scientific principles and the rewards of complying with authority, Galileo eventually agrees to recant his research and becomes a broken man.

With its themes of the power of knowledge, the fear that can come from knowing the truth, and the ways in which authorities can distort the truth to suit their own ends, *Leben des Galilei* clearly references many of the key issues of the era in which it was written, from the abuse of authority in Nazi Germany to the power of the scientific knowledge that led to the creation of the atomic bomb. And this is to say nothing of the work's ongoing relevance in the second decade of the twentieth century – an era characterized by an increasing gulf between those able to harness the benefits of a globalized knowledge economy and those who are not, by widespread manipulation of public opinion and by seemingly incessant claims of fake news.

The combination of a canonical, and indeed controversial, play text and a translator who is himself not averse to causing controversy makes Mark Ravenhill's 2013 version of Brecht's *Leben des Galilei* (translated as *A Life of Galileo*) a highly useful example of celebrity translation for the purposes of this book. But what's particularly interesting about this translation is the way in which Ravenhill largely appears to avoid imposing his own voice on his version of the play text, to the extent that much of Ravenhill's dialogue is strikingly similar to the literal translation from which he worked – something that will become clear from the examples given later in this chapter. There is therefore arguably a large degree of dissonance between the *audience's potential expectations* of Ravenhill's translation and what Ravenhill actually presents to spectators. In terms of relevance theory and Sperber and Wilson's concept of ostensive-inferential communication, we could say that there is significant divergence between the stimulus by the communicator (i.e. Ravenhill) and the way in which this is interpreted by the addressee (i.e. the audience) (Clark 2013: 113). This then leads to a cognitive environment that's not necessarily shared by the communicator and the addressee. I will demonstrate this by distinguishing between

1. on the one hand, elements of the celebrity translator's text that are 'motivated choice on the part of the writer' (Verdonk 2002: 9) (i.e. a translation that is intentionally designed to inject some of the celebrity translator's own voice into the text) and
2. on the other hand, elements that are not intended to be interpreted as the voice of the celebrity translator, but that might be mistakenly *inferred* by spectators to be such a choice (i.e. a translation that implies the same as the source text in terms of ostensive communication, or rather in this case, that implies the same as the literal translation).

In accordance with the rationale for exploring authors' motivations provided in the previous chapter, I will start by exploring Brecht's likely motivations for writing *Leben des Galilei*. I will then examine the likely motivations of both the literal translator (Deborah Gearing) and the celebrity translator (Mark Ravenhill) in translating their texts. This will enable us to examine their translations from their own respective points of view. Following this analysis, I will explore specific examples of each author's text (Brecht's, Gearing's and Ravenhill's) to illustrate the difference between an *intentional* celebrity voice (i.e. where Ravenhill appears to be intentionally injecting some of his own voice into his text) and an *unintentional* celebrity voice (i.e. where Ravenhill appears to be attempting to respect the source text but where this might be misinterpreted by the audience as being Ravenhill's own voice).

Bertolt Brecht's *Leben des Galilei*

Bertolt Brecht (1898–1956) wrote three different versions of *Leben des Galilei*, each in a very different place, set of circumstances and frame of mind. Each version has therefore tended to attract quite different interpretations of Brecht's communicative intentions given the varying political and social climates at the time of each iteration. What's more, *Leben des Galilei* has inevitably been constantly re-evaluated by scholars and audiences alike as political and social events (e.g. the end of communism and the reunification of Germany in the 1990s, or the financial crash of 2008 and the consequent era of austerity) provide new backdrops against which to assess Brecht's plays and political ideology.

The first version of *Leben des Galilei* was written towards the end of 1938 while Brecht was living in exile on the Danish island of Funen. According to modernism scholar John White, Brecht's decision to write *Leben des Galilei* was 'a response to an ominous chain of events triggered off by the very country which Brecht had been obliged to leave' (1996: 11), namely Germany's *Anschluß* of Austria, the occupation of the Sudetenland and the ill-fated Munich agreement. Importantly, White also points out that the play was not originally conceived in response to the nuclear age since this first version 'pre-dates not only the first use of atomic weapons but even public knowledge of the advances in nuclear physics that made their creation possible' (1996: 11), a fact that contradicts much current popular understanding about Brecht's original motivations when writing the play. This should not be taken to imply, however, that this first version of *Leben des Galilei* (now known as the *Danish version*) was inevitably intended as a critique of the rise of fascism in Germany and beyond at the time. Theatre scholar Cathy Turner argues that the Catholic Church in the play could stand for either the rise of fascism in the West or the rise of Stalinism in the East – an interpretation often overlooked by those who assume that Brecht was indiscriminately pro-communist in his political stance (2006: 146).

Here, it's worth pointing out that, in spite of his reputation as a political writer, Brecht actually came to politics relatively late. As theatre director and Brecht scholar Stephen Unwin points out, 'Like many of his generation, [Brecht's] response to the First World War was a kind of anarchist despair, lacking in political analysis or prescriptions for a better future' (2005: 27). His support for communism appears to have been triggered only in 1929 after seeing a banned May Day demonstration in Berlin being broken up by the police (Wizisla 2009: 6). By the late 1930s Brecht was already deeply disillusioned by the Soviet Union and its betrayal of socialist ideals, even if he was reluctant to admit this in public (Unwin 2005: 28). It would be a mistake, then, to view *Leben des Galilei* solely through the frequently assumed filter of Brecht's Marxist leanings.

A second version of *Leben des Galilei* (called simply *Galileo*) was written in English between 1944 and 1947 in collaboration with British actor Charles Laughton during Brecht's exile in the United States. The writing of this second version (now known as the *American version*) coincided with the dropping of the atomic bomb on Hiroshima in August 1945. This gave the play's examination of the uses of science a horrifyingly modern twist and 'made the relationship between society and science into a life-and-death problem' (Brecht 1993: 355). Indeed, in Brecht's own much-cited preface to the published second version, he states that 'the atom bomb is, both as a technical and as a social phenomenon, the classical end-product of [Galileo's] contribution to science and his failure to contribute to society' (1995: 201). For White, this leads to a much narrower interpretation of this and the subsequent third version of *Leben des Galilei*.

> An unfortunate by-product of the play's metamorphosis was the way in which a most un-Brechtian ossification to the work's reception set in, narrowing its import unduly to a less representative parable than it was in the 1938 version and fixing it in time as if it were forever tied to the events of 1945. (1996: 22)

It's interesting to note that many of the passages in the first version that satirize the Church are cut in this second version. As a result, the politics of the play become less focused. Here, then, we can assume (although not be completely certain) that Brecht's motivation was more one of challenging the role of science, and scientists, in society rather than of questioning totalitarian ideology and idealism per se, as was the case with the Danish version. As Turner suggests, Brecht is implying that 'a science which denies its political affiliation will be bound by default to the ruling ideology', and that 'it is only by consciously opposing [this ruling ideology] that science will not become subject to it' (2006: 147). In retrospect, the dialectic view that Brecht subscribes to here is in many ways the forerunner of post-structuralist thinking in the way that it questions many of the assumptions underlying scientific and cultural ideas.

The third and final version (the *Berlin version*) was written between 1953 and 1956 when Brecht was living in the newly created German Democratic Republic. He died during rehearsals for the play in August 1956, and therefore never saw this version in performance in front of an audience to be able to assess its reception. It's this version that is now considered the most authoritative version, and indeed the only one that the Brecht estate now allows to be performed or translated. And so it's also this version that Gearing used for her literal translation. Brecht's primary motivation with this supposedly definitive version of his play, which was published in 1957, appears to be to create the space for philosophical debate about the power of knowledge (and about the conflict between science and authority in general) rather than specifically between science and religion. Here, Brecht was presumably thinking primarily about the implications of the misuse of science from a Second World War and Cold War perspective by the time of writing this Berlin version – a backdrop that was scarcely imaginable at the time of writing the first version of the text in 1938. Such considerations would have included not only the tragic consequences of the discovery and use of atomic weapons but also the implications for science of the medical experiments conducted by the Nazi Party on concentration camp prisoners without their consent, information about which was only starting to become public knowledge in the years following the end of the war (e.g. in the 1947 Doctors Trial in the United States).

The Berlin version of *Leben des Galilei* also restores many of the passages in the Danish version that satirize the Catholic Church and its control over the accumulation and dissemination of knowledge. Yet the political events that took place between the first and third versions meant this latest version could now easily be interpreted as a somewhat different allegory. As Brecht scholars John Willett and Ralph Manheim point out, 'The parallels are too clear: the Catholic Church is the Communist Party, Aristotle is Marxism-Leninism with its incontrovertible scriptures, the late "reactionary" pope is Joseph Stalin, the Inquisition the KGB' (1995: xxii). Indeed, by the time this version of the play premiered in East Berlin in 1957, it would have been easy for East German audiences (and indeed audiences anywhere) to make these assumptions.

For the purposes of the following textual analysis of the Berlin version of *Leben des Galilei* and its translations, then, we can (fairly) reliably presume that Brecht's *most likely motivation* when writing this version of his text was to alert us both to the responsibilities that inevitably come with the power of knowledge and the uses to which that knowledge is put, and to the need for both the scientific community and civil society at large (including political and religious institutions) to uphold these responsibilities. Having said this, we should not allow ourselves to be constrained by specific interpretations relating to atomic warfare when analysing Brecht's work in a contemporary context. Indeed, by using the historical figure of Galileo as a metaphor for the relationship between science (in its broadest sense as knowledge, or *Wissenschaft*), society and authority, Brecht could be seen to be reminding us that this is a fundamentally timeless concern – and one that's as relevant today as it was in the seventeenth century or in post-war Europe. Certainly, these are themes that recur in much of Ravenhill's own work, as will be seen later in this chapter.

Deborah Gearing's literal translation of *Leben des Galilei*

The literal translation of *Leben des Galilei* that Ravenhill used to produce his own version was prepared by Deborah Gearing. Gearing is first and foremost a playwright and a youth theatre director. She first became involved in the theatre in Berlin in the late 1970s while working as a teaching assistant during her German degree at a UK university. Gearing subsequently worked as an actor in the UK, Germany and Switzerland (Gearing 2014: n.p.) before starting to write her own plays. *Leben des Galilei* is one of only a few literal translations for the theatre that she has produced commercially, preferring instead to work with theatre groups on socially driven projects.[1]

Gearing's literal translation of *Leben des Galilei* was initially commissioned for use by playwright David Edgar for his production of *The Life of Galileo* at the Birmingham Repertory Theatre in 2005. 'I started doing literals by accident,' says Gearing. 'My first play was on at the National Theatre. [The National Theatre's literary department] was looking for a translation for David Edgar's *Galileo* up in Birmingham and they found out that I was a Germanist.' Edgar was therefore Gearing's *implied reader*, in other words the person whom the text is aimed at and written for. Indeed Edgar was probably the *only* reader of the text at the time, although it was subsequently consulted by playwright David Hare (for his second version of *The Life of Galileo* in 2006) before being used by Ravenhill. As Gearing notes, her work has at least 'done the rounds' in that it's provided the basis for three very different versions of Brecht's play.

Gearing's text was required not only to convey her own interpretation of the source text to Edgar (who speaks no German) but also to explain the cultural nuances and the historical context that Edgar might not otherwise have fully understood. Certainly, examination of Gearing's text reveals her thoroughness in completing this task. As well as translating all the footnotes in the first Suhrkamp edition of *Leben des Galilei* (1962) and all of Brecht's stage directions (minimal though these often are), Gearing also takes pains to point out examples of rhyme, word play, emphatic word order, particularly formal language and so on in order to optimize Edgar's awareness of both the dramatic and the communicative effects of the source text. But at the same time, Gearing is clearly herself well aware of the practical limitations, and even contradictions, inherent in the task of producing a so-called *literal* translation. By her own admission, 'you still have to make choices, even if it's just three words, and you can't help but impose some of your own judgements in those choices'.

Importantly from the perspective of the translation scholar, these choices are sometimes explicit, such as in the following example from Act I:

Source text (Brecht [1955] 1963: 12)
   GALILEO: Eine neue Zeit ist angebrochen, ein großes Zeitalter, in dem zu leben eine Lust ist.

Literal translation (Gearing 2005: 9)
GALILEO: A new time/age is beginning, a great age, in which it is a delight/ pleasure to live.

Here, then, it's clear that, from the translator's perspective, the process of producing a literal translation *can* offer rewards beyond the financial. Gearing notes how she 'enjoyed doing the literal translation of *Galileo* because it was lovely to work with German and feel immersed in the language again'. At the same time, there's also the potential for considerable frustration by the process of literal translation, particularly if, like Gearing, literal translators also have their own training and experience in acting and playwriting. Certainly, Gearing appears to lament the perceived lack of scope for any creative input by the translator.

> I just went for a clean line. I didn't put myself into it at all. If I sat around with translating for longer, I think I'd probably make character choices. So the thing about a literal is that you don't want to spend too much time on it. You just want to get as close to the original as possible. It's quite a mechanical thing. You're just bashing it out. I did it quite quickly, but it's still a long job. And then you think, can I really give up my time to do this? I'm a playwright now. I should be writing my own plays. Why would I put all that effort into something I can't put anything of myself into?

Perhaps most importantly for Gearing at the time, her acceptance of the commission to translate *Leben des Galilei* for Edgar was also motivated by the opportunity that it gave her to raise her own professional profile. Indeed, it led to a commission to write a play for young people, *Rosalind: A Question of Life* (2006) for the Door (part of the Birmingham Repertory Theatre). Inspired by the work of the overlooked scientist Rosalind Franklin, who provided the photograph that led to the discovery of DNA, this play subsequently ran in parallel with Edgar's *The Life of Galileo*. As Gearing herself says, 'I guess that's what you are hoping for when you take on a literal – a foot in somewhere else.' This observation does not appear to be unique to Gearing as it could arguably also apply to literal translators with other backgrounds. For example, Charlotte Barslund combines producing literal translations of Henrik Ibsen's works with literary translation (see Chapter 6), actor Simon Scardifield has also translated from French, German and Spanish for the British stage, and Russianist Helen Rappaport's work as author, historian and consultant has also included occasional literal translations of Anton Chekhov, Maxim Gorky and Alexander Ostrovsky. Each of these may well also view (or have previously viewed) working on literal translations as a way of being noticed by – or at least staying on the radar of – publishers, playwrights, directors and so on.

With this in mind, however, it's interesting to note the lack of interchange between the literal and celebrity translator during Ravenhill's translation process. Gearing recalls that she did have some contact with Edgar, who got in touch with her to clarify a number of (now long-forgotten) issues with the text while he was writing his own version of *The Life of Galileo* for the stage. Ravenhill, on the other hand, did not make made any contact with her at all during his own writing process. Gearing suggests that Ravenhill was likely to have had at least some understanding of Germany and his own network of contacts in that country due to the fact that his work is frequently translated into German and staged in German-speaking countries. 'Mark knows lots of people in Germany, so he knows something of the context and has people he can ask.' At the same time, though, Gearing also appears to be acutely aware of the division of tasks between the literal and the celebrity translators (undoubtedly because of her own experience as a playwright) and the dangers of treading on one another's toes.

> You have to leave them the chance to find the rhythm. You can put a note to tell them that this rhymes with this in German, but I'm not going to make the choice as to what they do with it. Writing a play and doing a literal are two completely different tasks. My translation choices were based on my knowledge of German rather than my knowledge of how plays work on stage. I was doing the line-by-line version whereas David [Edgar] was looking at the bigger picture.

Ultimately, the relatively low remuneration and the lack of public acknowledgement of her involvement in Edgar's production made Gearing unenthusiastic about producing many more literal translations for other playwrights in her subsequent career – and understandably so given the rewards brought by her primary career as a playwright and director. Indeed, her only subsequent commercial translation work in the theatre was on John von Düffel's 2012 reworking of the Thebian trilogy (*Oedipus, Seven against Thebes* and *Antigone*) as *Ödipus Stadt* (*Oedipus City*) at the Deutsches Theater in Berlin, for which she and David Spencer provided the literal translation that formed the basis of the English surtitles (itself, an intriguing commission that adds an additional dimension to our understanding of the function of literal translation). 'I've said I'm not doing any more [literals] because it's a lot of work for not much money,' she insists. Indeed, the practical and emotional limitations that are imposed by the task of producing a literal translation for a celebrity playwright suggest that literal translators, whatever their background, may well often feel undervalued – and not only from a financial perspective. It should not be surprising, then, that Gearing appears to feel little, if any, ownership of the versions of *The Life of Galileo* that her work inspired.

> I went to see [Edgar's *The Life of Galileo*] and I didn't feel like it had very much to do with me at all. I've always assumed that playwrights work with several different literals, so I don't know how much of my work made it into the final play. It's not my work once I've handed it over. It's up to [the playwright] what he does with it.

Having said this, Gearing continues to carry out translations either for her own use (e.g. she directed performances of her own translations of Georg Büchner's *Woyzeck* and other Brecht plays by an ex-offenders group) or for colleagues in theatre (e.g. she co-adapted a piece from Franz Kafka's diaries for a professional production). In this sense, then, she remains strongly involved in and excited by theatre translation, albeit outside the context of celebrity translation. 'I've made [translation] work in my own context. Because translation has lots of contexts, just as theatre does. And I get to do the texts that I really want to do.'²

I will return in the final chapters of this book to issues around the practice of literal translation and the scope for giving theatre translators a bigger role in the process of creating theatre, as Gearing herself has done. In the meantime, let's now explore the background to Mark Ravenhill's version of *Life of Galileo*.

Mark Ravenhill's *A Life of Galileo*

British playwright Mark Ravenhill (1966–) has enjoyed international success and critical acclaim ever since his very first full-length play, *Shopping and Fucking*, appeared on the London stage in 1996. This and subsequent plays, such as *Faust Is Dead* (1997), *Handbag* (1998), *Some Explicit Polaroids* (1999) and *Mother Clap's Molly House* (2000), firmly established Ravenhill's reputation as a prime exemplar of *in-yer-face* theatre, defined by theatre scholar Alexs Sierz as 'a theatre of sensation [that] jolts both actors and spectators out of conventional responses, touching nerves and provoking alarm' (2001a: 4). These early works can be seen very much as scathing dramatizations of late twentieth-century British society, with themes such as excessive consumerism, moral vacuity and the transactional nature of relationships recurring at regular intervals. As playwright and theatre scholar Dan Rebellato notes, '(*Shopping and Fucking*) asks ... whether there is anything left in our lives that cannot be bought and sold' (2001: xi). In raising these and many other questions, 'Ravenhill is profoundly moral in his portraiture of contemporary society ... his vision is elliptically but recognisably social, even socialist' (2001: x). Sierz, however, also notes a more traditional, even sentimental, side to Ravenhill's early writing, suggesting that 'Ravenhill is not an angry young man, but a more paradoxical figure: his plays may explore contemporary life, using gadgets, pop culture icons and poststructuralist ideas, but his values are ... traditionally humanistic values' (2001a: 151).

Ravenhill's work since the turn of the century has become on the one hand much more abstract, experimental and ambiguous, and on the other hand much less overtly political. In 2007, for example, *Shoot/Get Treasure/Repeat* tackled the subject of the war on terror that characterized much of the first decade of the twenty-first century, but was less about the political context of war and more about how excessive media coverage of war can have a paralysing effect on democracy. *Over There* (2009), meanwhile, took as its theme the reunification of Germany and its effects on the populations of the two separate German states. While ostensibly a political theme, Ravenhill approached what he describes as the 'deep schism in the German identity' (2013b: x) from a more sociological or anthropological perspective, examining the effects of separation and reunification on twins as a symbol of how individual Germans were coming to terms with the changes in their country. Subsequent work such as *The Experiment* (2009) and *Ten Plagues* (2011) continued to provoke, and even shock, audiences and reviewers. Against such a controversial background, Ravenhill might have been seen by some as a somewhat surprising choice as the Royal Shakespeare Company's (RSC's) new Writer in Residence in 2012. However, as theatre critic Neil Dowden points out, 'since his sensational debut *Shopping and Fucking* in 1996 … he has developed into an all-round man of the theatre, sometimes directing and even acting, in addition to writing an impressive number of works in different genres, and collaborating with a rich array of artists and companies' (2013: n.p.).

It was during his RSC residency that Ravenhill produced his translation of *Leben des Galilei*. This was first performed as *A Life of Galileo* at the Swan Theatre in Stratford-upon-Avon on 31 January 2013. After a two-month run at the Swan, the same production toured several English cities in 2014. At the Birmingham Rep, the play formed part of a Brecht celebration curated by Ravenhill himself that also featured new versions of *The Threepenny Opera* and *The Mother* (the latter also translated by Ravenhill). Unlike the second piece of work completed during his residency, *Candide*, the adaptation of which was his own choice, Ravenhill was specifically asked to write a new version of Brecht's play for the RSC. Much like Gearing, then, his primary purpose was to fulfil a specific commission rather than to create a new work entirely from scratch. While this might seem to be a somewhat out-of-character task for a writer known primarily for developing his own characters, plots and messages, Ravenhill had previously argued in favour of the theatre rediscovering canonical works, pointing out how 'it's only by having a theatre culture that continues to explore and expand our relationship with the past, as well as presenting the best of the present, that we'll have a theatre that is fully alive' (2005: n.p.). Similarly, theatre-maker and dramaturg Dan Hutton observes Ravenhill's enthusiasm for dealing with big ideas in the theatre, and his dismay at how this is often discouraged in the British theatrical system. 'To hear a playwright speaking about … big ideas is a rarity in our corporate-sponsored world. As Ravenhill notes, there's an "anti-intellectualism" in British theatre, and although we may expect playwrights like Tom Stoppard or Michael Frayn to give us "an *In Our Time* sort of experience", there's a sense that younger playwrights are often discouraged from grappling with big ideas' (2014: n.p.).

More specifically, Ravenhill has also publicly expressed his admiration of *Leben des Galilei* as a theatrical work, suggesting that he embraced the challenge of translating Brecht with more relish than critics and audiences might possibly have concluded at the time given his stature as a playwright in his own right – perhaps as a way of paying tribute to the original work as much as adding his own stamp on it. For example, in a 2013 interview for the BBC with broadcaster Philip Dodd, he notes how 'every scene is almost a little experiment in theatre in itself [and] Brecht is playing with different permutations of space and language and objects and movement, so [it's] like a little dramatic laboratory' (Dodd 2013: n.p.). Having said this, it's also interesting to note that Ravenhill was also aware of how his translation might be received, given his own public persona and the reputation of his work. For example, in this same BBC interview (Dodd 2013), he makes the following important observations about his commission.

> No-one's ever asked me [to do a version of an existing play] before. They might have thought that I'd put lots of rude words in or something. I think it's completely unconscious, but there is still a sense that the heterosexual male will provide the neutral text, and that if a play has got an interesting feminist angle, if it's *A Doll's House* or something, then it would be interesting to have a woman. But I think

there's still a sense that somehow a gay man would stand between the original play and the audience. ... I think somewhere lurking in the collective subconscious of people commissioning is a sense of 'his isn't a neutral sensibility, he couldn't just deliver the original play to the audience, he would queer it up in some way'.

Ravenhill's observations about adaptations by gay playwrights raise interesting questions about what happens when a celebrity translator produces a text that does *not* conform to the theatrical system's or the audience's assumptions about what that text will be like (that, in Ravenhill's case as seen above, he will *queer it up*). This has important implications in the context of relevance theory. As we will see later in this chapter, a spectator's quest to derive cognitive effects and maximize relevance (as determined by the relevance-guided comprehension heuristic) may well lead him or her to assume communicative intentions that are not actually the case on the part of the author. In this respect, it's important to note that, while openly gay, Ravenhill has always distanced himself from the *gay playwright* label (see Sierz 2000: 151). But, of course, this is not to say that Ravenhill's sexuality will not influence the contextual associations and cognitive contexts of spectators attending a performance of *A Life of Galileo*, whether consciously or subconsciously.

Ravenhill himself has claimed that his primary intention when writing his version of *Leben des Galilei* was as follows.

> [My role was] to put the text into speakable English, and I cut it a fair bit too as it is rather repetitious at times. Brecht himself of course was happy to adapt other writers' work and shape it for his own ends, but I have stayed truthful to his intentions [*sic*] – I just wanted to avoid the stodginess which has weighed down some of the productions of Brecht that we have seen in this country in the past. (Dowden 2013: n.p.)

But while Ravenhill openly admits to editing the source text in his translation, he is less prepared to admit that his version of Brecht's source text contains any of his own recognizable voice – one defined by Sierz earlier on in Ravenhill's career as 'ironic, amused, slightly detached' (2001b: n.p.). In an interview with theatre-maker and student Billy Barrett in 2013, when asked whether audiences will recognize a distinctively Ravenhill resonance, Ravenhill replies as follows.

> I've tried as much as I can to capture what I think is the voice of the play and of Brecht's writing. ... The crude image of me is that somehow I'd up the number of swearwords and [create] *Galileo* plus swearwords and anal knifing. So there certainly isn't that. Maybe people who have a different knowledge of my work might recognise something. (Barrett 2013: n.p.)

Here, it's important to note that any exploration of Ravenhill's version of Brecht's source text (or indeed any other translators' versions of that text) needs to be viewed in the context of the Brecht estate's protectiveness of Brecht's work. According to David Johnston, the estate is 'notorious for being difficult to deal with for anyone who wants to make any change in the fabric of [Brecht's] plays' (1996: 139). Indeed, the estate previously refused to allow David Hare to publish his version of *The Life of Galileo* that was staged at the National Theatre in 2006, supposedly because it was unhappy with the cuts that Hare had made to Brecht's text (see Wootton 2006 and Taylor 2009). At the time, journalist Mark Lawson noted the irony of this given the play's theme of censoring knowledge, observing how 'rather as Galileo was silenced by the Vatican for daring to suggest that the Earth moves round the sun, the possibility arises that Hare is being kept from the printing presses for daring to suggest that the sun doesn't always shine out of Bertolt Brecht's backside' (2006: n.p.).

We can assume, therefore, that Ravenhill's motivation in translating the source text will of necessity also have been to produce a translation that will gain not only audience approval but also the approval of the Brecht estate. The restrictions imposed by the estate are bound to have had a considerable impact on Ravenhill's perceived freedom to inject his own voice into his work, and should not be underestimated when comparing either Ravenhill's text with Brecht's source text, or Ravenhill's translation with other celebrity translations of works that are either out of copyright or protected by less controlling estates. So Ravenhill is acting (and potentially even *forced* to act) within constraints imposed at a number of different levels when carrying out his translation of *Leben des Galilei*.

1. At the broadest level, Ravenhill is obliged to work according to the expectations imposed by the British theatrical system in terms on the one hand of audience, director and actor expectations of norms (e.g. the length of a typical play), and on the other hand of transactional value (e.g. value for money on the part of spectators, and financial rewards on the part of the producers and cast).
2. Within this system, Ravenhill is also expected to act within the framework imposed by the RSC in terms of having to adhere to its product and brand values as a 'the world's leading classical theatre company' (Arts Council 2014: n.p.), not least because of the level of public funding that it receives, which amounted to over £16 million in the 2013–14 financial year (Arts Council 2014).
3. At a more practical level, Ravenhill is required to respect certain budgetary, spatial and time constraints – for example, having to produce a text that can be performed with a certain cast size and on a stage of particular dimensions. And he is also is obliged to act within the limitations imposed by the Brecht estate, according to which, as seen above, he is not allowed to deviate significantly from the source text.
4. Finally, as part of these expectations and restrictions that arise within the theatrical system itself, Ravenhill undoubtedly also feels an obligation to act in a way that is commensurate with his own responsibilities to his work and with his professional standing as a reputable playwright. This not only encompasses the perceived expectations of producers, directors, critics, other playwrights and so on that he will create a work that is consistent with the quality of his previous plays, however that might be measured. It also encompasses his assumed responsibilities to his *client*, the RSC, in terms of justifying the fee that he will have earned from his commission.

A final influence that is also useful to mention here is the fact that Ravenhill's own work has been frequently translated for performance outside English-speaking markets, with *Shopping and Fucking* alone having been translated into ten other languages. This experience appears to have given him a particularly acute sensitivity to theatre in translation. 'I've found something to replace true, universal and timeless as the other part of the theatre paradox. Resonance for me now lies in the international. I am fascinated by the way a work mutates and is reborn through translation and re-production. ... I wonder what this will mean in other countries and cultures' (2009: xiii). Such sensitivity is also likely to have had an influence on Ravenhill's approach to translating *Leben des Galilei*. In particular, his appreciation of how a work might resonate in other cultures is almost certain to have informed his adaptation of Brecht's explicit and implicit references or allusions in the source text to forces such as the Catholic Church, communism and nazism. Likewise, his understanding of how his own voice as a playwright resonates in different ways across different audiences is also likely to have guided his translation choices. These issues will now be explored in the following sections.

Explicatures and implicatures

The distinction between the *explicit* and the *implicit* in communication, which is inherent in the notion of the search for relevance (whether in a literary text or a non-literary text), is described in relevance theory using the terms *explicature* and *implicature*. Such terms are fundamental to my discussion in the following sections of this chapter of the different 'layers' of meaning that spectators may infer in Ravenhill's translation of Brecht, so it's essential from the outset that readers are clear exactly what I mean when I talk about explicatures, implicatures and, in particular, weak implicatures.

Pragmatics and semantics scholar Robyn Carston has explored the processes involved in deriving explicatures and implicatures and concluded that there are essentially four different levels of communication in an utterance:

1. the *linguistically encoded meaning* of the utterance, which might also be termed the *literal* meaning by translation scholars;
2. the *proposition expressed*, which is the core conceptual meaning of the utterance (similar, therefore, to Grice's concept of *what is said*), as determined by a pragmatic process;
3. the *explicature*, which is an explicit development of a logical form encoded by an utterance; and
4. the *implicature*, which is an assumption communicated by the utterance that is not explicit. (2002a: 116)

In drawing these distinctions between different levels of communication, relevance theory essentially reminds us that what is encoded linguistically in an utterance will often fall far short of telling us not only what is said, but also what is actually meant and implied by what is said (see Boase-Beier 2004). More specifically in the context of play texts, which are written primarily to be *performed*, relevance theory, by focusing on the receiver of that text, takes account of the multiplicity of implicatures that each individual spectator might derive either during the performance (which, in theory, may be different from those of any other spectator) or at any time afterwards once that initial spontaneous interpretation is influenced by subsequent positive cognitive effects. And as already seen in Chapter 3, the implicature is the level at which stylistic devices used by the author influence communication because it's the level of communication that is open to interpretation (see Boase-Beier 2004: 278).

In relevance theory, explicatures and implicatures that are less obviously recoverable from an utterance or a text are called *weak explicatures* and *weak implicatures*, respectively. We could talk about these weaker explicatures and implicatures as being more difficult for receivers to recover in the sense that they require more processing effort. But rather than thinking about the level of difficulty that they involve, I prefer to focus on the fact that such weaker explicatures and implicatures are likely to be recovered in a more *random* fashion – in other words, some receivers may recover them and some may not. In the case of the theatre, we can say that interpretation of a weaker explicature or implicature in a play text will therefore depend entirely on the individual spectator's unique set of assumptions about the author's communicative intentions, as guided by his or her contextual associations with that author at the time. In theory, then, each spectator could recover a unique set of weaker explicatures and implicatures – including some that the celebrity translator may or may not have intended audiences to recover.

In this respect, it's important to stress that the different *layers* of interpretation that Carston identifies (linguistically encoded meaning, proposition expressed, explicatures and implicatures) are not necessarily intended in relevance theory to be seen as a sequential process. So, for example, the theory doesn't claim that receivers of an utterance have to first understand the linguistically encoded meaning, then the proposition expressed and then the explicit and implicit content of that utterance to arrive at a cognitive effect. As Carston points out, current understanding of cognitive processes proposes that 'the comprehension system ... is fast and automatic, and, more crucial to the position, it is domain-specific, in that it is activated exclusively by ostensive stimuli and employs its own proprietary concepts and processing strategies and routines' (2002b: 132).

Indeed, weak implicatures may sometimes actually be recovered more easily in a text than more explicit communication. And as already seen in Chapter 3, literary texts are often designed to be difficult for readers to process (again, see Pilkington 1996: 158). In such cases, more implicit communication in the form of weak implicatures could feasibly obstruct a more logical, rational or obvious interpretation – say, in the case of intentionally ambiguous or politically incorrect utterances in a text. The same is clearly true of play texts that might actively seek to challenge, provoke and disarm audiences, or might feature references such as 'in-jokes' that only certain types of spectators will be expected to understand. The key issue here is that, no matter how and when spectators infer something of the author's communicative intentions, their processing effort continues to be worthwhile in that it leads to a rewarding outcome, namely, an alternative interpretation or the dismissal of a previous interpretation. In other words, processing effort continues to deliver positive cognitive effects.

In the following sections, I will seek to demonstrate the *potential* layers of interpretation that audiences might feasibly infer from a number of textual examples in both Brecht's source text and Ravenhill's target text. I will then look at the differences in interpretation that might arise between Brecht's text and Ravenhill's translation. While my onion-like visualization of these layers of interpretation is necessarily a two-dimensional figure (see Figure 4.1), it's not in any way meant to imply that there's a fixed order of interpretations starting with the outer layer and terminating at the core of the onion. Rather, the aim is to show how the different layers might relate to one another, with the inner layers being the interpretation(s) inferred from more subtle cognitive effects – effects that may or may not be the result of the progressive build-up of more easily accessible contextual or cognitive effects.

Let me give an example here to show how this model can help us to explore how particular utterances in the source or the target text might be interpreted by audiences. For the sake of simplicity here, let's just look at a line from Brecht's source text, together with Gearing's literal translation – a line that represents what is perhaps one of the key ideas in Brecht's play, namely, the power of knowledge and the power wielded by those who withhold knowledge. This line appears in Scene 9, when Galileo tries to explain to a distraught former pupil, Mucius, why the pupil's book appears to condemn the Copernican theory about the rotation of the earth.

Source text (Brecht [1955] 1963: 81)
GALILEI: Wer die Wahrheit nicht weiß, der ist bloß ein Dummkopf. Aber wer sie weiß und sie eine Lüge nennt, der ist ein Verbrecher!

Literal translation (Gearing 2005: 75)
GALILEI: He who does not know the truth is simply an idiot. But he who knows it and calls it a lie is a criminal!

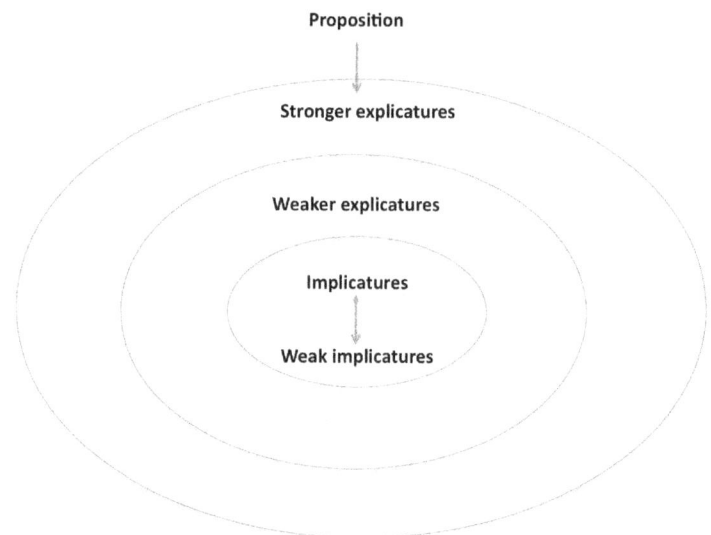

Figure 4.1 Visualization of layers of interpretation.

There are clearly a number of different ways in which audiences could interpret this line in the context of Brecht's play. Using the terms referred to above, we could say that the *proposition* that Galileo is expressing here is (i.e. what Galileo is actually saying) is essentially that to be ignorant of the truth is to be an idiot, but to refute the truth is to be a criminal. But the potential strong explicature and weak explicature (i.e. the forms of the proposition that are contextualized to a greater or lesser extent) and the potential implicatures (i.e. the implicit assumptions that are communicated) that audiences might infer from this utterance might include some or all of the inferences shown in Figure 4.2. And here, I mean potential in the sense that these are just some of many possible inferences. These different layers of interpretation could then be visualized as in Figure 4.3.

As pointed out in the previous chapter, the implication in each of the following examples is that individual spectators will derive their own unique interpretations of the text, guided by assumptions about the text and its authors that will be shared with other audience members. In each case, it's not my intention to propose that my suggested explicatures and implicatures are the *only* inferences that spectators will derive. Rather, I'm suggesting that they represent examples of *potential* inferences,

Stronger explicature	Galileo believes that the author of Mucius's book condemning Copernicus's theory is a criminal.
Weaker explicature	Galileo is condemning those who refuse to accept the truth.
Implicatures	Galileo rejects the Catholic Church's dismissal of his findings and, by extension, is seeking to stand up to all of those throughout history who have sought to distort or conceal the truth in order to further their own ends.

Figure 4.2 Potential explicatures and implicatures derived from Brecht's source text (Scene 9).

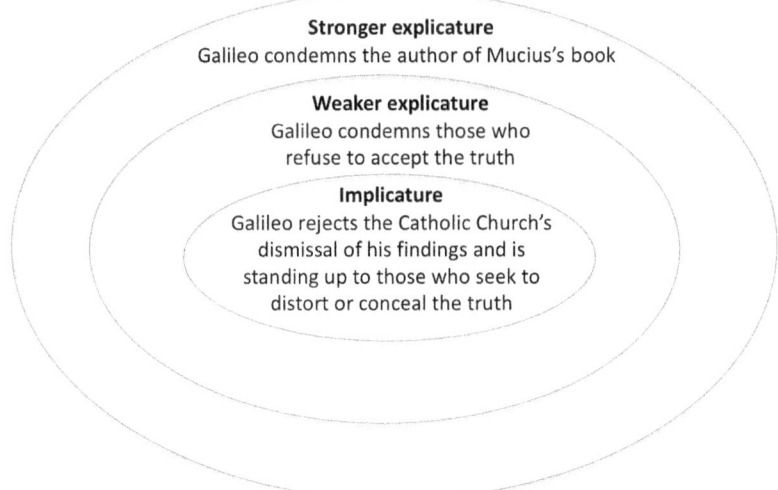

Figure 4.3 Visualization of layers of interpretation (Scene 9).

which then have ramifications for how these textual examples *might* be interpreted, either at an individual or at a group level.

Ravenhill's conscious celebrity voice

In the following sections, I would like to draw attention to what I've termed Ravenhill's *conscious* and *unconscious* voices in his adaptation of *Leben des Galilei*. By *conscious* voice, I'm referring to examples in his text where Ravenhill appears to actively inject some of his own voice into his translation – or, at least, what he believes audience expectations of that voice to be. By *unconscious* voice, on the other hand, I'm referring to examples in his text where Ravenhill has not actually altered the meaning of the source text (as seen by comparing his text with the literal translation), but where spectators might legitimately interpret more of a 'Ravenhill-esque' voice (i.e. one that appears to reflect the values associated with Ravenhill) because of the weight of their expectations of his work.

In terms of relevance theory and the notion of ostensive-inferential communication (see Chapter 3), we can describe this distinction between the intentional and unintentional voice as follows.

1. Where Ravenhill produces an utterance that makes it mutually manifest to himself *and* his audience that he intends by means of this utterance to make manifest to the audience a set of assumptions, we can assume that he expects the audience to perceive or infer this utterance in the way that he intended. This, then, is his *conscious* voice.
2. On the other hand, where Ravenhill makes it manifest to *himself* that he intends by means of this utterance to make manifest to the audience a set of assumptions, but where spectators are working with a different set of assumptions that are manifest to them (i.e. their cognitive environment does not coincide with Ravenhill's), we can assume that the audience will perceive or interpret this utterance in a way that is different from what Ravenhill intended. This is what I have termed his *unconscious* (i.e. potentially misinterpreted) voice.

Looking first at the *conscious* voice, the following extract from Scene 6 of Brecht's *Leben des Galilei* (Scene 5 in Ravenhill's version) provides a fascinating example of a conscious attempt by Ravenhill to inject some of his own voice into his translation. This text occurs at a point in the play when Galileo is being ridiculed by members of the Catholic Church for daring to suggest that the earth rotates around the sun rather than the other way around.

Source text (Brecht [1955] 1963: 58)
MÖNCH: Mir schwindelt. Die Erde dreht sich zu schnell. Gestatten
    Sie, daß ich mich an Ihnen einhalte, Professor.
GELEHRTE: Ja, sie ist heute wieder ganz besoffen, die Alte.
MÖNCH: Halt, halt! Wir rutschen ab! Halt, sag ich!
ZWEITER GELEHRTER: Die Venus steht schon ganz schief. Ich sehe nur noch
    ihren halben Hintern, Hilfe!

ZWEITER MÖNCH: Wenn wir nur nicht auf den Mond geschmissen werden! Brüder, der soll scheußlich scharfe Bergspitzen haben.
GELEHRTE: Stemm dich mit dem Fuß dagegen.
MÖNCH: Und schaut nicht hinab. Ich leide unter Schwindel.
DER DICKE PRÄLAT: Unmöglich, Schwindel im Collegium Romanum!

Literal translation (Gearing 2005: 54)[3]
MONK: I'm dizzy. The earth is turning too fast. Permit me to hold onto you, Professor.
SCHOLAR: Yes, she's (*the earth*) quite drunk again today, the old woman.
MONK: Stop, stop! We're slipping off! Stop I say!
SECOND SCHOLAR: Venus is all crooked. I can only see half her backside, help!
SECOND MONK: As long as we're not thrown up on the moon! Brothers, it's supposed to have terribly sharp mountain peaks.
FIRST SCHOLAR: Plant your foot against it. (*this? Unclear what?*)
FIRST MONK: And don't look down. I suffer from giddiness.
FAT PRELATE: Impossible, giddiness/swindle in the Collegium Romanum! (*this is a play on words: schwindel = giddiness also: swindle/deceive*).

Target text (Ravenhill 2013a: 30)
MONK: I'm giddy. The earth is spinning too fast. Allow me to hold on to you Professor.
SCHOLAR: Mother Earth, drunk again, the old crone.
MONK: Stop, stop! We're falling off! I said stop!
SECOND SCHOLAR: Venus is twisted. I can only see half her bottom, help!
SECOND MONK: As long as we're not pitched up to the moon! They say, brothers, that its mountain peaks are terribly sharp.
SCHOLAR: Dig your heels in deep.
FIRST MONK: And don't look down. I'm feeling dicky.
FAT PRELATE: Imagine, in the Collegium Romanum feeling dicky!

The last line in each of the above excerpts, in particular, potentially gives us an insight into both Brecht's and Ravenhill's likely communicative intentions. Here, the original German source text features a play on words on the German *Schwindel*, which as Gearing rightly notes in her literal translation has a dual linguistic meaning of both *giddiness* and *swindle*. Ravenhill, however, chooses an entirely different and highly contemporary play on words in his translation – one that mocks the Catholic Church's persistent attitudes to homosexuality even into the twenty-first century, and, dare I say it, alludes not so subtly to the various child abuse scandals that hit the Church from the start of that century onwards as well (see Keenan 2013). But I would argue that Brecht's and Ravenhill's respective plays on words might actually lead spectators to ultimately infer similar communicative intentions.

Of course, as Sperber and Wilson point out, 'we do not all construct the same representation because of differences in our narrower physical environments on the one hand, and in our cognitive abilities on the other' (1995: 38). This means, then, that not all audiences will respond in the same way to this line, either because they do not all share the same empathy with Brecht's or Ravenhill's political stance, humour or view of the Catholic Church, or because the implication is not immediately spotted when watching a live performance of the play – as opposed to the critical reflection that analysis of the written texts allows. But it's surely not unreasonable to assume that the *explicatures* and *implicatures* emerging from Brecht's source text (and explicitly demonstrated here in Gearing's literal translation) could be summed up in Figure 4.4. On the other hand, in Ravenhill's translation for the stage, there's an entirely different set of likely explicatures (see Figure 4.5), but the text arguably retains the ultimate implicature of swindle among members of the Catholic Church, and the importance of seeking the truth.

Looking at these layers of interpretation another way, the two likely interpretations can be visualized in Figure 4.6 to show that the ultimate implicatures in both the source and the target texts are essentially very similar.

Stronger explicature	A humorous play on words based on the double meaning of *Schwindel* (*giddiness* and *swindle*).
Weaker explicature	A satirical reference to the Catholic Church's refusal to accept Galileo's theories about the earth revolving around the sun because this contradicted its own view that the sun revolved around a stationary earth.
Implicatures	An admiration by Brecht of Galileo's questioning of the social order and willingness to stand up to the Church's swindle and abuse of its power in refusing to allow scientific advances that contradict its teaching to be made public – by extension, an admiration of individuals standing up to all forms of authority.

Figure 4.4 Potential explicatures and implicatures derived from Brecht's source text (Scene 6).

Stronger explicature	A humorous play on words between *dicky* (feeling shaky or weak in informal British English) and *dick* (slang for penis).
Weaker explicature	A satirical reference both to the Catholic Church's claimed resistance to homosexuality and to the cover-up of historical child abuse in the Church, the scale of which only became public knowledge in the early twenty-first century.
Implicatures	An attack on the Catholic Church's hypocrisy, and the way in which it has abused its power – by extension, an admiration for those who bring this hypocrisy to light and who stand up to the Church.

Figure 4.5 Potential explicatures and implicatures derived from Ravenhill's translation (Scene 5).

Mark Ravenhill's Version of Bertolt Brecht's Leben des Galilei 69

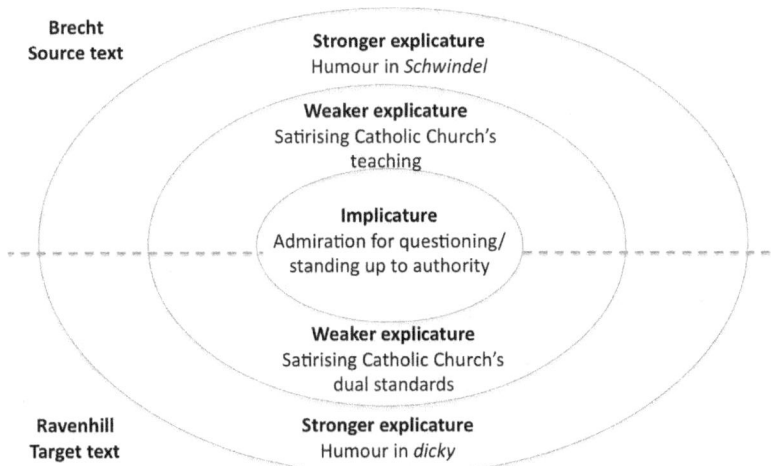

Figure 4.6 First example of the conscious voice.

This model demonstrates the potential *inferential equivalence* of Brecht's source text and Ravenhill's target text (i.e. the similarities between the inferences that receivers of each text are likely to draw) more effectively than a simple linguistic or stylistic comparison of those texts. The model also serves to justify Ravenhill's role as Brecht's celebrity translator in the sense that it shows how his status can lead to cognitive effects that closely replicate the response to the source text without there necessarily being any explicit equivalence in linguistic meaning whatsoever. Indeed, where audiences implicitly acknowledge the synergy between Brecht's and Ravenhill's contexts, the cognitive response is arguably multiplied, leading to even greater relevance (i.e. a greater number of cognitive effects for minimal processing effort). There is also likely to be a similar synergy between the reactions among those audience members who are more familiar with Brecht (and who process the text based on their understanding of Brecht's own context) and the reactions among those audience members who are more familiar with Ravenhill (and who process the text based on their understanding of his context). Such an assumption could, indeed, be tested by, for example, comparing the live responses of different audience profiles to seeing *A Life of Galileo* and noting the points at which they laugh, gasp or remain in shocked silence.

Of course, it's also possible that Ravenhill's translation here is designed to be something of a self-parody – a conscious attempt to *queer up* the text to conform to the audience's expectations of his work. Such a suggestion is not at all unthinkable given Ravenhill's previous form in this regard. Consider, for example, some of his characters in earlier plays such as *Shopping and Fucking* and *Mother Clap's Molly House*, or in the 2016 ITV situation comedy *Vicious* that Ravenhill co-created with Gary Janetti, which starred Ian McKellan and Derek Jacobi as stereotypically camp elderly gay couple. Indeed, the *dicky* pun could even be said to echo the verse of a song in Ravenhill's *Mother Clap's Molly House*, which plays on a similar pun in *prick*.

> The prick of Eros' arrow's sweet
> It enters swiftly in
> And once sweet prick is known to man
> His pleasure can begin. (2008: 27)

The use of songs in *Mother Clap's Molly House* in itself echoes Brecht's own use of songs in many of his plays as part of his *Verfremdungseffekt*, designed to make the audience question the ideas that he is raising in his work by forcefully reminding them that they are watching a piece of theatre. This additional layer of overlap between Brecht's and Ravenhill's work has interesting implications for the likely overlap in cognitive context among different types of audience members. At a more subtle level, Ravenhill has also been known to satirize the role of the playwright in his work, such as in his 2013 adaptation of *Candide* that followed *A Life of Galileo* at the RSC, in which he essentially deconstructs his own play by creating the character of a writer who is commissioned to write a screenplay of one of Ravenhill's own scenes.

From the perspective of relevance theory, it could be argued that such self-parody represents a particular *echoic* use of language. Although normally defined as 'utterances which express an attitude to a proposition that the speaker is not asserting but attributing to someone else' (Clark 2013: 203), Ravenhill's text here is potentially intended to be an attitude to a proposition that he's seeking to attribute to the receiver's *preconceived ideas of himself*. This adds a further layer of interpretation over and above the implicatures already discussed above.

Having explored a very overt example of Ravenhill consciously (i.e. as it would seem, intentionally) injecting some of his own voice into his translation, let's now consider a second example in *A Life of Galileo* that's perhaps a more *subtle* demonstration of Ravenhill's conscious voice, and one that might be noted only by those with a deeper understanding of Ravenhill's work (see Barrett 2013).

Sierz comments on an often underestimated sense in Ravenhill's work of a post-1980s, post-Thatcherite ennui in British culture centred around the perceived lack of political or social issues to fight for (or, perhaps, rather the lack of ability to fight for those issues).

> Ravenhill's plays suggest a sensibility (by which I mean a complex of feelings and ideas) that simply wouldn't have been possible in, say, the 1980s. ... The great British tradition of the state-of-the-nation play meets the contemporary reality of a globalised economy and nostalgia seems to sum up a distinctly contemporary sense of drift, uncertainty and confusion. Politically, few would have been able to write like this before the Fall of the Berlin Wall in 1989. (2008: n.p.)

With this in mind, let's now consider the following excerpt from Scene 13, when Andrea, the son of Galileo's housekeeper, attacks Galileo for recanting his teaching about the movement of the earth around the sun.

Source text (Brecht [1955] 1963: 113)
ANDREA: Unglücklich das Land, das keine Helden hat. Ich kann ihn nicht ansehen, er soll weg.

FEDERZONI: Beruhige dich.
ANDREA: Weinschlauch! Schneckenfresser! Hast du deine geliebte Haut gerettet? Mir ist schlecht.
GALILEI: Gebt ihm ein Glas Wasser!
ANDREA: Ich kann schon wieder gehen, wenn ihr mir ein wenig helft.
GALILEI: Nein. Unglücklich das Land, das Helden nötig hat.

Literal translation (Gearing 2005: 104)
ANDREA: Unhappy the land that has no heroes! I can't look at him. Get him away.
FEDERZONI: Calm down.
ANDREA: Old soak (*lit: wine skin*)(?)! Snail eater! Have you saved your own beloved skin? I feel sick.
GALILEI: Give him a glass of water.
ANDREA: I can walk now if you help me a little.
GALILEI: No. Unhappy the land in need of heroes.

Target text (Ravenhill 2013a: 68)
ANDREA: Unhappy the land that has no heroes! I can't look at him. Make him leave.
FEDERONZI [*sic*]: Calm.
ANDREA: Wine guzzler! Quail stuffer! Saved your own flesh? I feel ill.
GALILEI: Give him a glass of water
ANDREA: I can walk now if you help me.
GALILEI: No. Unhappy the land that is in need of heroes.

In this example, we can see that Ravenhill has clearly chosen to translate Andrea's *Weinschlauch! Schneckenfresser!* in a different way from the literal translation, but in a way that appears likely to be an attempt to find an utterance that Ravenhill believes will have an equivalent effect in his own voice. At the same time, the literal translation also represents an interpretation of Brecht's source text that arguably fails to convey all the shades of meaning that Brecht was most likely intending to convey. As such, Ravenhill possibly understood Brecht's text in different ways from those which Brecht possibly intended.

Brecht's term *Weinschlauch* (literally *wineskin*, as in the bag made from goatskin used to carry and dispense wine) has in this context the notion of a *bon viveur* or a *glutton* – someone who enjoys indulging in the finer things in life such as good wine, even if rather to excess. The term *Schneckenfresser*, meanwhile, is an ambiguous one in the German text. While ostensibly another reference to Galileo's Epicurianism (here, a love of eating snails), it is a particularly marked use of language in the choice of *Fresser*, which would normally be used to mean *eater* in the context of animals rather than human beings. Some spectators of the source text may possibly also detect a biblical reference here – the *Fresser* and *Weinsäufer* of Mt. 11.19 in Martin Luther's version, who in the King James Version is 'a man gluttonous and a winebibber'. As such, Andrea's utterance in the source text starts to take on more insulting connotations – of

Stronger explicature	Andrea is mocking Galileo's love of wine and snails.
Weaker explicature	Andrea is accusing Galileo of gluttony and of thinking only about himself (because he is only concerned about his own interests).
Implicatures	An attack on those who would rather sell their soul (to the Catholic Church) than stand up for what they actually believe in.

Figure 4.7 Potential explicatures and implicatures derived from Brecht's source text (Scene 13).

Galileo not only as a selfish glutton but also more figuratively as someone who is more concerned about stuffing his face than standing up for what he believes in. With this in mind, we could summarize the explicatures and implicatures of Brecht's original German text in Figure 4.7.

In Gearing's literal translation, meanwhile, these two terms are translated in a way that gives way to somewhat different connotations from those in the source text. Gearing's *old soak* has implications of excessive drinking of alcohol (to the extent of implying alcoholism) and arguably conveys much more of a value judgement than Brecht's *Weinschlauch*. Her translation of *Schneckenfresser* as *snail eater*, meanwhile, fails to convey all of the animalistic connotations of the source text, such that her implied reader (in this case, Ravenhill) is left to decide for himself what Brecht intended to convey in this term. As such, we might assume that the explicatures and implicatures of her text will probably not correspond entirely to those of Brecht's text – and, of course, none of us can ever be sure exactly what Brecht intended anyway.

Ravenhill's translation for the stage certainly does appear to give rise to a different set of explicatures from Brecht's text, even if the ultimate implicatures are still arguably closer to Brecht's text than Gearing's literal translation would have suggested. But this appears to have come about because of the way in which Ravenhill actively chose to depart from the literal translation – or, in other words, because of the way in which he consciously chose to insert something of his own voice into his text.

His *wine guzzler* certainly appears to come closer to the connotations of a *bon viveur* than Gearing's *old soak* might have given rise to, and could suggest that he sought a second opinion or carried out his own online research before deciding on his own translation. More intriguing, though, is his translation of *snail eater* as *quail stuffer*. The most likely explanation for the shift from *snail* to *quail* in Ravenhill's text is that he perhaps sees quails as having the same cultural significance to modern-day audiences as he assumes snails had in Galileo's time (or as he assumes Brecht assumed that they did), that is, a gourmet food that signals a certain level of culinary sophistication (see Sembhy 2013). In this sense, *quail* could be seen as a *domestication* of the German reference to snails (see Venuti 2008) in that it also implies a love of the finer things in life. Interestingly, the shift from *eater* in the literal translation to *stuffer* in the stage translation also aligns Ravenhill's text more with Brecht's *Fresser* – an amusing and wholly invented insult on the part of Ravenhill (unlike Brecht's *Schneckenfresser*, which in other contexts is a derogatory way of referring to the French), and one that also adds to the connotations of culinary sophistication in the way that it calls to mind the notion of *stuffed quail*.

Having said this, however, Ravenhill's translation adds *different* associations to his text that arguably give rise to different explicatures but broadly similar implicatures to those that may be inferred from Brecht's text. First, *quail* arguably has particular connotations for some people in contemporary UK culture, who could see it as a symbol of snobbishness or social climbing. To give just one example of this, journalist Tom Cole noted in his *Radio Times* review of a new cookery programme launched on British television in 2012 that 'foodies hoping to appear on Simon Cowell's new cookery show would be well advised to hide their quail's eggs and caviar as the media mogul has to some declared that *Food Glorious Food* "is not a show for snobs"' (Cole 2012: n.p.). Here, we can draw some clear parallels with characters in many of Ravenhill's earlier plays who are seduced by brand names, and who seek to conceal their true selves by appearing more sophisticated than they really are. Take, for example, actor Amy in Ravenhill's 2005 play *Product*, who is mocked by film producer James for fetishizing her Gucci luggage, Versace suit and Jimmy Choo shoes (Ravenhill 2008: 155).

Secondly, a common theme in Ravenhill's plays is the lack of ability of those on the left to bring about genuine social change – the fact that members of society do not sufficiently stand up to the negative effects of capitalism, but rather concentrate primarily on their own needs. Plays that touch on issues such as these would include *The Cut* (2006), which explores the self-deception of liberal Western societies in not confronting the consequences of their behaviour on other parts of the world, and the cycle of sixteen short works that Ravenhill wrote for the 2007 Edinburgh Fringe Festival entitled *Shoot/Get Treasure/Repeat*, which explore Western democracies' blindness to the personal effects of war.

As theatre journalist Richard Patterson notes in an interview with Ravenhill, 'What image do we present, Ravenhill seems to ask, when our major concerns are coffee in the morning, garden centres during the day, plenty of sleep at night, and a heaping helping of freedom and democracy?' (Patterson 2008: n.p.). Spectators who are familiar with this aspect of Ravenhill's work might well then detect a similar inherent accusation in Andrea's utterance – and then derive implicatures that are ultimately not so very different from those that audiences watching a performance of Brecht's text might infer from the insult, namely, that Galileo is too concerned about acting in his own interests (as seen in his over-indulgence in wine and quails) to stand up for what he knows to be fundamentally right. Against this background, then, the likely explicatures and implicatures in Ravenhill's text could be summed up in Figure 4.8.

Looking at these layers of interpretation using my onion device, the crossover between Brecht's source text and Ravenhill's target text, and the way that slightly different explicatures still lead to similar implicatures, can be visualized in Figure 4.9.

In both textual examples explored here, then, we can see how Ravenhill does indeed appear to consciously inject some of his own voice into his text, but that in neither case does this fundamentally alter the meaning that Brecht most likely wished spectators

Stronger explicature	Andrea is mocking Galileo's love of wine and quails.
Weaker explicature	Andrea is accusing Galileo of pomposity and of not being true to himself (by failing to defend his discovery and failing to act in the interests of science).
Implicatures	Andrea is attacking those who sell out rather than stand up for what they believe in – who no longer uphold true values and only pay lip service to their ideals.

Figure 4.8 Potential explicatures and implicatures derived from Ravenhill's translation (Scene 13).

Figure 4.9 Second example of the conscious voice.

to infer from his source text. The fact that this should be possible appears to be a combination of

1. the synergy between Brecht and Ravenhill in terms of their social and political values, and the relatively strong salience that these values have among the respective followers of both playwrights, and
2. the synergy in terms of potential cognitive states between those spectators who are more familiar with Brecht and those spectators who are more familiar with Ravenhill (i.e. the fact that both playwrights are likely to appeal to spectators who themselves share similar values, even if their relative awareness of the source-text playwright and the celebrity translator might vary considerably).

From the point of view of relevance theory, then, the celebrity translator's and the source-text playwright's communicative intentions here are likely to be *broadly similar*, even if the stimuli used to make manifest their assumptions to the audience are quite different. On the other hand, the cognitive environments of different sectors of the audience (the Brecht followers and the Ravenhill followers) are likely to be quite different depending on which contextual associations are more salient – those derived from their understanding of Brecht or those derived from their understanding of Ravenhill. As a consequence, their specific assumptions about the text and the writer in each case mean that they will filter those stimuli in different ways to arrive at the same interpretation.

At other points in Ravenhill's text, however, the cognitive filters applied by those audience members who are particularly familiar with Ravenhill's work may actually *prevent* them from interpreting his stimuli in the way in which he most probably intended to be interpreted. This is because of those spectators' specific expectations about what the text *should sound like* – expectations which are, of course, raised whenever the text does indeed echo Ravenhill's voice. These assumptions can then lead them to seek such resonance even where it's not actually intended. Such unintended interpretations serve to create what I have termed Ravenhill's *unconscious* celebrity voice.

Ravenhill's unconscious celebrity voice

Having shown the effects of the celebrity translator consciously injecting some of his own voice into his translation, I'd now like to consider as a comparison the likely effects of a different scenario. In this section, I will explore the potential reception of textual examples that represent a more neutral translation – examples where the translator is more concerned about remaining overtly *faithful* to the voice of the source-text playwright than about creating a text in his own image, but where receivers of the translated text might infer a different meaning from that which the celebrity translator most likely intended.

Let's first consider the following extract from Scene 1 of Brecht's *Leben des Galilei* and Ravenhill's *A Life of Galileo*, in which Galileo is pleading with the bursar of his university for a salary increase.

Source text (Brecht [1955] 1963: 16)
GALILEI: Ich lehre und lehre, und wann soll ich lernen? Mann Gottes, ich bin nicht so siebengescheit wie die Herren von der philosophischen Fakultät. Ich bin dumm. Ich verstehe rein gar nichts. Ich bin also gezwungen, die Löcher in meinem Wissen auszustopfen. Und wann soll ich das tun? Wann soll ich forschen? Herr, meine Wissenschaft ist noch wißbegierig!

Literal translation (Gearing 2005: 13)
GALILEI: I teach and teach, and when should I learn? Man of God, I am not such a clever clogs (*coll: siebengescheit –smart aleck, too clever by half,*) as the gentlemen from the philosophy faculty. I am stupid. I understand nothing at all. And so I am forced to plug the holes in my knowledge. And when should I do that? When should I research? Sir, my science is still eager for knowledge!/ anxious to learn!

Target text (Ravenhill 2013a: 10)
GALILEO: I teach and I teach and when am I supposed to learn? I'm not as stuffed with knowledge as the gentlemen of the philosophy faculty. I'm stupid. I understand nothing. I need to fill up all those gaps in my knowledge. And when am I going to do that? When will I research? My science is hungry to learn.

Here, it's clear that Ravenhill's translation follows the literal translation extremely closely, with often only slight stylistic improvements made in order to give Galileo's speech a somewhat more modern, colloquial tone – for example, the use of contractions and the avoidance of *should* to express a sense of obligation in a question. Such close adherence to the literal translation (and thereby the source text) extends to the transfer of the meaning of Galileo's original polemic about his salary as a mathematician, and of Brecht's implicit questioning of the value attached to mathematical knowledge and progress by Galileo's employer – which by extension can be seen as a questioning of authority in general.

From the perspective of a contemporary audience, however, this passage is arguably open to two (or possibly even three) different interpretations depending on the spectator's specific cognitive context.

1. First, among those receivers who have some awareness either of Brecht's source text or at least of Brecht's political stance (whether such awareness is born out by reality or not), Galileo's speech *could* be interpreted in Ravenhill's translation in the way that they assume Brecht intended it to be understood, that is, as a demonstration of the battle over ownership of knowledge and control of information.
2. Second, for those receivers who are more familiar with Ravenhill's context as a playwright, and his own left-leaning, anti-establishment stance, such an extract might easily be taken at face value to be a comment on more contemporary issues, such as the funding (and indeed status) of higher education or the arts in the UK.
3. Third, again among those receivers who are more familiar with Ravenhill, this part of Galileo's speech might be understood at a deeper level to be a dismissal of the postmodernist view that reality (and therefore knowledge) is not something to be shared: what Rebellato calls 'the privatisation of public knowledge' (2001: xvi).

Indeed, before and after his version of *A Life of Galileo* was first performed, Ravenhill wrote or spoke on various occasions about the state of arts funding in the UK and his suggestions for an alternative model of funding (see Ravenhill 2007, 2010 and 2013c). So it's not entirely unreasonable to assume that such comments, appearing in publications or on websites such as the *Guardian*, the BBC and the *World Socialist Web Site*, to name but a few, might have attracted the attention of those theatregoers who are supporters of Ravenhill's causes or fans of his previous work as a playwright. As such, then, these spectators will have viewed Ravenhill's *A Life of Galileo* through a different cognitive filter from those who were attracted to the play more because of their interest in the work of Brecht.

More significantly perhaps, it's also possible that many of those spectators who went to see Ravenhill's version of *A Life of Galileo* may well have been familiar with another recurring theme in some of his early plays, such as *Shopping and Fucking* (1996) and *Some Explicit Polaroids* (1999) – namely, that of the ownership of reality and knowledge in a postmodern world. As Rebellato points out, 'Ravenhill's characters recite ... postmodern platitudes, insisting that nothing should ever mean anything, that truth is no more valuable than lies, that we should never think of the big picture' (2001: xvi). Without knowledge of Brecht's source text, then, followers of Ravenhill might easily assume here that he is celebrating Galileo as an anti-postmodern hero because of the way in which the latter seeks to carry out research so that he can subsequently share his knowledge with the world.

In pointing out these different interpretations, I'm not in any way claiming that these meanings are mutually exclusive, or that the two audience groups that I've described (the Brecht followers and the Ravenhill followers) are themselves mutually exclusive – far from it, there's likely to have been a significant overlap in terms of political leaning and concern about social issues between the Brecht and the Ravenhill groups of followers. Rather, the point that I wish to make is that the *greater relevance of Ravenhill* in receivers' cognitive contexts (using the term *relevant* in the technical sense used in relevance theory, see Sperber and Wilson 1995: 265) means that Galileo's speech is *more likely* to be processed within the context of their awareness and understanding of Ravenhill. This is because the unconscious effort required to achieve this cognitive effect is smaller than the effort that would be required to process it within the context of their awareness and understanding of Brecht (which is less salient and therefore more difficult to process).

Thinking again, then, in terms of the likely explicatures and implicatures of Brecht's source text (shown here in Gearing's literal translation), the potential interpretation of Galileo's speech in this extract could be summarized in Figure 4.10.

Of course, such meanings might be revised by receivers of this text as the play progresses and as Brecht is seen to attack Galileo for refusing to stand up for his profession against the might of the Catholic Church. But for the sake of the argument here, I'll restrict my analysis to the likely cognitive context of receivers during Act I of Brecht's play rather than at the end.

Stronger explicature	Galileo rejects the power that his employer exerts over his pursuit of mathematical understanding.
Weaker explicature	Brecht is mocking the dominance of philosophical over scientific thought at the time within the Catholic Church.
Implicatures	Brecht admires Galileo's attempts to defend his profession and his beliefs, making him a metaphor for the power of the individual to resist the distortion of or control over knowledge and information that was in evidence both in Galileo's time and in Nazi Germany.

Figure 4.10 Potential explicatures and implicatures derived from Brecht's source text (Scene 1).

Stronger explicature	Galileo rejects the power that his employer exerts over his pursuit of mathematical understanding.
Weaker explicature	Ravenhill is mocking the dominance of philosophical over scientific thought at the time within the Catholic Church.
Implicatures	*If Brecht is more salient to the receiver:*
	Brecht admires Galileo's attempts to defend his profession and his beliefs, making him a metaphor for the power of the individual to resist the distortion of or control over knowledge and information that was in evidence both in Galileo's time and in Nazi Germany.
	If Ravenhill is more salient to the receiver:
	Ravenhill is using Galileo's plea for a larger salary to highlight the lack of importance placed in contemporary society on learning and broadening the mind, and:
	1. to criticize the way in which education and the arts are reduced to the status of commodities, and therefore not given the level of funding that they deserve,
	and/or
	2. to attack the postmodernist idea that reality is not shared and that there is no such thing as absolute truth.

Figure 4.11 Potential explicatures and implicatures derived from Ravenhill's source text (Scene 1).

In Ravenhill's translation for the stage, meanwhile, the explicatures can be assumed to be the same as in Brecht's text, but there's potentially a very different emphasis in the implicatures that are inferred depending on the cognitive context of the receiver of the text, as seen in Figure 4.11.

As before, by mapping one set of interpretations onto the other (see Figure 4.12), the level of overlap between the source and the target texts is still very great, but at a very different level from that seen in the previous text examples.

In contrast to the textual examples explored in the previous section, then, where the explicatures were very different in the source and target texts, but the implicatures were actually very similar, here the opposite is true. The explicatures are broadly identical in both texts, but the implicatures derived from Ravenhill's text vary significantly depending on the cognitive mindset of the receivers – or in other words, depending on the extent to which their cognitive context is dominated more by Brecht or more by Ravenhill while watching a performance of Ravenhill's version.

A second example of this unconscious voice occurs in Scene 14 of *Leben des Galilei*, and in Scene 13 of Ravenhill's *A Life of Galileo*, where Galileo is trying to justify why he recanted his view that the sun, and not the earth, is at the centre of the universe.

Source text (Brecht [1955] 1963: 126)
GALILEI: Ich hatte als Wissenschaftler eine einzigartige Möglichkeit. In meiner
   Zeit erreichte die Astronomie die Marktplätze. Unter diesen ganz besonderen

Umständen hätte die Standhaftigkeit eines Mannes große Erschütterungen hervorrufen können. Hätte ich widerstanden, hätten die Naturwissenschaftler etwas wie den hippokratischen Eid der Ärzte entwickeln können, das Gelöbnis, ihr Wissen einzig zum Wohle der Menschheit anzuwenden! Wie es nun steht, ist das Höchste, was man erhoffen kann, ein Geschlecht erfinderischer Zwerge, die für alles gemietet werden können.

Literal translation (Gearing 2005: 116)
GALILEO: I had a unique opportunity as a scientist. In my time astronomy reached the market places. In these quite special circumstances the steadfastness of one man could have provoked great upset. If I had resisted, scientists could have developed something like the hippocratic [*sic*] oath of doctors, the vow to use/apply their knowledge for the good of man alone! As it now stands, the most that man can hope for is a race of innovative dwarves who can be rented for everything.

Target text (Ravenhill 2013a: 77)
GALILEO: As a scientist, I was presented with a unique opportunity, astronomy had reached the market square. One man standing strong could have shaken the world. If I'd held out, scientists might have made a promise, and oath, to use their knowledge solely for the good of humanity! Now all we've got is a race of inventing pygmies who can be sold to the highest bidder.

As with the previous example, at first glance the source and target texts appear largely similar, with Ravenhill's most obvious alteration being to reduce the length of Galileo's utterance, and in particular removing the reference to doctors' Hippocratic Oath. But the part of the text in which I'm most interested from the perspective of the *unconscious*

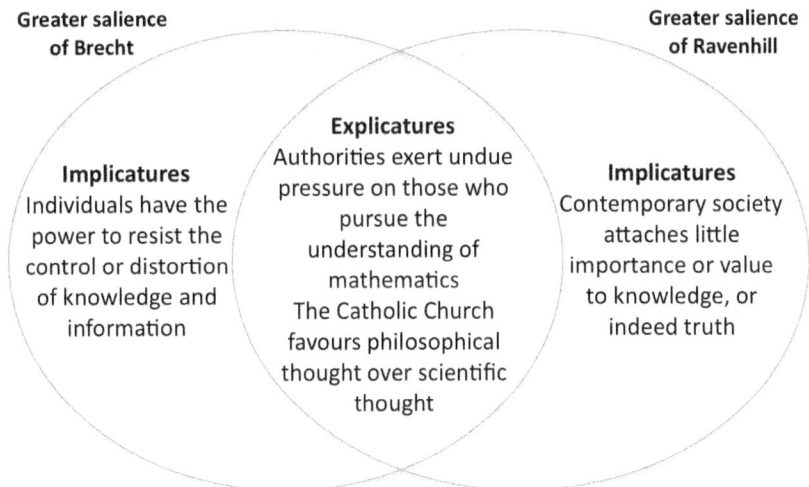

Figure 4.12 First example of the unconscious voice.

celebrity voice is the final sentence, in which Galileo bemoans the extent to which scientists are from now on condemned to selling their knowledge as a transaction rather than making it available for the general good.

In a performance of Brecht's source text, it will surely be clear to most, if not all, spectators that this is a reference to the dropping of the atomic bomb on Japan in 1945 – an act that, as already seen above, Brecht described as 'the classical end-product of [Galileo's] contribution to science and his failure to contribute to society' ([1980] 1995: 201). While some scholars have since criticized Brecht for essentially blaming Galileo for Hiroshima (see, for example, Hayman 1983: 297 and McCullough 1992: 121), others have taken a more sympathetic view. Author Jan Needle and Brecht scholar Peter Thomson, for example, note that while putting the blame on Galileo might be something of an overstatement, 'not to overstate at that time would have been shameful' (1981: 170).

However history might judge Brecht's own judgement of his central character in *Leben des Galilei*, it remains the case that the play has become inextricably caught up in the debate surrounding the way in which scientific knowledge is applied and the dangers that can arise from the misuse of such knowledge. Again, as already seen earlier in this chapter, this was an issue at the time Brecht was writing his final version of the play in relation not only to the atomic bomb but also to other scientific experiments that had been carried out in Nazi Germany. For contemporary audiences, meanwhile, their cognitive context with regard to this issue might also include more modern-day debates surrounding the ethics of, say, developing weapons of mass destruction, cultivating genetically controlled crops or experimenting with human cloning. In any event, then, the reference to 'a race of innovative dwarves who can be rented for anything' is likely to resonate strongly.

Ravenhill's reference to 'a race of inventing pygmies who can be sold to the highest bidder', meanwhile, is also likely to cue similar associations with the misuse of science across all audience types, whatever their specific cognitive context. It's certainly unlikely that any audience members would *not* note the atomic bomb inference in this utterance if they were aware of the approximate time period when Brecht wrote the play, even if they're not necessarily entirely aware of Brecht's background or frequently assumed political stance. More particularly within the context of Ravenhill, however, there's arguably a strong possibility that this utterance could *also* be understood in a slightly different (and complementary) way, namely as a reference to the way in which market forces now represent true power (i.e. the fact that those that bid the highest have the most power), and the way in which contemporary society commodifies and puts a monetary value on everything, including knowledge.

This is a theme that Ravenhill had previously addressed on many occasions, both in his plays and in his interviews or speeches that have been quoted in the media. In his own work, for example, we only need to look at his first play, *Shopping and Fucking*, to see what literature scholar Dominic Head describes as 'a graphic depiction of alienated urban youths filling meaningless lives with conspicuous consumption, whether food, sex or drugs, in a society where every relationship has been reduced to money' (2006: 921). In his 1998 play *Handbag*, meanwhile, Ravenhill portrays characters whose only view of education is that it will enable their children to earn more money than they themselves can.

> **MAURETTA:** We work so that he can have a future. He's got to have an education, he's not going to end up like …
> **LORRAINE:** What? What?
> **MAURETTA:** He's not going to be a two-pound-an-hour person. (2001: 212)

With this in mind, then, the likely interpretation of Galileo's speech as it appears in Brecht's source text (shown here in Gearing's literal translation) could be summarized in Figure 4.13. In comparison, in Ravenhill's translation, we can surmise the explicatures and implicatures summarized in Figure 4.14 depending on the cognitive context of the audience.

As already pointed out above, I'm not in any way claiming in this distinction that those spectators who receive Ravenhill's text through the cognitive filter of their understanding and experience of Ravenhill's work will overlook or ignore the atomic bomb inference when processing this text. The point I do wish to make, though, is that

Stronger explicature	Galileo laments the way in which scientists will rent out their knowledge.
Weaker explicature	Brecht is lamenting the misuse of knowledge, and of the power that such knowledge brings.
Implicatures	Attack on the role that scientists played in the invention of the atom bomb, and a condemnation of Galileo as a traitor for paving the way for its invention.

Figure 4.13 Potential explicatures and implicatures derived from Brecht's source text (Scene 14).

Stronger explicature	Galileo laments the way in which scientists will sell their knowledge to the highest bidder.
Weaker explicature	Ravenhill is lamenting the misuse of knowledge, and the way in which it can be bought and sold.
Implicatures	*If Brecht is more relevant to the receiver:*
	Attack on the role that scientists played in the invention of the atom bomb, and a condemnation of Galileo as a traitor for paving the way for its invention.
	If Ravenhill is more relevant to the receiver:
	Attack on the market-dominated society in which power equates to spending power, and in which everything is commodified and given a price, even knowledge itself.

Figure 4.14 Potential explicatures and implicatures derived from Ravenhill's translation (Scene 13).

such associations will also be supplemented by other, more contemporary inferences that may well be at least as salient (or, from the perspective of relevance theory, at least as *relevant*) to these spectators.

As before, then, if I map one set of meanings on the other (see Figure 4.15), we can see a similar pattern to the previous example. Here, it's again clear that there are broadly identical explicatures in both the source text and Ravenhill's translation, but that the implicatures are quite different depending on the cognitive context of the receiver and the extent to which either Brecht or Ravenhill is more dominant when receiving Ravenhill's text in performance. But in both these examples it's vital to understand that whether Ravenhill actually *intended* this connotative meaning to be implied in his version of Brecht's text is actually less important than the fact that it *might be interpreted* in this way by some members of the audience. And by extension, it will be clear that the cognitive context of spectators plays a much more important role in determining the connotative meaning of a play text when that text is translated by a *celebrity* translator than when it's translated by an *unknown* translator. Indeed, in these examples of *unconscious* voice, the interpretation by the audience is actually the *only* important factor in determining how the text is received. That's because spectators' expectations effectively *outweigh* the intentions of the author – or in other words, because the text is received in a way that is determined more by the audience than it is by either the source-text playwright or the translator.

This relevance-theoretical account might not be unique to celebrity translation since the same conclusions could also be drawn when analysing reception of *any* text by a well-known author with a distinctive voice (Seamus Heaney's *Beowulf* would be a good example here). But given that celebrity translators usually adapt texts written by playwrights who are themselves celebrities in their own right, this account appears particularly useful as it suggests a *battle for cognitive effects* between the celebrity

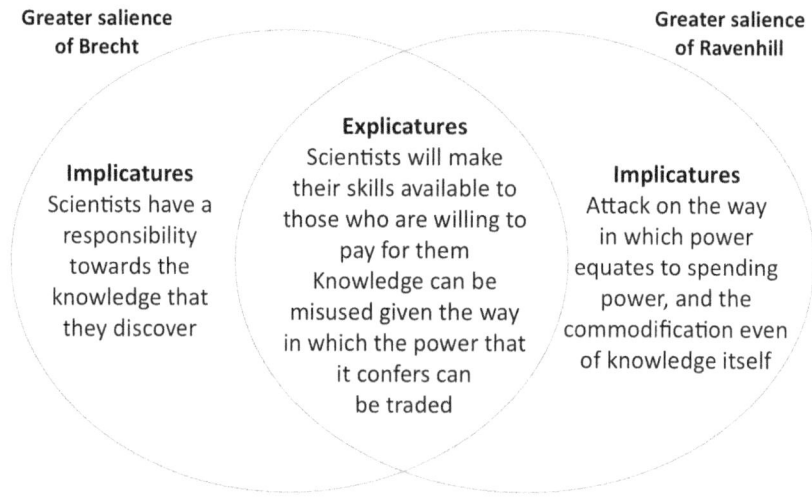

Figure 4.15 Second example of the unconscious voice.

translator's text and the celebrity source-text author's text. And it's the relative balance of each author's salience (or in other words, the extent to which associations with that author dominate in an individual spectator's cognitive environment) that determines which author wins the battle for that particular spectator's attention.

By extension, it could also be said that celebrity translation offers theatre audiences the opportunity to derive a *greater wealth* of cognitive effects from a performance than would be the case if a canonical work were translated by an unknown translator. And if we assume that more cognitive effects translates into a more thought-provoking and therefore more intellectually rewarding experience in the theatre, then my championing of celebrity translation starts to appear justified from both a theoretical and a practical perspective.

Celebrity translation and complementary contexts

What conclusions can we draw, then, from this relevance-theoretical analysis of *A Life of Galileo*? It perhaps shouldn't be a surprise that some of those conclusions may be the opposite of those that might be drawn from a more text-based theoretical analysis of the same text.

First, we can see that the greater the overlap of *implicatures* in the models discussed in earlier sections of this chapter (Figures 4.6, 4.9, 4.12 and 4.15), the more the target text can be considered a faithful translation of the source text – again, using the term *faithful* in its translation-theoretical sense to imply equivalence, however we might choose to define that in practice. That's because the greater similarity or emphasis in implicatures suggests that the text has similar cognitive effects on the audience. This may then often lead scholars (and indeed some audience members, if they're familiar with the source text) to an evaluation of the source and target texts that is very different from an assessment of those texts that is based more on an analysis of their textual equivalence.

Second, it is now clear that the greater the overlap of implicatures in these figures, the more we can assume that there is some *complementarity* between the audience's associations with the source-text playwright and their associations with the celebrity translator in terms of their inherent beliefs, values, causes and so on. As a consequence, then, we can also conclude that the greater the overlap of implicatures, the more successful the collaboration with the celebrity translator is likely to be from an artistic (and ideally also a commercial) point of view. This complementarity has important implications both for the choice of celebrity translator and for how a celebrity translator's text is marketed. For example, it could help theatres to determine how much emphasis should be given to the celebrity translator in publicity material compared with that given to the source-text playwright. It could also help those theatres to decide which audiences should be targeted in online and traditional direct marketing campaigns (and see Chapter 7 for more thoughts on how this could actually work in practice).

Third, it goes without saying that both explicatures and implicatures will inevitably vary between audience types, depending on the number of cognitive effects that the source-text playwright's and celebrity translator's respective texts give rise to.

Even though the cognitive environment of spectators who are more familiar with Brecht may well overlap significantly with the cognitive environment of spectators who are more familiar with Ravenhill, it's the *dominant* cognitive environment (i.e. the associations that are more salient) that ultimately determines the interpretation of the celebrity translation. Again, this has important implications for the marketing of celebrity translations and the types of spectators that should best be targeted in communication. For example, in the case of Ravenhill's translation of Brecht, it might help theatre marketing departments to decide whether they should prioritize the targeting of spectators who had previously attended productions of plays by other in-yer-face playwrights, or whether they should focus resources more on targeting those who had previously attended other plays by German playwrights.

Finally, we should remember that celebrity translation in the theatre is by its very nature more concerned with *equivalence of emotional effect* than equivalence in communicative meaning per se. While this could be said to be true of any form of literary translation, the issue here is that the equivalent effect of celebrity translation has as much to do with the text receiver's understanding of (and interest in) the complementarity between the source-text playwright's context and the celebrity translator's context as it has with the precise meaning of the source and target texts themselves. This will become clearer in my subsequent case studies.

5

Roger McGough's version of Molière's *Tartuffe*

Introduction

Jean-Baptiste Poquelin, better known by his stage name Molière (1622–73), first staged his play *Le Tartuffe ou l'imposteur* in Versailles in 1664. The work was controversial from the outset. Banned after its very first performance because of the vitriolic response it received from the Catholic Church in France, it has continued to this day to spark debate about what Molière was really trying to say to his audiences.

The plot of *Tartuffe* is a farcical one. Imposter Tartuffe pretends to be a pious man, such that his host, Orgon, falls under his spell and refuses to hear a bad word said against him. Orgon looks up to Tartuffe so much that he seeks to marry his daughter Mariane to the fraudster – to the horror of Mariane herself and the family. In an attempt to show Orgon what Tartuffe is really like, the family traps Tartuffe into declaring his desire for Elmire, Orgon's wife. Their plan initially backfires when Tartuffe declares himself guilty and Orgon accuses his son, Damis, of lying in order to blacken Tartuffe's name. As recompense for the suffering Tartuffe has endured over the accusation, Orgon hands over all his worldly possessions to Tartuffe. It's only when Orgon is persuaded to eavesdrop on a meeting between Tartuffe and Elmire and discovers for himself that Tartuffe is indeed trying to seduce his wife that he seeks to banish Tartuffe from his house. Tartuffe now reveals his true colours and tries to blackmail Orgon by claiming that he has evidence that Orgon assisted a traitor. Just as it looks as though Orgon will be arrested after being denounced by Tartuffe, it transpires that the king has heard of Tartuffe's treachery towards Orgon and demands Tartuffe's arrest instead. The family therefore escapes dispossession, and the play ends with Orgon announcing that Mariane is to marry her fiancé Valère instead.

English translations of *Tartuffe* might never have been banned, but over the years they have certainly still attracted more than their fair share of controversy among translators and drama enthusiasts. By the time Roger McGough's adaptation was first staged in the UK in 2008, there had already been over thirty different English translations of the play, including a number of translations more loosely based on Molière's source text.[1] With this in mind, then, there might appear to have been little artistic or commercial need for yet another English translation of *Tartuffe*.

It was, nevertheless, against this background that the Liverpool Everyman Theatre commissioned Roger McGough CBE (1937–) to produce a new adaptation of *Tartuffe* in 2007. Most importantly for the purposes of this chapter, McGough's translation contains many examples of his own distinctive voice that is already widely familiar from his own works of poetry. Indeed, the very fact that McGough is best known for being a poet rather than a playwright surely helps to create the expectation of a heightened voice that's inevitably different from that of an author known more for writing in prose.

Another factor that makes McGough's *Tartuffe* an interesting case study in the context of an exploration of celebrity translators is that, unlike the other translators explored here, McGough did not work from a literal translation of the source text but rather with a selection of published translations. Such a variety of reference material in different languages, different verse forms and different time periods clearly gives McGough a richer vein of language from which to craft his own adaptation of *Tartuffe*. And it perhaps heightens the urge to create a translation in his own image as a way of differentiating it from the many and varied versions that have gone before.

As in the previous chapter, I will begin by exploring Molière's and McGough's motivations for their respective works as a way of analysing their likely communicative intentions. I will then introduce the concept of *encyclopaedic entries*, which Sperber and Wilson (1995) use to explain how receivers of communication infer the meaning of utterances or texts. This provides a useful model for investigating the contextual assumptions that might be activated by concepts in McGough's translation and for demonstrating how these might serve to convey his distinctive voice. In applying this model to a series of textual examples in his translation, I'll explore the various different ways in which I believe McGough's voice is likely to be inferred by audiences attending a performance of his version of *Tartuffe*.

Molière's *Tartuffe*

An exploration of Molière's likely motivations for writing *Tartuffe* helps us not only to deduce his most probable communicative intentions but also to explore the potential responses to the play among audiences at the time. As was the case with Ravenhill's *A Life of Galileo*, we need to acknowledge at least some of the political and ideological context in which the play was originally conceived in order to appreciate Molière's most likely rationale for writing the piece in the first place and to understand the critical and popular response that the work received at the time.

Few scholars would probably doubt that Molière's likely motivation for writing a comedy about religious hypocrisy was to challenge, and even shock, his audience by virtue of the sheer audacity of his subject matter. Literary scholar Hugh Gaston Hall reminds us that 'to Molière's contemporaries every aspect of religion was an absorbing topic, but that one did not write about it in a comedy' (1960: 7). The fact that the play was banned after its first public performance could therefore hardly have been a surprise to its author, not least because one of his earlier plays, the 1662 comedy *L'École des femmes*, had already raised the hackles of the French establishment. As Molière biographer Virginia Scott points out, 'Flag flying, and, one might say, thumb to nose, he entered the fray a second time' (2000: 158). This time, however, Molière's work was to strike at the very heart of French society and stoke discord among even its most powerful members.

Here, we should bear in mind how relevant the content of the play was to the subjects of Louis XIV, the France's king at the time of its first performance. In the seventeenth century, for example, France witnessed an enduring conflict over the very nature of Christianity and its role in society. This was also the time when the Jansenist movement emerged, which emphasized the importance of divine grace and the notion of the *chosen few*. Jansenism's teaching frequently clashed with that of the Jesuit order, which played an important role in the Counter-Reformation movement and went on to become more of a modernizing force in the Catholic Church. It's also important to acknowledge how pertinent the notion of a *faux dévot* was at the time. According to Molière scholar Antoine Adam, the *dévot* had been a social type since the beginning of the seventeenth century in a similar way to the monk or the hermit of the Middle Ages (1962: 298). The idea, then, of someone with rather dubious connections to the Church being accommodated by a family to lead their prayers and hear their confessions was not as far-fetched at the time as it might appear to modern audiences. Moreover, given that devoutness was seen as a way of gaining power and becoming one of the chosen few, it should not be surprising that the unscrupulous sought to feign it.

Over and above the pertinence of the theme of *Tartuffe*, which in itself was a guarantee of attracting attention, we should also take into account how *true to life* the plot of the play is likely to have seemed to be to audiences at the time. Gaston Hall notes an alleged case not long before Molière wrote *Tartuffe* of a *faux dévot* seducing the wife of one of Molière's neighbours after being given shelter in the household (1960: 8). It would not be unreasonable, then, to assume that this was the most likely inspiration behind the events in Act III, Scene 3, in which Tartuffe attempts to seduce Elmire, the wife of his host Orgon. Similarly, it would also be reasonable to suppose that reports in 1667 of how the actor Bendinelli was betrayed by a priest staying in his home (1960: 8) will have been in Molière's mind when writing his revised version of *Tartuffe*.

At the same time, it's important to acknowledge *Tartuffe*'s resonance with dramatic traditions in the French theatre at the time of its first performance, not least its intended status as a *comedy*. Molière is arguably concerned more with depicting comic situations than with pointedly satirizing the religious establishment itself or particular groups within it (even if the Jansenists and the Jesuits will have no doubt delighted in seeking out lines in the play that could be considered satirical of the other). In this sense, then, *Tartuffe* bears much more than a passing resemblance to the long-standing theatrical tradition of farce, whose physical humour and absurdity remains popular to this day in theatre, television and film, both in France and across the Anglophone world. Consider, to give just one example, the enduring international appeal of French actor and playwright Jean Poiret's 1973 farcical play *La Cage aux Folles*, which has enjoyed various incarnations as a Franco-Italian film of the same name (1978) and, as *The Bird Cage*, a Broadway musical (1983) and a Hollywood Film (1996) starring Robin Williams and Gene Hackman. More UK-specific examples would include Alan Ayckbourn's plays such as *Bedroom Farce* (1975) and *Taking Steps* (1979), and Michael Frayn's *Noises Off* (1982), to say nothing of the farcical elements of the traditional British Christmas pantomime.

Likewise, Molière's characters' direct and indirect pronouncements on the corrupting influence of power, money and religion, and his ultimate plea for moderation, remind us that *Tartuffe* is in many ways a play about the value of reasoning and finding common ground – a sentiment that obviously has clear relevance across cultures and time frames. This perhaps explains the success of modern-day productions of the play before and since McGough's version that have transposed the setting to, say, the political establishment in contemporary Washington, DC (Harold Leaver's 2007 production using Ranjit Bolt's 1991 translation), the fashion world in twenty-first-century Paris (a 2009 production adapted and directed by Preston Lane), or the British Asian community in modern-day Birmingham (Anil Gupta and Richard Pinto's production for the RSC in 2018).

In considering Molière's motivation for writing *Tartuffe*, it's also worth mentioning the most obvious feature of Molière's text, namely, the twelve-syllable *alexandrine*. We should remember that this mode of expression would not have been considered unnatural to the literate theatre audiences watching a performance of *Tartuffe* in the seventeenth century, and the cadence of the verse will have been one of the familiar ways in which writers were able to add a comic or tragicomic dimension to their plots and their characters. Clearly, we cannot say the same of modern dramatic comedy or tragicomedy, and must therefore infer a somewhat different intention on the part of McGough in his decision to use rhyming verse for his adaptation of *Tartuffe*. I will explore the effects of McGough's rhyming verse in detail later in this chapter.

Lastly, it should be noted that *Tartuffe* was defined at the time of its writing as a social comedy in the *intermediate style*, in other words a style between the high style of classic epic and tragedy and the low style of popular diction (Gebauer and Wulf 1995: 114). The implication here is that the play was aimed at the lower aristocracy and the *haute bourgeoisie*. At the same time, Molière violates what are now considered the rules for such social comedies (as codified by poet and critic Nicolas Boileau in 1674 in *L'Art poétique*) by ridiculing characters across all the social strata (and not merely the stock character of the comic servant), yet in a way that focuses less on their social standing and more on their behaviour from a moral perspective (Gebauer and Wulf 1995). This is, of course, an issue that continues to preoccupy much drama from across the literary spectrum even today.

Roger McGough's *Tartuffe*

Roger McGough is best known as a writer and performer of poetry, having published more than fifty collections of poetry since the late 1960s. During the course of his career, however, he has also been an actor, playwright and musician. Born on the outskirts of Liverpool, McGough has remained associated with his home city throughout his working life. He made his first appearance on stage as an actor at the Liverpool Playhouse in 1963, and his first play was performed at the Liverpool Everyman Theatre in 1967. In the late 1960s, McGough was also a member of the Liverpool pop group The Scaffold, which had a UK number one hit with *Lily the Pink* in 1968. Since 2002, meanwhile, he has presented the BBC Radio 4 programme *Poetry Please*, the longest-running radio programme devoted to poetry in the world.

McGough's poetic voice has been variously described as reflecting 'a talent for an original use of poetic language, the inverted cliché, the ironic metaphoric trope and neologistic devices' (Wright 2003: v), epitomizing 'the working-class Liverpool of his childhood ... down-to-earth, unpretentious, dry, witty, ironic and sceptical' (O'Reilly 2008: n.p.), and embodying a 'subtle, surreal, zany twist' (Brown 2009: n.p.). McGough himself, meanwhile, describes his own verbal style thus: 'I like recycling things, looking at a word and playing with it. It's repartee, and I like being a juggler and catching people off guard. And it's good to mix things up' (Feay 2014: n.p.).

McGough's adaptation of *Tartuffe* was originally commissioned by Liverpool Everyman and Playhouse artistic director Gemma Bodinetz. She gave McGough a clear remit to breathe new life into a play that was already regularly performed in various versions. As Bodinetz says, 'I wanted to do a European classic ... but I wanted it to have a Liverpool heartbeat. ... Reading [*Tartuffe*], it felt like Roger and Molière were a match made in heaven – the wit, the irreverence, the scepticism ... the joy of language that they both share just felt perfect' (YouTube 2011: n.p.). In other words, McGough's role was to be more than simply one of translator from the very outset – he was the lynchpin that ensured that a landmark production for this theatre got off the ground in the first place, even without his having an existing pedigree as a translator, let alone a translator of Molière.

Having said this, it should nevertheless be noted that McGough had already had a long association with French literature by the time he first embarked on translating Molière. He studied French at the University of Hull in the late 1950s, during which time he not only wrote his first poetry but also 'attempted his first translations of Molière' (McGough 2008: xi). Moreover, following the critical acclaim and commercial success of his adaptation of *Tartuffe*, McGough has gone on to adapt Molière's *Le Malade imaginaire* as *The Hypochondriac*, first performed at the Liverpool Everyman Theatre in June 2009, and *Le Misanthrope*, which opened at the Liverpool Playhouse in February 2013.

Unlike the other celebrity translators explored in this book, McGough chose to rely on previous published translations of the play rather than a literal translation. His primary source was the prose translation published by Dover Press that claims to be 'based on the eighteenth-century translation from the French by H. Baker and J. Miller' (2000: vi). He also made some additional reference to existing translations for the stage by Richard Wilbur (1963), Christopher Hampton (1983), Liz Lochhead (1985) and Ranjit Bolt (1991, revised 2002). Importantly, however McGough's translation of *Tartuffe* confidently treads a different path both from those texts that adhere much more rigidly to the source text (e.g. Baker and Miller, or Wilbur) and from those that are much freer adaptations (most notably Lochhead's Scots version set in Scotland at the end of the First World War), while nevertheless retaining a healthy respect for the source text and its author. As he himself comments, 'I have this photograph of Molière on my desk and want to make sure that what I do reflects him, it's his story, and I just imagine him here with me and think, that's how he would have done it.'[2]

McGough's more confident style, which is arguably very much in his own image, is perhaps not surprising given the fact that he adapted *Tartuffe* after a career as a poet in his own right lasting more than forty years. In fact, McGough openly admits that his experience both as a poet and in the theatre had a positive influence on his adaptation of *Tartuffe*.

> My own work was definitely a help in doing *Tartuffe*. I've written plays and done a lot of theatre work, but I couldn't have done this in my thirties, and I wouldn't have attempted it. I've reached a stage in my life for some years now where I find it easier to write in verse than prose, so this is the right time for me to be doing this.

Tartuffe therefore represented a professional challenge at a time in McGough's career when he had already achieved considerable success with his own original poetry. With such a level of trust in his own abilities as a poet (if not necessarily as a linguist or a translator), we should perhaps not be surprised that McGough appears less concerned about remaining faithful to the source text than some of the other writers who have adapted *Tartuffe* during their respective careers as playwrights or translators.

From the perspective of a translation scholar, the differences between McGough and other writers in terms of their translation approach can be easily explained by the different balance of skills that each adaptor brought to the task at the time. For example, while writers such as Wilbur or Bolt might have been more confident as linguists than as poets at the time of their respective Molière translations, the opposite applies to McGough. This might help to explain why McGough gave himself greater licence for playfulness with the source text. His own justification for this is refreshingly honest,

> If you're a linguist, you'll be so careful and obsessed with the text and getting it right. Because who are you doing it for – for other translators to look at and pick at? But I came to this with a sense of naivety – 'who are you, Roger, tackling one of the great dramatists, you're daring to do it?' And once I tried it, it took me over and I loved it. And as long as I felt that Molière would approve I just got on with it.

Over and above the notion of what might be the *right* way to translate a text, which is reminiscent of the concept adhered to by nineteenth-century classical philologists of there being a correct way to interpret a classic text (Turner 2014: 304), McGough's concern for gaining Molière's approval is an important admission since it raises the issue of allegiance to the author, which has been an important topic of debate among literary theorists since the 1960s (see Roland Barthes's 1967 essay 'Death of the Author', Barthes 1977 and Michel Foucault's 1969 essay 'What Is an Author?', Foucault 1977). Essentially, then, it could be argued that McGough has both the authorial expertise and the public profile that allow him to more confidently become the *inferred author* of his adaptation of *Tartuffe* than would be the case for some of the other translators or adaptors of Molière. This then has important implications for the extent to which McGough's own voice is inferred not only by audiences but also by other agents in the theatrical system (not least the commissioner of the production), whether this voice is consciously implied or not.

Again from the perspective of the translation scholar, we should also acknowledge how much the discipline of translation studies evolved in the decades leading up to McGough's 2008 adaptation. While McGough would make no claims to being a translation studies scholar himself, it remains the case that he was most likely consciously operating in the literary polysystem that was prevalent at the time (see Even-Zohar 2004: 199), that is, a theatrical translation culture in the UK in the early twenty-first century that perhaps more actively embraced revaluation of canonical works than might have been the case in previous decades – whether as a legacy of post-structuralist and postmodern thinking about literary creation and authorship, or as a more sure-fire way of balancing artistic and commercial considerations in their programming. As adaptation studies scholar Yvonne Griggs points out, 'We are now more likely to view canonical texts not as works of individual genius but as cultural artefacts that are reliant for their construction and consumption on more than the writer's imaginative outpourings' (2016: 10).

Finally, the *saleability* of McGough, even when adapting a work as marketable in its own right as *Tartuffe*, is a factor that should not be underestimated when evaluating McGough's approach to translation. Importantly, McGough himself makes a ready distinction between his visibility as a marketing tool and his visibility as the adaptor of Molière's words. On the one hand, he is, not surprisingly, aware of the role that his public profile played in the commissioning and subsequent promotion of his adaptation of *Tartuffe*:

> Gemma Bodinetz asked me to do *Tartuffe* because she liked my poetry and she thought I had a similar soul, as it were, to Molière. And me being well known and well loved in Liverpool, she probably thought that commercially if he does it, it'll be good. When it was first advertised it was Molière's *Tartuffe* adapted by Roger McGough. And then it became more like Roger McGough's Molière's *Tartuffe*. That was purely commercial, it was nothing to do with me. ... But my being involved in it was never not going to be transparent, that was always part of it.

Somewhat contradictorily, however, McGough is also extremely conscious of the assumption, or even expectation, that his work would *sound* like his own work, and that the voice inherent in his poetry would be audible in his adaptation of Molière. 'I didn't want it to be my voice because I think sometimes my own poetry can be so ironic, and I didn't want that.'

Here, as in the previous chapter, we should remember that it's essentially irrelevant (at least as far as my analysis is concerned) whether the translator *intends* his or her voice to be inferred or not. More relevant is the fact that audiences are likely to infer this voice irrespective of the translator's *actual* or *claimed* intentions (which may or may not coincide). So it's at this point, then, that I'd like to introduce the concept of *encyclopaedic entries*. This concept offers us a useful means of exploring how audiences might arrive at an interpretation of McGough's translation of *Tartuffe* via the different ways in which they infer his voice in the text.

Encyclopaedic entries

The notion of *encyclopaedic entries* first emerged from studies of the lexicon and how associations with words are structured, organized and stored in the mind according to different *scripts* or *frames* (see Schank and Abelson 1977 and Minsky 1977). Encyclopaedic entries can essentially be defined as the information filed in a receiver's memory about a specific *concept* (i.e. a specific label, or address in the mind) relating to the external objects, events or properties that instantiate that concept. In other words, they comprise the assumptions that surround that concept, whether they are real or imagined, or whether they are central or incidental to the concept. Such entries are therefore one of three types of entry that go to make up the meaning of a concept, alongside the logical entry (the deductive rules that apply to the logical form of that concept) and the lexical entry (information about the natural-language form of that concept, that is, the word or phrase that expresses it).

To give an example of these different types of entries, let's consider an ad hoc concept (i.e. a concept that has occasion-specific meanings) that's particularly pertinent here – the ad hoc concept THEATRE*.[3] The *logical* entry for the concept THEATRE might contain rules that enable the receiver to deduce by a process of computation that the communicator is referring to a building, a performance of a theatrical work, or an artistic genre, but not exactly which one of those three was meant. The *lexical* entry for the concept THEATRE will contain information about the word whose meaning is the concept (e.g. that THEATRE is rendered in English by the noun *theatre*). The *encyclopaedic entries* for the concept THEATRE, meanwhile, include all the representations that enable the receiver to access contextual assumptions with regard to that concept. These assumptions would enable the receiver to determine which of the meanings of THEATRE the communicator intended (which may or may not be one or more of those suggested above). Such assumptions might also trigger the receiver's associations with his or her previous experience of the theatre, with the type of person who goes to the theatre, or with particular theatrical works, and so on (see Sperber and Wilson 1995: 89).

Sperber and Wilson's application in relevance theory of the notion of encyclopaedic entries broke new ground in linguistic theory in that it viewed such entries as the *very basis* for understanding communication. This is because Sperber and Wilson see encyclopaedic entries as a way of describing the *inferences* that receivers derive from an utterance (1995: 65–177). In other words, they are less concerned with the logical or purely lexical part of meaning than with the *pragmatic* dimension of meaning. Here, we need to remind ourselves that relevance theory aims at a causal-mechanistic account of communication. According to this account, receivers rely on their contextual assumptions to deduce the meaning of an utterance – what Robyn Carston refers to as an 'inferential system which blindly performs its computations on the input it is given, using the logical elimination rules which constitute its proprietary database' (2002a: 7). Relevance theory therefore assumes that receivers infer *their own meaning* from an utterance, and that they can 'construct their own implicatures and metaphors as communication shades off into cognition' (MacKenzie 2002: 25).

Now, part of this proprietary database is made up of the receiver's background knowledge or cognitive context. In relevance theory (and in accordance with current thinking in the field of cognitive linguistics), this cognitive context is described as comprising a system of 'cross-referenced encyclopaedic entries attached to particular conceptual addresses' (Carston 2002a: 7). These entries are then activated by ostensive stimuli (such as an utterance, or any other sensory stimulus) to determine the inferred meaning of that stimulus.

Let's look at an example of this process. The following text is taken from McGough's translation of *Tartuffe* and occurs in Act V, Scene 2, when Damis criticizes his father, Orgon, for trusting Tartuffe.

Target text (McGough 2008: 66)
DAMIS: I hear that blatherskite's been threatening you.
After all you've done for him. Can this be true?

The ad hoc concept BLATHERSKITE* might activate a range of encyclopaedic entries that we could visualize in the 'mind map' in Figure 5.1. The idea here and throughout this chapter is to depict the associations that receivers may make with each ad hoc concept and to portray the potential hierarchy of receivers' contextual assumptions. The maps are not intended to be prescriptive – in other words, they're not meant to imply that this the *precise order* in which encyclopaedic entries will be activated. Nor

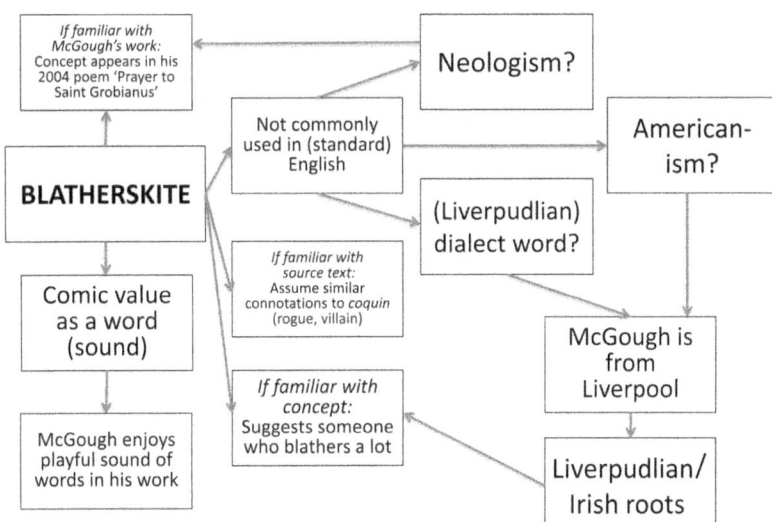

Figure 5.1 Potential encyclopaedic entries attached to concept BLATHERSKITE*.

are they intended to be comprehensive and to imply that these are the *only* entries that will be activated. Rather, they're designed merely to demonstrate how receivers *might* infer meaning from McGough's text.

Here, then, it's probably not unreasonable to make the following assumptions.

1. There will be some audience members who might be familiar with and understand the meaning of the concept BLATHERSKITE* because they have previously heard it in other contexts, and that a sub-group of these audience members may even recall that it features in one of McGough's poems, although this context is unlikely in isolation to have given many hints as to the precise meaning of the concept.

   Prayer to Saint Grobianus
   The patron saint of coarse people
   ... Have pity on we poor wretched sinners
       We blatherskites and lopdoodles
       Lickspiggots and clinchpoops
       Quibberdicks and Quakebuttocks ... (2004: 351)

2. There will be other audience members, meanwhile, who will have never heard this concept before, and who must therefore infer its meaning either from the context (which might suggest something along the lines of *rogue, swindler, thief* and so on), and that, again, within this group, there will be those who assume that it might be a word from a dialect of English with which they're not familiar, and others who assume that it is a neologism.

3. Within one or both of these groups of audience members, there may be some (even if only a small minority) who are extremely familiar with the French source text, to the extent that they might be able to make a link between BLATHERSKITE and the term that Molière used, *coquin* (most often translated as *rogue* or *rascal*).

4. Within one or both of these groups of audience members, there may be also some who assume that BLATHERSKITE is a Liverpudlian dialect word due to their associations with *blather* – a word which is arguably more common in some dialects of Northern England than elsewhere – and the relatively easy semantic leap from *skite* to *shite* to create a semantic unit. (As an aside, *blather* is in fact believed to come from the Old Norse *blathra*, meaning *to talk nonsense*, and first appeared in Scots in the sixteenth century. It remains a feature of Scots and Hiberno-English, which is the term used to describe the range of English spoken by people whose mother tongue is Irish – see Dolan 1999: 24. It also features occasionally in some Northern varieties of English, either as *blather* or as *blether*, while in Southern England, it has more often become reduced to *blithe,* and is used especially in its adjectival form *blithering* – see Oxford Dictionaries 2016: n.p.)

As seen in Chapter 3, and of particular importance when exploring a receiver's immediate response to a multi-sensory experience such as seeing a play performed in a theatre, the crucial factor here is the relative *accessibility* of those contextual assumptions. In other words, the most accessible (i.e. the most immediate) assumptions are the ones that are most important in determining how a stimulus is processed. In the above example, then, it could of course be argued that spectators might make a mental note of the concept BLATHERSKITE* and Google the term, look it up in a dictionary, check the source-text word, ask their peer group if they are familiar with the term, or any combination of these acts. If this were the case, the consequent expansion of a spectator's encyclopaedia could give rise to an almost limitless number of contextual assumptions, particularly given the way in which encyclopaedic entries are constantly cross-referenced and updated. But for the purposes of this analysis, I'll restrict my exploration to those entries that are likely to be activated *most spontaneously* at the time of receiving the stimulus, with a particular focus on those entries that may or may not be activated as a result of pre-existing assumptions about the celebrity translator.

Again, then, with regard to the above example, spectators might realistically assume any of the following:

1. The concept is an invented one (i.e. a neologism), and this is consonant with McGough's playful use of language that frequently involves inventing words for comic effect (as in the poem cited earlier).
2. The concept is embodied in a dialect term, and presumably one that is peculiar to McGough's home city of Liverpool, given that associations with Liverpool are likely to weigh heavily in the contextual associations surrounding McGough and his work. (In fact, BLATHERSKITE is originally a Scots word that has since become more common in North American varieties of English than in British colloquial usage, allegedly as a result of its use in the Scottish song *Maggie Lauder*, which became popular among American troops during the War of Independence, see *Oxford Dictionaries* 2016: n.p.)
3. The concept is part of McGough's existing idiolect and therefore requires prior familiarity with and appreciation of McGough's work to be spontaneously understood.

As already seen in Chapter 3, whether such assumptions are correct or not is immaterial from the perspective of relevance theory. Likewise, the fact that spectators might access incorrect encyclopaedic entries that then lead them to false assumptions is again irrelevant. All that matters is that receivers of the concept are able to make *their own assumptions* as to McGough's communicative intention, and that this then satisfies their need for relevance. In fact, it's when receivers are *more* dependent on guesswork for drawing their inferences (i.e. when they have no encyclopaedic entries stored in their memories in relation to that concept) that their associations with that celebrity translator might be spontaneously activated to fill this void simply because of the lack of any other viable explanation (see the assumption above about 'McGoughisms').

In the following sections of this chapter, I will apply Sperber and Wilson's notion of encyclopaedic entries to various textual examples in McGough's target text as a way of comparing the range of possible meanings or interpretations that might be inferred by spectators. Here, it's vital to understand that this is a very different task from comparing meanings in a logical or conceptual sense. Such an exercise would imply that we can reasonably infer the meanings intended by the respective authors – something that's ultimately impossible to do, as already seen in Chapter 3. In other words, I will be exploring the *likely cognitive responses* to these text examples based on everything I can reasonably infer *either* from McGough's motivations for writing his text (and his likely or claimed assumptions about Molière's motivations for writing his text) *or* from my own assumptions (which may or may not be correct) about the cognitive contexts of different audiences.

I'm going to start by exploring the potential encyclopaedic entries attached to a number of *specific concepts* that feature in McGough's adaptation of *Tartuffe* (networks of signifiers, puns and a single example of anachronism). In each case, I will seek to demonstrate how the cognitive effects derived from these concepts are influenced by existing cognitive associations with McGough – associations that are made by virtue of his status (or more specifically, his voice) as a well-known poet in his own right. I will then apply the concept of encyclopaedic entries to some of the *comedic devices* that feature repeatedly in McGough's text (the use of particular verse forms, sociolects and idiolects, and repeated exoticizations). Here, I will be building on work by other scholars that suggests that concepts that trigger encyclopaedic entries are not limited to lexical items. As neuroscientist Antonio Damasio points out, a concept can consist of anything that might be triggered or activated in the receiver's mind by the presence of an external stimulus, or in other words, any of 'a wide variety of representations … that together define the meaning of the entity momentarily' (1989: 26).

McGough and translated concepts

Underlying network of signification

Translation scholar and philosopher Antoine Berman notes that literary texts contain 'a hidden dimension, an "underlying" text, where certain signifiers correspond and link up, forming all sorts of networks beneath the "surface" of the text itself' (2004: 284). Here, Berman's notion of *signifiers* (as opposed to linguist and semiotician Ferdinand de Saussure's more fixed notion of signifiers) is similar, in some ways at least, to Sperber and Wilson's notion of *concepts*, as defined earlier in this chapter, that is, a label or address under which various types of information can be stored and retrieved and which may appear as a constituent of a logical form (1995: 86).

While such a comparison of the terminology of literary critical theory, on the one hand, and cognitive linguistics, on the other, might be fraught with danger in many other contexts, Berman's notion of underlying networks of signification does still provide us with an interesting framework within which to assess translation. Examples of such underlying networks might include the way in which an author chooses to use certain *concepts* (or *signifiers*, if we prefer to use Berman's terminology) in unexpected places, to use concepts that by their very nature cue other concepts, or indeed to avoid concepts where they might otherwise have been expected. The destruction of such underlying networks of signification is one of the twelve ways in which Berman believes that translators negate the foreign in literary texts, known as his twelve 'deforming tendencies' (2004: 280).

Perhaps the most obvious example of an underlying network of signification in *Tartuffe* is the way in which Molière uses religious references to develop and intensify his theme of religious hypocrisy. It's telling, however, that McGough destroys much of this network by frequently using much more neutral language in his adaptation. In Act IV, Scene 7, for example, in which Tartuffe is attempting to seduce Orgon's wife, Elmire (unaware that Orgon is hiding in a chest in the room), we find several references to Tartuffe's supposed piety that lose their more spiritual associations in McGough's translation.

Source text (Molière [1669] 2003: 149)
TARTUFFE: Tout conspire, Madame, à mon contentement:
J'ai visité de l'œil tout cet appartement;
Personne ne s'y trouve; et mon âme ravie.

My literal translation
TARTUFFE: Everything conspires, Madame, to my satisfaction:
I have surveyed this entire apartment;
There is no one there; and my soul is ravished.

Target text (McGough 2008: 62)
TARTUFFE: All is clear, madame, and rampant, the bull is at the gate... Let Eros triumph...

Here, we see how Molière's reference to Tartuffe's *âme ravie* – his *ravished soul* – becomes lost in McGough's translation. And while McGough's reference to the Greek God Eros does at least retain Molière's sense of Tartuffe's hypocrisy, he also thereby avoids (whether consciously or not) the implication of religious hypocrisy that is usually seen as central to Molière's play. As a result, McGough's Tartuffe is ultimately seen as a figure of fun – a hedonist rather than necessarily a sinner. Relating this to the notion of encyclopaedic entries, the ad hoc concept EROS* might here give rise to the contextual assumptions among spectators shown in Figure 5.2.

The suggestion that McGough's translation activates encyclopaedic entries that more readily position Tartuffe as a comic rather than a hypocritical character fits with the supposition that spectators will be actively seeking humorous references in McGough's work by virtue of their pre-existing expectations of that work. At the same time, though, we should not forget that the humour in the farcical situation of Orgon hiding in the chest while Tartuffe seduces his wife will also have been very obvious to audiences of Molière's original work. Indeed, Molière is considered by many scholars to have been one of the driving forces in bringing farce to the Parisian stage, even if there is still some debate as to whether this constituted a *revival* of French traditions of farce dating back to the Middle Ages, or whether it was more a direct result of the influence of Italian *commedia dell'arte* (Wadsworth 1987: 77). In this sense, then, McGough is in fact reflecting what we can assume to have been Molière's intended voice as much as inserting his own voice.

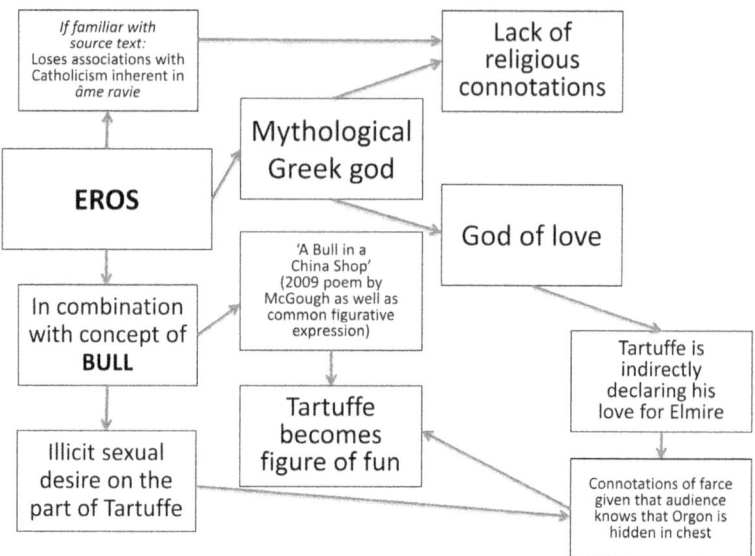

Figure 5.2 Potential encyclopaedic entries attached to concept EROS*.

On the other hand, McGough also inserts some religious references into his adaptation of *Tartuffe* where none existed in Molière's source text. For example, in Act I, Scene 5, when Orgon tells his brother-in-law, Cléante, of Tartuffe's remorse at accidentally killing a bee (a flea in Molière's original), Cléante replies as follows, in a riposte lacking in the original source text.

Target text (McGough 2008: 15)
CLÉANTE: With full military honours, I'll be bound!
           And a gravestone suitably inscribed:
           'Here lieth a bee
           No longer busy
           RIP.
           Death, where is thy sting?'

The encyclopaedic entries that might be triggered in this case by the ad hoc concept BEE* are summarized in Figure 5.3.

In this example, we can observe how actual, metaphorical and even onomatopoeic associations can be cued from a single concept. It's also interesting to consider how each of these might potentially lead audiences to infer some of McGough's distinctive voice in his translation – either spontaneously (as an obvious example of word play and play on the sounds of words), upon reflection (as a mischievous biblical reference) or more obliquely among those already familiar with Molière's work (as a personal criticism of Tartuffe's hypocrisy that has been consciously inserted into the translation). In this respect, it's important to note that, perhaps because of his own religious convictions, about which he had previously talked openly (see McGough 2012: n.p.), McGough

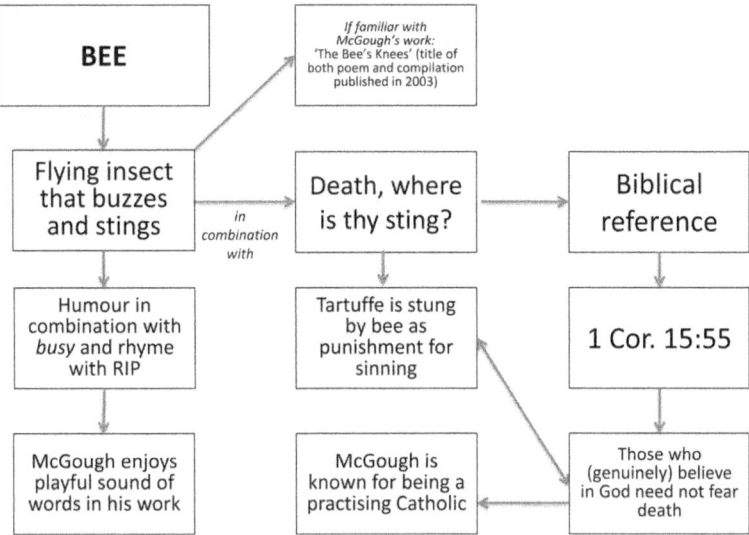

Figure 5.3 Potential encyclopaedic entries attached to concept BEE*.

claims to have actively sought to avoid the anti-religious slant that permeates other translations or adaptations of *Tartuffe*. This is because he believes that this is not what Molière intended, in spite of the backlash from the Catholic Church with which the work originally met.

> The thing about *Tartuffe* and a lot of the other adaptations I've seen, and why Molière got into trouble, is that it's seen as a very anti-clerical, anti-Christian, anti-Catholic piece, which Molière denied. And as a Catholic myself, I sort of felt that Molière was saying that Tartuffe was perhaps a sinner who would confess that he'd sinned and enjoyed his life. So with Cléante, I didn't want to make him a fool like he is in some translations, where he's seen as a bit of a pompous ass defending the faith. But I didn't do that, so I think that made it a stronger piece, more in line with what Molière was saying.

Against this background, it becomes clear that, rather than destroying Molière's underlying network of signification, McGough is actually creating his very own network. This network will then be understood by receivers of his translation in different ways depending on the different encyclopaedic entries that are triggered. So, if receivers associate McGough with a particular type of humour (however they might choose to define it), the cognitive effects of the utterances explored here will be dominated by the comic dimension of, say, Tartuffe's amorous advances or a buzzing bee. These utterances will then be processed in the context of their associations with McGough's voice – for example, associations of being whimsical or mischievous. If, on the other hand, receivers have some awareness of McGough's religious convictions, then they may alternatively or additionally infer some of the sentiments in the above citation. As a consequence, they might derive cognitive effects that focus more on the questioning of morals rather than the questioning of religion (and specifically Catholicism) per se.

The key conclusion here, then, is not simply that changes to specific concepts in the source text (whether by omission, expansion or any other approach to translation) will alter the way in which the target text will be received because of the different encyclopaedic entries that will be triggered compared with those triggered by the source text. Rather, it's more that the encyclopaedic entries triggered by these concepts can either individually or cumulatively create a distinct underlying network of signification – a different, *hidden* dimension that, in the case of the celebrity translator, starts to become an integral part of how that translator's voice is inferred in his or her text.

Puns

Pragmatics scholar Agnieszka Solska notes that the assumptions stored under the encyclopaedic entries of concepts are 'of particular importance in the case of puns, many of which tend to be autonomous, self-contained texts' (2012: 392). The dynamic model of context that is fundamental to relevance theory's description of how utterances are understood (Sperber and Wilson 1995: 118) implies that receivers of utterances will attempt to select or construct the appropriate senses of the word or words that are being used to create the pun from the context. As a result, they 'end up constructing … an explicature consisting not of one but of two equally valid propositions' (Solska 2012: 394). What this means, then, is that receivers will juxtapose two distinct concepts that share the same *lexical* entry but different *logical* and *encyclopaedic* entries. This applies whether the pun is based on two *homophones* (two lexical entries with the same pronunciation but different meanings) or on a *polyseme* (a lexical entry with two or more meanings).

Let's now explore two different puns in McGough's *Tartuffe*. First, in Act III, Scene 6, when Damis tries to convince Orgon of Tartuffe's treachery, McGough's pun on the homophones *wretch* and *retch* adds a wholly new dimension of cleverness to Molière's dialogue.

Source text (Molière [1669] 2003: 120)
ORGON: Tais-toi, pendard!
 À Tartuffe. Mon frère, eh? Levez-vous, de grâce.
 À son fils. Infâme!
DAMIS: Il peut…
ORGON: Tais-toi.
DAMIS: J'enrage! Quoi? Je passe…

My literal translation
ORGON: Shut up!
 To Tartuffe. My brother, eh? Rise, for Heaven's sake.
 To his son. Villain!
DAMIS: He can…

| ORGON: | Shut up. |
| DAMIS: | I am enraged! What? I am being taken for... |

Target text (McGough 2008: 46)
| ORGON: | You wretch. |
| DAMIS: | I will in a minute. I've swallowed so much bile watching him wind you up – he's vile. |

Figure 5.4 shows the potential encyclopaedic entries attached to the ad hoc concept WRETCH/RETCH*.

Similarly, an example of a polysemous pun occurs in Act IV, Scene 5, when Orgon is hiding in a chest to spy on Tartuffe while the latter is attempting to seduce Orgon's wife, Elmire. In an effort to give Orgon a cue to emerge from the chest and expose Tartuffe, Elmire tries coughing to alert her husband.

Source text (Molière [1669] 2003: 144)
| TARTUFFE: | Vous toussez fort, Madame. |
| ELMIRE: | Oui, je suis au supplice. |

My literal translation
| TARTUFFE: | You are coughing loudly, Madame. |
| ELMIRE: | Yes, I am in torment. |

Target text (McGough 2008: 60)
| TARTUFFE: | You have a bad cough, Madame. |
| ELMIRE: | Yes, I've something on my chest. |

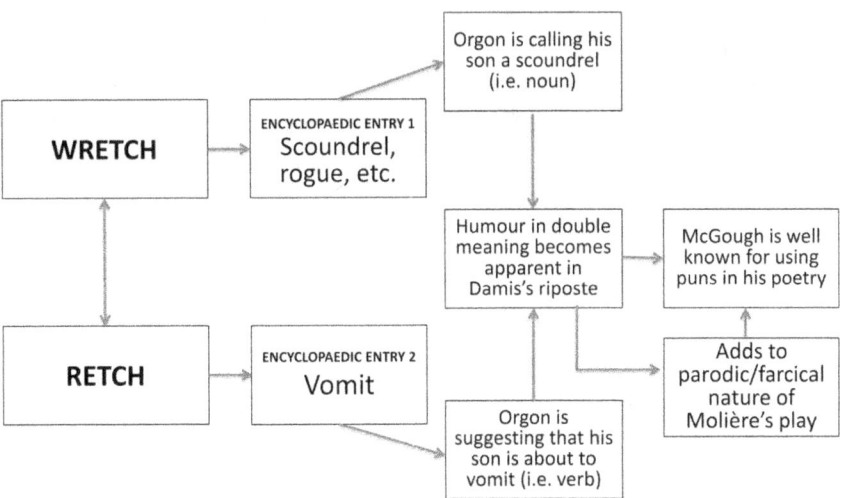

Figure 5.4 Potential encyclopaedic entries attached to concept WRETCH/RETCH*.

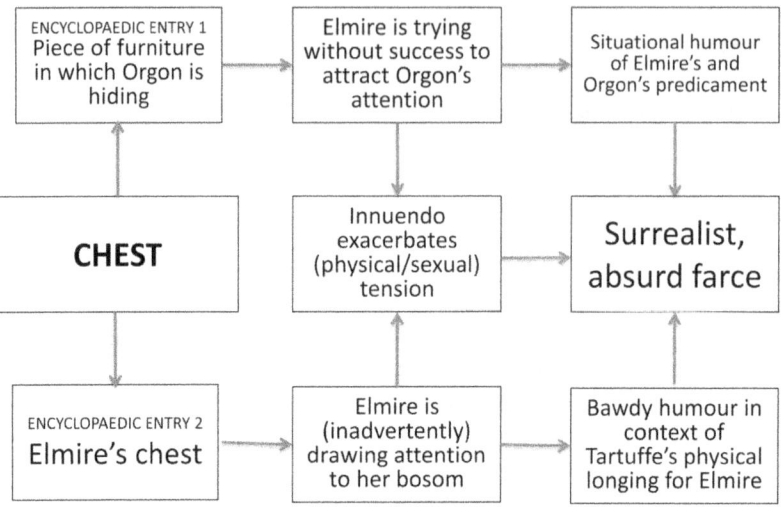

Figure 5.5 Potential encyclopaedic entries attached to concept CHEST*.

Here, the innuendo inherent in the ad hoc concept CHEST* (the piece of furniture in which Orgon is hiding and Elmire's bosom) is likely to trigger a number of encyclopaedic entries, as seen in Figure 5.5.

Here, it becomes clear how audiences might easily detect a type of humour that is bawdier than might necessarily be associated spontaneously with McGough given his body of work to date (although not necessarily bawdier than many might associate with Molière). But at the same time, such humour ultimately conjures up a sense of surrealism and absurdity that is very much in keeping with the style of much of McGough's poetry. In this respect, then, we could say that receivers of McGough's *Tartuffe* are guided towards discovering a new dimension of McGough's voice (bawdiness) via his familiar punning device. This reminds us that a celebrity's voice is not a fixed entity but rather a fluid concept that changes with each successive piece of work by that celebrity, whether that work is a translation or not.

Anachronism

Lawrence Venuti talks about 'the inevitable problem of anachronism in translation', by which he is referring to the way in which translations 'cannot simply restore past sounds and listening experiences for readers who do not have sufficient access to the foreign context' (2013b: 189). While Venuti is thinking here more in terms of the loss of context when translating from one time period to another as well as from one culture to another, I would like to draw attention to an example in McGough's adaptation of a wholly anachronistic *concept* – and to show how exploration of the encyclopaedic entries attached to that concept can potentially help us to see anachronism as a way of positively engaging audiences rather than being an inevitable problem for the translator.

The particular textual example that I would like to look at can be found in Act IV, Scene 3, when Orgon challenges his daughter Mariane's claim of preferring life in a convent to a life of being married to Tartuffe.

Source text (Molière [1669] 2003: 135)
ORGON: Ah! voilà justement de mes religieuses,
Lorsqu'un père combat leurs flammes amoureuses!
Debout! Plus votre cœur répugne à l'accepter,
Plus ce sera pour vous matière à mériter:

My literal translation
ORGON: Ah! This is exactly what women who become nuns are like,
When a father fights their amorous flames!
Get up! The more your heart shies away from accepting it,
The more you will deserve it:

Target text (McGough 2008: 53)
ORGON: Oh what sadistic games love-sick girls like to play,
making parents suffer when they don't get their own way.
Rejecting the lure of suicide, they make the first enquiry
to enter the nearest convent, or if Daddy's rich, the Priory.

Here, the reference to *the Priory* is clearly a complete anachronism if the joke is understood as McGough presumably intended, that is, as a reference both to (1) another type of religious institution in which Mariane might prefer to live as an alternative to marrying Tartuffe and to (2) the Priory Hospital Roehampton, a private psychiatric hospital in south-west London that was only established in 1872. On the other hand, some audience members might not immediately understand that the ad hoc concept PRIORY* is a humorous reference to this hospital and simply infer the first of the above two meanings from that concept. In this case, then, the anachronism goes unnoticed and these audience members fail to understand the joke because they fail to access all the encyclopaedic entries attached to the concept PRIORY* in this context.

Of course, the fact that McGough chooses to refer to a nineteenth-century institution in an adaptation of a seventeenth-century French play is one that might be questioned by some translation scholars because of the way that it fails to respect the culture or time period of the source text. But from the audience's perspective, we can see in Figure 5.6 that McGough's translation might yield a rich variety of contextual associations that more than outweigh the anachronistic connotations that the concept might give rise to at a logical level – at least among those spectators who understand the joke.

Importantly, the fact that the concept PRIORY* has the effect of an 'in-joke' is not at all dissimilar to Molière's own playful humour, which often involved oblique references to social or political events or individuals that would only be understood spontaneously by those spectators who were particularly aware of the issues being discussed in Paris at the time. Consider, for example, Molière's allusions in *Tartuffe* to the Bendinelli affair discussed earlier in this chapter, which only those spectators

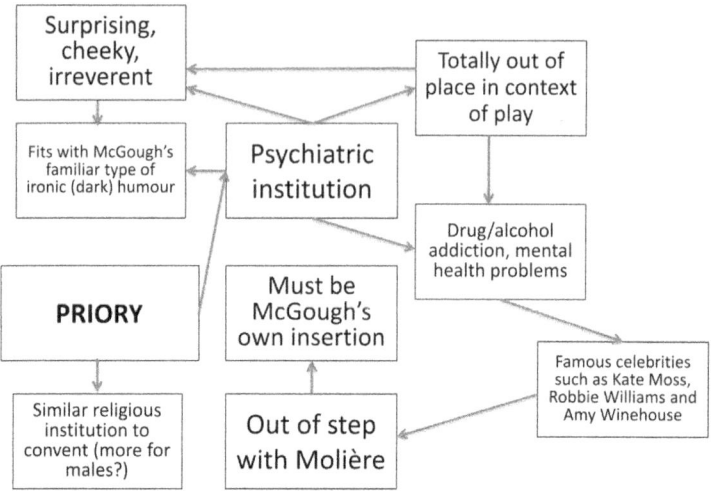

Figure 5.6 Potential encyclopaedic entries attached to concept PRIORY*.

who were aware of the betrayal suffered by Bendinelli will have picked up on. In this respect, it's interesting to note that McGough felt that response to his Priory joke varied across the theatres in which *Tartuffe* was performed, with audiences in theatres further from London often less likely to spontaneously understand the reference to the Priory Hospital than those closer to the capital.

Here, it's obvious that McGough appears to take a mischievous delight in challenging his audience's sensibilities, yet without going so far as to damage the integrity of the source text and its author. 'I thought, if Molière were at my side going through it with me, would he let me get away with it, and I think he would. But I wouldn't do anything that would hurt him or that I don't think he'd approve of.' And of course we should also acknowledge that spectators are unlikely to process McGough's mischievous anachronism purely at a rational level. Such humour will probably be greeted more by knowing laughter (either at the time of the joke or sometime after the event) than by any concerns about a lack of respect for Molière and his text. After all, topical social, cultural and political references are already an inherent part of much of British mainstream culture, whether in the broadcast media in programmes such as BBC One's *Have I Got News for You* and BBC Radio 4's *The News Quiz*, or on stage in the traditional Christmas pantomime. Such references are therefore ultimately unlikely to be received by audiences in the way that the more spontaneous encyclopaedic entries identified above might suggest.

McGough and comedic devices

Verse forms

As Adrian Pilkington points out, verse forms can in themselves affect how texts are received, either because metre can force the receiver to expect a certain stress pattern (which may often be different from that of normal speech patterns) or because some metrical patterns are more effective than others in enhancing particular effects, such as the comic effects in the verse metre of limericks or in the predictability of the iambic pentameter (2000: 133). Similarly, poetry scholars Tom Furniss and Michael Bath suggest that metrical regularity creates 'a visual and aural framework or pattern' within which all the linguistic effects of a text are played out (2007: 15). As part of this framework, any rhymed words are therefore not merely random lexical items at the end of a line but rather a foregrounded feature of the text that reinforces the metrical structure, draws attention to these items and the relationship between them, and adds to the aesthetic quality of the text.

Molière's *Tartuffe* is written entirely in twelve-syllable rhyming couplets known as alexandrines in which each syllable has a more or less equal metrical weight. alexandrines allow rhymes in an inflected language such as French that would be less admissible in a non-inflected language such as English. To give some examples taken from a speech by Cléante in Act I, Scene 5, we see Molière rhyming *eux* with *yeux*, *simalgrées* with *sacrées* and *distinction* with *dévotion*. Each of these examples highlights the greater flexibility of rhyme in French than in English, or what poetry translation scholar Clive Scott terms the 'different degrees of rhyme' that French recognizes (2011: 72). Scott also points out that 'the French alexandrine works with a much greater awareness than the English iambic pentameter of the significance of positions on its own scale, this largely because of the syntactic self-sufficiency of the alexandrine and the fixedness of its caesura' (1986: 84). As a consequence, the position of a particular syllable in a line can in itself automatically create certain expectations and have certain prosodic effects that could not be replicated in another language or another verse form. It's for this reason that Scott dispels the notion that there might be an equivalent for the French alexandrine in other languages, and argues that free verse remains the most appropriate translational medium for poetry (1997: 35).

Bolt, meanwhile, has a more aesthetically driven aversion to the alexandrine, misciting poet Alexander Pope's condemnation of the verse form ('A limping Alexandrine ends the song/Which, like a wounded snake, drags its slow length along' (*sic*)) to make the point that 'the alexandrine, for whatever reason, simply isn't acceptable to an English ear' (1994: 19). Unlike Scott, however, Bolt suggests that the iambic pentameter is a viable English equivalent for Molière's alexandrine. Such a suggestion might have some historical justification in that the iambic pentameter was regularly used in much English drama performed at the time of Molière (most obviously in many of Shakespeare's plays and sonnets). But it overlooks the fact that, for contemporary British audiences at least, the iambic pentameter has arguably since become as associated with satirical rhyme as with works of long-standing literary merit. Examples here include W. S. Gilbert and Arthur Sullivan's parody of Alfred Lord Tennyson's *Princess Ida* in their operetta of the same name, or the comedic delivery of lines in faux-Shakespearian style in episodes of TV shows such as *Star Trek* and *Doctor Who* (TVTropes 2015: n.p.). The effects of using the iambic pentameter in English translations or adaptations of Molière are therefore potentially divisive. On the one hand, such a style could serve to highlight the quirkiness and wittiness of Molière's source text, giving it an added comic dimension that could arguably be said to ennoble the original play. On the other hand, however, it also potentially imparts what Bolt calls a 'patness to the proceedings' (1994: 19), that is, a more noticeable, indeed possibly even obtrusive, cohesiveness that risks excessive predictability and therefore dullness.

No doubt aware of the predictability associated with the iambic pentameter, McGough employs a variety of different verse forms in his adaptation of *Tartuffe*, including a constant switch from verse to prose for the dialogue spoken by Tartuffe himself. The use of this device is perhaps most markedly felt in Tartuffe's first lines in the play, which come in Act III, Scene 2.

> **Source text (Molière [1669] 2003: 104)**
> TARTUFFE: Laurent, serrez ma haire avec ma discipline,
> Et priez que toujours le Ciel vous illumine.
> Si l'on vient pour me voir, je vais aux prisonniers
> Des aumônes que j'ai partager les deniers.
>
> **My literal translation**
> TARTUFFE: Laurent, put my hair shirt away with my scourge,
> And pray that Heaven may always enlighten you.
> If anyone comes to see me, I am going to the prisoners
> Alms that I have to distribute the monies.
>
> **Target text (McGough 2008: 38)**
> TARTUFFE: Laurent! Rub some fresh stinging nettles into my hair shirt, will you? And can you put away the scourge... The one I use for self-flagellation. Should anybody call I have gone to prison to distribute, among those poor unfortunates, my last few coins.

McGough's own rationale for letting Tartuffe speak in prose is that it reinforces the character's distinctive tone and personality.

> I decided at some point to give Tartuffe his own voice and make him speak in prose. It could have been these long chunks of stuff that I had to rhyme, or it could have been that he's a class apart. There's a darker side to him, and in prose he can be more lascivious and less playful than the others.

So, if we now describe this switch from verse to prose as the ad hoc concept SWITCH FROM VERSE TO PROSE*, the encyclopaedic entries that might be triggered by this concept could be summarized in Figure 5.7.

Here, it's useful to remind ourselves that such a switch from verse to prose and back again in dramatic texts is nothing new – indeed, the device was frequently used by Shakespeare in many of his plays to indicate a change of emotion or mood within a scene. At the same time, while literary theorist Roman Jakobson explicitly links verse features to poetic function, he also points out that such features are not unique to literary texts as they can also be found in, say, political speeches, advertising messages or football chants (1960, 1968). This suggests, then, that McGough's switch from verse

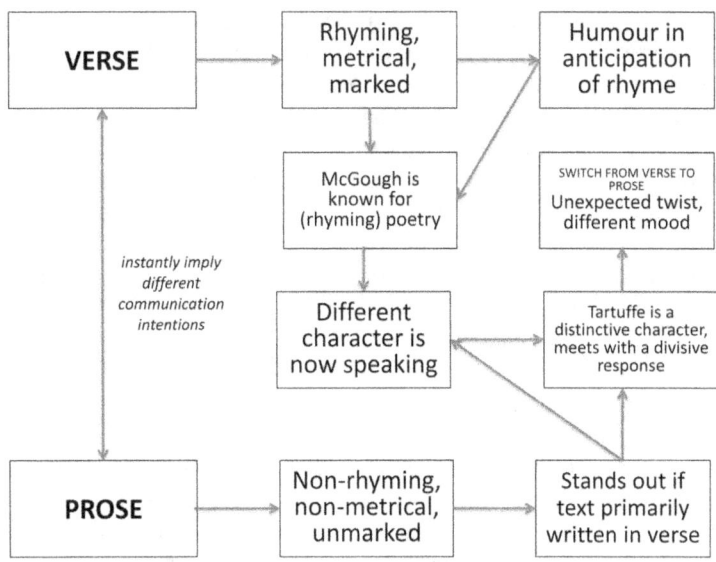

Figure 5.7 Potential encyclopaedic entries attached to concept SWITCH FROM VERSE TO PROSE*.

to prose and vice versa may in many cases trigger associations in the minds of the receivers of *Tartuffe* that extend way beyond any theories or concepts that poetry or literary scholars might have to offer on the subject.

It's also important to note Pilkington's suggestion that 'metrical variation ... allows for the speedier and lengthier activation of the assumptions stored at the encyclopaedic entries of the concepts involved' (2000: 137). This suggestion is based both on the claims made in relevance theory about processing effort and contextual effects, and on ideas about lexical access (i.e. the way in which speakers select the words that correspond to the concept or concepts in the utterance that they wish to express) taken from psycholinguistic theory (see Caramazza 1997, Roelofs, Meyer and Levelt 1998 and Levelt, Roelofs and Meyer 1999). While these latter ideas are beyond the scope of this book, Pilkington's argument that verse and prose potentially activate encyclopaedic entries in different ways would appear to support my claim that McGough's switching from verse to prose and back again will in itself trigger a variety of poetic effects because of the range and richness of the encyclopaedic entries that this device activates in receivers' memories – and will do so even if the specific encyclopaedic entries that are activated in the process are more difficult to determine in terms of how quickly and for how long they are activated.

Now, of course, we should remember that an author such as McGough might be popularly perceived among the general public as a poet who often writes in verse – if nothing else, because of the likely popular perception that *all* poetry is in verse of some kind. But irrespective of how accurate this perception might actually be if one were to analyse his entire body of work, it could also be argued that the prose sections in *Tartuffe* (i.e. when Tartuffe himself speaks) will potentially activate more and richer encyclopaedic entries than the verse sections simply because they are *unexpected* from someone popularly known primarily as a poet. Here again, then, we have an example of how McGough's voice does not have to be predictable or derivative for it to generate cognitive effects.

A second verse device used by McGough is *enjambment* (the continuation or *run-on* of a sentence, or even a word, beyond the end of one line to create a rhyme). This device not only makes his dialogue much more naturally speakable – it is also typically used to great comic effect. According to linguistics scholar Geoffrey Leech, this comic effect is the result of 'a tension between the expected pattern and the pattern actually occurring' (1969: 123), or in other words the abnormal relationship between the syntactic unit and the rhythmic measure. This compares with an end-stopped line, in which the last syllable coincides with a grammatical break in a sentence and always with the end of a word. More specifically, cognitive linguist Frank Kjørup distinguishes four different types of syntactical displacement: *run-on*, where there is no pause between one line and the next; *enjambment*, where the reader temporarily stops before straddling the obstacle posed by the end of the line; *versificational pseudosyntax*, where the syntax has to be broken to continue from one line to the next; and *versificational garden path*, where the reader is tricked into believing that the line has come to an end, only to discover in the next line that the syntax continues to unfold (2008: 87–91).

An example of enjambment (which Kjørup might describe as either run-on or enjambment depending on how the actor chooses to deliver the line in question in performance) can be found in Act III, Scene 3, where Elmire uses her charms in an attempt to persuade Tartuffe not to seek her daughter's hand in marriage.

Source text (Molière [1669] 2003: 114)
ELMIRE: D'autres prendraient cela d'autre façon peut-être;
            Mais ma discrétion se veut faire paraître.
            Je ne redirai point l'affaire à mon époux;
            Mais je veux en revanche une chose de vous:

My literal translation
ELMIRE: Some might perhaps take it another way;
            But I wish to show my discretion.
            I will say nothing about the matter to my husband;
            But in return I wish to have one thing from you:

Target text (McGough 2008: 43)
ELMIRE: Ah me, the pitfalls of being fair of face!
            The curve of the hips, the feminine grace
            can all too often lead to arousal.
            But nevertheless, I know my spouse'll
            be alarmed, and as I don't want you harmed
            I'll be discreet. But in return I want something from you.

As before when looking at specific ad hoc concepts, the encyclopaedic entries attached to the ad hoc concept ENJAMBMENT* could be summarized in Figure 5.8.

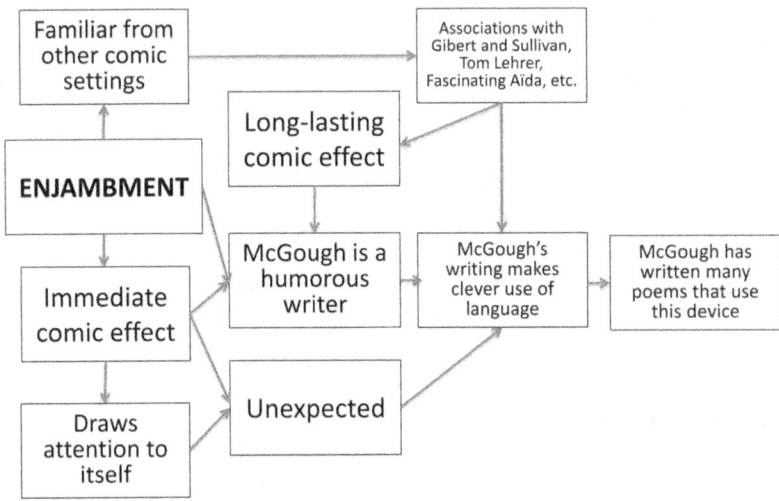

Figure 5.8 Potential encyclopaedic entries attached to concept ENJAMBMENT*.

The key point to notice in this example is the extent to which this concept relies on *surprise* for its comic effect. The surprise derives from the fact that the syntax is at odds with where the line appears to end (in this case, after *spouse*, or possibly also after *alarmed*). Of course, the comic effect of enjambment is highly dependent on how the lines are delivered by the actor, and is likely to be optimized if the actor shares the audience's surprise – that is, if she plays the line in a way that suggests that she herself has only just noticed the rhyme of *arousal* and *spouse'll*.

Here, then, we have a device that perhaps only a small minority of spectators might know by name, but that in terms of its poetic effects and cognitive associations, may still ultimately enhance reception of McGough's distinctive voice, whether directly through associations with other poems by McGough that feature this device (e.g. 'First Day at School', 'The Lesson' or 'Let Me Die A Youngman's Death', to name just a few) or indirectly through recall of other comic writers who use the same device. In either case, the key conclusion that we should draw is that such a specific stylistic device can have a similar effect to the use of particular lexical items in terms of the way in which it can activate specific encyclopaedic entries.

Sociolects and idiolects

Molière gives Dorine, Mariane's servant, a distinctive style of speech (a distinctive *sociolect*) as a way of differentiating her from the other characters in *Tartuffe*, all of whom come from a different social class. As Gaston Hall points out, 'Her words at once place her socially in a popular comic type and, by giving voice to the socially unsayable, suggest the irrepressibility of her temperament which appears also to represent that of human nature itself' (1960: 54). Indeed, the difference between Dorine's speech and that of her masters is such that Molière feels obliged to excuse Dorine's vulgarity in Act

I, Scene 2, by explicitly adding the stage direction *c'est une servante qui parle* ([1669] 2003: 55).

It's also this very instance of vulgarity that offers a particularly good example of McGough's strategy for translating Dorine's sociolect:

Source text (Molière [1669] 2003: 55) f
DORINE: À table, au plus haut bout il veut qu'il soit assis;
          Avec joie il l'y voit manger autant que six;
          Les bons morceaux de tout, il faut qu'on les lui cède;
          Et s'il vient à roter, il lui dit: "Dieu vous aide!"
                                      C'est une servante qui parle.

My literal translation
DORINE: He wishes to seat him at the highest end of the table;
          He will joyfully watch him eat as much as six people would;
          He must be given all the best bits of everything;
          And if ever he belches, he tells him: 'May God help you!'
                                              A servant speaking.

Target text (McGough 2008: 9)
DORINE: And yet there he is, top of the table next to his master,
          Eating more and eating faster.
          Belching and burping like a camel in distress,
          And what does Orgon say? 'God bless.'

Importantly, McGough gives Dorine an even more comic role in his version of *Tartuffe* than Molière does in his. As the down-to-earth, outspoken voice of reason, Dorine is allowed to speak her mind more freely than the more socially constrained aristocratic characters in the play. McGough's Dorine also has much greater licence to use humour (e.g. 'belching and burping like a camel in distress', 2008: 9) and to send up characters such as Orgon and Cléante. For example, in the line that comes immediately after those quoted above, Orgon is described by Dorine as thinking that 'the sun shines out of [Tartuffe's] pantaloons' (McGough 2008: 9). More subtly, the fact that McGough's Dorine speaks in a verse form with a highly irregular metre would appear to imply that she has a lower level of sophistication than that of her masters – and this is something that McGough clearly had in mind from the outset. 'I didn't know when I wrote [*Tartuffe*] who was going to be cast in it, but I almost had an idea early on that Dorine was a sort of a Lancashire girl, with a Polly James type of voice' (Polly James is a British actor born in Blackburn, Lancashire, who is best known for her role as Beryl in the BBC comedy series *The Liver Birds* during the late 1960s and early 1970s).

Dorine is also responsible for the only neologism in Molière's source text, *tartuffié* (Molière [1669] 2003: 87). Most English translators of *Tartuffe* from Baker and Miller in 1739 to Hampton in 1983 chose to anglicize Molière's neologism as *tartuffed*, although Wilbur and Lochhead notably prefer *tartuffified*. But McGough's own neologism,

Tartooth, is an ongoing comedic reference to Dorine's inability to pronounce Tartuffe's name correctly. In fact, the *Tartooth* device features as many as fourteen times throughout McGough's adaptation. On many of these occasions, Dorine is corrected by other characters in a way that is reminiscent of British pantomime-style audience participation. Again, this device serves at first glance to accentuate Dorine's lack of sophistication and status within the household, but at a deeper level also reminds us that Dorine's ultimate role in the play is to highlight the comic egotism of characters such as Orgon.

Figure 5.9 shows how we might envisage the encyclopaedic entries attached to Dorine's sociolect if explored as the ad hoc concept DORINE'S SOCIOLECT* and as demonstrated in the above examples. As with my other textual examples, this is based on my assumptions about what audiences might infer as McGough's intention rather than what I know to have been his intention based on his own comments mentioned earlier.

We can also gain some useful insights by exploring how McGough often gives different characters their own individual *idiolects* (particularly stylized speech habits) to a much greater extent than Molière himself does. For example, at the very end of Act V, Scene 8, when Cléante implores Orgon not to seek revenge on Tartuffe for his behaviour, Orgon replies in a style more akin to modern British farce.

Source text (Molière [1669] 2003: 178) f
ORGON: Oui, c'est bien dit: allons à ses pieds avec joie
             Nous louer des bontés que son cœur nous déploie.

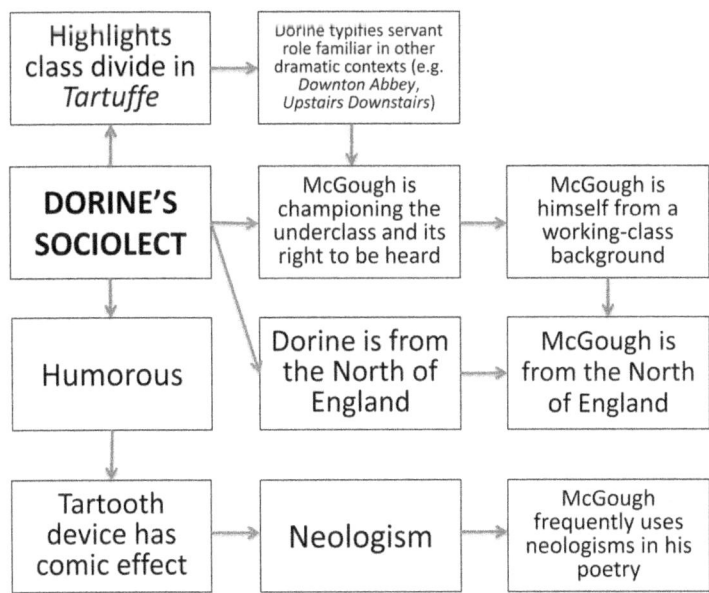

Figure 5.9 Potential encyclopaedic entries attached to concept DORINE'S SOCIOLECT*.

My literal translation
ORGON: Yes, well said: let us throw ourselves at his feet with joy
           And praise the goodness that his heart shows towards us.

Target text (McGough 2008: 81)
ORGON: Well said, Cléante, as ever you make good sense,
           and soon to the palace I shall get me hence
           to prostrate myself before our sovereign
           and thank him most sincerely for his boverin'...

Here, we could envisage, for example, that such a way of speaking might activate encyclopaedic entries associated not only with farce as a dramatic genre but also with contemporary British comic writers whose characters' idiolects are based on an exaggerated version of what is known (pejoratively, for the most part) as a *chav* idiolect. *Chav* is defined in the *Oxford English Dictionary* as 'a young lower-class person typified by brash and loutish behaviour' (Oxford Dictionaries 2015: n.p.). A typical feature of the speech of this social group (and one that is stereotyped by characters featuring in British comedy in the early twenty-first century such as Catherine Tate's Lauren Cooper in *The Catherine Tate Show* and Matt Lucas's Vicky Pollard in *Little Britain*) is the use of 'th-fronting', whereby the 'th' sound in words such as 'three' becomes a 'f' ('free') and in words such as 'bother' becomes a 'v' ('bovver'). Indeed, Lauren's favourite phrase 'am I bovvered?' led to 'bovvered' being named the *Oxford English Dictionary*'s Word of the Year in 2006 (Phillips 2006: n.p.).

Tate's character may well have been one of the very first associations in many audience members' minds when they heard Orgon say 'boverin'' in a performance of McGough's translation only two years later in 2008. And among British audiences, at least, this may then potentially also trigger other cognitive effects that arise as a consequence of McGough's assumed mockery of the upper classes or of *faux sophisticates* – again, dimensions that might serve to enhance associations with McGough's own voice given public perceptions of his own social background and 'the working-class Liverpool of his childhood' (O'Reilly 2008: n.p.).

Repeated exoticization

I would now like to draw attention to two very different comedic devices that appear in McGough's adaptation of *Tartuffe* and explore how these might trigger a variety of encyclopaedic entries in *repeated* usage. I would describe both of these devices as *exoticizing* rather than *foreignizing* devices in that they produce what Venuti terms 'a translation effect that signifies a superficial cultural difference' yet that does not 'question or upset values, beliefs and representations' in the target culture (2008: 160). In each case, McGough appears to be playfully mimicking the humour that is already popularly associated with British TV comedies such as *Allo, Allo* or *Benidorm* and that mocks the way people misuse or mix up words or phrases from other languages.

The first of these repeated devices is McGough's frequent use of French words and phrases, including 'vite, vite' in Act I, Scene 1 (2008: 8), 'zut alors' in Act I, Scene 2 (2008: 9), 'un, deux, trois' in Act II, Scene 4 (2008: 35), 'bâtard' in Act III, Scene 1 (2008: 37), 'pardonnez-moi' in Act III, Scene 3 (2008: 40), or 'mot juste' in Act V, Scene 4 (2008: 74), to name but a few, and of invented phrases such as 'relaxez-vous' in Act I, Scene 2 (2008: 9), 'mélange à trois' in Act IV, Scene 5 (2008: 61), or 'as sure as œufs are œufs' in Act V, Scene 2 (2008: 66). Here, the comic effect of using French, particularly anglicized French, is clearly reminiscent of the writing of journalists such as Miles Kington, who began writing a regular column for *Punch* during the 1970s that used *Franglais*, a fictional language blending English and French in a comical way. The column led to five books that popularized the Franglais genre more widely – *Let's parler Franglais!* (1979), *Let's parler Franglais again!* (1980), *Parlez-vous Franglais?* (1981), *Let's parler Franglais one more temps* (1982) and *The Franglais Lieutenant's Woman* (1986). Another, perhaps less extreme, example of the use of anglicized French can be found in the work of Michael Wright, whose *C'est la folie* column in *The Telegraph* in the early 2000s reflected on British expat life in rural France.

In capitalizing on this device, McGough's text is likely to trigger cognitive effects both among those spectators who understand the ironic misuse of French terms or the malapropisms, and among those who recall their own clumsy attempts at speaking French due to their limited grasp of the language. There's clearly also a sense in which McGough is parodying the way in which non-native speakers of English might interject words or phrases from their own language when speaking English, or the way that English speakers might pepper their speech with foreign words (often used incorrectly) in an attempt to appear more linguistically gifted or sophisticated than they actually are. McGough is thereby gently mocking the foreign while simultaneously allowing British audiences to laugh at themselves – a type of humour that is arguably strongly akin to Molière's own sense of irreverence in the way that he mocks the aristocracy and the clergy (see Gaston Hall 1960: 19).

The second device used repeatedly (four times) by McGough that has no equivalent in the source text is his 'old English saying' interjection, which playfully deconstructs certain idiomatic expressions in English. This occurs as follows:

1. in Act I Scene 1 (McGough 2008: 8), when Madame Pernelle is reacting to Cléante's and Dorine's suspicions about Tartuffe;

    MME PERNELLE: There is an old English saying that goes, 'The one who laughs at the beginning, does not laugh for as long as the one who laughs at the end,' which roughly translated means...

2. in Act IV, Scene 3 (McGough 2008: 54), when Elmire is trying to persuade Orgon to trick Tartuffe by hiding under the table;

    ORGON: They have a saying in English: 'There can be no smoke without something burning,' which, roughly translated, means...

114 *Celebrity Translation in British Theatre*

3. in Act IV, Scene 5 (McGough 2008: 59), when Tartuffe is attempting to seduce Elmire;

TARTUFFE: They have a saying in English: 'Behaviour shouts louder than language,' which roughly translated means…

4. in Act V, Scene 1 (McGough 2008: 65), when Cléante is consoling Orgon about his predicament.

ORGON: Huh! There's an old English saying…
CLÉANTE: 'And hogs might take to the air'?
ORGON: That's the one.

Here, there are clearly different levels of irony at work:

1. the irony of supposedly French characters misquoting English idioms to a British audience (i.e. reminding audiences of the foreign),
2. the irony of using British pantomime-like humour in a play set in France (i.e. domesticating the text to appeal to British audiences), and
3. not least, the irony of repeating 'roughly translated' in a loose translation of a canonical work of drama – at least among those spectators who are more familiar with Molière's source text, or who have a greater appreciation of the role of the translator, or who are more likely to recognize self-referentiality as a feature of postmodern literature (see Aylesworth 2015).

In the case of each of these devices, the encyclopaedic entries potentially triggered by the concept REPEATED EXOTICIZATION* could be summarized in Figure 5.10.

The irony that emerges from both devices in repeated usage helps to enhance audiences' inferences of McGough's voice at different levels:

1. first, because of the way in which it reminds spectators familiar with McGough's poetry that much of his existing work is designed to be interpreted ironically;
2. second, because of the way in which these devices call attention to the fact that McGough's role here is one of *translator* rather than creator of his own original source text (irrespective of how familiar spectators might be with any of his original texts); and
3. third, because of the way in which McGough's work and persona have been largely shaped over the course of several decades by his very *Britishness* and his wry observations of peculiarly British ways of behaving and making conversation (perceptions of which might be the result of having heard McGough being interviewed or presenting *Poetry Please* in the past as much as being familiar with his work to any great extent).

Sperber and Wilson describe ironic utterances as examples of *echoic interpretation*, that is, when interpretation achieves relevance by informing the receiver that the author has something in mind when uttering a particular thought (e.g. an opinion on what

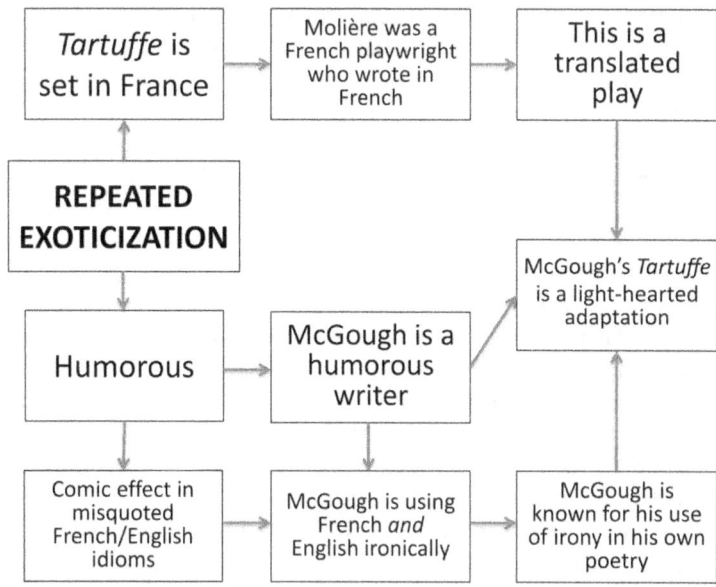

Figure 5.10 Potential encyclopaedic entries attached to concept REPEATED EXOTICIZATION*.

someone else thinks) (1995: 238) In this sense, then, we could also conclude that the irony ultimately results from the way in which McGough humorously represents his attitude to the task of translation and playfully switches between bringing his text to the spectator and bringing the spectator to his text (see Schleiermacher 2004). I'll return to the concept of echoic interpretation in Chapter 7, where I explore the way in which reviews and blogs might influence the way in which spectators receive a performance of a play translated by a celebrity translator.

Celebrity translation and linguistic peculiarities

The study of an *extreme* example of celebrity translation such as McGough's version of *Tartuffe* (i.e. a translation that is markedly different from the source text and that contains a myriad of examples of the celebrity translator's own particular style) demonstrates the extent both to which translation can refresh a classic source text for a contemporary audience and to which celebrity translation can place a new slant on a frequently translated canonical work. Indeed, this study reveals the potential, in both dramatic and commercial terms, for celebrity translation to be considered as a genre in its own right – as a subset of the genre of canonical drama that pushes the boundaries of translation to create what are essentially wholly new works.

As with my previous case study, the notion of the *complementarity* between the source-text playwright and the celebrity translator again appears to be key in determining the success of the collaboration, with Molière's and McGough's respective texts clearly proving to be much more similar in terms of the emotional response that they generate among spectators than any textual comparison might suggest. The notion of encyclopaedic entries allows us to delve more deeply into the likely explicatures and implicatures derived from the celebrity translator's text and to indicate the extent to which audiences may hear the celebrity translator's voice in his or her text by pointing out from where these implicatures might be derived – whether from previous work by that celebrity, or from more general cultural associations. In this sense, then, this case study also helps to confirm the usefulness of relevance theory as a framework for evaluating celebrity translation.

The use of encyclopaedic entries to help describe the effect of textual devices as well as specific lexical items also appears to be an enlightening exercise – and one that could be more widely applied by scholars. While such analysis remains largely theoretical in its scope and application, it nevertheless provides us with useful insights about how audiences relate to devices such as verse form, puns, sociolects and so on, and most importantly how each of these manifests itself in the minds of spectators as an integral dimension of a celebrity translator's style and voice.

Of course, the great advantage that McGough had when producing his celebrity translation was that his ultimate source material (Molière's original play) is no longer protected under copyright law, which under British law currently expires seventy years after the end of the calendar year of the author's death. This meant that McGough had greater artistic freedom to *play* with the source text than Mark Ravenhill did when translating *Leben des Galilei*, the rights to which, as seen in Chapter 4, are still owned and protected by the Brecht estate. My analysis does, however, demonstrate that there are other factors at play here that possibly gave McGough greater licence to *stretch* the source text in his translation. In no particular order, such factors might include:

1. McGough's perception of his own critical standing (among directors, critics, audiences and so on) and the consequent freedom that he felt this gave him to inject much of his own voice (as defined in Chapter 1) into his work;
2. the remit that McGough was given to refresh Molière's text, which itself is a function both of McGough's own status in artistic circles (i.e. as one of the UK's best-known poets) and of the vast number of existing translations of that text (which almost by definition implies that any new version is expected to be significantly different from those versions that have gone before if it is to stand out), and
3. perhaps not least, the commercial expectations placed upon McGough's work compared with Ravenhill's (i.e. the fact that it was commissioned by a theatre with fewer resources than the RSC and therefore more urgently required to deliver a guaranteed return on investment).

In the following chapter, I will explore a different type of celebrity translation again – one that relies more on cumulative associations with a celebrity translator's personal, dramatic and stylistic concerns, and one that progressively builds spectators' individual constructs of voice via increasingly weak implicatures.

6

Simon Stephens's version of Henrik Ibsen's *Et dukkehjem*

Introduction

Henrik Ibsen's *Et dukkehjem* (*A Doll's House* or, in its translations for the US market, *A Doll House*) was first performed in Copenhagen in December 1879. The play quickly became a cause célèbre across much of Europe, triggering fierce debate about women's rights and emancipation – and often well before such issues reached the top of political agendas. *A Doll's House* is also Ibsen's most frequently translated play. By 2013, one year after the first production of Simon Stephens's adaptation, *A Doll's House* had already been translated into fifty-six languages, with 1,538 productions recorded in seventy-six countries (Fauskanger 2013: n.p.).

The plot of *A Doll's House* is a straightforward but (at the time of its publication, at least) socially explosive one. Nora and Torvald Helmer appear to live a life of perfect social respectability in Norway in the 1870s, but beneath this veneer of respectability lies a terrible secret that Nora has been keeping from her bank manager husband. Torvald is unaware that Nora borrowed a substantial amount of money from his employee Nils Krogstad to finance an extended stay in Italy designed to help Torvald to recuperate after a serious illness. At a time when women were unable to borrow money in their own right, Nora forged the signature of her dying father, but made the mistake of dating the signature after her father's death.

Krogstad then tries to blackmail Nora by threatening to tell Torvald about the debt unless she is able to persuade her husband not to dismiss Krogstad from his job at the bank. He writes a letter to Torvald and deposits it in the Helmers' letterbox. Nora manages to distract Torvald for one night by persuading him to help her rehearse the tarantella, a dance she is due to perform at a party the following evening. In spite of an intervention by Nora's friend Kristine, who manages to persuade Krogstad to stop the blackmail, Nora allows Torvald to read the letter after they return home from the party. Initially furious with his wife for potentially damaging his reputation, Torvald then forgives Nora. But Nora tells Torvald that their marriage is over and that she no longer wishes to live with him in what she feels is an oppressive doll's house. Torvald appears to have a last-minute revelation about what love really means, but it's already too late, and the play ends as Nora slams their front door shut, ready to start a new life on her own without her husband and children.

Literary and theatre critics might now typically agree that *A Doll's House* is one of the landmarks of nineteenth-century drama. Indeed in 2001, the contribution that *A Doll's House* has made to theatrical history was acknowledged by UNESCO when it added the play to its Memory of the World register and described Nora as 'a symbol throughout the world, for women fighting for liberation and equality' (UNESCO 2001: n.p.). But the play's reception at the time it was first performed was much less favourable. Perhaps not surprisingly, critical reaction appears to have focused on the dramatic motivation for Nora's actions in leaving her husband and children. While the controversy surrounding the plot of *A Doll's House* might have abated during the twentieth century and beyond, the debates as to what Ibsen was actually trying to communicate in the play remain fierce to this day. Was he aiming to spur the embryonic feminist movement into action? Or was his message a more general one about the emancipation of all human beings, male or female? These questions and more have occupied Ibsen scholars ever since *A Doll's House* was first published, as they pore over the playwright's plays, letters and speeches in an attempt to unearth his true intentions. Scholars best known in English-speaking countries in this respect include, to name but a few, British Ibsen translator and biographer Michael Meyer (1967 and 1985), British academics and authors James McFarlane (1961, 1989 and 1994) and Janet Garton (1994, 2004 and 2014), American scholars Gail Finney (1989 and 1994) and Joan Templeton (1989 and 1997), Swedish academic and literary critic Egil Törnqvist (1995), Norwegian literary historian Kristian Smidt (2000) and Norwegian academic and author Toril Moi (2006).

British playwright Simon Stephens's version of *A Doll's House* was first performed at the Young Vic theatre in London in 2012 and immediately met with widespread critical acclaim. But over and above its qualities as a piece of theatre, Stephens's version of the play is particularly intriguing as an example of celebrity translation. That's because his voice appears to be quite understated at the level of specific textual elements, but much more obvious at a more holistic level, that is, when assessing the text in terms of its cumulative effects – or, in relevance theory terms, the chains of weak implicatures that it triggers. Fortunately, there is a wealth of interview material available online with the actors, director and Stephens himself. This material provides useful insights into the translation process from literal to performable text, and from written performable text to text in performance.

As with my other case studies that feature in this book, I will begin by investigating Ibsen's likely motivations for writing *A Doll's House*, taking into consideration the lack of consensus and the caveats with regard to authorial intention mentioned above. I will then explore the literal translator's and celebrity translator's potential motivations for producing their own texts. Following this, I will propose an analytical framework based around the concept of weak implicatures as a way of assessing the likely cognitive effects of Stephens's style on spectators in the theatre, and subsequently illustrate these effects by means of examples from Stephens's text. My overall aim will be to show how relevance theory can help us to account for the way in which stylistic devices and recurrent motifs can *cumulatively* create a sense of authorial voice.

Henrik Ibsen's *Et dukkehjem*

Henrik Ibsen (1828-1906) might be one of the most widely performed and translated European playwrights, but he has not always enjoyed unequivocal acclaim among critics. Ibsen's status in the European canon has been particularly called into question in English-speaking countries, where there has been frequent disparagement of his plays' dialogue, storylines and lack of theatricality in performance. This in turn has affected how, when and by whom Ibsen has been translated into English for the British stage since the late nineteenth century up to the present day.

A Doll's House (1879) is one of several Ibsen plays categorized as his *problem* or *critical realism* plays – other plays in this category would be *Samfundets støtter* (*Pillars of Society*, 1877) and *Gengangere* (*Ghosts*, 1881). Literary scholar Bjørn Hemmer suggests that each of these works 'concentrates on some phase in the contemporary situation where a latent crisis suddenly becomes visible', thereby enabling Ibsen to 'embody contemporary social problems through the medium of an individual's destiny' (1994: 71). Ibsen's characters are thus designed to be representative of specific social types, and their situations are used to exemplify a wider social malaise. This then enables the playwright to convey a message that has general social validity. According to comparative literary critic René Wellek, this not only breaks with the pervading form of characterization in romanticism but also implies that there is a 'didactic, moralistic and reformist' purpose to theatre (1963: 253).

Through the prism of realism, then, Ibsen is presumably imparting a moral message in *A Doll's House* about the importance of truthfulness, reminding us that we can only be free if we are true to ourselves. Nora's truthfulness according to the realists is in wanting to find out who she really is so that she can be true to herself – 'å komme efter hvem der har rett, samfunnet eller jeg' (Ibsen [1879] 2013: 142), translated by Meyer as 'to satisfy myself which is right, society or I' (1985: 101), but rather tellingly omitted from Stephens's version of *A Doll's House* (see later in this chapter for more discussion of Stephens's take on Nora's dismissal of society). At the same time, Ibsen also clearly encourages audiences to consider the motives that lie beneath the behaviour of the play's characters and to relate those dynamics to what was happening in Norwegian society at the time. In this sense, then, *A Doll's House* adheres to the naturalist tenet of portraying the struggle between competing hereditary and environmental forces – such as the biological distinction between male and female versus the roles that society forces men and women to play.

Over and above these differing post hoc scholarly perspectives on Ibsen's motivations, other views have been proffered over the years from Marxist, Freudian, modernist and post-structuralist perspectives. Eleanor Marx (daughter of Karl and herself an Ibsen translator) considered Nora's miracle as Marxist change and Nora's domestic situation as a metaphor for the exploitation and oppression of workers (cited in Durbach 1994: 234). Meanwhile, theatre scholar Freddie Rokem interprets the eroticism between Nora and Dr Rank from the perspective of Freud's views on female sexuality (1997: 225). Literary scholar Toril Moi offers a modernist take on Ibsen's work between *A Doll's House* and *Fruen fra havet* (*The Lady from the Sea*, 1888). She believes that this body of work conveys the characteristic themes of Ibsen's modernism, namely, 'the situation of women; the relationship between idealism and scepticism; and the use of marriage as figure for the ordinary and the everyday' (2006: 10). In Elfriede Jelinek's 1979 play *Was geschah, nachdem Nora ihren Mann verlassen hat oder Stützen der Gesellschaft* (*What Happened After Nora Left Her Husband, or Pillars of Society*), Nora wanders into the text of Ibsen's 1877 play *The Pillars of Society*, only to discover that 'any attempt on [her] part to change her life by slamming shut the door to the "doll's house" is sabotaged from the outset because it is conceptualized from within the power framework Nora tries to escape' (Kiebuzinska 2001: 93). And finally, Lucas Heath's 'sequel' to A Doll's House, *A Doll's House Part 2, or Whatever Happened to Nora?*, which premiered at the Golden Theater in New York City in 2017, adds a different perspective again. In Heath's play, Nora has become a successful feminist author championing causes such as the elimination of marriage. She returns to her former marital home for the first time in fifteen years to seek a divorce from Torvald, without which she remains a criminal under Norwegian law. But Torvald refuses to sign the necessary papers, thereby highlighting Nora's ultimate inability to escape the strictures imposed by patriarchal society in spite of her revolutionary views.

Ibsen's own communicative intentions in *A Doll's House* have also frequently been called into question by scholars over the years because of some of the statements that he himself made on the controversy unleashed by the play in the years following its publication. Most importantly, many scholars point to a speech that Ibsen gave to the Norwegian Association of Women's Rights in 1889. During this speech, he insisted that he was 'more of a poet and less of a social philosopher' and that he was not 'even very sure what women's rights really are' (Worrall 1994: xli). These (and other) remarks have been variously interpreted over the subsequent decades as, at one extreme, an admission on Ibsen's part that *A Doll's House* is in no way a feminist tract, and, at the other extreme, a mere triviality in a career that demonstrated a passionate interest in the issues of the day (including what became known as *the woman question*) and a body of work that showed a huge empathy for women's struggle for freedom and equality.

Supporters of the anti-feminist argument include Ibsen biographer and translator Michael Meyer, who famously came to the conclusion that '*A Doll's House* is no more about women's rights than Shakespeare's *Richard II* is about the divine right of kings or *Ghosts* about syphilis' (1967: 329). James McFarlane, another highly respected Ibsen scholar, included the remarks that Ibsen made in the speech cited above in his commentary on *A Doll's House* that appears in the *Oxford Ibsen* series. The remarks were cited under the heading 'Some Pronouncements by the Author' (1961: 456), as if Ibsen were referring directly to this work rather than making some general comments about his lack of interest in nailing his colours to the feminist mast. Theatrical critic, producer and playwright Robert Brustein, meanwhile, believed that Ibsen was 'completely indifferent [to the woman question] except as a metaphor for individual freedom' (1962: 105).

Ibsen scholar Joan Templeton, on the other hand, is one of the best-known feminist critics to argue that Ibsen was actually *pro*-feminism. Following earlier work by academics such as Inga-Stina Ewbank (1979), Gail Finney (1989) and Janet Garton (1994) that started to explore Ibsen's relationship to feminism, Templeton's 1997 book *Ibsen's Women* systematically traces gender patterns and the portrayal of women from

Ibsen's earliest plays to the end of his career, and explores how the women in Ibsen's life influenced the portrayal of women in his work. Her argument is that Ibsen's empathy with the feminist cause is easily demonstrated both by the influence that feminist women had on his life (such as his independently minded wife Suzannah and his friend Camilla Collett, regarded as Norway's first feminist writer) and by the way in which this influence is seen in his female characters – most notably Lona Hessel in *Pillars of Society*, Hilde Wangel in *Bygmester Solness* (*The Master Builder*, 1892), Helene Alving in *Ghosts* and, not least, Hedda in *Hedda Gabler*.

It's also surely rather telling that all the participants in the first performance of *A Doll's House* in London either were already associated with the British feminist cause or had achieved or would achieve prominence in the country's socialist movement. The role of Nora, for example, was played by Eleanor Marx (Finney 1994: 89), who went on to become a translator of Ibsen herself after learning Norwegian specifically for that purpose (Anderman 2005: 83). Here, it must be remembered that socialism and feminism were familiar bedfellows at the end of the nineteenth century. Consider, for example, Ibsen's remark in an 1885 speech to the working men of Trondheim: 'the transformation of social conditions which is now being undertaken in the rest of Europe is very largely concerned with the future status of the workers and of women. That is what I am hoping and waiting for, that is what I shall work for, all I can' (cited in Finney 1994: 89).

I would certainly tend to agree more with the view of scholars such as Templeton, Finney and Garton that Ibsen's life and work were strongly influenced by the mounting pressure for change in women's rights that he observed throughout his career, and not least in the public response to *A Doll's House*. To suggest as Meyer did that the theme of *A Doll's House* is nothing more than self-discovery seems at best naïve and at worst rather offensive to those who seek to champion Nora as a role model for emancipation – and indeed to those who rightfully point out that the pressures faced by Nora are still real for many women even in twenty-first-century European society (see Cracknell 2012). But of course, whether Ibsen would actually identify himself as pro-feminist, pro-women or simply pro-equality for all is difficult to judge given both the level of development of the feminist movement at the time of his writing, and the prism of feminism and post-feminism through which we now assess his work. So, however interesting it might be, this is a debate that lies outside the scope of this book. But what *is* of particular interest here, though, is the way in which issues associated with women and feminism are addressed by Stephens in his version of *A Doll's House*. These will be explored later in this chapter.

As a final point, it's worth considering how Ibsen's unique literary qualities influence perceptions of his communicative intentions. Directors, actors and audiences appear to have traditionally expected Ibsen in translation to sound as if he had written in a standard idiomatic form of spoken language, presumably because of the realist label he was saddled with in English-speaking markets. But in fact Ibsen's Dano-Norwegian is more of an inventive form of language that's not meant to appear as a standard way of speaking. Technically, Ibsen's language is very close to modern-day *Bokmål*, or *book language*, the written form of Norwegian used by the majority of the population, as opposed to *Nynorsk*, or *New Norwegian*, which is the other official form of written

Norwegian. *Nynorsk* was developed in the mid-nineteenth century to be an alternative to Danish, which was widely used in writing in Norway at the time. Paradoxically, *Nynorsk* preserves more of the forms of Old Norwegian, which was spoken in Norway until the union with Denmark in the sixteenth century (see Törnqvist 1995: 50).

McFarlane suggests that 'an absence of humour, an absence of free imagination, an absence of glamour, an absence of what is loosely called "style" even, add up to nothing; but in the case of Ibsen they seem to multiply up to what has very suitably been called his "spell"' (1989: 56). Ibsen translator William Archer, meanwhile, concurs that '[Ibsen's] meaning is almost always as clear as daylight; the difficulty lies in reproducing the nervous conciseness, the vernacular simplicity, and, at the same time, something of the subtle rhythm of his phrases' (1904: x). Dramatist and essayist Arthur Miller appears to be one of few critics who appreciated that, far from being a writer of prosaic and joyless language, Ibsen actually creates his own *sprogtone* (*language tone*) in his texts, which '[packs] with suggestion an apparently flat and colourless style' (Ewbank 1998: 59), yet which when translated into English may result in 'a somewhat banal and melodramatic' style (Anderman 2005: 99). Examples of this *sprogtone* include the following.

1. Ibsen makes frequent use of modal adverbs such as *jo* (which corresponds loosely to the English *after all*), *nog* (*still* or *yet*) and *vel* (usually used to suggest *presumably*). In combination, these adverbs serve to imply a strong sense of doubt, caution and uncertainty that would normally be conveyed in English more by intonation.
2. His choice of second-person pronoun (the informal *Du* or the formal *De*, which correspond more or less to the German use of *Du* and *Sie*, at least at the time of Ibsen's writing) is designed to denote a level of intimacy or distance between characters and the relative status that one might attach to the other. This choice is used to dramatic effect in *A Doll's House* to highlight Torvald's discomfort at hearing his subordinate Krogstad calling him *Du* in front of others, even though they have known each other since their studies at law school.
3. Ibsen makes constant use of adjectives with a definite article but unaccompanied by nouns. The most obvious example of this in *A Doll's House* is the repetition (no less than nineteen times) of *vidunderlig* (*miraculous*), *det vidunderlige* (*the miraculous*) and *det vidunderligste* (*the most miraculous*). In English, however, these variations on *vidunderlig* are often rendered as *the miraculous thing*. According to Anderman, this tends to make the concept 'more specific and less open to audience interpretation and imagination' (2005: 101).
4. Similarly, Ibsen reveals a fondness for compound words. In particular, he has a tendency to use compound words to build an intricate pattern of symbolism that is then woven throughout the text. Examples of this include *livsløgn* (*life lie*, as in the German *Lebenslüge*), *gengangere* (*something or someone that walks again*, the Norwegian title of the play *Ghosts*), *hjertekulde* (*heart-coldness*) and, in *A Doll's House*, *lykkebarn* (*fortune's child*, or *child of happiness*).
5. He also enjoys using double entendre to imply sexual tension between his characters. An example of this in *A Doll's House* is the dialogue between Nora and Dr Rank in Act III, when Nora offers to light Dr Rank's cigar for him. Nora's 'La

meg gi Dem ild' (Ibsen [1879] 2013: 124) (literally *Let me give you fire*) and Rank's subsequent 'Sov godt. Og takk for ilden' (Ibsen [1879] 2013: 124) (*Sleep well. And thank you for the fire*) inevitably lose their sexual connotations when *fire* is translated into English as *light*.

With such issues in mind, I am keen in the following sections of this chapter to avoid too many direct comparisons between the source text and Stephens's adaptation (or indeed between Charlotte Barslund's literal translation of the source text and Stephens's text) at the level of individual textual examples. Interesting though such comparisons might be in terms of showing how dialogue in the theatre has changed between the late nineteenth century and early twenty-first century (and thereby highlighting a shift in norms of behaviour), they do not necessarily help to further my search for a distinctive celebrity voice beyond being able to demonstrate, say, that Stephens's version sounds particularly English or particularly modern. As Gideon Toury reminds us in his discussion of translation norms, comparison of source and target texts (and indeed of various target texts) is not about evaluating the relative merits of those texts but rather about identifying trends of translation behaviour within the sociocultural constraints specific to the translator's culture, society and time (1995: 54).

In contrast to my two other case studies in this book, then, I will seek in the following sections of this chapter to examine both Ibsen's source text and Stephens's target text at a more holistic level, investigating the *cumulative* effect of specific stylistic devices or tropes used by the celebrity translator to build an impression of a distinctive authorial voice. But before then, it's useful to consider the motivations of the other two agents in this translation process – literal translator Barslund and Stephens himself.

Charlotte Barslund's literal translation of *Et dukkehjem*

Charlotte Barslund is a professional translator from Danish, Swedish and Norwegian into English. Her published work includes translations of novelists such as Vigdis Hjorth, Ane Riel, Jonas T. Bengtsson, Samuel Bjork, Peter Adolphsen, Karin Fossum, Per Petterson, Carsten Jensen, Sissel-Jo Gazan and Thomas Enger. She has also translated plays for the stage (such as Ingmar Bergman's version of Ibsen's *Ghosts*, which was performed at the Barbican Theatre in London) and for radio (such as August Strindberg's *The Pelican* which was broadcast on BBC Radio 3 in 2005). On top of this, Barslund has also completed literal translations of the majority of Ibsen's plays, which she sells to British theatre companies on an ad hoc basis.

Unlike Deborah Gearing, literal translator of *Leben des Galilei*, Barslund's career has always been in translation rather than playwriting or acting. Following a degree in English and Drama, Barslund completed a master's in Scandinavian Translation and wrote her dissertation on Ibsen. So it was on this basis that she established her credentials as a theatre translator, and in particular as a translator of Ibsen's work. She justifies her preference for being 'behind the scenes' thus: 'for me, to be just one character was too limiting, I wanted to be in control of all of them. So being a translator is perfect. I love translating dialogue and creating characters through dialogue. That's where my heart lies.'[1] This background in both literary and theatre studies gives her not only a particularly nuanced perspective on the role of the literal translator in the process of drama production but also a high degree of sensitivity towards Ibsen's language and stagecraft. This sensitivity is evident in her enthusiastic championing of Ibsen in translation, both for the stage and for academic study. 'I've always loved the Ibsen literals, I think they're fantastic things to do. When you look at the structure of an Ibsen play you can really see how it works and why it's so good, it teaches you so much about drama.'

Barslund's primary role as a literary translator in her own right appears to have a marked influence on her approach to literal translations for the theatre. First, it's clear that she sees literal translations as more than merely functional texts but also as literary texts in their own right.

> When a theatre asks for a literal, although that's what they say they want it's not what they need. Because there are so many adaptations, they want to go back to the urtext, but the urtext doesn't make as much sense as they think it does. You try not to take too many decisions, but you have to because it wouldn't make semantic sense if you translated metaphors or similes literally.

Second, as well as adding notes to explain specific references or the dual meaning of certain words, Barslund also seeks to add value at a broader cultural level. For example, she relishes the opportunity to demonstrate her in-depth knowledge of Ibsen's theatrical devices and cultural context by, say, offering her thoughts on props or providing insights into Scandinavian history and heritage if requested. 'I make sure I always translate all the stage directions and give explanations if it's a specific cultural habit. Like bringing the Christmas tree in on the eve of the 24th and then the children come in and strip it. So you need to explain why that happens, because it's enormously symbolic.'

At the same time, however, it's also evident that Barslund is under no illusions about the status of literal translators in the British theatrical system. The fact that she has established a successful business selling off-the-peg literal translations of Ibsen's plays perhaps enables her to distance herself from the end products created by each successive celebrity translator on the basis of her work – and indeed to avoid any sense of being ignored, irrelevant or undervalued in the translation process. For her, the merit of her work is a different one from that of the finished play text. As she rightly reminds us, 'People have their own ambition. And they've usually read several versions of the play and have their idea of how they want to do it. They're looking to you to provide them with an ingredient, that's all.' Similarly, Barslund appears to bear little grudge towards the celebrity translators themselves, who may sometimes claim glory for work into which they themselves have had less input than might be publicly acknowledged. Her outlook in this respect is a remarkably pragmatic one.

> I do often hear my own translation word for word. And it's very flattering of course. Because you can sometimes end up doing an adaptation for the sake of it. And not all writers have a strong enough vision to go off-script. Or they just want

to do a better version of the original without intoning something that isn't there. So those versions tend to look more like the literal because they're meant to, they trust the text as it is.

In this respect, for example, Stephens himself has admitted that he relied heavily on Barslund's literal translation for his own version of *A Doll's House*, admitting that 'the Ibsen literal was to an extent actable so it was just about refining and refocusing' (2014c: n.p.).

Indeed, while Barslund is adamant that her paymaster in her role as literal translator is Ibsen rather than the celebrity translator, and that as far as she is concerned the source text is already the perfect version of the text, she is also realistic enough to accept that there is little artistic or commercial need for new adaptations of Ibsen's work if these are not to offer a new interpretation of Ibsen's text. As she points out, 'When you do a celebrity Ibsen, you have to change it, otherwise there's no point, it's got to be your version and Ibsen is a springboard for you.' In this sense, then, Barslund's professional and commercial motivations (to have as many British theatres as possible pay for one of her literal translations) most likely outweigh any more idealistic intentions of preserving the sanctity of the source text, no matter how in awe she might be of Ibsen's talents as a dramatist. 'I just provide the raw material, so I don't get upset if they change it. The end-result is this creative team's take on it, and maybe you've seen other people do it better, but there's always something about each new version that's enjoyable.'

Ultimately, it would be difficult to disagree with Barslund's conclusion that literal translations are 'both very rewarding and very frustrating' – rewarding in the sense that she clearly relishes her role in keeping Ibsen very much alive on the British stage, but frustrating in sense that such a role is not accorded greater recognition in either artistic or financial terms. On the other hand, it's also gratifying as a translation scholar and practitioner to note both that Barslund's work will continue to be in demand as long as the culture of commissioning a new adaptation for each new production persists, and that her off-the-peg business model will no doubt reap much greater financial rewards for her in the long term than the typical piecework approach to paying for translation might ever be likely to do. Perhaps this is something to which the frequent critics of the practice of celebrity translation should pay greater attention.

Simon Stephens's *A Doll's House*

Simon Stephens (1971–) is the most prolific British playwright of his generation. Born and brought up in Stockport, he made his first attempts at writing drama while studying history at the University of York in the late 1980s and achieved his first professional production in 1998 when *Bluebird* was staged at the Royal Court in London. He became Playwright in Residence at that theatre in 2000–01, and went on to forge an extremely productive career that saw him write thirty-six plays in the space of little more than twenty years. As a result, Stephens's celebrity credentials within theatre circles are unquestionable. He has won two Olivier awards (for Best New Play for both *On the Shore of the Wide World* in 2006 and *The Curious Incident of the Dog in the Night-Time* in 2013) and a Tony Award for Best Play (for the Broadway production of *The Curious Incident of the Dog in the Night-Time* in 2015). Moreover, he has been widely written about by British theatre scholars, including Jacqueline Bolton (2008, 2013 and 2014, to mention just a few), David Lane (2010), Dan Rebellato (2005 and 2010) and John Bull (2018).

Stephens is also no stranger to translation and adaptation. His own plays have been translated into over a dozen languages (Bolton 2013: 102). And while professing no foreign-language skills himself, he has also written English adaptations of Norwegian playwright Jon Fosse's *I Am the Wind* (2011), Chekhov's *The Cherry Orchard* (2014) and *The Seagull* (2017), Brecht's *The Threepenny Opera* (2016), as well as Ibsen's *A Doll's House* (2012). On top of this, *The Curious Incident of the Dog in the Night-Time* was an adaptation of the novel of the same name by Mark Haddon, *Blindsided*, *Birdland* and *Carmen Disruption* (all 2014) were each inspired by classic works (*Medea* by Euripedes, *Baal* by Brecht and *Carmen* by Georges Bizet, respectively). Meanwhile, *Obsession*, his 2017 play co-adapted with Dutch writer Jan Peter Gerrits, was based on Lucino Visconti's 1943 film *Ossessione*, which was itself an adaptation of James M. Cain's novel *The Postman Always Rings Twice*. As Stephens points out, adapting other people's work is 'a rich source of material and actually a classical way for playwrights to work. … Rather than imagining source material afresh, we assimilate from others and reimagine it and always have done. The vanity of thinking we can think of our own stories is modern' (2016: 32).

Although similar in terms of age to the in-yer-face generation of British playwrights (see Chapter 4), Stephens prefers to categorize himself more as a post-millennial, post-in-yer-face playwright. While his work ostensibly shares some of the features of in-yer-face drama in terms of some of its themes, imagery and language, the 'gritty realism' (Bolton 2013: 104) of Stephens's plays belies a more compassionate and optimistic view of his characters and the society in which they operate than could often be said for in-yer-face playwrights such as Sarah Kane, Anthony Neilson and Mark Ravenhill (see Sierz 2001a). Lane, for example, describes Stephens's *Bluebird* as portraying 'a pre-millennial metropolitan landscape, populated by individuals determined to live through broken and damaged lives with a mixture of humour, pathos and blind hope' (2010: 32). Years later, *Motortown* (2006), *Pornography* (2007) and *Punk Rock* (2009) offered an angrier view of society, but still one in which characters are often allowed to glimpse and aspire to a kinder and more compassionate future.

Perhaps most importantly for the purposes of this case study, it's clear that Stephens sees characters in his plays as more than a metaphor for a particular message. They are actually the very lifeblood of the dramatic situation that he is portraying. He himself suggests that his background in history might inform the way in which he develops his characters. 'The characters in my plays carry the burden of the past around with them. … The historian, like the dramatist, fixates on behaviour and its causes and its consequences' (cited in Innes 2011: 446). Moreover, Stephens's concept of the audience needing to understand and recognize something of themselves in the behaviour and actions of his characters echoes Ibsen's motivations for writing work such as *A Doll's House*. It also distances Stephens from his in-yer-face predecessors' overt desires to disquiet and outrage their audiences. Bolton explains Stephens's approach to characterization and the type of narrative in which these characters typically operate as follows.

> Stephens's construction of character and narrative invites audiences into a process of observation, selection and comparison in order to interpret a story from the individuals, events, dialogue and images presented to them. The invitation to engage empathetically with the drama … might better be read as a provocation, an entreaty or a dare to the audience to recognize themselves and/or their loved ones. (2013: 105)

This implies a role for the audience that goes beyond being mere receivers of Stephens's text and the meaning that *he* intends spectators to infer via his own brand of naturalism. Rather, he actively invites spectators to construct their own version of his dramatic fiction – one that resonates with their own experiences, aspirations and concerns. Such an unconscious acknowledgement of the relevance theory account of how humans infer communicative intentions (albeit phrased in different terms) provides an illuminating backdrop to my discussion in the subsequent sections of this chapter. Stephens's invitation to empathize also contrasts sharply with the views of some other playwrights about the role of the audience – the views of Brecht, for example, who felt that spectators should question rather than empathize. It also tells us a lot about Stephens's likely perception of his role as the translator of another playwright's constructions – one of imagining and then attempting to reconstruct the way in which the source-text playwright engaged with his or her audiences at the time.

Given these observations, Stephens's commission to write a new version of Ibsen's *A Doll's House* would appear to be an inspired match. While not Stephens's idea, he certainly appears to have been enthusiastic about the project from the outset.

> The genesis came from Carrie Cracknell, the director, who was and remains fascinated by the sexual politics surrounding Nora and representations of Nora and the meaning of her narrative now 120-odd years after its writing. But it was brought to me by [playwright and theatre director] David Lan who was excited not only by Carrie's enthusiasm for it, but also by the thoughts of Jon Fosse on the way Ibsen was being represented in England. (Stephens 2014c: n.p.)

(See later in this chapter for discussion of Fosse's view of how Nora has traditionally been represented on the British stage.)

In spite of his stature as a bold, confident playwright in his own right, and of the relish that he clearly shows for reimagining Nora for the twenty-first century, Stephens claims a surprising reluctance to deviate too far from Ibsen's original text.

> I think I attacked it originally with the intention of really reconsidering the thing. … And the more I sat in his head and had him glowering at me from my screensaver, and the more that I sat in that play, the more I felt that it would be a mistake to do that and the only thing to do was be truthful to his imagination and truthful to his vision. (cited in Dally and Hemming 2012: n.p.)

Yet having said this, Stephens *does* significantly alter Ibsen's source text in the way in which he reframes the play's famous ending. Whereas every other English-language version of *A Doll's House* adheres to the structure of the source text in the final scene (Nora leaves, Torvald gives his final speech and then we hear the door downstairs slam shut), Stephens's Nora first closes the door to her apartment before slamming the downstairs door, and in between Torvald is given only one word ('Nora') as he waits, buries his face in his hands and then gets up to go to the apartment door (Stephens 2012b: 110).

As well as being aware that *A Doll's House* is now inevitably viewed through the prism of a century or more of women slowly moving towards equality in the eyes of the law, Stephens also consciously views the play against a background of an increasingly atomized society – one characterized by the frequent breakdown of constructs such as the family unit and the sanctity of marriage. These are themes throughout much of Stephens's original work both before and since working on *A Doll's House*, so we should not be surprised that they are woven into this adaptation as well. But here it is clear that Stephens takes this idea of a modern interpretation of *A Doll's House* to a different level – one that moves beyond the debate about whether Ibsen was championing the feminist cause or talking more about the authenticity of the individual (whether female or male), and that asks us to focus more on the issue that Nora raises towards the end of the play when she questions whether there really is such a thing as society.

> What's fascinating to me now a hundred and forty years on is that I think we're looking at the rights of the individual from an altogether different perspective. There's a line at the end of the play when Nora … says that she's not entirely sure if she thinks there's any such thing as society. And I remember thinking, gosh, I'm sure I've heard a woman say there's no such thing as society before. … Maybe it's time to reconsider our commitment to owning ourselves, and to reconsider the possibility that we ought to commit to society to just the same extent that we've been committing to ourselves as individuals. (cited in Dalley and Hemming 2012: n.p.)

For any readers who may be too young to recognize the allusion here, Stephens's observation that 'I'm sure I've heard a woman say there's no such thing as society before' is a reference to a comment made by British prime minister Margaret Thatcher in an interview with Douglas Keay in 1987 – a comment that subsequently gained notoriety as the defining statement of Thatcher's neoliberal political ideology. Here, Stephens's use of the term 'before' is interesting since it suggests that Nora's comment is made subsequent to Thatcher's remark. In fact, from the perspective of a British theatre audience in the early twenty-first century, relevance theory would indeed propose that Nora's utterance triggers implicatures relating to Thatcher in such a way as if the latter had been the first of those two women to make such a comment.

As an aside, this is exactly the same process that will lead to other implicatures being triggered if spectators recognize in *A Doll's House* any other contextual associations with previous works by Stephens – or indeed subsequent works if they watch a performance of *A Doll's House* after the event (for example, online on the Digital Theatre website).

Clearly, such contextual associations cannot be attributed to Ibsen's own 1879 source text. But this doesn't mean that audiences question the chronology of the cognitive effects that are experienced during a performance. Theatre scholar Bruce McConachie suggests that such cognitive processes in the theatre are the result of Gilles Fauconnier and Mark Turner's *conceptual blending* referred to in Chapter 3. Here, theatre audiences blend the actor and the character together into one image and one concept of identity, space and time in order to enable their immersion in the performance (2008: 43). To this, I would add that audiences also blend the source-text playwright and the translator together into one image and one concept of voice – something which is hopefully becoming clearer with each successive case study in this book.

But to return to Stephens's comment above, we should not take his suggestion that Nora's story should be examined at a broader societal level to imply that he does not take a side in the debate over whether Ibsen is a flag-bearer for feminism or for universal human rights. Rather, Stephens appears to be wholly aware that his Nora will inevitably be viewed through the prism of feminism because he feels that this is the automatic reaction of British audiences given the play's history in the UK (as discussed earlier in this chapter). As such, it becomes his duty as the adaptor to promote a different perspective from that which other translators into English might have adopted in their portrayal of Nora. What's more, in the same way that academics and reviewers have been eager to assess Stephens's Nora through the prism of his previous work, it's almost inevitable that *spectators* will not only compare Stephens's Nora to other Noras that they may be aware of (whether in performance or otherwise) in other adaptations of *A Doll's House*. They will also (either consciously or unconsciously) seek in Stephens's Nora something of the other strong, if not exactly feminist, female characters that Stephens has created in his previous work.

In the following sections, then, I will analyse particular thematic and stylistic dimensions of Stephens's adaptation of *A Doll's House* in order to determine the extent to which Stephens's voice might be inferred by spectators watching a performance of the play. Beforehand, however, let's explore relevance theory's notion of weak implicatures, which provides a useful framework within which to assess what these spectators might infer depending on their cognitive contexts. Building on the discussion in Chapters 4 and 5 of contextual associations and how these can influence the voice that spectators might identify in a celebrity translation, such an exploration will help to explain how textual and extratextual associations might combine *cumulatively* to create a sense of a distinctive celebrity voice that exists over and above individual linguistic choices.

Chains of weak implicatures

Literary texts by their very nature contain a very large number of *weak* implicatures. They are texts that invite the reader to think about (and indeed take responsibility for) what is being communicated. They are also texts that encourage a wide range of different interpretations – interpretations which may or may not coincide with what the author was trying to imply. This means that, theoretically at least, a literary text can be inferred in a different way by every single reader (see Sperber and Wilson 1995: 236;

MacKenzie 2002: 24 and Furlong 2007: 336). The weak implicatures of a text essentially give rise to what receivers would perceive as the author's *style* (i.e. the linguistic choices made by that author), and what scholars would term the stylistic or poetic effects that the text has on those receivers (i.e. the ways in which those receivers are able to engage with the text) (Boase-Beier 2020: 58). These weak implicatures are not necessarily consciously intended, but result from the cognitive context of the author of that text, and they are processed (or not as the case may be) by the receiver against his or her own cognitive context.

In previous chapters, I've already explored how individual words or utterances in translated play texts can trigger a wide variety of weak implicatures. But what about the implicatures that are triggered by the effect that a play text has at a more holistic level, particularly when that text is assimilated in the context of a live theatrical performance? Clearly, the potential for weak implicatures in such a scenario is theoretically almost limitless, even if in practice the common cultural and aesthetic understanding among spectators and the interactive relations both between spectators and the stage and between different spectators might serve to limit those implicatures.

In any event, spectators' inferential processes will be guided, and the mutual cognitive environment will be enlarged, by stimuli beyond the text itself. Such stimuli might include the actors (both when speaking the lines in the text and when following the author's stage directions), the set, the lighting, the physical characteristics of the theatre itself, other audience members and so on (see Pavis 1982 and Elam 2002). Important and interesting though such refracted stimuli might be in the real world, I must limit myself in this book to those stimuli that the celebrity translator is able to have at least some control over – namely, the text itself, and the features contained within that text that give rise to contextual, poetic effects.

What I'm particularly interested in here, then, are those weak implicatures that are triggered by the celebrity translator's text because of the *cumulative* effect of particular thematic tropes or stylistic devices on spectators. Such tropes or devices might in isolation give rise to only a few weak implicatures, but in combination might cue much more powerful contextual associations with, say, the translator's existing work or dimensions of his or her personality. This notion of the cumulative effect of weak implicatures chimes with Anne Furlong's concept of cumulative or non-cumulative readings, which are the outcome of productive re-reading of a text (2008). This concept reflects the distinction that Furlong makes between *spontaneous* and *non-spontaneous interpretations*, where a spontaneous interpretation is 'an interpretation that is adequate for the effort expended' and a non-spontaneous interpretation is one that 'has as its goal optimal interpretation' (2008: 290). In turn, Furlong's distinction in many ways echoes psychologist Daniel Kahneman's notions of fast and slow thinking, which are based on the idea that we use two fundamentally different modes of thought to understand stimuli – System 1, which is fast, automatic and intuitive (i.e. spontaneous), and System 2, which is slow, deliberate and effortful (i.e. non-spontaneous) (2011: 19–108). Such distinctions also arguably reflect Brecht's view of the importance of thinking about performance in the theatre as well as experiencing it (see Chapter 2). This is something with which Stephens would no doubt also concur given his comments about the importance of provoking spectators into seeing something of themselves in the characters he creates – which may or may not be something that those spectators are able to articulate by themselves, or even be consciously aware of.

I'm essentially talking here about a spectator's first and only reception of Stephens's text – in other words, I'm assuming that most of any given audience have not previously seen the play, or read the published version of Stephens's text, which may or may not be an accurate assumption. But this concept of spontaneous and non-spontaneous interpretation remains a useful one for my analysis since it supposes different levels of expectations of relevance. We could therefore distinguish, for example, between the spectator who goes to see *A Doll's House* without any previous knowledge of either Ibsen or Stephens and who simply seeks a stimulating evening in the theatre (and who will aim for an adequate interpretation of Stephens's text), and the spectator who is a long-standing admirer of Stephens's work and highly familiar with his previous plays, and who will be more prepared to expend considerable cognitive effort in deriving an interpretation – and to take responsibility for that interpretation. This clearly has implications both for the *number* of weak implicatures that the spectator infers and for the *cumulative effect* of those weak implicatures. Of course, this separation of audience members is in reality more of a spectrum, with most spectators falling between these two extremes. Spontaneity is in this context, then, a *relative* construct rather than a binary distinction.

In both the source and target texts explored here, the chains of weak implicatures created by Ibsen and Stephens lead, with repetition and reinforcement (and, of course, with the willingness of the audience to put the effort into deriving those implicatures in the first place), to what I would term *higher-order implicatures* – representations that are still implicit, but that cumulatively become more readily accessible to receivers because of the series of contextual associations that are triggered. This increased accessibility gives rise to increased relevance, which in turn affects the plausibility of those implicatures (see Sperber and Wilson 1995: 201). And following on from this argument, it also becomes clear how Stephens's and Ibsen's different dramatic voices may often lead to spectators deriving quite different chains of weak implicatures in the target text from those that are derived in the source text. The most obvious example of this is the different way in which both authors use metaphors in their respective texts. While Ibsen's frequent use of extended metaphors inevitably gives rise to a number of chains of weak implicatures, Stephens often either breaks the chain of implicatures that spectators of Ibsen's source text will typically construct (essentially destroying what Berman would term the underlying network of signification, see Chapter 5) or creates his own chains of implicatures.

A particularly vivid illustration of an extended network of contextual associations in *A Doll's House* is Ibsen's repeated use of *vidunderlig* (*wonderful* or *wondrous*), which occurs no fewer than nineteen times in the source text in either adjectival or noun form. Initially used by Nora to simply express her delight at the household's lack of financial worries (Ibsen [1879] 2013: 14), she gradually moves towards what Törnqvist calls 'the more mystifying *det vidunderlige* and from there to the climactic substantival superlative *det vidunderligste*' (1995: 57). The progression in this underlying network of signifiers from being a relatively prosaic expression of pleasure to an encapsulation of the pinnacle of happiness mirrors Nora's ongoing and increasingly frustrated search for her own wonder – namely, the wonder of a true marriage.

In his own version of *A Doll's House*, on the other hand, Stephens alternates between *wonderful* and *miracle* throughout his text, which in itself destroys the accumulation of weak implicatures that the source text triggers with its consistent repetition of words based on *vidunderlig*. But having said this, there's also a greater sense in Stephens's text that the miracle that Nora is seeking is a more tangible one, namely, a secure home with her husband and children – a place where she can feel emotionally and materially comfortable and which gives her the security she clearly craves. Here, it's telling that Ibsen uses the Dano-Norwegian word *ægteskab*, based on *ægte*, meaning *genuine* or *honest*, to signify marriage (literally *state of honesty*). Stephens's Nora, meanwhile, appears more to desire something more akin to the more modern Norwegian concept of marriage as *samliv*, or living together (cf. Törnqvist 1995: 61). This then triggers a *different* chain of weak implicatures from that which Ibsen's text gives rise to, and one that potentially fundamentally changes our understanding of Nora's motivations for leaving her husband and family.

To give a more concrete example of how chains of implicatures are constructed and can affect the way in which spectators of *A Doll's House* will infer Stephens's communicative intentions, let's look at the way in which Stephens makes ongoing use of turns of phrase that are for the most part peculiar to British English. In doing so, he injects cues of a particular type of Englishness into his work – cues that are obviously lacking in the Dano-Norwegian source text. At the level of what Short calls the character–character level of dramatic discourse (1989: 149), I have identified in Figure 6.1 some of the utterances that will cumulatively create an impression of Englishness in Stephens's characters (my italics in each case, both here and in all the following figures in this chapter).

The point here is not to imply that spectators are hereby constantly reminded that Stephens is an English-speaking playwright (which would not in itself constitute a weak implicature), but rather that he is actively choosing to give his characters' dialogue a *distinctively English voice* (and thereby cumulatively create a domesticating effect) for a particular dramatic reason. Such a reason might be any one or several of the following:

1. to emphasize the class differences between characters,
2. to imply an imbalance of or struggle for power between two particular characters (compare, for example, the way in which Ibsen uses the formal and informal *you* in his text),
3. to suggest controlling behaviour on the part of a particular character,
4. to foreground an ironic tone of voice, or
5. to surprise audiences by juxtaposing different stylistic registers (e.g. Stephens's 'boring old fart' in the second text segment in Figure 6.1).

As already indicated, whether such inferences are intentional or not is not an issue in relevance theory. As Sperber and Wilson remind us, relevance theory does not accept that there's a 'clear-cut distinction between wholly determinate, specifically intended inferences and indeterminate, wholly unintended inferences' (1995: 199). The indeterminacy of the possible implicatures suggested in the following sections of this chapter merely indicates the level of confidence that individual spectators have

Ibsen's source text (Ibsen [1879] 2013)	My literal translation	Stephens's target text (Stephens 2012b)
STUEPIKEN: Frue, her er en fremmed dame NORA: Ja, la henne komme inn. (14)	MAID: Madam, there is a lady, a stranger. NORA: Yes, let her come in.	HELENE: Mrs Helmer, there is a lady here, a stranger. NORA: A stranger, *good Lord, how exciting!* (12)
NORA: De gamle kjedelige menneske kab bli for meg hvor han er. (32)	NORA: The tiresome old person can stay where he is as far as I am concerned.	NORA: That *boring old fart* can get out of my head now. (22)
NORA: Jeg har en sånn umåtelig lyst til å si: død og pine. (38)	NORA: I have such an immense urge to say: death and torment/ damnation (*equivalent to* well, I'm damned).	NORA: I have a terrible urge to go right up to him and whisper in his ear: *'Bloody hell!'* (26)
NORA: Jeg tror (Torvald) har noe å bestille. RANK: Og De? (78)	NORA: I think (Torvald) has got to get something done. RANK: And you?	NORA: (Torvald) is finishing some business for the bank. RANK: Terribly important business, I have no doubt. And what about you, Nora? Are you *dreadfully busy* as well? (60)
RANK: Med døden i hendene? – Og således å bøte for en annens skyld. Er det rettferdighet I dette? (80)	RANK: With death in my hands? – And thus making amends for another's sin? Is there justice in this?	RANK: Am I demonstrating a lack of reason as I face my own death? *Oh how miserably inconsiderate of me!* (*sarcastically*) (61)
KROGSTAD: Hvorledes vil De kunne forhindre det? (90)	KROGSTAD: How will you be able to prevent it?	KROGSTAD: *How the devil* are you going to stop that from happening? (70)
HELMER: Men kjære Nora, du ser så anstrengt ut. Har du øvet deg for meget? (98)	HELMER: But dear Nora, you look so strained. Have you practised too much?	TORVALD: Nora, darling. You look exhausted. Have you been *overdoing the practising a little*? (76)
RANK: Du bør ikke si henne imot. (102)	RANK: You should not contradict her.	RANK: *I wouldn't* contradict her *if I were you*, Mr Helmer. (79)
KROGSTAD: Och vet De hva jeg her går og gjelder for? (110)	KROGSTAD: And do you know how I am said to be here?	KROGSTAD: *Have you got the slightest idea* what people say about me? (84)
HELMER: Jeg har ikke på lenge sett ham i så godt lune. (118)	HELMER: I have not seen him in such a good mood for a long time.	TORVALD: I've not seen him in such a good mood for a very long time. He was *positively jolly*. (89)
RANK: Nå, man får jo ikke noe for ingenting her i livet. (122)	RANK: Well, one cannot have anything for nothing here in this life.	RANK: There is *no such thing as* an action without consequence in this life, Mr Helmer, *old chap*. (92)
HELMER: Ville da det ha vært for deg? (136)	HELMER: Would that have been any good for you?	TORVALD: *I'm afraid I don't really see the point of that*. (103)

Figure 6.1 Chain of weak implicatures implying Englishness.

in their belief that *their* interpretation is an accurate reflection of Stephens's thoughts. And it should not in any way be taken to imply how correct those beliefs might be, or what proportion of spectators might adopt those beliefs.

At this point, then, it will be clear that the distinctiveness of an author's voice is not just about the attitudes that they are felt to espouse (as is the case with Mark Ravenhill, see Chapter 4) or the verbal tics for which they become recognized (as is the case with Roger McGough, see Chapter 5). It's also about the themes that they are constantly drawn back to in their work. As Stephens himself says, 'It is a myth that a writer needs to reinvent themselves with every play or find a new subject or do something new. The great writers return to the same questions obsessively. Having identified these themes, we can take ownership of them and so consciously find new ways into them' (2016: 181). Even more tellingly, Stephens also notes how 'writers have obsessions which they return to. It's like we're trying to solve something that we can never solve' (cited in Wonfor 2012: n.p.). In Stephens's case, three of those obsessions would appear to be the varying levels of sympathy shown towards his female characters; his frequent focus on society's damaged, frail characters; and the constant search for home by many of his characters.

I will now explore each of these three themes, or obsessions, in turn and show not only how Stephens's adaptation of *A Doll's House* carries resonances of some of his *previous* work at a thematic level but also how in some cases the issues that he focuses on in his version of *A Doll's House* become manifest in some of his own *subsequent* work.

Stephens and sympathies for Nora

Stephens's own work has a relatively consistent focus on female characters who are in one way or another lost, confused and seeking to escape their immediate surroundings and situation. So it should not be surprising that Stephens was drawn to adapting *A Doll's House*, whose Nora is one of European theatre's most famously vulnerable women. As Stephens himself notes, 'The myth of the brave individuals struggling in the face of impossible odds (is) a myth I've based a lot of plays upon' (2016: 47). The central dilemma of Ibsen's play, namely, how to be true to yourself while at the same time being a marriage partner and a parent, is one that continues to resonate in European societies, and not just for women. 'In a sense,' says theatre critic Caroline McGinn, 'Nora's famous dramatic exit is something many parents do five days a week' (cited in Rustin 2013: n.p.).

Against this background, I'm interested here in exploring the extent to which Stephens's sympathy (or lack of sympathy) for Nora echoes the sympathy (or lack of it) he feels for some of his own female characters, such that spectators of his adaptation of *A Doll's House* might consciously detect some similarities in his characterization and thereby infer some of Stephens's own dramatic voice in his translation. As explained in the previous section of this chapter, the theoretical device that I will use to attempt to illustrate this is the concept of chains of weak implicatures. In Figure 6.2, I have selected (in the order in which they appear in the play) a series of utterances that feature in

No.	Ibsen's source text (Ibsen [1879] 2013)	My literal translation	Strong implicature	Stephens's target text (Stephens 2012b)	Potential chain of weak implicatures
1	NORA: Herefter kan vi leve ganske annerledes enn før, – ganske som vi vil. Å, Kristine, hvor jeg føler meg lett og lykkelig! Ja, for det er dog deilig å ha dyktig mange penge og ikke behøve å gjøre seg bekrymringer. Ikke sant? (18)	NORA: From now on we can live quite differently than before – just as we like. Oh, Kristine, how relieved and happy I feel. Yes, for it is splendid to have heaps of money and not need to worry. Isn't it?	Nora admits to her friend Kristine that she loves the pleasures that money can bring.	NORA: It's going to change everything for us. We can live exactly as we've always wanted to. You've no idea how relieved I feel. *You've no idea how much money he's going to make.* (14)	We see Nora as materialistic and obsessed by status.
2	NORA: Si meg, doctor Rank, alle de som er ansatte i Aksjebanken, blir altså nu avhengige av Torvald? RANK: Er det det De finner så uhyre morsomt? NORA: La meg om det! Ja det er riktignok umåtelig fornøyelig å tenk på at vi – at Torvald har fått så megen innflyelse på mange mennesker. (36)	NORA: Tell me, Dr Rank, all those who are employed at the Joint Stock Bank, are they now dependent on Torvald? RANK: Is that what you find so hugely funny? NORA: Let me, let me. Yes, it is indeed so immensely funny to think that we – that Torvald has got so much influence over many people.	Nora is unsympathetic towards Dr Rank.	NORA: You must tell me, Dr Rank. Are all of the people who work at the Savings Bank so dependent on Torvald? RANK: Is that your idea of something funny? NORA: Oh, don't you worry about that. Don't you worry about that. *I just find it rather entertaining to think about all the people that Torvald has power over.* (25)	We now also see Nora as manipulative and hungry for power over others.
3	KROGSTAD: Blir jeg utstøtt for annen gang, så skal De gjøre meg selskap. [*Han hilser og går ut gjennem forstuen.*] NORA: [*en stund eftertenksom, kaster med nakken*]. Å hva! Å ville gjøre meg bange! Så enfoldig er jeg da ikke. (54)	KROGSTAD: Should I be expelled for the second time, then you will keep me company. [*He bows and goes out through the hall.*] NORA: [*thoughtful for a while, then tosses her head*]. Oh, what! He wants to get me upset. But I'm not that stupid.	Nora rebuffs Krogstad's threat that she will also suffer if he is found out.	KROGSTAD: You can do whatever you like, but if I am thrown into the gutter for a second time then I will bring you down there with me. Have a very good day and may I take this opportunity to wish a very happy Christmas to you and your family. *He leaves. She stands for a while watching the space he has left. She shakes her head. She laughs.*	We see Nora as uncaring and unsympathetic to Krogstad's plight. Our sympathies are more with him than with her.

Figure 6.2 Chain of weak implicatures implying Stephens's sympathies for Nora.

Figure 6.2 (Continued)

No.	Ibsen's source text (Ibsen [1879] 2013)	My literal translation	Strong implicature	Stephens's target text (Stephens 2012b)	Potential chain of weak implicatures
4	NORA: Er det virkelig så slemt, det som denne Krogstad har gjort seg skyldig i? HELMER: Skrevet falske navne. Har du noen forestilling om hva det vil si? NORA: Kan han ikke har gjort det av nød? (59)	NORA: Is it really so bad what this Krogstad became so guilty of? HELMER: Wrote false names. Have you no idea what it means? NORA: Could he not have done it out of necessity?	Nora stands up to Torvald in defence of Krogstad.	NORA: Will you tell me what Krogstad did that is so awful? TORVALD: He forged signatures. NORA: Did he? TORVALD: Do you understand how bad that is? NORA: *Maybe he had no choice.* (44)	We see Nora start to realize the seriousness of her own forgery, but in the light of her uncaring attitude towards Krogstad feel little sympathy for her.
5	BARNEPIKEN: De små ber så vakkert om de må komme inn til mamma. NORA: Nei, nei, nei; slipp dem ikke inn til meg! Vær hos dem du, Anne-Marie. BARNEPIKEN: Ja, ja, frue. (60)	NURSE: The little ones are begging so hard to be allowed to come in to mother. NORA: No, no, no; don't let them come in to me. Stay with them, Anne-Marie. NURSE: Yes, yes, madam.	Nora is rude to the nurse after she suggests that the children would like to see their mother.	ANNA: is something wrong? NORA: I simply want you to play with the children, *which I think is what you're paid to do, is it not?* ANNA: Very good. (46)	We find Nora's attitude towards Anna and towards her own children unappealing.
6	NORA: Spør de titt efter meg? BARNEPIKEN: De er jo så vant til å har mamma om seg. NORA: Ja men, Anne-Marie, jeg kan ikke herefter være så meget sammen med dem som før. (62)	NORA: Do they ask after me a little? NURSE: They are so used to having mother around them. NORA: Yes but, Anne-Marie, I cannot henceforth be with them as much as before.	Nora suggests that she has already decided to leave her family.	NORA: They're not still asking after me, are they? ANNA: They're used to having you around. NORA: Yes. Well. *I'm afraid they're going to get used to not having me around quite so often any more.* (48)	We question Nora's lack of regret about leaving her children.
7	NORA: Nu vil Torvald at jeg skal være neapolitansk fiskerpike og danse tarantella, for den lærte jeg på Capri. (64)	NORA: Now Torvald wants me to be a Neapolitan fisher girl and dance the tarantella that I learned in Capri.	Nora explains to her friend Kristine that she will dance for her husband at the party.	NORA: Did you know that I could dance the tarantella? *I don't imagine that you did, did you?* I learnt it in Capri. (50)	We find Nora's sneering attitude towards her friend distasteful.
8	HELMER: Langsommere, langsommere. NORA: Kann ikke annerledes. HELMER: Ikke så voldsomt, Nora! NORA: Just så må det være. (100)	HELMER: Slower, slower. NORA: I cannot do it differently. HELMER: Not so violent, Nora! NORA: It has to be just like this.	Nora stands up to Torvald by refusing to dance more slowly.	TORVALD: Slow down. A little slower. NORA: I can't go any slower. TORVALD: Don't be so violent Nora. NORA: *I can't help myself. I have to be violent.* (77)	We wonder who might be at the receiving end of Nora's urge to be violent.

No.	Ibsen's source text (Ibsen [1879] 2013)	My literal translation	Strong implicature	Stephens's target text (Stephens 2012b)	Potential chain of weak implicatures
9	HELMER: Så, så, så; ikke denne oppskremte villhet. Vær nu min egen lille lerkefugl, som du pleier. NORA: Å ja, det skal jeg nok. (104)	HELMER: Come, come, come; not this startled wildness. Now be my own little lark, as you usually are. NORA: Oh yes, I will still be [your lark].	Nora pretends to Torvald that she will continue to play her role as the dutiful wife.	TORVALD: Calm down. You're getting yourself wound up. I want my skylark back. NORA: *Oh, she will come back, I promise you, Torvald.* (79)	We continue to sympathize more with Torvald as we realize what Nora's true intentions are with regard to her family.
10	NORA: Du skal ingenting forhindre. Det er dog i grunnen en jubel, dette her, å gå og vente på det vidunderlige. FRU LINDE: Hva er det du venter på? NORA: Å, det kan ikke du forstå. (104)	NORA: You will prevent nothing. It is, however, basically a celebration to go and wait for the wonderful thing. MRS LINDE: What are you waiting for? NORA: Oh, you could not understand.	Nora dismisses Kristine's question about her plans.	NORA: I'm not going to try to prevent anything any more. I'm just going to wait. Something wonderful is going to happen. KRISTINE: What are you talking about? NORA: *You wouldn't understand. Even if I told you.* (80)	We feel anger towards Nora as she increasingly alienates those who might be able to help here, such as her friend Kristine.
11	HELMER: Han kan gøre med mig, hvad han vil, forlange af meg hva det skal være, byde og befale over meg, som det lyster ham; jeg tør ikke kny. Og så jammerlig må jeg synke ned og gå til grunne for en lettsindig kvinnes skyld! NORA: Når jeg er ute av verden, så er du fri. HELMER: Å ingen fakter. Slike talemåter hadde din far også. (130)	HELMER: He can do what he wants with me, tell me how things should be, order and command me as he pleases; I dare not murmur. And so wretchedly must I sink and perish due to the fault of a frivolous woman. NORA: When I'm out of this world, so are you free. HELMER: Oh, no gestures. Your father had such platitudes as well.	Torvald feels sorry for himself because he will be so beholden to Krogstad, but Nora dismisses his concerns.	TORVALD: He can do whatever he wants with me now. He can ask whatever he wants. NORA: *When I'm dead he won't be able to do a –* TORVALD: Oh, don't be so pathetic. You sound exactly like your father. (98)	We sympathize even more with Torvald's predicament in the light of Nora's melodramatic and uncaring response.
12	HELMER: Forlate ditt hjem, din mann og dine born! Og du tenker ikke på hva folk vil si. NORA: Det kan jeg ikke ta noe hensyn til. Jeg vet bare det blir nødvendig for meg. (140)	HELMER: To leave your home, your husband and your children! And you don't think about what people will say. NORA: I cannot take that into consideration. I only know that it is necessary for me.	Nora insists that her own needs are more important than the needs of her husband and children.	TORVALD: You can't leave your husband. You can't leave your children. NORA: Why not? TORVALD: What will people say about you? NORA: *I don't care about that.* (105)	We ultimately question Nora's selfishness and coldness towards her husband and children.

Stephens's adaptation, and that might reasonably be said to have a cumulative effect on spectators' inferences about Stephens's attitude towards Nora and her actions.

Stephens himself admits that his interpretation of Nora is somewhat different from that which is seen in many other English translations of *A Doll's House*. He suggests that this is mainly due to conversations with Fosse, whose work Stephens had already translated prior to his adaptation of *A Doll's House* (see earlier in this chapter). In particular, Stephens claims to have been struck by Fosse's observation that Ibsen's play had never been received in Norway as a celebration of female emancipation at all. He compares this with what he perceives as the typical British representations of Nora in the late nineteenth century, which held her up at the time as 'a kind of flag-bearer for women's rights' (Stephens 2014b: n.p.). Stephens also believes that Ibsen himself never intended Nora to be seen as a feminist icon either. As such, he is siding with Meyer's interpretation of Ibsen's communicative intentions more than with that of scholars such as Finney and Templeton (again, see earlier in this chapter). 'In the letters and in the lectures and in the journals he kept he talks of his frustration with people who represent Nora as being symbolic of female emancipation. Because for him she never was' (2014c: n.p.). Stephens's interpretation is that Ibsen was struggling at the time to develop a sense of his own authenticity and to counter the way in which he was 'objectified and commodified' in Norwegian literary circles (2014c: n.p.). He feels it was this that was the real driving force behind Ibsen's development of Nora, rather than any overt desire to highlight the feminist cause. 'If Nora is nothing but an emblem for female emancipation she's not a human being therefore, and I think she's much more interesting than that, so my impulse was to try to reclaim that. And part of reclaiming that humanity involved dramatising that selfishness and thoughtlessness as honestly as her capacity for clarity and bravery' (2014c: n.p.).

Irrespective of how 'accurate' Stephens's interpretation of Ibsen's intentions might be, his interpretation influences not only his portrayal of Nora but also how this portrayal is potentially received by audiences. Here, it's clear from the segments italicized in Figure 6.2 (and particularly from segments one to three and five to seven) that spectators will almost inevitably perceive Nora as a rather selfish and thoughtless character – and, if they're familiar with other adaptations of Ibsen's work, as a *more* selfish and *more* thoughtless character than she has previously been portrayed on the British stage (and particularly if those adaptations present Nora from a more modernist or more feminist perspective). As Stephens himself suggests, 'I think the way she treats Doctor Rank is unbelievably cruel. I think the way she treats Mrs Lind is just unbelievably selfish and unthinking, her capacity for savagery in the way that she lashes out at the servants is consistently high-handed and her treatment of Krogstad in the end is ungenerous and unthinking and lacks empathy' (2014c: n.p.).

Importantly, scholars and critics alike have also noted how different Stephens's Nora is from those typically seen on stage in the English-speaking world. Theatre translation scholar John Bull, for example, suggests that Stephens's version of the play makes Nora a much more aware (particularly sexually aware) woman than she had been in previous versions of *A Doll's House*. 'Stephens's version highlights very strongly both Torvald's sexual obsession with his wife, and Nora's skilful management of this obsession' (2018: 292). By way of examples, Bull cites a number of Stephens's stage directions in Scene

1, none of which appears either in the source text or in any English-language version of the play from William Archer's translation onwards (e.g. 'He struggles to take his eyes off her. She enjoys him watching her' [Stephens 2012b: 4] and 'She kisses him. He checks the maids are not within earshot and kisses her back' [Stephens 2012b: 5]). Bull also notes how, later in this first scene,

> Nora explains to Kristine why her husband has banned her from eating chocolates in a way that both accepts and simultaneously questions the terms of the ban, which she explains – again entirely without precedent – is not about health issues (the parental figure concerned for the welfare of his 'child') but about sex, something which makes the following stage direction (*She puts a chocolate in his mouth*) deliberately unsubtle in view of Dr Rank's infatuation with her. (2018: 292)

Guardian critic Michael Billington, meanwhile, focuses on Nora's newly found exuberance, as evident from her excessive excitement about Torvald's new job (segment 2 in Figure 6.2) and from her aggressive, violent dancing (segment 8). As a consequence, the tarantella scene, which, according to Moi, is designed to be 'a graphic representation of a woman's struggle to make her existence heard, to make it count' (2006: 238), becomes in Stephens's version an act of hysterical vanity. 'She reacts with reflex excitement to every mention of the word "money", maintains a hopelessly idealistic view of her husband, Torvald, almost to the last, and seems half in love with easeful death as she dances to a standstill in the famous tarantella. And, when the truth finally dawns about her dependence on Torvald's self-serving egotism, she resorts to downright violence' (Billington 2012a: n.p.).

Such changes in Nora's attitudes and actions noted by Bull and Billington would certainly support the view that Stephens's Nora is likely to be perceived as a more egotistical and manipulative character than Ibsen himself perhaps ever intended. Stephens's changes would also appear consonant (whether consciously or not) with what Templeton terms the *feminist backlash* interpretation of Nora, in which she is dismissed as 'an irrational and frivolous narcissist; an "abnormal" woman, a "hysteric"; a vain, unloving egoist who abandons her family in a paroxysm of selfishness' (1989: 29). So, whereas Törnqvist believes that 'Nora does not leave her family to discover her true self merely for her own sake' but rather leaves 'in the conviction that self-knowledge is a prerequisite for being a true wife and mother' (1995: 43), Stephens's Nora appears to be acting wholly out of self-interest and as a reaction to the constrictions of family life and marriage.

Of course, without knowing how many spectators attending a performance of Stephens's *A Doll's House* were familiar with any of the many other versions of Ibsen's play that have been performed on the British stage over the years, it's difficult to determine to what extent Nora is perceived as egotistical and manipulative in her own right, and to what extent such perceptions are comparative notions – in other words, perceptions that emerge when comparing this Nora with any of the other Noras that they may have previously been aware of. This suggests, then, that the point of reference that might be *at least as pertinent* here is actually not any of these other Noras, but rather some of Stephens's other female characters in his previous work. That's because it could well be the case that a greater proportion of audiences came to see Stephens's *A Doll's House* because of the draw of Stephens himself (i.e. because they had enjoyed at least some of his previous work) than because of the appeal of Ibsen. So how might spectators' perceptions of Nora be influenced by their contextual associations with these other women created by Stephens before he created his own version of Nora?

Even only a cursory glance at some of Stephens's previous plays and at much of the critical response to those plays reveals that Stephens certainly has some history of developing female characters for whom audiences are not always meant to feel much sympathy. And yet at other times he has created female characters whom he delights in portraying as succeeding against all odds, particularly if their family background and childhood environment conspire against such success. This means, then, that both Stephens's unsympathetic and sympathetic female characters might actually serve to shape audiences' inferences about his portrayal of Nora. As a consequence, the cumulative effect of the chain of implicatures identified above is likely to be further strengthened, either because there's a synergistic effect in the way in which spectators identify *similarities* between Nora and other female characters in Stephens's work or because the *contrast* between the associations with Nora and the associations with another character turns Nora into a kind of *anti-character* within Stephens's repertoire.

The first useful place to look for female characters that have some similarity to Nora is in the plays by Stephens that have most obvious parallels to *A Doll's House* – *Port* (2002) and *Harper Reagan* (2008). Rebellato describes these as two of a number of plays by Stephens that are 'domestic, somewhat naturalistic dramas … depicting the effect on ordinary people of violence, scandal, and loss' (2010: 574). Other plays by Stephens that might also fit this description include *Herons* (2001), *One Minute* (2003) and *Country Music* (2004).

Port tells the story of Racheal, who lives in Stephens's own hometown, Stockport. We follow her falling in and out of love with her environment as those people she loves let her down or leave her behind. The play's action unfolds in an almost documentary form that focuses on the extraordinary in the ordinary. As *Guardian* theatre critic Susannah Clapp notes,

> Lives in the theatre are so often seen through the prism of a decisive incident, or a series of critical moments. The life that is told here – a life that belongs to a voluble, intense female person – develops through slight, inconclusive episodes whose importance becomes apparent only later. This is as close to biography as you will get on stage. (2013: n.p.)

Racheal has one obvious similarity to Nora in that she also ultimately decides to leave her environment and change her life. Ever since she was a young girl, she has dreamt of escaping Stockport with her mother.

> **RACHEAL:** We could go now. We could just leave. Wouldn't need no bags or anything. Nothing like that. Just start driving. Go to Grandad's and not come back. Go to country. Go to Disney World Florida. Couldn't we though, Mum? I reckon that'd be a top idea. (Stephens 2005: 250)

Unlike Nora, however, spectators are left in no doubt that Racheal will achieve her goal. As Clapp observes, 'Having seen her thwarted energy you believe she can. What could have been sentimental is stirring. The sun falls on her face, where for the first time an enormous smile radiates' (2013: n.p.). Already then, we can see greater sympathy for Racheal's dreams of escaping Stockport than we ever find in Stephens's text for Nora's desire to escape her home environment. Racheal's positive outcome (not dissimilar to Stephens's own escape from Stockport to go to university in York in the late 1980s) contrasts with Stephens's (possibly not entirely serious) suggestion that Nora's departure will be less successful. 'There's part of me that thinks [Nora's] going to go back next day, hung over and apologetic' (2014b: n.p.).

Stephens himself sees *Port* as a play about 'making sense of what it is to love and to face disappointment ... about making sense of growing up in the battered north ... about making sense of the juxtaposition of energy and lethargy in one place at the same time. But, more than that, it's a play about making sense of the inevitability of death and, through that, the urgency of living a life with eyes as wide open as you can get them to be' (2013b: ix). While the Helmers' privileged lifestyle in late-nineteenth-century Norway might have little in common with Racheal's life in turn-of-the-millennium Stockport, Stephens's observation that his play is about making sense of the juxtaposition of energy and lethargy chimes with Nora's experience of living in her 'doll's house'. Consider, for example, the contrast in Nora's mood between segment 5 (when she appears too tired to play with her own children) and segment 10 (when she embraces the possibility that a miracle is about to happen) in Figure 6.2. But in *Port*, Racheal channels her energy in a more constructive way, seeing her hometown through new eyes after being away and desperately seeking signs of hope emerging from the environment of her childhood spent with friends such as Danny.

> **RACHEAL:** When I was a kid I used to think [the clock tower in Merseyway] was massive. Fucking big skyscraper. I couldn't understand how come, when they had programmes about the tallest buildings in the world, I couldn't understand why they never mentioned the clock tower in Merseyway. I went back in there at the weekend. It's tiny. Very squat. Really short. I was quite disappointed. Noticed the viaduct.
> **DANNY:** The viaduct?
> **RACHEAL:** I never really paid any attention to it before. I never really noticed it. But I was looking at it, on my way into town. It's actually, y'know, it's quite impressive. There's something about it. (Stephens 2005: 316)

This dialogue is typical of much of Racheal's way of speaking – a clumsy but wholly sincere observation on urban life that points to a character that Stephens himself describes as 'open-eyed, tough, brilliantly optimistic' (2013a: n.p.). Unlike Nora, our sympathies for Racheal rely on her very abilities to see the best in her environment and the people within it. Another poignant example of this is her attempt to empathize with her brother, who has been in prison.

> RACHEAL: You know what I think. I think that nobody or nothing should make you cry. Ever. And I'm sorry because I know that there are some things that I just don't know about prison and about what it was like and what now. I do get you. And I didn't always but I do now. And I love yer. And I do think that you will be all right. (Stephens 2005: 335)

Both *Port* and *A Doll's House* are about how their central female protagonists deal with issues such as the loss of a parent, the confines of marriage and the ease with which families can fall apart. Why, then, is Stephens's Racheal portrayed so much more sympathetically than his Nora? The most obvious explanation would be that Stephens himself identifies more with working-class families such as Racheal's than with more privileged middle-class families such as the Helmers, and as a result champions the former's triumphs more than the latter's. While Stephens clearly delights in showing us how Racheal succeeds in the face of all the problems that life throws at her through no fault of her own, we can also imagine him delighting in Nora experiencing the very opposite – a fall from grace in spite of all the advantages that she has enjoyed in life. Underlying this greater distance from the world of the Helmers is perhaps also the fact that these characters are not Stephens's own in the sense that they were originally created by another writer, and that they are not in Stephens's possession in quite the same way as characters that he has developed on the page entirely by himself.

It could, of course, be argued from the perspective of relevance theory that a playwright's characters never actually belong to the playwright who created them, but rather to the spectators who create their own image of those characters. But the point I'm seeking to make here is a more general one – namely, that, while translators' characters are bound inevitably to contain some of that translator's voice (at least if we accept the view that the translator's voice is heard in every translation, see Hermans 1996: 27), this does not have to imply that the translator will always empathize with the source-text author's characters in the same way that the source-text author might. So when audiences familiar with *Port* watch Stephens's *A Doll's House*, the lack of sympathy that they are potentially encouraged to feel for Nora (as evidenced by the chain of weak implicatures identified earlier) could well trigger contextual associations with Racheal by virtue of her complete *oppositeness* to Nora. This then serves to create rewarding poetic effects through the *collision* of wholly contrasting cognitive effects – one of empathy and one of apathy.

We can contrast the associations that Racheal might trigger with the associations that might be triggered by another of Stephens's female characters, Harper Regan (in the play of the same name first performed in 2008). At first glance, Harper would appear to bear many similarities to both Nora and Racheal in that all three women feel compelled to flee their physical surroundings as a way of escaping the detrimental effect that their environment has on their sense of freedom and self-worth. But while Racheal seeks to escape her working-class background, Harper seeks to escape the anguish of her middle-class family when she leaves her husband and family behind in Greater London and returns to her Manchester roots to visit her parents. Here, she's forced to confront the toxic secret at the heart of her comfortable family life (namely, that her husband, Seth, has taken pornographic pictures of children playing in a park) and finally find peace with herself. Lesley Sharp, the actor who played Harper in the play's initial run at the National Theatre in London, describes Harper as 'a woman who's confused about how she feels about her life. ... She's supposed to be a wife and a mother, but she goes on a very dark journey. By the end, she goes home and sees the truth of her situation, her relationship and who she is' (cited in Trueman 2013: n.p.).

Harper's journey is clearly similar to Nora's in that both feel the need to step out of their environment to discover who they really are. Here, Stephens acknowledges the influences on *Harper Regan* of classical Greek drama such as those of Euripedes. 'I wanted to write a play about a quest. I wanted to write a play which was dominated by a heroic central protagonist. And I wanted to write a play in which a transgression within a family had cursed that family and the quest was an attempt to solve that curse, or to ease it, or to heal it' (cited in Bolton 2008: 4). The fact that Nora's dramatic journey is triggered by her own offence and Harper's by the offence of another does not detract from the fact that both characters remain defined by the extraordinary circumstances in which they find themselves as a result of those offences. Like Nora, Harper's inner life and turmoil shapes everything that she does and says. The spectre of her past hovers over each of her reactions, from the most prosaic to the most profound, including those that she does not articulate in words.

Consider, for example, even the opening lines of *Harper Regan*.

ELWOOD: If you go I don't think you should come back.
  A terribly long pause. As long as they can get away with. They stand incredibly still.
HARPER: I don't know what to say.
ELWOOD: No. (Stephens 2011: 205)

In these lines alone, Stephens not only implicitly sets up the key theme of his play, described by Bolton as 'an empathetic exploration of the sexual drives which, consciously and unconsciously, influence behaviour' (2008: 6). He also employs a dramaturgical feature that he frequently uses throughout his work – that of throwing the audience off-balance and unnerving them before unveiling the true nature of the relationship between his characters. This scene unfolds to become one in which we see that Harper is actually asking her employer, Elwood, for time off to visit her sick father. In the process of this disclosure, we are invited to be fascinated by and fearful of the sexual tension between the two characters in equal measure.

As discussed earlier in this section, such sexual tension is, of course, equally evident (and equally unnerving) in Stephens's depiction of the relationship between Nora and Dr Rank, and of the triangular relationship between these two characters and Torvald – one which is also frequently imbued with fascinating and fearful silences. Stephens observes how his favourite moment in his version of *A Doll's House* is 'when Torvald leaves Rank and Nora on the sofa alone to get his cigar. They sit in silence. They can't speak. The level of love and sadness and fear of death in them is utterly extraordinary and moves them beyond words' (2016: 67).

Stephens's portrayal of subtly unnerving sexual tension (coupled with painfully long periods of silence) in both *Harper Regan* and *A Doll's House* will surely not go unnoticed among audiences familiar with both plays, and would certainly be noted by spectators who are familiar with some of those other English translations of *A Doll's House* that, as pointed out by Bull earlier in this section, do not suggest anywhere near as much sexual awareness on the part of Nora as Stephens does.

Another dimension of Harper Regan that is strongly reflected in Stephens's Nora is the relationship that both characters have with what they perceive as *truth*. Against the background of her husband's supposed paedophilia and her father's concealed sexuality, Harper declares towards the end of the play, 'I've decided I'm going to do my best to try to stop lying all the time. Too many people do that, I think' (Stephens 2011: 291). Like other characters in Stephens's own plays written before and after *Harper Regan* (such as, say, Peter in *On the Shore of the Wide World*, 2005, Lilly in *Punk Rock*, 2009, and Steve in *Marine Parade*, 2010, to name but a few), Harper seeks her own peace through telling the truth, both to others and to herself. As Stephens says, 'In these characters' attempts to be honest there is a kind of dignity' (2011: xix).

Stephens's Nora, meanwhile, is also arguably fixated on the notion of truth to a greater extent than Ibsen's Nora. In the above chain of implicatures, for example, we see Nora switch from having a rather ambivalent attitude towards truth in segment 4 to sneering at the faux authenticity of her relationship with Torvald in segment 11. If we compare Stephens's Nora's defiant outburst following her discovery of the seriousness of her fraudulent forgery of her father's signature at the end of Act I ...

> **NORA:** It's not true. It's not true. It's not true. It's not true.
>
> (Stephens 2012b: 46)

... with Ibsen's Nora's search for a more logical solution in which possibility is privileged over truth ...

> **NORA:** Å hva! Det er ikke så. Det er umulig. Det ma være unmulig.
>
> (Ibsen [1879] 2013: 60)
>
> *My literal translation: Oh what! It isn't so. It's impossible. It must be impossible.*

... it's not unlikely that Stephens's audiences will infer a more heartfelt, but also more misguided, quest for honour and self-respect in his Nora than might be the case for more literal translations of Ibsen's text (e.g. Meyer's rather stoical 'It's nonsense. It must be. It's impossible. It must be impossible,' 1985: 54). Ultimately, Stephens's Nora seeks to see herself for who she truly is. And like the Nora whom Stephens's audience sees, she is unlikely to find anything other than cold comfort in that truth. For while audiences will undoubtedly applaud Racheal and Harper for embarking on their own journeys of self-realization, Stephens offers us less evidence that Nora will find peace once she arrives at her own truth – nor are we necessarily invited to wish her a peaceful conclusion.

A final character created by Stephens that I would briefly like to explore in this context is Cathy, the main female character in his 2014 play *Blindsided*. Presented to the public for the first time almost two years after Stephens's Nora first appeared on stage, Cathy is an example of a character who has been influenced *by* Nora, rather than the other way around. As Stephens himself says, 'I think the influences of the two plays on one another were unconscious. I was drawn to a trapped, dislocated young female character responding to a cumulated pressure with an action of extremity, perhaps. I think I was working on *Blindsided* some time after *A Doll's House*, but it got into my blood, that play.'[2] And here, we should, of course, bear in mind that the time at which Stephens was writing *Blindsided* was most probably the same time at which *A Doll's House* was enjoying its first run at the Young Vic theatre. Given the media attention that the Young Vic production attracted, including many interviews with Stephens himself, it would seem wholly likely that the two works were occupying Stephens's attention at the same time.

Blindsided was Stephens's most party-political play to date at the time it was first performed at the Royal Exchange Theatre in Manchester. We witness what Bolton calls the 'deracination of social, cultural and generational bonds' that Thatcherism unleashed on UK society following the 1979 election (2014: iii). And while the social revolution in nineteenth-century Norway that Ibsen foresaw in *A Doll's House* is in no way directly comparable to the ideological reorientation seen in the UK during the 1980s, there's nonetheless a sense in which both Nora and her husband Torvald on the one hand, and Cathy and her partner John on the other, are all in their own way metaphors for societies on the cusp of radical social upheaval. Both couples act not only as protagonists but also as victims of this upheaval. Moreover, both couples' stories remain unfinished, leaving spectators to decide what the ultimate fate of all four characters is from their position as more knowing observers of what was to come in their respective societies.

While Nora, unlike Cathy, might never have killed any of her children, there are some telling parallels between the way in which Stephens interprets Ibsen's Nora and the way in which he develops his own character Cathy. Most importantly, Stephens clearly appears to follow a path in both plays that culminates in us having some sympathy, but little empathy, with the leading female character because of the means by which they both seek to undo the damage caused by their relationships. As *Guardian* theatre critic Lyn Gardner concludes in her review of *Blindsided*, 'This is not a play that you respond to with your brain; it's a play that you feel in your bones. The characters are undeniably odd and yet undeniably alive. Alienated and not always lovable, they are nonetheless compulsively watchable, contrarily human' (2014: n.p.).

Spectators who see *Blindsided* after *A Doll's House* will almost certainly recognize in Cathy the same desperate need to be loved and feel secure that Nora reveals. Compare, for example, Nora's love of the material security that Torvald provides for her (see segment 4 in Figure 6.2) with the absoluteness of Cathy's love for John.

CATHY: When I'm with you, I don't worry about the things that have happened to me and I don't worry about the things that are going to happen to me. I don't worry about Ruthy (her daughter). I feel I'm kind of just there.
JOHN: I've known you three days Cathy.
CATHY: I can get rather attached to people quite suddenly. (Stephens 2014a: 12)

Similarly, Nora's claim to her friend Kristine in segment 10 about her life being about to change finds its echo in Cathy's sinister admission to her friend Isaac that she has a plan to surprise her boyfriend John (the plan, as we discover later, being to murder her daughter).

> **CATHY:** I came up with a brilliant idea. I can't tell you what it is because it'd really surprise you and you'd probably try and stop me or you'd tell the police and then things would just go from bad to worse.
> **ISAAC:** Cathy why would I tell the police?
> **CATHY:** You wouldn't really. But I bet you'd try and stop me… (Stephens 2014a: 62)

Ultimately, of course, even if their crimes are in no way comparable, both Nora and Cathy are characters 'whose transgression is against the unfeeling and unsympathetic laws created by male-dominated society, but whose deeper motives are honourable and admirable' (McFarlane 1989: 236). The crisis that both of them face is therefore not entirely of their own doing, and the emancipation that emerges from their respective crises again reminds us of their emotional strength more than their emotional frailty. The same thing cannot be said of some of the men in Nora's life, as we shall now see.

Stephens and emotionally damaged characters

Emotional frailty is, of course, at the heart of much powerful drama of any era and in any language. And one of Ibsen's frequent themes in this respect is the frailty that results from what McFarlane terms the 'ironic disparity' between what a character thinks and what other characters in that situation (and the audiences observing it) know to be the reality – 'where a character, because of some delusion or misapprehension or prejudice or ignorance or mental sickness or hypnotic suggestion cannot or will not grasp the realities of the case' (1989: 91). In Stephens's work, meanwhile, emotional frailty is framed more in terms of his characters' 'childlike sense of wonder at the world' (Rebellato 2005: 176). This then invites an idealistic view of that world that, on the one hand, saves those characters from confronting the worst aspects of their lives but, on the other hand, breeds a dysfunctional relationship with reality that can sometimes lead to implosion.

The character in *A Doll's House* who best exemplifies such ironic disparity and dysfunctional idealism is Nora's husband, Torvald. Characters in other plays by Ibsen who would also fit this description include Helene Alving in *Ghosts* (1881), Hjalmar Ekdal in *Vildanden* (*The Wild Duck,* 1884), Hedda Gabler in the play of the same name (1890), and Halvard Solness in *The Master Builder* (1892), to name just a few. In the chain of implicatures shown in Figure 6.3, we can see in both the source and target texts how Torvald goes from gently belittling Nora to aggressively infantilizing and ridiculing her as the reality of their relationship slowly dawns on him.

No.	Ibsen's source text (Ibsen [1879] 2013)	My literal translation	Strong implicature	Stephens's target text (Stephens 2012b)	Potential chain of weak implicatures
1	HELMER: Er det lerkefuglen som kvidrer der ute? (...) HELMER: Er det ekornet som romsterer der? (6)	HELMER: Is it the lark bird twittering out there? (...) HELMER: Is that the squirrel rummaging there?	Torvald belittles Nora by comparing her to a bird/squirrel.	TORVALD: Is that *a little swallow* out there? (3) (...) TORVALD: Can I hear *a chaffinch* fluttering around my house? (4)	Torvald constantly dismisses Nora as a less powerful partner in their relationship.
2	HELMER: Har nu lille spillefuglen vært ute og satt penge ver styr igjen? (8)	HELMER: Has the little bird been out and squandered money again?	Torvald scolds Nora for spending too much of his money.	TORVALD: Has my hamster been spending all of *my money* again? (4)	Torvald actively seeks to control Nora.
3	NORA: Er jeg ikke også snill at jeg føyer deg? HELMER: Snill – fordi du føyer din mann? Nå, nå, du lille galning, jeg vet nok du mente det ikke så. (70)	NORA: Am I not also nice to indulge you? HELMER: Nice – because you indulge your husband? Well, well, you little rogue, I know you didn't mean it like that.	Torvald puts Nora down and reminds her of his power over her.	NORA: You're lucky I like indulging you so much. TORVALD: Lucky? I'm your husband. *It's your job to indulge me.* (55)	Torvald starts to slowly destroy Nora's sense of her own self-worth.
4	HELMER: Tror du at du er meg mindre kjær fordi du ikke forstår å handle på egen hånd? Nei, nei; stött du deg bara til meg; jeg skal råde deg; jeg skal veilede deg. Jeg måtte ikke være en mann hvis ikke nettopp denne kvinnelige hjælpeløshet gjorde deg dobbelt tiltrekkende in mine øyne. (134)	HELMER: Do you think you are less dear to me because you don't understand how to act on your own? No, no; just lean on me; I shall advise you; I shall direct you. I should not be a man if precisely this female helplessness did not make you doubly attractive in my eyes.	Torvald criticizes Nora for being a woman who is unable to think for herself.	TORVALD: I actually find your lack of insight and lack of ability to know what to do rather attractive. *It makes me realise that I am a man and you are a woman.* (101)	Torvald's abuse takes on a new dimension as he seeks to dominate Nora intellectually.
5	HELMER: (En mann) har liksom satt henne inn i verden på ny; hun er på en måte blitt både hans hustru og hans barn tillike. (134)	HELMER: (A man) has somehow put her into the world anew; she has in a way become his wife and his child at the same time.	Torvald infantalizes Nora by reminding her how much he looks after her.	TORVALD: In a way it's like I've given you a new life. In a way it's a little bit like you're my wife and you've also *now become my child*. (101)	Torvald exerts his control over Nora by seeking a parental role over her.
6	TORVALD: Du er syk, Nora; du har feber; jeg tror nesten du er fra sans og samling. (142)	TORVALD: You're ill, Nora; you've got a fever; I almost think you're mad (*literally beyond sense and concentration on*).	Torvald tells Nora that he thinks she is mentally disturbed.	TORVALD: You're ill, you're *going out of your mind*. (106)	Torvald subtly undermines Nora by questioning her sanity.

Figure 6.3 Chain of weak implicatures implying emotionally damaged characters.

One of the most overt ways in which Ibsen's Torvald belittles his wife is his constant reference (particularly in Act I) to Nora as an animal (see, for example, segments 1 and 2 in Figure 6.3) –as a *lerkefugl (lark*, seven times), *spillefugl ('play bird'*, four times), *sangfugl (songbird*, twice), *spøgefugl ('jester bird'*, once), *fugl (bird*, once) or *ekorn (squirrel*, three times). On one occasion Nora also refers to herself as a *lark* and a *squirrel* (Ibsen [1879] 2013: 12). Stephens's version, meanwhile, features fewer (fourteen) references to Nora as an animal, made either by Torvald or by Nora in response to or in anticipation of Torvald belittling her. But Stephens's choice of animal is somewhat different – he makes six references to *swallow*, five to *skylark*, two to *hamster* and one to *chaffinch*. Moreover, the context of these references is often much more overtly passive-aggressive than in Ibsen's text (see later in this section). These instances (just a few of many that slowly serve to build a tension between Torvald and Nora) also show us how Stephens's version takes on a particularly sinister tone that ultimately results in Nora being the one who questions her own sanity rather than Torvald.

To give another example of how Stephens ramps up Torvald's emotional failings, we see in Ibsen's source text how duty, combined with fear and a sense of his own inadequacy, drives Torvald to defend his own professional position and his role in the household. This represents *his* only hope of freedom and self-fulfilment, just as Nora's only hope is to escape. Once Torvald sees that Nora is no longer willing or able to play the role of the subservient wife, this inevitably forces him to question his own role, values and behaviour. But whereas in Ibsen's version Torvald is often simply conforming to a caricature of male social and moral behaviour in a patriarchal and class-ridden culture (albeit a particularly extreme one), the emotional turmoil and moral weakness of Stephens's Torvald is also conditioned by Stephens's portrayal of the impact of societal and familial pressures on Torvald's life – such as, say, the pressure to look after his family financially, or the pressure to seek promotion at work.

Stephens thereby gives Torvald's frailty a much bleaker dimension than Ibsen does. As Bolton says, 'Characters in Stephens's plays … demonstrate an ongoing improvisation of moral, societal and familial values, an improvisation engendered by the twentieth century's erosion of such ideological certainties such as organized religion, elected government and the nuclear family' (2013: 103). A particular consequence of this erosion is Stephens's characters frequent inability to connect with one another. Stephens himself points out that he is often drawn to duologues or monologues as a means of distilling the worlds of his characters. 'There are many reasons for this, but among them must be an interest in dramatising a world that seems to be more atomised and fractured than it has been in the past and subsequently scorched by a need and an inability to connect' (2009: xxi).

Torvald's inability to connect with Nora is certainly a theme that Stephens utilizes to the full in his version of *A Doll's House*, as seen in all the segments in Figure 6.3. What's more, the exchange between the two characters in the final part of Act III of Stephens's text (when Nora announces her desire to end their marriage) reveals an even more dysfunctional relationship between the two than Ibsen's dialogue does – and one that's likely to result in spectators' sympathies veering much more dramatically between Torvald and Nora than a different audience might during a performance of the source text. In particular, Stephens's Torvald is arguably even more lacking in emotional intelligence than Ibsen's Torvald. We can see this, for example, in the even more sinister dialogue in segments 3 and 4 in Figure 6.3, which reveals Torvald's total lack of empathy for Nora's situation and an inability to see the world from any perspective other than his own.

Such manipulation of Nora under the pretext of seeking to preserve the appearance of a wealthy and righteous household does, in many ways, mirror the way in which many other characters in Stephens's plays value outward demonstrations of material success above all else. Bolton, for example, describes how Stephens's 2009 play *Pornography* 'dramatizes the devaluation and insidious erosion of qualities such as tolerance, trust, generosity, kindness and empathy. Values and lexicons forged in the crucible of consumer capitalism infiltrate private as well as public spheres, co-opting everyday relations into miniature narratives of transaction and exploitation' (2013: 119). We can also compare Torvald's lack of emotional literacy to the behaviour of Peter in Stephens's Olivier award-winning play *On the Shore of the Wide World* (2005). Here, it's only as his father Charlie lies dying that Peter appears able to articulate his resentment towards him for maltreating his mother – just as Torvald only starts to realize his own capacity for change as he sees his marriage to Nora falling apart.

> **PETER:** Alex told me [you hit Mum]. Christopher [*Peter's other son*] saw you.
> **CHARLIE:** What kind of a – I don't believe you're – I never hit your mother. Not ever.
> **PETER:** I don't believe you. I believe Christopher more than I believe you. He makes you look like a liar.
> **CHARLIE:** Peter, I –
> **PETER:** I wanted to tell you. I can't be like you any more.
> **CHARLIE:** What are you talking about?
> **PETER:** You know. I should have told you a long time ago. (*Pause*) I should be going. (Stephens 2011: 99)

Described by Billington as 'a deeply English play about our national capacity for evasion' and one that ultimately reminds us how 'families are often bound together by guilt, shame and secrecy' (2005: n.p.), there are many resonances here with the Helmers' family life that spectators who are familiar with *On the Shore of the Wide World* will recognize – the sparse conversations that constantly seem to be holding something back, the restrictions imposed by having to constantly live up to others' expectations and the cathartic effect of unburdening a lifetime of frustrations onto those we are meant to be close to.

On top of this, Stephens's Torvald also shows stronger hints of a disturbing mental imbalance than is apparent in Ibsen's Torvald – to the extent that, in a modern-day context, his behaviour would potentially be considered a form of emotional abuse. Consider, for example, the stages Torvald passes through in the segments in Figure 6.3 – from behaving in a passive-aggressive way to exerting overt control and manipulation, followed by an attempt at reconciliation before trying to transfer his own loss of sanity onto Nora. Such emotional abuse, nowadays commonly referred to as *gaslighting*, would now been recognized in the UK as a crime under the Serious Crime Act of

2015. This Act created a new offence of controlling or coercive behaviour in intimate or familial relationships that carries a maximum sentence of five years' imprisonment, a fine or both (Home Office 2015: n.p.). Again, this type of behaviour is something of a regular theme in Stephens's work, and one that may well resonate with spectators of *A Doll's House* who are familiar with situations that occur in some of his earlier plays – for example, the abuse suffered by Billy at the hands of a gang of teenagers on his council estate in *Herons* (2001), Bennett's bullying of Tanya and Chadwick in *Punk Rock* (2009), and Sian's manipulation of Jonathan in *Wastwater* (2011).

Importantly, Stephens acknowledges that he accentuated the connotations of mental illness in his version of *A Doll's House* as a way of optimizing the credibility of Torvald's behaviour towards Nora in Act III.

> I remember working on [Act III] and thinking this is where we lose the audience. … And so there were two decisions made about that, one was the introduction of the possibility that Torvald's illness, which is very vague and unspecific in the literal, very probably was a kind of mental breakdown, so there's a character with a backstory of erratic psychological behaviour. And the other thing was to really amp up the amount of booze he'd had. (2014c: n.p.)

The role of alcohol and alcoholism in shaping a character's physical and emotional behaviour is certainly a theme that Stephens has explored previously in his own work on several occasions. Examples of characters in whose lives alcohol looms large include Billy's mother in *Herons*, Jamie in *Country Music* (2004), Peter in *On the Shore of the Wide World*, Danny in *Motortown* (2006), and virtually all the characters in *Three Kingdoms* (2011). So it should be no surprise to spectators familiar with this work that it emerges again in *A Doll's House*. And Stephens himself is well aware of why this is so.

> I come from a family of alcoholics. My dad died when he was fifty-nine of alcohol-related illness. … As a writer that's something you're going to return to and obsess about. … So it's not surprising that in my version [of *A Doll's House*] themes that have haunted me like compassionate consideration of mental illness and an interrogation of alcoholism and the presence of alcoholism in our culture … should be underlined and revealed. (2014c: n.p.)

References to alcohol are indeed more prevalent in Stephens's version of *A Doll's House* than in Ibsen's source text. Indeed, they potentially serve to create another small chain of weak implicatures, as can be seen in Figure 6.4.

Here, it's clear how Stephens's version accentuates the theme of alcohol far more than Ibsen's version does. Segments 2 and 3 in Figure 6.4 have no equivalent in the source text at all, and segment 1 contains an explicit reference to the amount of wine that Torvald has ordered for Christmas Eve, which again doesn't feature in Ibsen's text. This, then, is a very obvious example of Stephens injecting something of his own voice or agenda into his version – perhaps as a result of the belief that alcohol fuels Torvald's anger towards Nora on discovering the letter from Krogstad, or is behind Nora's decision to leave her family. This would appear consistent with Stephens's suggestion

No.	Ibsen's source text (Ibsen [1879] 2013)	My literal translation	Strong implicature	Stephens's target text (Stephens 2012b)	Potential chain of weak implicatures
1	HELMER: God vin har jeg bestelt. Nora, du kan ikke tro hvor jeg gleder meg til i aften. NORA: Jeg også. (14)	HELMER: I have ordered good wine. Nora, you cannot believe how I am looking forward to this evening. NORA: Me too.	Torvald has ordered some good wine so that they will enjoy Christmas Eve.	TORVALD: I'm rather excited about tonight. NORA: I am too. TORVALD: I did take the liberty of ordering one or two rather decent bottles of wine, I'm afraid. NORA: Or three. Or four. (10)	Torvald makes it clear to Nora that he intends to drink heavily on Christmas Eve.
2	(does not appear in the source text)			TORVALD: So. We're having a party now, are we? NORA: Yes. We are. We're going to drink champagne now until the morning rises. (79)	Torvald and Nora both appear to be slowly getting drunk.
3	(does not appear in the source text)			RANK: *The wine, tonight, was just splendid –* TORVALD: *The champagne, especially.* RANK: *Beautifully dry. Méthode champenoise. It is almost incredible how much of it I managed to wash down.* NORA: *Almost as much as Torvald, I'm sure.* RANK: *Is that right?* NORA: *And now he's really a little bit drunk.* (91)	Alcohol will play a role in Torvald's and Nora's subsequent argument, and in Nora's and Dr Rank's sexually suggestive behaviour towards one another.

Figure 6.4 Chain of weak implicatures implying drunkenness.

(cited in the previous section) that Nora will return home the next day, hung over and apologetic.

Irrespective of any awareness of alcohol and alcoholism being a thread running through much of Stephens's previous work, this theme of alcohol will become obvious to spectators of Stephens's version if they read the interview with Stephens contained in the programme for the London productions of *A Doll's House* entitled 'Drinking and Madness – Simon Stephens on *A Doll's House*' (an extended version of which is available online, see Stephens 2014c). This is an example of what Gérard Genette would term *epitext* (i.e. a paratextual element outside of and at some distance from the primary text), and of how epitexts can play a strong role in shaping reception of that primary text (1997: 344). It would certainly be interesting to speculate to what extent this interview *might* have influenced spectators' spontaneous inferences from Stephens's text in situ, that is, in the theatre itself, either before the start of the play or during the interval, or immediately afterwards.

In the meantime, however, I'd like to explore how one final theme throughout much of Stephens's work might be inferred in his version of *A Doll's House* – the recurrent topic of home, homecoming and what home really means.

Stephens and the constant search for home

The concept of home was a regular theme in Ibsen's own work, both literally and symbolically. Whether in the context of the marital or family home (as in *A Doll's House*), the home town or home country (as in *Peer Gynt*), or the artificially created home (the seamen's home in *Ghosts*), the relationship that Ibsen's characters' have with home is perhaps as complex and ambivalent as Ibsen's own relationship with Norway – the country of his birth yet one he lived away from for twenty-seven years. Certainly, there's often a sense in Ibsen's work of an escape from home being the only way to achieve self-reliance: 'to flee the place that stunts one's growth, stifles one's breath, distorts one's values and kills one's opportunities' (McFarlane 1989: 240).

This is certainly something with which Stephens would also undoubtedly identify. His own home town, Stockport, features in a number of his plays, both as a place that his characters are desperate to escape from in order to seek a better life (e.g. William in *Punk Rock*, Alex in *On the Shore of the Wide World* and Cathy in *Blindsided*) and also as one that his characters sometimes also return to in the hope of finding a more authentic version of themselves (e.g. Rachael in *Port* and Harper in *Harper Regan*). Likewise, characters in other plays also seek to move from and to other cities to discover where home is – for example, Danny in *Motortown*, who returns home to London after fighting in the Iraq war, or Sally in *Marine Parade* (2010), who seeks to escape London to return home to Newcastle. In all of these plays, Stephens shows 'a fascination with the potential and the struggle of individuals to negotiate transience, to locate and communicate a self, to understand and to be understood' (Bolton 2013: 101). This is sometimes achieved by means of the spatial environment that those individuals find themselves in or back in, and that they in many cases learn to understand as home –

whether this is an individual building, a community of individuals or the city in whose streets their lives are played out. At the same time, as director Sarah Frankcom notes, it's also often achieved in the way that Stephens's work examines 'what you can learn by journey[ing], what people experience from changing their circumstances ... how journeys can be your undoing or how they can be your salvation' (cited in Bolton 2013: 110).

Let's now explore in Figure 6.5 a chain of weak implicatures in Stephens's version of *A Doll's House* to see how audiences might infer this theme the constant search for (a) home if they are familiar with Stephens's previous work.

Looking at Ibsen's text in Figure 6.5, it's difficult not to agree with McFarlane's view that, in spite of Nora's delight in her house as a symbol of her husband's professional success, this particular home represents a claustrophobic trap from which she is perhaps destined to escape. 'For the married woman of Nora's day, the "home" could be just as disabling as for the child; Nora finds herself reduced to the level of a home-comfort, something that merely contributes to the husband's domestic well-being and flatters *his* ego at the cost of destroying hers. She becomes a possession' (1989: 242). In this respect, the very fact that Ibsen called his play *Et dukkehjem* (*A doll's home*) and not *Et dukkehus* (*A doll's house*) suggests that Ibsen is reminding us that Nora and their children are being treated as playthings for Torvald's delight in what is supposed to be a place of refuge, comfort, security and love. In fact, the term *dukkehjem* at the time of writing the play was used more to describe a small, neat home. It was only as a result of Ibsen's play that it took on a more pejorative connotation (Törnqvist 1995: 54) – something that modern-day spectators of the play in translation would be unlikely to infer unless they were particularly familiar with the Dano-Norwegian of Ibsen's time.

In Stephens's version, meanwhile, Nora and Torvald's home is likely to be understood less as a metaphor for claustrophobia and control, and more as a place in which characters seek to assert their own identity, and in which they discover the incompatibility of their respective identities. In segment 2 in Figure 6.5, for example, Stephens's text inevitably carries with it greater connotations of Nora actively shaping her home to suit her own needs, tastes and perceived status – and not least because it's inferred at a time of even more conspicuous consumption than in Ibsen's time, and in an era in which opportunities for home beautification are much greater than they would have been in the nineteenth century. Likewise in segment 5, Torvald's attempts to sexually arouse his wife after she has danced for him might nowadays appear more like the ramblings of a drunk than the coercive voice of a domineering master. Finally, the fact that Stephens's Nora reminds us of *where she has come from* indicates a more circular concept of her impending journey back to her roots than Ibsen's less emotive reference to her *old homestead*.

And whereas Ibsen's text is likely to suggest an enforced and not entirely satisfying journey of self-discovery on the part of Nora (a return to a place of little excitement, but one that will at least enable her to view her life in a simple and honest environment uncluttered by material trappings), Stephens's Nora is more likely to be inferred as a woman on the verge of a challenging voyage of genuine self-realization – one that will enable her to find a sense of purpose and (re)discover her true identity. Of course, as we saw earlier in this chapter, this is not to say that Stephens wants us to *like* the real

No.	Ibsen's source text (Ibsen [1879] 2013)	My literal translation	Strong implicature	Stephens's target text (Stephens 2012b)	Potential chain of weak implicatures
1	FRU LINDE: Bare så usigelig tom. Ingen å leve for mer. Derfor hold jeg det ikke lenger ut der borte i den lille avkrok. Her må det dog være lettere å finne noe som kan legge beslag på en og oppta ens tanker. (22)	MRS LINDE: Just so unspeakably empty. Nothing to live for any more. So I couldn't stand it any more in the little backwater. Here it must be easier to find something that will absorb one's attention and occupy one's thoughts.	Mrs Linde was bored and sought a more interesting life in the city.	KRISTINE: *I couldn't stand being at home*. The place started to feel so horribly remote. I thought it would be easier to find work here. I need work that will challenge me. I need something that can make me think. (17)	Home as a stifling environment that Kristine is desperate to escape.
2	NORA: Sorgløs! Å kunne være sorgløs, ganske sorgløs! Å kunne leke og tumle seg med børnene; å kunne har det smukt og nydelig i huset, all ting således som Torvald setter pris på det. (32)	NORA: Carefree! To be able to be carefree, quite carefree! To be able to play and tumble with the children; to have everything beautiful and lovely at home, everything just as Torvald appreciates it.	Nora is relieved to be free of her financial burden and to live a carefree life.	NORA: I'm free to do anything I want to do. To play with my children all day if I want to. *To stroll around a beautiful and neat and elegant home*. To have everything exactly the way Torvald likes it. (22)	Home as a symbol of security and status.
3	HELMER: En sånn dunstkrets av løgn bringer smitte og sykdomsstoff inn i et helt hjems liv. Hvert åndedrag som børnene tar i et sånt hus, er fylt med spirer til noe stygt. (60)	HELMER: Such a ring of fumes of lies brings infection and disease into a whole home's life. Every breath that the children take in such a house is filled with, grows into something horrible.	Torvald is critical of Krogstad for lying to cover up his forgery.	TORVALD: *To lie in a family home diseases the place*. It contaminates it. The children can, they can breathe it. (45)	Home as a place of openness and honesty.
4	NORA: Torvald holder jo så ubeskrivelig meget av meg; og derfor vil han eie meg ganske alene, som han sier. I den første tid ble han liksom skinnsyk bare jeg nevnte noen av de kjære menneskene der hjemme. Så lot jeg det naturligvis være. (68)	NORA: Torvald thinks so indescribably much of me; and so he wants to possess me all on his own, as he says. At first he was somehow jealous even if I just mentioned some of the dear people at home. So of course I let it be.	Nora is willing to lose contact with her friends from home so that Torvald will no longer be jealous.	NORA: (Torvald) is so unthinkably fond of me that he wants to keep me all to himself. *He used to be quite jealous if I even mentioned the names of anybody from back home*. So I stopped mentioning them. (52)	Home as a reminder of childhood/youth and of belonging.

No.	Ibsen's source text (Ibsen [1879] 2013)	My literal translation	Strong implicature	Stephens's target text (Stephens 2012b)	Potential chain of weak implicatures
5	HELMER: Da forestiller jeg meg at du er min unge brud, at vi nettopp kommer fra vielsen, at jeg for første gang er alene med deg, – ganske alene med deg, du unge skjelvende deilighet! (120)	HELMER: I imagine that you're my young bride, that we are just coming from the wedding, that I'm alone with you for the first time, you young trembling loveliness.	Torvald is aroused by Nora's dancing and tries to force himself on to her.	TORVALD: I imagine that you are my young bride and we have only just been married that night and *I am taking you to my home for the first time*. That I will be alone with you for the first time. (90)	Home as a place of control (for both Nora and Torvald).
6	NORA: I morgen reiser jeg hjem, – jeg mener, til mitt gamle hjemsted. Det vil det være lettest for meg å komme inn i et eller annet. (140)	NORA: Tomorrow I shall go home – I mean to my old homestead. It will be easiest for me to get into one or another thing.	Nora decides to return to the place of her youth in order to seek some stability.	NORA: *Tomorrow I'll go back home. To where I came from.* It will be easier for me to find something to do there. (105)	Home as a place of refuge and a simpler life.
7	NORA: Jeg kan ikke bli liggende natten over i en fremmed manns værelser. (146)	NORA: I cannot spend the night in a strange man's room.	Nora makes it clear to Torvald that she feels no emotional attachment to him.	NORA: I can't spend the night *in a stranger's house*. (108)	Home as a place of emotional closeness.

Figure 6.5 Chain of weak implicatures implying a search for home.

Nora that lurks under the surface of the Nora we see in his version of *A Doll's House*. Rather, he wishes us to at least admire her search for a place (physical or otherwise) with which she can find a true connection.

There's an obvious connection between the way in which Stephens articulates the theme of home and homecoming in *A Doll's House* and the way in which he explores the same theme in one of his other plays, *The Curious Incident of the Dog in the Night-Time*. This latter work is also an adaptation, but this time an intralingual adaptation of Mark Haddon's 2003 book of the same name. Stephens's play opened at the National Theatre in July 2012, just a few weeks after *A Doll's House* opened at the Young Vic. It transferred to the West End in March 2013, and ran there until June 2017. The play, like the book, tells the story of the journey that fifteen-year-old Christopher undergoes in search of the killer of his neighbour's dog and explores how we cope with the shocks that can tear our familiar world apart. It won praise (not least in the form of an Olivier Award for Best New Play in 2013) for its touching depiction of the world as seen through the eyes of a boy with behavioural problems (commonly assumed to be the result of Asperger's syndrome, although Haddon himself has always refused to confirm this, see Singh 2015: n.p.).

While *The Curious Incident of the Dog in the Night-Time* and *A Doll's House* might not obviously share a similar audience, there is arguably considerable potential, at least at a hypothetical level, for London theatregoers to have seen both plays – and possibly also to have seen them in quick succession if they are particularly interested in Stephens's work. With this in mind, it's interesting to note, as Stephens himself does, that both plays share an *identical* line of dialogue.

> Two years ago, *A Doll's House* and *The Curious Incident of the Dog in the Night-Time* were in rehearsal at the same time. I noticed that both plays had the same line in them. 'I could never spend the night in a stranger's house.' Possibly this was because I am a lazy writer. But rather I think it's because both texts, generated by other writers and responding to specific sources – Mark Haddon's novel and Henrik Ibsen's play – resonated in some way with what I found myself returning to as a writer. I write again and again about characters needing to leave home but terrified of its impossibility; or struggling to live away from home; or having left home being unable to ever return. (2016: 180)

This begs the question as to whether Stephens's work on Ibsen's play influenced his work on his version of Haddon's book, or whether it was actually the other way around. In any event, Stephens's recurrent themes of home and family (and the attachment and detachment that his characters experience in relation to these) are such common tropes in his work (whether his original plays or his adaptations) that audiences may immediately recognize them in either or both of these productions – and even more so if they attended performances of both within a short period of time.

As an aside, it should also be noted how much *A Doll's House* and *The Curious Incident of the Dog in the Night-Time* are both 'an obsessive interrogation of honesty and dishonesty' (Stephens, cited in Rees 2012: n.p.) – in *A Doll's House* because of the trauma caused by the lies that Nora felt forced to tell, and in *The Curious Incident of the Dog in the Night-Time* because of Christopher's inability to lie (an acknowledged trait of those with Asperger's syndrome). Here, there's clearly potential for a synergistic effect, with the themes of the search for home and the search for honesty combining to create an overarching theme of home being the one place in which we should be able to be totally honest with others and with ourselves – something that Torvald alludes to in segment 3 in Figure 6.4, and something that Christopher, whose home is ultimately the world in which he lives alone with his thoughts, also demonstrates vividly.

The questions of what home really is, whether we can actually leave it, and whether it is ever possible to return to it, have run throughout Stephens's original work since his 1998 play *Bluebird*. It should not be surprising, therefore, that they feature heavily in his adaptations as well. Stephens tackles this theme in his own work from a number of different perspectives – from a bleak assessment of the impact of urban brutality on teenagers' sense of belonging in *Herons*, to an examination of the need to reconnect with an estranged family in *Harper Reagan*, and an intense exploration of the impact on a character of having to return home due to a death in the family in *Song from Far Away* (2015). In this latter play, we watch how the only character, Willem, reflects on the distance that he feels from his family, even when forced to be the same physical space as them. Having returned to Amsterdam from his home in New York for his brother's funeral, Willem recounts some home truths that his father told him shortly before his departure.

> **WILLEM:** I was washing up after dinner when Dad came in. He asked me if I was staying at the Lloyd again tonight. I told him I was. He said that was probably for the best. I asked him why. 'I know you never liked Pauli. The way you talked about him when you were children. And when he got older all he wanted was for you to ask him to go and see you and stay with you for a while. Of course you didn't. But he was your brother, Willem. You come back home. You won't stay at the house. You go to the funeral. You stare at everybody. You don't even try to look sad.'
> (Stephens 2015: 18)

This contrast between the home and the house (between Willem's actual home in New York and his temporary home in the Lloyd Hotel in Amsterdam), and the historical, geographical and physical barriers that we can choose to erect to help us define our own sense of home are also heard strongly throughout Stephens's adaptation of *A Doll's House* (see all the segments in Figure 6.4). They perhaps culminate in Nora's realization in Act III that her home life with Torvald has been built on a lie.

> **TORVALD:** Are you trying to tell me that you've never been happy here?
> **NORA:** Never. Not happy.
> **TORVALD:** You ungrateful, unreasonable –
> **NORA:** I've been cheerful. That's not the same. You've always been very kind to me. But none of this was real, you know? This wasn't really a house. It was a playroom. I've been your doll. (2012b: 104)

Bolton's analysis of these different ways in which Stephens depicts home could almost serve as a description of the plot of *A Doll's House*.

> The ways in which individual identities are shaped by history and geography constitute a red thread running throughout Stephens's œuvre. Place is often depicted in these plays as a kind of expression of the self, a proposition treated, however, with some caution: the sense of identity, purpose and belonging imparted by 'home' can at the same time delimit and deny opportunities for change, growth and renewal. (2013: 103)

Stephens's own explanation of why he constantly returns to this theme is one that is ultimately rooted in far more personal reasons. In a similar way to how his father's alcohol-related death has driven the ongoing presence of alcohol and mental health issues in his work, Stephens's own move away from, but constant return to, his hometown Stockport in his work, combined with his subsequent experience of being a father, have clearly also shaped his interest in building a myth around the concept of home. As he himself says, 'Maybe it's to do with parenting. Maybe it's to do with the things that we keep from our children. Maybe it's to do with something broader in our political culture. Maybe it's just something writers have' (cited in Rees 2012: n.p.).

Such a view on the motivations for emphasizing the concept of home in his original plays and his adaptations alike has strong echoes of the Darwinian perspective on literature, namely, that literary works, as products of the adapted mind, reflect and articulate the four basic behavioural systems – survival, sex and mating, parenting and kinship, and group living (Buss 2016). Indeed, literary historian Asbjørn Aarseth has suggested that Ibsen himself was highly interested in Darwin's scientific ideas and that these had a strong influence on his plays (2005: 1–10). It's known, for example, that Ibsen visited J. P. Jakobsen, the translator into Danish of Darwin's two key works, *On the Origin of the Species* (1859) and *The Descent of Man* (1871), while living in Rome in 1878, one year before *A Doll's House* was published (Aarseth 2005: 3). Yet irrespective of whether Darwinism genuinely did influence either Ibsen or Stephens, it remains the case that both playwrights' foregrounding of the theme of the home in their work is perhaps one of the most obvious ways in which we recognize their respective dramatic voices. Here, *home* essentially becomes what evolutionary biologist Richard Dawkins would term a *meme*, that is, a 'unit of cultural transmission' (2016:249).

Celebrity translation and cumulative associations

As Ewbank reminds us, translating Ibsen is never as straightforward as many translators have perhaps believed. 'In Ibsen, tidying up the apparently irregular – in grammar and syntax as well as vocabulary – can play havoc with the verbal structures which he so carefully built. Translations are the more successful, and the more helpful to actors and students, the more they have the courage to show something of Ibsen's strangeness' (1988: 65). Analysis of Stephens's adaptation of Ibsen certainly reveals that he had more than enough courage to show something of Ibsen's strangeness. Such courage undoubtedly comes from being such a renowned playwright in his own right but is also likely to be a function of his particular sensitivity to the issues highlighted in this chapter – to the vulnerability of characters in relationships that are not built on authenticity, to the frailty of characters that have been in some way damaged by their past, and to the problems that so many people have in reconciling the pull–push factors of home with the excitement of making a fresh start elsewhere.

As this chapter has shown, Ibsen's and Stephens's respective versions of *A Doll's House* both rely heavily on extended metaphors around the themes of power, control and belonging, and the impact that the quest for these has on the play's characters and their relationships with one another. It's this closeness to the *poetic effects* of the source text that ultimately led to Stephens's work being critically acclaimed as a 'sensible, sensitive and spirited' version of Ibsen's play (Cavendish 2012: n.p.), but that also, and perhaps somewhat contradictorily, lends Stephens's version its own contemporary relevance and resonance with audiences. As Stephens himself points out, 'It is through metaphor that as audiences we come to understand ourselves. It is through metaphor that we examine our empathy. This examination is, finally for me, the key function of theatre. It is an empathy machine. Its machinations make us better at being human' (2016: 295).

As a consequence, it should not be a surprise that the conclusion we can draw from this case study is that the notion of the *voice of the celebrity translator* extends beyond the attitudinal or verbal peculiarities that characterize that translator's way of writing. It also encompasses more broadly both

1. the *intensity of the poetic effects* of the text that the translator gives to the actors performing that text, and the ways in which such effects cumulatively serve to create a sense that the translator's characters and his depiction of their interaction with one another is very much in his own image, and
2. the *aesthetic merits* of the translated text in terms of its originality and artistry, and the way in which it forces spectators to think in a different way about society and culture – in the case of Stephens's *A Doll's House* to think in a different way about, say, feminism, social change and indeed about Ibsen himself.

At the same time, such notions of what constitutes *voice* in the theatre remind us that, more than any other artistic endeavour, theatre-making is a collaborative effort. As a result, voice in the context of celebrity translation will almost always be inferred as much more than simply a combination of contextual associations with the two authors involved in the process – or, if there's also a literal translator hidden away behind the scenes, the three authors involved in the process. It will also encompass elements of the voice of the actors, the director, the theatre itself and many other influences besides – all of which are, both in themselves and in combination with one another, responsible for triggering their own cognitive effects and able to lay claim to their own aesthetic merits.

I will come back to this issue in the following chapter when I reflect in more detail on the benefits and constraints of concentrating on the page version of a theatre text rather than the stage version. But in the meantime, let's move the discussion away from the purely theoretical and see if there is any evidence in the real world for how celebrity translators might influence audiences' perceptions of a translated play.

7

From the theoretical to the empirical

Testing hypotheses in the real world

The theoretical discussion throughout this book assumes that different spectators will have different cognitive contexts and that by categorizing these different contexts we can start to see how spectators might perceive the explicatures and implicatures of a translated text in different ways. The notion of a range of different cognitive contexts in any one given audience group appears wholly sensible and unquestionable in the sense that no two individuals are likely to share *completely identical* cognitive contexts. Even if spectators might share the same cultural background, interests, viewpoints and so on, their different life experiences will inevitably lead to them interpreting a text in somewhat different ways. Such differences might be as trivial as, say, the difference between reading or not reading a particular press article by a celebrity translator prior to seeing the play in performance, or, in the case of Mark Ravenhill's version of *A Life of Galileo*, as significant as, say, having or not having ancestors who suffered persecution during the Nazi era.

Having said this, as already seen in Chapter 1, the very notion of celebrity by definition implies that there are dominant discourses or influences in contemporary culture that lead to particular groups of individuals in society sharing similar perspectives on an individual in the public eye. It's not important, at least for my argument here, whether such perspectives are real or imaginary, demonstrable or inferred. What does matter, however, is that we can assume the existence of a group of spectators with *relatively* homogenous attitudes towards and beliefs about a celebrity translator. That is because without this construct there would be no cultural, artistic or commercial value attached to one individual over any other – or in other words, there would be no celebrities. Indeed, the commissioning of celebrities as translators (over any unknown translators) would surely defy logic if they were not to bring with them a distinctive, and therefore identifiable, set of expectations.

But again, the notion of a celebrity translator actively altering a spectator's cognitive context remains only a theoretical idea unless we are able to assess what that cognitive context is actually made up of in terms of expectations of the celebrity translator, expectations of the source-text playwright and expectations of a multitude of other factors. Such expectations might arise as a result of the actors appearing in the production (e.g. whether they're already known to a spectator, and from where) to the physical experience of the staging itself (e.g. what the theatre tells us about the prestige attached to the source-text playwright and the celebrity translator, or what the sets tell us about the production budget). But how can we possibly measure what a spectator's cognitive context consists of, and how these different contexts subsequently influence reception of the translated text? In the following sections, I will consider a number of ways in which this might be possible at a practical level.

Researching audiences

Theatre audience research has been explored by a number of academics over the years. Examples include Suleiman and Crosman 1980, Ben Chaim 1984, Dolan 1988 and 2005, Campbell 1996, Bennett 1997, Tulloch 2005 and McConachie 2008, to name but a few. Until the turn of the twenty-first century, much of this research focused on the study of the audience as a cultural phenomenon – a study that, on the one hand, explored the consumption of theatre against a background of audience's different social experiences and, on the other hand, sought to understand the relationship between the theatrical event (i.e. what the audience has come to see) and the local, situated context (i.e. the theatre in which the audience watches that theatrical event), which is of course different for every performance.

Against this background, it's not surprising that there has been little agreement among scholars about how research among audiences should be conducted, and indeed whether such research is likely ever to yield any useful insights about the reception of theatre. Theatre scholar John Tulloch points this out very clearly.

> The [theatrical] event is … an audience event insofar as multiple horizons of expectations are renegotiated before, during and after the theatrical performance. Thus, any flat methodology, such as the familiar quantitative theatre audience surveys … is likely to miss important aspects of the 'live' relationship of negotiation between occasion and place. An audience participates in a performance processually, across a changing temporality before, during and (sometimes long) after the performance. (2005: 7)

In addition, media scholar David Gauntlett reminds us that 'people's brains do not usually contain ready-made lists of "what I think" about any number of issues. … The brain certainly can rise to the challenge of dynamically generating instant answers to an interviewer's questions, but it is not always likely that these responses will be wonderfully impressive, meaningful or "true" to the interviewee's more precise feelings' (2007: 185).

In the context of each of the case studies explored here, then, any attempt to interview spectators about their contextual associations with the source-text and target-text playwrights before and after going to see the play in question assumes that spectators are not only *aware* of those associations but also able to *articulate* them. And in many cases this is probably an unrealistic assumption. That's because individuals are only readily able or willing to articulate those associations and beliefs that they and others are aware of. Other levels of awareness (the unconscious associations) will require more projective questioning techniques before they can be uncovered, which is almost impossible to achieve in a questionnaire-based research methodology, whether such questionnaires are administered face to face, over the telephone or online. This suggests that direct, structured interviews with spectators might not give us a very accurate picture of an audience's cognitive context, and could potentially lead to quite misleading findings. This is to say nothing of the fact that such interviewing could only really be conducted in a very narrow window of time, that is, immediately before and after seeing a performance, to capture spontaneous rather than post-rationalized responses.

Alternatively, we could adopt an ethnographic approach and observe audiences as they are watching a performance of the play. This would enable us to validate some of our assumed implicatures – for example, if, say, we heard certain sectors of the audience laughing more than others at Ravenhill's *dicky* pun explored in Chapter 4. But such an approach is only really appropriate for assessing communal rather than individual responses to communication. It's likely to be difficult, if not impossible, to separate out the responses that are due to spectators' pre-existing contextual associations and those that are due to the reactions of fellow audience members – or what sociologists would term a *ripple effect* (see Long 2001: 65). So actually neither of these two research approaches appears to me to be particularly practical or indeed particularly valuable in isolation.

At best, there would appear to be some value in conducting analysis of *audience types* attending a performance of a celebrity translation versus a translation by a non-celebrity. The aim here would be not so much to try and identify different clusters of spectators sharing similar cognitive contexts but rather to explore my hypothesis that the distinctive set of expectations surrounding a celebrity translator will attract a different audience from that which might be expected from an unknown translator. Analysing different audience types should, in principle at least, be much easier than analysing different cognitive contexts as there are obviously certain tangible characteristics such as demographic data that can be collected and evaluated more easily and more objectively than, say, attitudinal data. While factors such as likely age, socioeconomic status and lifestyle can only ever give us a partial insight into likely mindsets or beliefs, they may at least provide some kind of concrete benchmark against which to make value judgements about particular clusters of individuals. Such judgements can then help to fine-tune more theoretical assumptions or hypotheses about different audience types.

For example, I might hypothesize that *A Life of Galileo* translated by Ravenhill would attract a younger, more socially aware audience because of the pull of Ravenhill himself. This would then support my argument that celebrity translators will potentially attract spectators with cognitive contexts that are different from those who might otherwise attend a play by a given source-text playwright and translated by an unknown translator. But comparing two sets of data would only give us wholly reliable results if they related to spectators of the same play, performed at the same theatre, with the same catchment audience, and at exactly the same time – and with one audience attending a version translated by a celebrity and the other audience attending a version translated by a non-celebrity. This is, of course, a wholly unlikely real-world scenario, and one that could only be replicated in the context of a customized (and hugely expensive) research project.

Perhaps the closest we might ever get to such a situation would be in the case of a theatre festival – such as Birmingham Rep's 2014 Brecht festival mentioned in Chapter 4, which featured Ravenhill's *A Life of Galileo* alongside three other Brecht plays, two of which were translated by non-celebrities. Even here, though, any comparison of audiences is unlikely to yield entirely accurate insights given the different appeal of those different plays, to say nothing of the appeal of the different casts, the ticket prices, the days of the week on which performances were held, whether the productions were new or not and so on – or in other words, all those factors that go to make up the context of theatre production and reception.

Ultimately, then, any demographic and attitudinal data will not in itself give a *precise* indication of individual spectators' or groups of spectators' likely cognitive contexts. So, in the case of Brecht and Ravenhill again, even though we might be able to hypothesize about issues such as, say, spectators' likely political leanings or awareness of twentieth-century political history, we cannot predict with any great certainty what associations spectators might have with one or the other playwright. At best, all we can really do is make assumptions based upon our own entirely subjective analysis of the data. Likewise, without any proven benchmark of a *typical* Brecht or Ravenhill audience (if indeed such an audience actually exists), we cannot say with complete certainty that the involvement of a celebrity translator has *definitely* had an influence on audience profiles or compositions.

So are there any other empirical ways of 'measuring' the influence that a celebrity translator has on audiences? In the next sections, I'll argue that there are.

Analysing reviews and blogs

If we accept that audience research is unlikely to deliver any useful insights into spectators' cognitive contexts, is there at least a practical and relatively reliable way of evaluating the *external influences* that might go towards shaping these different cognitive contexts, and thereby towards influencing the way in which audiences might receive a play translated by a celebrity versus a non-celebrity? One of the external influences that might consciously or unconsciously shape spectators' cognitive contexts is the *opinions of reviewers and bloggers* to which they are exposed before attending a performance of a play. This shaping of their cognitive contexts will then influence the relative extent to which those spectators infer the source-text playwright's and the celebrity translator's voice in that play.

Of course, any analysis of reviews and blogs also remains a somewhat theoretical exercise since it assumes that these external influences are more significant than other influences either on spectators' reception of the performance or on their decision to see that performance in the first place. In the real world, spectators' individual and collective mindsets and decisions will inevitably be shaped by a multitude of other uncontrollable and subjective factors, such as word of mouth, the desire to see particular cast members on stage, loyalty towards their local theatre, special discounts on ticket prices, and much more besides. At the same time, this approach to gauging external influences can go *at least some way* towards explaining why celebrity translators might attract either a different audience from an unknown translator or an audience whose members have a different cognitive context (both individually and collectively) from that of spectators watching a play translated by an unknown translator.

There is certainly some justification for this approach in terms of translation theory. The distinction between individual and collective cognitive contexts largely mirrors Mona Baker's distinction between private (ontological), shared (collective) and public narratives. Just as shared narratives ('stories that are told and retold by numerous members of a society over a long period of time', Baker 2006: 29) and public narratives ('stories elaborated by and circulating among social and institutional formations larger than the individual', Baker 2006: 33) feed into the ontological narratives of individual members of society, so our individual cognitive contexts are shaped by shared and public consciousness. Moreover, 'shared narratives ... require the polyvocality of numerous personal stories to gain currency and acceptance, to become "normalized" into self-evident accounts of the world' (Baker 2006: 30). This clearly helps to explain both the usage and the usefulness of reviews and blogs – not only for audiences as a way of feeling part of a community but also for the reviewers and bloggers themselves as a way of gaining traction and influence.

With this in mind, I conducted word frequency and content analysis of a corpus of 16,926 words made up of

1. twenty-five reviews of Roger McGough's *Tartuffe* that appeared online on the websites of British national and local press titles or on other websites (sevenstreets. com, timeout.com, britishtheatreguide.info, whatsonstage.com, thesphinx.co.uk and brighton.co.uk) aimed at more specific audiences such as students, visitors or theatre enthusiasts,
2. nine blogs (either personal blog sites or sites such as thereviewshub.com or reviewsgate.com that act as a platform onto which bloggers are invited to post their own articles) and
3. eight preview articles that appeared on the websites of British national and local press titles.

This spectrum of material therefore comprises different levels of context, from the personal (blogs) to the group (websites for targeted audiences) and finally the general (national press). This again reflects Baker's typology of ontological, collective and public narratives.

McGough's *Tartuffe* was first performed at the Liverpool Everyman Theatre from 9 to 31 May 2008. The same production then toured a small number of English cities in 2011 – Liverpool (8 to 17 September), Cambridge (20 to 24 September), Newcastle-upon-Tyne (27 September to 1 October), Richmond, Surrey (4 to 8 October), Exeter (11 to 15 October), Brighton (18 to 22 October), Ipswich (25 to 29 October) and Watford (1 to 5 November) (English Touring Theatre 2011: n.p.). The relatively small number of venues and the limited time span over which the play was performed mean that the press coverage was limited to local Liverpool press and broadsheet national press for the initial Liverpool run, and local press in each of the eight provincial cities and two new reviews in the broadsheet national press (*The Independent* and *The Times*) for the subsequent tour of English cities. I can therefore be reasonably confident that my sample comprises the entire set of press reviews that were written for *Tartuffe* (barring any in local or regional press that may have appeared at the time but that were never or are no longer accessible online).

Blogs are more difficult to access online since they tend to appear lower down in Google search results. This is due to the fact that individuals are less likely to pay for a premium listing or engage in search engine optimization (the process of maximizing traffic to a website by ensuring that it appears as high as possible in search engine results) than the owners of press websites. Spontaneous visibility of blogs depends therefore on the specific keywords that bloggers have tagged. Here, I have selected blogs that appeared within the first three pages of the Google search results for *McGough*, *Tartuffe* and *blog*, but ignored those that appeared lower down the list (at least at the time of my search). The rationale for this is that low-visibility blogs are less likely to influence spectators' reception of a play than high-visibility blogs – an argument that is perhaps not entirely watertight in that regular theatregoers may have their own favourite bloggers whom they search for by name rather than by play title or theatre, but one that is arguably sufficiently robust for the purposes of this exercise.

Other online sites such as sevenstreets.com, timeout.com, british-theatreguide.info, whatsonstage.com, thesphinx.co.uk and brighton.co.uk represent something of a hybrid between traditional press titles (i.e. titles that are still also available in hard copy) and personal blogs. Run by groups of journalists or volunteers, these sites are often geared towards either specific local audiences (e.g. thesphinx.co.uk is a site for students in Liverpool, while brighton.co.uk targets visitors to Brighton) or specific interest groups (e.g. whatsonstage.com is a site where avid theatregoers can read about and book tickets for current productions). They are therefore likely to generate a significant amount of trust among their particular communities.

My textual analysis was limited to word frequency and content analysis as a way of analysing the overall themes of my corpus. As well as being particularly interested in the prevalence of terms relating to McGough's voice, I was also keen to identify specific examples of verbatim citations of lines from the play. This is because the citing of lines actively encourages spectators to rationalize or intellectualize their cognitive responses to those lines in advance of hearing them during the play itself. It's also likely to mean that these spectators will also consciously or unconsciously listen out for similar examples of humour, word play, double entendre and so on during the play. In other words, they are essentially *primed* to respond to the text in a certain way.

Of course, audiences do not blindly follow what reviewers and bloggers say when responding to a play – even if there are countless examples in the theatre of poor reviews killing off a production before spectators have had a chance to make up their own minds (see Wardle 1992 and Blank 2007). But it does remain the case that reviews and blogs are the most easily measurable influence on public opinion, and specifically on spectators' cognitive contexts. After all, spectators might not agree with a review that they have read, but may still be influenced (whether knowingly or not) by its content, particularly if it triggers a cognitive response by activating pre-existing encyclopaedic entries in their memories – for example, by reminding them, say, that McGough is fond of word play in his work. Again, this is not to say that reviews or blogs represent the *most important* influence on spectators, but rather that they are the influence that is most accessible to analysis after the performances have taken place.

The computer program that I used for my analysis was AntConc (Anthony 2014), a freeware multiplatform tool for carrying out corpus linguistics research. AntConc was developed by Professor Laurence Anthony of the Center for English Language Education in Science and Engineering at Waseda University in Tokyo, Japan. Anthony is also a visiting researcher at Lancaster University in the UK. Among other things beyond the scope of my analysis here, this program allows users to count all the words in a corpus and present them in an ordered list (the word list tool), show search results in context to see how words or phrases are commonly used in the corpus (the concordance tool), and see the collocates of a search term to investigate non-sequential patterns of language (the collocates tool). For my purposes, its main advantages are that it enables users not only to explore the *frequency* with which reviewers and bloggers use relevant words or concepts (e.g. *translation* and its derivatives, such as *translate*, *translator*, *translated*, etc.) but to explore the *immediate context* in which references to, say, humour or word play are discussed.

The most obvious finding from my analysis, and perhaps also the one that's most telling, is that the corpus contains not only many more references to McGough than it does to Molière but also very little reference to translation. This can be seen clearly in Figure 7.1, which shows the overall word frequency in a word cloud format (i.e. the more frequently a word appears in the corpus, the larger it appears in the figure).

This greater emphasis on McGough rather than Molière becomes even more telling if we explore the frequency of *any* reference to McGough (*McGough, Roger, McGough's* or even *McGoughiere*) versus any reference to Molière (*Molière, Moliere, Molière's* or *Moliere's*). This reveals 186 mentions of (Roger) McGough compared with just fifty-six mentions of Molière. The fact that the celebrity translator is mentioned more than

Figure 7.1 Frequency of words appearing in reviews and blogs.

three times as often as the source-text playwright surely tells us something about the relative interest in McGough among reviewers and bloggers, and the assumptions that those reviewers and bloggers make about the relative interest among audiences. As if to confirm this, it's also useful to note that the term *translation* (or derivatives thereof) appears only fourteen times in all the files analysed, compared with forty references to *adaptation* (or derivatives thereof) or twenty-seven references to *version*.

Already, then, we can see how this focus on McGough and his own distinctive language and style contrasts strongly with the typical tendency of reviewers of translated prose (and readers of translated prose, come to that) to fail to attribute the language or style of translations to the translators themselves. The assumption here is usually that such language and style are a feature of the source-text author's writing rather than the translator's. As translator and author Esther Allen points out, reviewers of translated texts all too often treat translators as 'the inevitably inept servant of an author's sovereign will' (2014: 27). So, reviewers may celebrate the voice of the assumed author, but still dismiss translation as 'an unfortunate and detrimental process' (2014: 27). Importantly, this effective prioritization of style over content (as seen in the word cloud in the relatively low frequency of words relating to *Tartuffe*'s storyline) also provides a rare example of reviewers' adherence to Lawrence Venuti's first rule for reading translations: 'don't read just for meaning, but for language too; appreciate the formal features of the translation' (2004: n.p.).

It's also immediately apparent even at first glance that reviewers or bloggers often appear to be making a comparison with some *imaginary* version of Tartuffe written entirely in a form of objective, matter-of-fact English (if such a thing can ever be said to exist) – a version into which McGough has injected his own style, humour and personality. Consider, for example, such relativist language as *egged up* (Peter 2008) (compared with which *Tartuffe*, I wonder?), *fresh yet remarkably faithful* (Walker 2008) (faithful to which *Tartuffe*, exactly?), and *imbued ... with modern meaning* (Jones 2008) – as opposed presumably to Molière's outdated meaning? This would appear to be an example of what Jean Boase-Beier is referring to when she talks about translation as a conceptual blend – where the translation stands in a documentary relation to the source text, but also exists as a literary text in the target-language culture in its own right (2011: 67). As a blend, a translation will 'have effects on the minds of both its writer and its reader as a result of the combination of voices, languages, styles and cultures in the translated work, that are neither in the original work itself nor would be in an original work by the English translator' (2011: 68).

Here, however, McGough's text also stands in a documentary relation to all the *previous English translations* of *Tartuffe*. Indeed for many reviewers and bloggers, these other English texts are more likely to be their point of comparison than the original French source text, of which they may often have little, if any, knowledge or experience. As a result, then, we have here an example of a *triple-layer*, or *three-dimensional blend* comprising the Molière's source text, McGough's target text and the imaginary translation of *Tartuffe* with which McGough's version is compared. Indeed, it might also be argued that the blend comprises even more layers or dimensions than this, given that it will also comprise elements from the other translations consulted by McGough (by Wilbur, Bolt, Lochhead and so on – see Chapter 5).

If we look at the data more closely, then, it becomes obvious how often reviewers and bloggers make reference to *how McGough's voice is heard* in his translation, to the extent that it would appear quite likely that many readers will be left with a relatively clear idea of what to expect from the text in performance. Solely in terms of word frequency, for example, we can detect regular use of *comic/comedy* (fifty-one occurrences), *fun/funny* (thirty-three), *laugh/laughter* (twenty-eight), *wit/witty* (twenty-two), *farce* (nineteen), *satire/satirical* (twelve), *hilarious* (ten) and *humour/humorous* (ten). But of greater importance is the fact that these are often used less to describe the genre of the play or Molière's source text and more to describe McGough's own style. Take, for example, the following instances of the use of *wit/witty*. Here, and in all the following citations, the italics are my own.

1. This is an adaptation by Roger McGough, vigorously egged up, full of *witty* rhymes and jokes specially designed for English audiences. (Peter 2008: n.p.)
2. Tartuffe à la McGough is an absolute triumph – of *wit* and invention, of fop, fool and philanderer. (Jones 2008: n.p.)
3. In their zest and *wit*, McGough's lines, sometimes deliciously set up, at other time sprung on us with a mischievous artlessness, set a cracking pace. (Walker 2008: n.p.)
4. The play has been adapted by the brilliant Roger McGough with skill, side-splitting humour, *wit* and unbelievably clever rhymes. (Guest 2011: n.p.)

More specifically, the adjectives or adverbs used to describe McGough's wit or humour are likely to have a strong influence on the way in which spectators subsequently process a performance of *Tartuffe*. Here, descriptors such as *clever/cleverly* (eleven occurrences), *sharp* (two), *cheeky* (three) and *side-splitting* (three) offer a subjective opinion of McGough's humour that audiences may or may not agree with, but one that at least provides them with a benchmark against which to assess their own responses. Consider, for example, the uses of *clever* in the following.

1. It's hugely enjoyable, the infinitely inventive, *clever* and at times tongue-in-cheek cheesy verse driving the pace along merrily from one delicious set piece to the next. (Jones C. 2011: n.p.)
2. McGough has a gift for comic quasi-verse, but is never afraid to milk the comic potential of a truly execrable rhyme – and equally importantly, he never pushes his running gags or *clever* anachronisms too far. (Smith 2011: n.p.)
3. The dialogue, delivered in verse, is both *clever*, funny and at times plays with some deliberately bad, groan-inducing rhymes. (Clarke 2011: n.p.)

Here, it might appear that writers are often almost setting a challenge for spectators to identify and correctly interpret each of the comedic references. As journalist David Guest points out, 'Some of the wily rhymes are well signposted, while others sneak up unexpectedly causing such mirth that you are in danger of missing the next verbal treat' (2011: n.p.). Clearly this level of concentration has implications for the number and intensity of cognitive effects that the text will have on spectators who have read any reviews or blog posts prior to attending the performance.

At the same time, though, we should not forget that, for most spectators, attending a performance of *Tartuffe* is still likely to be first and foremost a relaxing and entertaining experience rather than one of heightened intellectual concentration. As Brecht points out, 'The one important point for the spectators ... is that they should be able to swap a contradictory world for a consistent one, one that they scarcely know for one of which they can dream' (1964: 188). In other words, cognitive effects are not necessarily only derived from conscious confirmation of, say, previously held assumptions, beliefs and even contradictions – say, the previously held belief that McGough's text will feature a number of neologisms. They are also derived from a more unconscious assimilation of the escapist fun of McGough's text – for example, the sense of delight experienced in spotting one of McGough's anachronisms or puns and being able to share in this delight with other spectators.

With this in mind, it's striking how often the reviews and blogs analysed here tend to repeatedly cite the same examples of McGough's wit. Consider, for example, the following line from Act I, Scene 5, (McGough 2008: 13), when Cléante is mocking Orgon for having fallen for Tartuffe's deceit, which is mentioned in no fewer than sixteen of the forty-two articles or posts.

> CLÉANTE: What is it about this interloper
> that goads you into faux-pas after faux-pas?

Likewise, the 'Here lieth a bee' line (Act V, Scene 1, McGough 2008: 15) and the repeated 'old English sayings' device (both already discussed in Chapter 5) are each mentioned by four separate writers. Even the reference to The Priory (Act IV, Scene 3, McGough 2008: 53), which McGough himself thought often passed unnoticed by audiences (again see Chapter 5), is specifically mentioned by two different writers.

1. The flow of Molière's razor-sharp dialogue is newly sprinkled with everyday expressions and allusions, including a reference even to The *Priory*. (Walker 2008: n.p.)
2. Although the audience didn't always get the references, such as mentioning the *Priory* as an alternative to the convent, we all seemed to be having a good time. (Evans 2008: n.p.)

Here, there will obviously be a strong synergistic effect if spectators read more than one review or blog before attending a performance of *Tartuffe* and both pieces mention the same pun or play on words.

As an aside in this respect, evaluation of the press material published by the Liverpool Everyman Theatre for its 2008 and 2011 productions of *Tartuffe* (and kindly provided by the theatre for my examination) reveals that none of the press releases contained any mention of these textual examples. So we can assume that the reviewers of the Liverpool performances did actually attend the play and were not simply recycling material distributed by the theatre. Of course, in our Google-dominated world, it's entirely possible that reviewers writing for the local press in the other English towns in which *Tartuffe* was performed in 2011 may have *borrowed* some ideas from the reviewers of the Liverpool productions, and that this might explain the consistency in the textual examples cited. For the purposes of this analysis, however, let's give them the benefit of the doubt and assume that this was not the case.

Finally, I'd like to draw attention to the fact that reviews and blogs can themselves sometimes *explicitly* refer to a playwright's voice, such that readers may potentially receive a play in a different way from that which might otherwise be the case. In this corpus, for example, we can find specific reference to McGough's voice (using the term in a very similar sense to that defined in Chapter 1) in two of the reviews.

1. In many ways it has become McGough's play. One can almost hear the inflection of his *voice*, the intonation and the accent. In fact I would [love] to hear him read it. (Young 2011: n.p.)
2. It's both a strength and weakness of Gemma Bodinetz's production that everybody – bar Colin Tierney's shifty-eyed Tartuffe, who talks in uncouth prose – sounds like a bit of the same McGough poem. Which is what they are, in a sense, but the *voices* are so overwhelmingly McGough-ish that the characters lose a certain amount of definition. (Time Out 2011: n.p.)

In addition, McGough himself is also cited in a review in *The Journal* on the subject of voice, claiming, 'I put [other people's translations] aside and let the characters speak, as it were, and I found I was able to give *voice* to them' (Hodgson 2011: n.p.). And while McGough does not presumably mean to imply that these characters then speak with his own voice, it's not unreasonable to assume that readers of this review might infer from such a comment that McGough was suggesting that he gave the characters a voice by injecting some of his own familiar authorial style (see Chapter 1).

Of course, without a valid benchmark for comparison over and above the imaginary English version of *Tartuffe* discussed previously, it's difficult to judge whether McGough's voice is actually an *ersatz* Molière voice (since neither reviewers nor spectators are likely to have a clear perception of the source-text playwright's authorial voice unless they have studied Molière's work in detail), or whether the character definition in McGough's *Tartuffe* is any less or any more sharply perceived than it would have been to theatregoers in the seventeenth century watching a performance of Molière's original play (which even the most serious scholars of Molière might struggle to demonstrate). In any event, irrespective of whether spectators are primed by the views or observations expressed above to *actively* hear McGough's voice or merely to infer a consistent voice *by default*, the fact remains that such reviews and blog posts are likely to sensitize readers to the issue of voice. This will then potentially encourage them to focus on the 'McGoughisms' in the text to a much greater extent than would have been the case if they had not read these articles before attending the performance.

Overall, then, this analysis tends to support my hypothesis that spectators' cognitive contexts are consciously or unconsciously shaped by the opinions of reviewers and bloggers to which they are exposed before attending a performance of a play. As a result, there appears to be sufficient evidence that such reviews and blog posts *do* influence the way in which those spectators infer the celebrity translator's voice in that play and thereby *do* help to construct public discourse around the celebrity translator's work. At the broadest level, reviews and blog posts give potential spectators a general framework within which to interpret a play by first of all defining its genre (in this case, a comedy) and placing it in a particular space and time (e.g. an adaptation of a classic French play) – essentially offering a set of guidelines that first and foremost enable potential audiences to decide whether they wish to purchase tickets to see that play or not. Such guidelines may in themselves also act as filters influencing the encyclopaedic entries that are triggered by the performance of that play, although arguably to no greater extent than a cursory exploration of a theatre's forthcoming programme or the recommendation of an acquaintance might also do.

In terms of generating expectations of the celebrity translator's voice, however, reviews and blogs also appear to have the potential to play a key role in activating *specific cognitive associations*, either because of the way in which they trigger existing awareness of that celebrity's voice (e.g. by referring overtly to McGough's humour at a general level) or because of the way in which they highlight actual examples of this voice, citing directly from the text to validate their broader observations. This *planting* of specific puns or plays on words in readers' minds will not only sensitize those readers to these specific examples of text when they hear them in performance. It will also encourage them to listen out for other examples of *similar* uses of language throughout the play. Indeed, there's likely to be a significant multiplier effect here, with pre-sensitization to one example of McGough's wit leading to spectators becoming even more receptive to other examples of his humour. This is to say nothing of the multiplier effect of word of mouth, whereby spectators themselves repeat some of the clever uses of language to others when recommending the play. Such perpetuation of ideas is perhaps more significant in the case of celebrity translation than other types of translation since the notion of celebrity creates its own momentum and makes it easier (and safer) for spectators to recommend the play to their peer group.

This actually represents a particular type of echoic reception or interpretation. Here, relevance is achieved by virtue of the cognitive effects that result from what has been reported by the reviewer or the blogger and the spectator's attitude towards it – or what has subsequently been reported by the spectator and the receiver's attitude towards it (see Sperber and Wilson 1995: 238). This echoic reception is also magnified in the environment of the theatre, where the response of other audience members helps spectators to activate their own encyclopaedic entries and cognitive processes, and provides reassurance that they are undergoing a similar inferential process to other audience members in order to arrive at a similar interpretation of the text. This would explain why some audience members might only start to laugh in the theatre when they hear other spectators doing the same.

Finally, it's clear that reviews and blog posts are likely to generate significantly different cognitive processes depending on the reader's pre-existing awareness and appreciation of the celebrity translator. Among those spectators who specifically choose to see *Tartuffe* because of McGough's involvement, prior exposure to reviews and blogs is likely to lead to even more intense scrutiny of the performance, and a greater sense of satisfaction, when the anticipated voice is actually inferred – or in other words, when the cognitive effects mean that relevance is achieved more readily. Among those spectators who are less aware of McGough, meanwhile, reviews and blog posts are more likely to fulfil the role of establishing a set of *interpretive guidelines* that both enhance the number and intensity of cognitive effects derived by spectators (via pre-sensitization to certain dimensions of McGough's voice) and give those spectators a sense of being able to *share in the public narrative* by reducing the amount of processing effort that's required for the text to achieve relevance.

But, again, can we ever actually demonstrate empirically that spectators' cognitive contexts are genuinely shaped by external influencers such as reviewers and bloggers, or does this remain simply a theoretical notion? In the absence of being in a position to scan spectators' brains before, during and immediately after a performance (and before and after exposure to such external influences), we will still be reliant on what these spectators are able to tell us about their responses towards that performance. And as we have already seen in the previous section, that's not easy to achieve via audience research. But what if we were able to follow what spectators were *spontaneously* saying about a play, without the intervention of a traditional interviewer?

Analysing social media responses

Prompting spectators to tell us their *genuine* feelings about theatrical performances and the inferences that they draw from such performances is a challenge that has long vexed theatre scholars. This is either because such responses inevitably change during and after that performance (and particularly once spectators become exposed to the influence of other agencies, such as peers, reviewers, bloggers and so on) or because spectators would in any case most likely be unable to articulate many of those feelings to a third party (such as an interviewer or a focus group moderator). And this is assuming that they were aware of those feelings in the first place.

Such a view, however, really applies only to more traditional (i.e. twentieth-century) ways of thinking either about the spectator as a passive agent in the theatrical process or about the scope for tapping into spectators' responses. Researchers' abilities to gauge genuine audience reactions have been typically constrained by the application of a limited repertoire of audience research tools that focused on observation (e.g. ethnography, see Marinetti and Rose 2013), behavioural measurement (e.g. use of skin response apparatus or 'applaudimeters' to track cognitive responses, see Heim 2016) or field research (face-to-face quantitative or qualitative audience surveys, see Tulloch 2005).

Theatre scholar Caroline Heim has explored the changing role of theatre audiences in the twenty-first century and offers a fresh reading of mainstream audiences that brings *spectators*' voices to the fore – a reading that gives rise to the notion of the 'audience as performer' (2016). Heim's argument is that the core of all theatre is the encounter – 'the encounter of the actors with the audience, the actors with each other, the audience members with each other', with each group having a reciprocal influence on the other (2016: 3). It is these encounters with other agencies that construct the individual as a performer, and each performer has a repertoire of actions at his or her disposal – the actor's is to perform on stage and the spectator's is to perform by responding to what is happening on the stage and to how other members of the audience are responding to the actors and to one another.

Audience performances, then, not only include clapping, laughing, booing and so on in response to what the actors are doing. They also encompass talking to other spectators in the interval, tweeting about the performance on their way home and blogging about their experience the day after, to give just a few of many possible responses that modern technology allows. It's this notion of the audience as performer that has inspired my methodology for researching spectators' responses to Stephens's adaptation of *A Doll's House*.

I conducted qualitative analysis of the Twitter posts (tweets) that were sent by audience members while or after attending a performance of Simon Stephens's adaptation of *A Doll's House* on the London stage in 2012 and 2013, either at the Young Vic (from 29 June to 4 August 2012, and again from 28 March to 20 April 2013) or at the Duke of York's Theatre (from 8 August to 26 October 2013). My aim here was to gain all the *spontaneous* responses to the play as soon as possible after seeing its performance – in other words before such responses might have been conditioned by internal, post-rationalized reflections or by external influences such as those mentioned above (exposure to peer-group responses, reviews, blogs and so on). This is not to say that such spontaneous responses are not also already conditioned by existing discourses and preconceptions. Rather, the distinction I wish to make is between more subconscious, instinctive responses and more considered responses that emerge when exposed to external stimuli.

To this end, I included in my research sample all those tweets that included the Twitter handle @youngvictheatre or @dukeofyorks plus the hashtag #adollshouse in their message, *or* that included #youngvictheatre or #dukeofyorks plus #adollshouse (or the variant #dollshouse in both cases). In my analysis I examined only those tweets that were sent in response to a performance (i.e. not those sent in anticipation of a performance), during the dates that performances were given and, as far as it was possible to tell from the time of posting, either during or immediately after the performance. I excluded any tweets that were not sent by regular audience members, such as tweets from the Young Vic itself, other theatres, ticket and casting agencies and the media, and from tweeters who might have a non-typical perspective, such as actors, academics, parents of children who featured in the production, and so on. This resulted in a total usable sample of 168 tweets.

For the purposes of my study of celebrity translators, the most important finding emerging from this analysis is that Stephens is mentioned in 12 of these 168 tweets, either in the body of the tweet or in the handle @StephensSimon. These tweets were as follows:[1]

1. Saw great @StephensSimon Ibsen #adollshouse yesterday evening @youngvictheatre – definitive Nora from Hattie Morahan. Fantastic set design too.
2. @youngvictheatre @StephensSimon #adollshouse was just amazing. Oh Nora! I really know how you feel sometimes...
3. @youngvictheatre Just seen Ibsens play #adollshouse English language version @StephensSimon it was fantastic #hattiemorahan is INCREDIBLE!
4. @StephensSimon @youngvictheatre Version of A Dolls House is unbelievable – acting, adaptation, staging, wow wow wow #ADollsHouse

5. @youngvictheatre's #ADollsHouse was such an amazing, charged performance. Can @StephensSimon do no wrong?
6. Excellent evening hanging over gallery @youngvictheatre for #ADollsHouse. Was utterly mesmerised throughout. Great job @StephensSimon et al!
7. @StephensSimon finally got to see #ADollsHouse at @youngvictheatre tonight – really great stuff. Congrats, sir.
8. Absolutely adored #adollshouse – sharp, fresh & relevant. Gorgeous design, beautifully directed. Thank you @youngvictheatre & @StephensSimon
9. #ADollsHouse at @youngvictheatre grips like a thriller, lands like a punch. Fantastic new version by @StephensSimon is funny & lethal.
10. @StephensSimon version of #ADollsHouse @youngvictheatre is excellent! Powerful acting & fantastic direction. Great set too! Don't miss it!
11. @StephensSimon's version of #Ibsen's #ADollsHouse @youngvictheatre June 28. Go see!
12. #dollshouse @youngvictheatre w/ @StephensSimon & #hattiemorahan More than I ever believed that play could be. Was transfixed every minute!

Such a relatively low proportion of tweets that mention the celebrity translator might appear to contradict my hypothesis that a playwright such as Stephens will attract an audience to the theatre who might otherwise not go to see a play by Ibsen. But to put this figure into perspective, it's worth comparing this with the number of tweets about other Ibsen adaptations that ran in the UK at a similar time to Stephens's version of *A Doll's House*. First, if we look at theatregoers' tweets about Brian Friel's adaptation of Ibsen's *Hedda Gabler*, which was performed at London's Old Vic Theatre in 2012 shortly after the end of the first run of Stephens's *A Doll's House* at the Young Vic down the road, we see that Friel was mentioned only once in a total of forty-four tweets selected more or less on the same criteria as those mentioned earlier. This is surely a surprise given Friel's own profile as a dramatist in his own right and the extent to which he put his own stamp on Ibsen's text – for example, in the way he suggests that Hedda is almost possessed by the devil, which according to Michael Billington is an intrusion that 'seriously affects the balance of the play' (2012b: n.p.). Second, if we compare Stephens's *A Doll's House* with the different version of the same play performed by the UK Touring Theatre in 2014, it's telling to note the complete lack of any mention of the play's translator, in any of the tweets from the audience, any of the audience feedback posted on the company's website (UK Touring Theatre 2014: n.p.) or in any of the press reviews of the production throughout its thirty-two-date tour of the UK.[2]

It's perhaps not surprising that most of the focus in the tweets about Stephens's *A Doll's House* is on the performance of Hattie Morahan as Nora (in all three productions). Other frequent themes include the revolving set, the availability of £10 seats at the Young Vic, and the performance of other cast members (most notably Dominic Rowan as Torvald and Nick Fletcher as Krogstad). But importantly, the comments about Morahan are often more about her characterization of Nora than they are about Morahan's acting per se (to the extent, obviously, that such a distinction can ever be possible). It could be argued, then, that the following tweets are as much about Stephens's craft as a playwright as about Morahan's craft as an actor, thereby suggesting that Stephens plays a bigger role in spontaneous responses to his adaptation than the number of actual mentions of his name would suggest.

1. An exquisitely constructed character with powerful thought and velocity
2. I can't imagine ever witnessing such a disturbingly moving Nora again
3. Utterly insightful portrayal of interior life of a marriage and how it unfolds when things don't go to plan

Contemporary relevance in general is also a common theme in post-performance tweets, and one that also suggests that Stephens's status and heritage as a modern-day playwright is more in evidence than might initially appear to be the case.

1. 5* for @youngvictheatre #ADollsHouse As relevant today as when it was written. Have we really made the progress we'd like to think we have??
2. Blazing production directed by CarrieCracknell play continues to strike a chord
3. Surprised by just how contemporary #adollshouse @youngvictheatre felt – totally blew me away

A similar pattern can be observed in the comments submitted directly to the Young Vic in 2012 in response to a post-performance email sent out to audience members soliciting feedback on their experience of the play. Here, in the fifteen reviews on the Young Vic's website (Young Vic 2012: n.p.), Stephens is mentioned in only one review (and my correspondence with the marketing department at the Young Vic reveals that there are no longer any records of the other feedback that was received at the time).

> This cast deserves recognition on a grand scale, particularly Hattie Morahan, Dominic Rowan and Nick Fletcher. ... This version of IBSEN'S great play was by Simon Stephens, directed by Carrie Cracknell, and *they all deserve CREDIT*.

This comment in itself (my italics) does, of course, highlight the collaborative nature of live theatre productions, and serves to remind us that the critical and commercial success of a translated play is by no means a function of the quality of the translation in isolation.

At the same time, even if Stephens's name is not mentioned explicitly, there is certainly plenty of evidence from audience members' feedback that the themes discussed in the preceding chapter *do* emerge relatively spontaneously (again, my italics). And even if such replies were actively solicited by the Young Vic, they still represent open-ended responses in which respondents are allowed to talk about whatever they wish in relation to the performance.

1. At A Doll's House at The Young Vic last night and saw a truly great performance by Hattie Morahan as Nora; in turns *sexy, kittenish, exuberant, manipulative and loving* we witnessed Nora change from girl to woman and it was wonderful to behold! ... Dominic Rowan also superb as Torvald giving *a study in baffled hypocrisy* ... It took a little time to get used to the revolving set – the technical

rehearsal must have been a nightmare – but all the rooms were small adding to the *claustrophobic nature* of the piece. Great stuff!
2. The Young Vic put on a fantastic version of Ibsen's *A Doll's House*. Hattie Morahan was brilliant as the *initially ditzy and increasingly tragic* Nora, and the cast and director really brought out both the humour and the horror of this fascinating play. I loved the revolving set, like a giant Doll's House, and the costumes which created an eerie, timeless atmosphere
3. First class production and acting. Nora's is a huge part. The ending is a little unconvincing, *her change of attitude is almost instantaneous and it shows* but a great play and the production surely would have pleased Ibsen.

Such comments support the argument in Chapter 6 that a celebrity translator's voice is also inferred via the thematic echoes that spectators hear during a performance and not just in the style of that translator's text. They also suggest that we can further distinguish between the *intensity* of the cognitive effects triggered by the translator's text (as seen, for example, in the comments about Morahan's dramatic impact as Nora) and the *breadth* of the cognitive effects triggered by that text – as seen in the comments about how the production encourages spectators to think more holistically about the aesthetic merits of this version, both in its own right and in comparison with other translations that they may have previously seen in performance.

This research methodology does, of course, have a number of limitations. Most importantly, the sample of both Twitter users and spectators who responded to the Young Vic's request for feedback is wholly self-selecting. It involves a conscious effort on the part of each of those individuals to offer a point of view, whether entirely spontaneously (as in the case of the tweets) or when prompted (as in the case of those who responded to the email from the Young Vic soliciting feedback on the performance). This, in itself, suggests that these spectators will have been more involved in the performance of *A Doll's House* that they attended than those spectators who did not choose to make their views 'public'. And of course, these spectators probably also have a greater affinity with communication technology than those who did not respond in these ways, which also suggests that they might not be entirely representative of audiences as a whole. Such limitations are, however, an inherent weakness of practically all audience research (except for ethnographic research) in the sense that respondents have to be actively willing to contribute, and so by definition therefore might be seeking to air a more polarized view than the norm – for example, wanting at one extreme to extol the praises of the production and at the other extreme to vent their displeasure. These limitations can therefore be overlooked for the purposes of this exercise.

This does not mean that there's no merit in conducting face-to-face audience research. After all, such research would, in principle, yield much richer insights than could ever be derived from what at the time of posting were tweets of a maximum of 140 characters – again, because it would allow us to understand more about the context of production and reception (see Pavis 1993). But, over and above the difficulties in getting spectators to express their genuine feelings, the practical challenges of conducting interviews or focus groups *immediately* after participants have watched the performance in question do impose a serious limitation. This is to say nothing of the costs that such in situ and in-person research would incur, which, when weighed up against the ease of analysing tweets, might ultimately mean that such research will never be as resource-efficient as the methodology that I have selected here in terms of cost per insight.

In defence of analysis of the written text

Having declared an emphasis on the reception of plays in performance in my aims for this book, I am acutely aware that out of practical necessity I have focused primarily on published play texts rather than plays in performance or at least the final scripts for those performances. I am also conscious of the fact that the published versions of the plays that I have analysed in my case studies are not necessarily the same as the versions that ultimately reached the stage. For example, Stephens and his director Cracknell trimmed a significant amount of text from the published version of *A Doll's House* during rehearsals to ensure that the text in performance did not exceed the allotted timeframe. But is my reliance on published texts really so contrary to my avowed focus on the reception of those texts?

It is, of course, the case that all theatrical performances, whether of translated or original plays, are about much more than the play text itself. As pointed out throughout this book, the many elements of the theatrical performance (the actors, the director, the stage designers, the lighting technicians, the make-up artists, the theatre staff, the designers of the theatre building and so on) all influence the relationship between the text in performance and the spectator. Likewise, no two versions of a text in performance will ever be wholly identical, either because of the variability of so many of these non-textual elements or because of the role that the audience itself plays in co-creating a live performance through spectators' individual and communal responses to the theatrical experience (see Heim 2016).

In this sense, then, it would be difficult not to agree with Susan Bennett that textual analysis can only represent part of the complex network presented to the audience in live theatrical performance (1997: 143). And as Roland Barthes reminds us in his description of the 'polyphonic system of information', 'at every point in a performance you are receiving (at the same second) six or seven items of information (from the scenery, the costuming, the lighting, the position of the actors, their gestures, their mode of playing, their language), but some of these items remain fixed (this is true of the scenery) while others change (speech, gestures)' (1979: 29). Similarly, Stephens's own thoughts on authorial voice are also extremely apposite in this context.

> Theatrical experiences are never pure articulations of any kind of authorial voice. The author's intentions, as revealed in their plays, are only ever starting gestures towards an evening in the theatre. This gesture will be refracted through the prisms of theatre architecture, social geography, audience make up, audience size, design, casting and rehearsal. (2016: 229)

If a play is translated, such gestures are obviously further refracted through the prism of the translator. And in the case of *A Doll's House* and many other translated play texts, they are yet further refracted through the prism of the literal translator.

Here, as already noted earlier, we should also not underestimate the influence of emotional contagion on theatre spectators. Emotions are catching in all contexts, but perhaps especially in the theatre, where the audience's focus on the performance on stage serves to bring individual spectators' emotional states more into alignment than would be the case in almost any other social setting. As McConachie points out, 'The empathy activated by our mirror system puts us in touch with the intentions and emotions of others, allowing us to catch their emotions ourselves' (2008: 95). In other words, the power of the theatre as an artistic medium is largely due to the fact that we typically experience it in the company of others. And while my analysis of the tweets sent by spectators of Stephens's *A Doll's House* reflects such an audience effect, my more theoretical analysis of the published texts of each of my three case studies is clearly of necessity more oriented towards *individual spectators'* likely cognitive contexts and inferences.

Having said this, I would argue that it's unwise to see the page versions and the stage versions of a play text as two wholly *separate* and *opposing* entities. The processes of creating a written version of a play text and then translating that written version into performance, or of a playwright adapting an existing play text and a director then adapting it for the stage, are at the same time separate and yet wholly interconnected processes. And as John Bull points out, 'The way in which these binaries operate is perhaps the most significant development in contemporary theatrical adaptation' (2018: 294). Likewise, while the text is only part of what audiences respond to in live performance, it's nonetheless the very lynchpin on which all the other elements of performance (the acting, directing, staging, etc.) depend, and as such is surely worthy of analysis in its own right. After all, as Susan Bassnett reminds us, 'language is the heart within the body of culture, and it is the interaction between the two that results in the continuation of life-energy' (2014: 25).

It's surely also the case that the distinction between watching and reading a text is nowadays not as clear-cut as might have previously been the case. In a social-mediatized world, in which we can give and receive immediate feedback on all kinds of experiences, the notion that, for example, we read, listen to music or watch TV in private is an increasingly delusional one if we can immediately share our emotional responses with others or check our own responses against those of other individuals who have experienced the same literary or artistic output. As a result, we should not assume that emotional contagion only applies to activities experienced en masse. Similarly, in an increasingly atomized social environment, we should also not underestimate either the role that social media plays in giving each individual spectator his or her own critical voice, or the influence that this will have on our willingness to take other spectators' emotional responses on board now that the internet provides us with a multitude of platforms for expressing an alternative opinion. Here, Bennett's view, expressed as recently as the late 1990s, that 'a performance is … unlike a printed work, always open to immediate and public acceptance, modification or rejection by those people it addresses' (1997: 67) already appears somewhat archaic in a world in which the distinction between public and private response appears increasingly blurred.

This argument not only helps to explain my rationale for concentrating on published play texts rather than texts in performance for the purposes of this book. It also raises some interesting questions about our culturally assumed common sense of the aesthetic (see Chapter 2). Here, it's interesting to reflect on the extent to which we consciously or unconsciously allow ourselves to be influenced by others' interpretations (which is the implicit assumption in any consideration of acknowledged artistic merit, or what might popularly be considered *good taste*), versus the extent to which we genuinely interpret communication on the basis of our own unique set of contextual associations. Relevance theory already accounts for the *group response* effect that this assumed common sense of the aesthetic gives rise to. That's because it acknowledges how the responses of others (including those responses experienced at the time of or prior to the communicative act in question) feed into our contextual associations. So, even if in theory there can be as many different responses to a play text (or any other act of communication) as there are receivers, in practice we usually filter our own inferences through our awareness and assessment of others' actual or assumed responses. We thereby arrive at an interpretation that represents a compromise between our own world view and our assumed socially acceptable view – one that gives us enough sense of our own individuality, but also sufficient reassurance that we share the same cultural values and level of artistic discernment as other members of our community.

At the same time, the fact that we are now all potential 'keypad critics' suggests that the notion of a common aesthetic sensitivity, while not exactly starting to break down, may well be becoming more fragmented and more consumer-driven. This not only has implications for how we view the phenomenon of celebrity translation in general – that is, whether we see it as commercially exploitative or as culturally enlightening. It also has ramifications for the range of translated drama that UK audiences might be willing to explore as we move increasingly towards a world in which the cultural agenda may be set as much by spectators' *actual* demands as by the cultural system's *assumptions* about those demands. And as we will see in the following chapter, we underestimate audiences' willingness to explore 'the foreign' at our peril.

8

Going forward

Harnessing the value of celebrity translation

I intentionally chose to explore three very different case studies in this book – one (Roger McGough's *Tartuffe*) by a highly popular poet with a very recognizable written and spoken style; one (Simon Stephens's *A Doll's House*) by a prolific contemporary playwright whose work constantly revisits familiar tropes; and one (Mark Ravenhill's *A Life of Galileo*) by a well-known and often controversial playwright from the in-yer-face generation. While it would be impossible to claim that these three different approaches to celebrity translation represent the *only* approaches seen in the UK's theatrical system, I trust I have clearly demonstrated that, on the basis of these examples at least, celebrity translators' voices *are* likely to be often inferred (either directly or indirectly) by spectators. What's more, the application of relevance theory has helped us to understand that the extent to which the celebrity translator's voice is inferred depends on the extent to which spectators' cognitive contexts are or are not dominated by contextual associations with that translator before, while and after seeing his or her work in performance.

So, can we also conclude as a result that celebrity translators *do* inject some of their own voice into their translations, either intentionally or unconsciously? Certainly in the case of the three celebrity translators explored in this book, it would appear that each of them *does* inject some of his own voice into his translation in his own individual way. In the case of McGough's *Tartuffe*, we can clearly identify the various ways in which the celebrity translator's own authorial voice will be very easily inferred by audiences given their likely familiarity with McGough's existing work and public profile. In Stephens's *A Doll's House*, meanwhile, the celebrity translator's voice is heard much more in the way in which certain themes typically associated with Stephens are emphasized, creating a strong sense of the celebrity translator advancing his own agenda in his work. Finally, the celebrity translator's voice in Ravenhill's *A Life of Galileo* is a more subtle one, inferred either through clever 'in-jokes' or through social, political or cultural references that may or may not have been intended on the part of the author. Of course, such observations from these three case studies do not in themselves amount to a suggestion that celebrity translators *always actively inject* some of their own voice into their work in order to optimize artistic or commercial acclaim, even if this might still be a justifiable interpretation in certain cases. Rather, the conclusion that we should draw is that the celebrity translator's voice is more of a *pull factor* for audiences (in other words, something that spectators themselves actively seek out) than a *push factor* on the part of the celebrities themselves or the commissioners of celebrity translations (i.e. something that is actively imposed on the translation and performance process).

This conclusion also helps us to assess how the synergy between the source-text playwright's voice and the celebrity translator's voice affects reception of the translated text by audiences. On the basis of the three case studies explored in this book, it's clear that the celebrity translator is likely to be more successful in *commercial* terms (i.e. more successful in attracting bigger audiences) if there is an obvious synergy between the source-text author and the celebrity author. This is obviously due to the fact that a more kindred relationship between these two agencies makes it easier to sell the work to potential producers, critics, theatres and audiences – the 'match made in heaven' that Bodinetz refers to when talking about Molière and McGough (in McGough 2013: n.p.) and that will undoubtedly have attracted spectators to the theatre to see one of McGough's Molière adaptations who might otherwise never have considered going to see a performance of a classical French play.

But on the other hand, it could be argued that the *artistic* success of celebrity translation (which may or may not also equate to commercial success) might be more easily guaranteed when there is a less obvious affinity between the source-text playwright and the celebrity translator. This is because there is greater potential for dramatic tension and surprise and for groundbreaking work in performance when there is greater dissonance between these two agencies in terms of their experience, values, agenda and so on. Stephens's adaptation of *A Doll's House* is the example explored in this book that comes closest to this notion of a potential dramatic discord between source-text playwright and celebrity translator in terms of their respective bodies of work, if not necessarily in terms of their likely artistic intentions.

Given the rather conservative nature of much of British theatre, it's perhaps not surprising that the majority of examples of celebrity translations in recent years would appear to demonstrate at least some synergy between the source-text playwright and the celebrity translator, and that the more challenging approach of selecting a translator who has no obvious affinity with the source text or the source-text playwright is more typically avoided. While the commercial rationale for this is entirely justifiable, such safe behaviour in the commissioning of translation runs the risk of creating reliable but undemanding theatrical experiences that fail to stimulate audiences. If we see one of the fundamental aims of translation as being to open an audience's eyes to new stories, new cultures and new ways of seeing the world, then we should also be encouraging theatres to do the same when commissioning translated play texts.

The question as to whether celebrity translators might always attract a different audience to translated drama from unknown translators is a more difficult one to answer. Given the limitations imposed by audience research, it's difficult to provide wholly convincing evidence that a celebrity translator will *definitely* attract more spectators or different spectators to a production compared with an unknown translator. Textual analysis of the likely inferences among spectators who attend a play because of the *pull* of the celebrity translator does, nevertheless, allow us to conclude that audiences *will* derive more cognitive effects from a translation by a celebrity translator than from a translation by a non-celebrity translator. This will then enhance the likelihood of that translation achieving both commercial and artistic success as spectators spread the word about their theatrical experience among their social circles.

In terms of the external, or extratextual, influences that might impact on the inferences that spectators draw from a performance of a play translated by a celebrity translator, it's clear that not only reviewers and bloggers but also spectators themselves play a vital role in influencing reception of a celebrity translation – and indeed in attracting spectators to the theatre in the first place to watch a performance of a celebrity translation that they might otherwise not have considered. In an era in which traditional top-down models of publicizing and reviewing theatre appear increasingly redundant, and in which individual spectators have a public platform for voicing their views in the shape of social media, there is scope for much more immediate and more visceral responses to celebrity translation to circulate and influence reception by subsequent audiences (consider, for example, the tweets about Stephens's *A Doll's House* made during the interval of a performance), whether such influences are genuine spectator responses or planted by the theatres themselves.

The extent to which a celebrity translator does or should act as a marketing tool to increase ticket sales is one that in itself raises many interesting questions about the visibility of translation and of translators at both a scholarly and a practical level. Should leverage of celebrity be discouraged for the sake of literary and artistic integrity, or should we celebrate the way in which celebrity translators increase the visibility of the act of translation and showcase the genre of plays in translation? Analysis of the likely cognitive state of the celebrity translator's audience sheds a more positive light on the phenomenon of celebrity translation that goes beyond the rather cynical *bums on seats* assumption about the practice. It also challenges some of the more negative social and ideological associations with the practice among those stakeholders in the theatrical system (and in the field of translation studies too, come to that) who are tempted to dismiss celebrity translation as an embarrassing example of Anglophone cultural insularity. That's because it ultimately reminds us that translators do indeed 'participate in very decisive ways in promoting and circulating narratives and discourses' (Baker 2010: 12).

At the same time, it also remains the case that the translator himself or herself is unlikely ever to be the *only* draw for audiences, however much of a celebrity he or she may be. Celebrity attracts celebrity, so a prestigious translator is likely to attract (and also be attracted to) a prestigious cast, director, theatre and so on. The translator's text is only one of a number of factors influencing either the artistic or the commercial success of a production or the reception of that production. Translation scholars may see the championing of translated theatre as a valid and necessary cause in a market such as the UK in which foreign theatre remains dominated by the canonical playwrights who feature in my case studies in this book. But ultimately we should remind ourselves that theatre audiences respond to *performances* rather than to translators or translations, and our desire to see more foreign plays on the British stage is only partially served by a focus on promoting greater interest in the translation process itself or the translator(s) involved in that process.

Of course, any initiatives designed to encourage greater interest in foreign drama are to be welcomed. And this is equally the case whether these initiatives are promoted by theatres (e.g. the RSC's 2017 Chinese Translations Project, billed on the Company's website as 'a cultural exchange bringing Chinese classics to a modern western audience', see Royal Shakespeare Company 2017: n.p.), theatre companies (such as London-based Foreign Affairs, which focuses on 'pushing artistic, social and creative boundaries through translation, ensemble work and performance in unconventional venues', see Foreign Affairs 2017: n.p.), or translation scholars (e.g. Margherita Laera's project on Translation, Adaptation, Otherness: Foreignisation in Theatre Practice, see Research Councils UK 2016: n.p.).

But we should not forget that an overt focus on the translation process itself presupposes a conscious search for otherness or foreignness that British audiences might not necessarily admit to when deciding what to go and see at the theatre. As author and translator Maureen Freely notes in the context of the UK's growing interest in translated literature (albeit from an embarrassingly low base), 'the fact that translations are selling more is because these books are interesting and are books that people know they need to read' (Wright and Freely 2017: 105). The same argument applies to the theatre. Audiences attend plays because they know, hope or have been told that a play is interesting and one that people know they need to see – and not simply because it's a translated play.

A new perspective on the notion of voice

Our associations with any authors, whether we choose to define them as celebrities or not, certainly extend beyond the page. Moreover, when those authors are translated by figures who are also well known in their own right, our associations with the creator of a text become even more plentiful. In an era in which all authors have the potential to become known for more than what they write or how they write, the possibilities are endless. Authors are no longer solitary figures of mystery – if indeed they ever really were. They are saleable commodities as much as anything else, ushered from one literary festival to another, and obliged to have their own websites, Facebook pages and Twitter feeds to ensure that their product sells. Suddenly we know so much more about them, their behaviour and their attitudes than what we might ever be able to infer solely from their work. Even dead authors do not escape the celebrity treatment at a time of so many 'biopics' or dramatizations of their lives on our cinema screens. How many people, I wonder, hear the voice of British actor and author Stephen Fry in their heads when they read Oscar Wilde, or see Australian actor Nicole Kidman in their minds when they read Virginia Woolf?[1]

In contemporary culture all authors, whether they like it or not, are not just writers – they are *brands*, in part created by their body of work, in part created by their publishers to help sell that work, and in part created by the fact that, once successful, they essentially become a centre of media attention and thereby a media construct in their own right. In the world of marketing, a brand is essentially a product with an identity. In the case of literature, an author's *product* is his or her text, and the set of product features or characteristics that make the product work and fulfil its remit as a piece of literature can be summed up as the author's *style*. The *branding* is then the *voice* that readers infer from that text and that gives that author his or her own particular literary identity. So can we borrow anything from the way in which marketers specifically define branding to help us define voice?

There are probably as many theories about what constitutes a brand as there are marketing experts, but it's generally agreed, give or take a few differences in terminology (see Ogilvy 2007; Godin 2011 and Kotler and Keller 2016, to name but a few), that there are five key elements to branding: story, positioning, personality, associations and promise. And each of these can apply as much to an author as to any other saleable product.

For as well as *telling* stories, authors also generate a story about *themselves*, whether consciously or unconsciously. We generally know, for example, the territory that they belong to in terms of genre or the issues they typically deal with in their writing. We also probably know what their *positioning* is because we have an idea of their perspective, ideology, outlook on life, attitude towards their stories and so on. We can then in turn construct a *personality* from everything we know about those authors as writers and more generally as human beings. We can also build a set of *associations* from everything that we infer from their distinctive, idiosyncratic way of writing – this is essentially the *fingerprint* that Mick Short discusses (1996: 329, see also Chapter 1), which is typically a function of being well known and well recognized as an author. Finally, if an author is worth reading or studying, then he or she must deliver some kind of *promise* – a promise of particularly appealing poetic effects, or a particularly satisfying intellectual reward that then gives rise to critical acclaim or kudos (which of course is different from simply being well known).

These five elements provide us with a framework for defining what gives an author his or her own voice. Rather than dimensions of voice, I prefer to imagine these five elements as *pillars*, as this reminds us that an author needs all five elements in place to support a strong voice, otherwise that voice is lost (see Figure 8.1). The foundation that supports each of those five pillars is the author's textual style (i.e. the set of product features and benefits that make the author's product, or text, distinctive). That's because without style there can be no voice – and without the bedrock of a distinctive style, none of the other pillars that combine to constitute voice will stand up to any scrutiny.

Building on the idea that translation is always a blend of voices, it follows by definition that the celebrity translator's voice in any given play-text translation must always be rooted in some way in the source-text playwright's voice. This is not only because the translation is always based on the translator's assumptions about the source-text playwright's communicative intentions, as conveyed by his or her style. It's also because readers of the translation can probably not avoid inferring at least some of the source-text playwright's voice even if they are unable to read anything that that author has written in his or her own language. Simply by virtue of being classified as famous, from a previous era or foreign, a source-text playwright will give rise to contextual associations, even if these might only remain relatively weak for some members of the audience.

While the notion of a blend of voices might be a highly theoretical construct, it can at least help us to think about the different ways in which the celebrity translator and source-text playwright complement or do not complement one another. And this is to

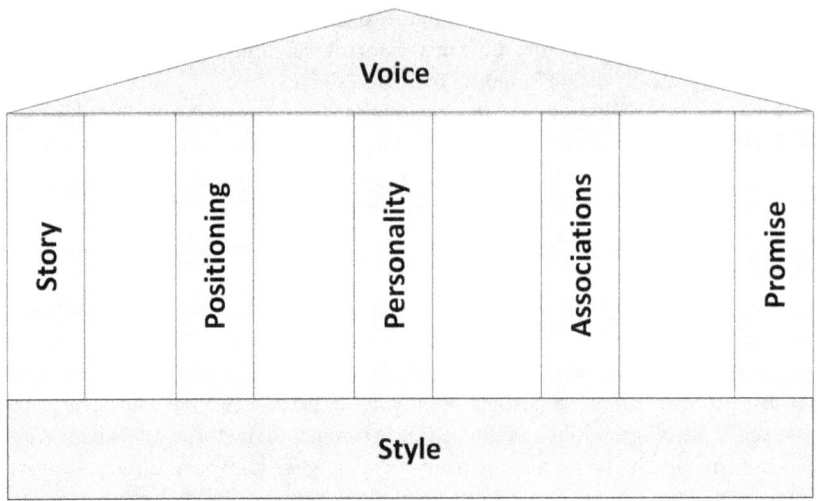

Figure 8.1 Pillars that construct voice.

say nothing of the way in which it can help us to move on from endless debates about the virtues or otherwise of translator visibility. It also reminds us that the rationale for working with a celebrity translator is that such a translator has much more *brand capital* than an unknown translator – or in other words, that his or her pillars are more solid. This capital hopefully helps to ensure that a production enjoys a greater public profile and higher level of artistic integrity than it would in the case of an unknown translator.

Rethinking the theatre translation process

The process and ethics of theatre translation in the UK, and in particular the practice of using literal translations, have already been subject to considerable comment and criticism over the years among UK-based scholars (including, to name just a few, Bassnett 1985, 1998 and 2011, Upton 2000, Perteghella 2004a and 2004b and Brodie 2018), translators (e.g. Rappaport 2001; Gregory 2009 and Bolt 2010), playwrights (e.g. Hampton 2011; Stephens 2014c and 2014d, and Hare 2016) and journalists (e.g. Logan 2003; Haydon 2014 and Lawson 2014). Likewise, the cases for greater status (and financial reward) for literal translators, more collaboration between translators and other agents in the theatrical system, and more public awareness of the value of theatre translation in the broader cultural environment have been argued time and time again, and do not need to be re-explored here.

Implicit in much of the criticism of the use of literal translations, particularly among translators and scholars, is the invisibility of the literal translator compared with the often monolingual celebrity translator – yet another example, so it is claimed, of the undeservedly low status attached to the art of translation compared with the accolades heaped on the celebrity. It's certainly the case that literal translators are at best often relegated to the bottom of a list of credits in a production, and at worst not mentioned at all. Take the example of Stephens's *A Doll's House*, the programme for which listed literal translator Charlotte Barslund below every other person involved in the production. Deborah Gearing, meanwhile, was given a slightly higher-profile credit for her literal translation for Mark Ravenhill's *A Life of Galileo* in the programme for the RSC's original Stratford-upon-Avon production in 2013, but was then not mentioned at all in the programme for the production's subsequent nationwide tour.

Of course, much of this agonizing about the lowly status of the literal translator echoes the dismay voiced about the status of translators in general, whether they work as theatre, literary or commercial translators. Particularly with regard to literary translation, this perceived lack of status is to a large extent symptomatic of the bigger issue of literary translation not being seen as a creative process. This is in spite of the various arguments advanced over the years by translation scholars that translators should be acknowledged as creative writers in their own right (see Boase-Beier and Holman 1998; Bassnett and Bush 2006; Perteghella and Loffredo 2007 and Wright 2016). The macro problem, here, obviously, is that translation itself is a largely invisible activity, either because of publishing practices, which typically foreground the author of the source text rather than the author of the target text (at least in Western societies), or because the skill of transferring a text from one language to another is one that is generally poorly understood, especially in predominantly monolingual cultures such as the UK.

Having said this, it's also the case that both the academy and the theatrical system often do little to promote the process and art of theatre translation to the wider public. Scholar, journalist, theatre critic and literary translator Joseph Farrell, for example, describes the literal translator as 'some unfortunate drudge ... commissioned to provide that most mysterious thing – a literal translation – to which a star name will add the glitter of lilied phrases and wittily turned dialogue' (1996: 54). Such a view is hardly likely to encourage linguists into the field of theatre translation. Similarly, theatre scholar and translator Maria Delgado suggests that 'translators too often just serve to provide a first draft which a [well-known] writer then appropriates' (cited in Zatlin 2005: 26). True though this may be, Delgado's pronouncement fails to acknowledge the fact that the literal translation remains a literary work in its own right, even if one with a very different *skopos* from the celebrity translator's text for the stage. If such views persist among translation practitioners themselves, it's little wonder that other agents in the theatrical system, including audiences, fail to have more interest in or respect for the behind-the-scenes translator.

Here, it would appear that scholars' and translators' repeated focus on issues such as foreignization versus domestication or translation versus adaptation does little to further the ultimate goal of theatre translation, namely, to bring foreign-language theatre to a wider audience and enrich the target culture. This is to say nothing of the impression that such inward-looking process-dominated discussion is likely to have on theatre audiences in the way that it potentially perpetuates the popular perception that the theatrical system is highly ego-driven. This is not to say that there is no value in championing the specific role of the theatre translator more widely. Rather, it's about reminding ourselves that this role needs to be presented and praised as part of a much broader network of collaboration (see Perteghella 2004a) rather than as an end in itself. And following the line of thought developed by Caroline Heim (2016), this network of collaboration needs to actively involve audiences as well. Here, translators and translation scholars could learn a lot from Stephens's collaborative approach to stagecraft, which is driven as much by pragmatism as idealism.

> Theatre in its metabolism is an optimistic art form, because it's built on collaboration. I have to be able to give my play to [the director] and say, I don't think you're going to fuck it up. He has to give it to the actors and trust them not to fuck it up. Then we have to show it to an audience and trust they will accept it with an openness of mind. (2012a: n.p.)

We should certainly not feel *forced* (as scholars, translation practitioners or spectators) to agonize about the virtues of the actual process of translation or the visibility or otherwise of the translation or the translator. The bigger issue that we need to explore is how to get more audiences interested in translated theatre (i.e. theatre from cultures that speak different languages from our own) in the first place. Once this is achieved, interest in and respect for the translator and the translation process (both in artistic and financial terms) will surely be guaranteed. As Geraldine Brodie reminds us (her italics), 'Teamwork … *provided that it is exposed to view*, brings the act of translation into focus, reminding the user of the intercultural shift taking place' (2018: 160).

Quite how realistic in the short term such a shift in attitudes might be in a market such as the UK is, sadly, still open to question. This is especially so in an era both of reduced public support for the arts, which inevitably reduces the scope for the theatrical system to take risks, and of increasing mechanization of the translation process, which is already having an impact on translation for the theatre. As translation and theatre scholar Mark O'Thomas points out, London's Royal Court Theatre has already made occasional use of machine translation with regard to specific scripts and communications.[2] It's therefore not entirely unimaginable that, as its accuracy improves, machine translation might soon be used to carry out initial screening of scripts submitted in languages other than English and perhaps even the first draft of an entire literal translation. While such a concept might initially appear abhorrent to literary translators (to say nothing of the impact that it would have on their income stream), I would tend to concur with O'Thomas that use of machine translation in the theatre does at least allow greater access to works that might otherwise never get onto the commissioner's radar due to linguistic or financial constraints. As such, then, increasing experimentation with machine translation in the theatrical system should actually be seen as a positive development, and one that could potentially facilitate exposure to a broader range of translated theatre in the UK than is currently the case (see also O'Thomas 2017).

In the face of both of these trends, we need to rethink the role of the literal translator and the value that he or she can bring. Phyllis Zatlin, US academic and theatre translator, has already suggested that 'the translator's contribution may be similar to that of a dramaturg … a consultant to a theatre company who knows the text well and can clarify details for the actors and director' (2005: 5). Building on this suggestion, it's clear that literal translators should also be given greater scope to play a much more visible role as cultural consultants in a broader context, as well as greater credit for the value that they can add to the overall process of creating theatre.

Of course, the notion of translators as cultural facilitators is as old as translation studies itself, and Bassnett and Lefevere's call for the study (and thereby the practice) of translation to be framed as the study (and thereby the practice) of cultural interaction was made as long ago as the 1990s (1998: 6). Whether the academy has yet to fully respond to this call is perhaps a matter for debate. It's certainly the case, at least in the UK, that there are still insufficient opportunities for systematic cross-disciplinary study of language, cultural studies, translation studies and theatre studies. Such study could help to train a new generation of theatre translators, multilingual playwrights and directors, as well as inspire more culturally aware audiences, critics and producers to explore foreign-language theatre beyond the European canon. Here, Sophie Stevens's 2014 project at King's College London, which involved conducting theatre translation workshops with secondary school students to enhance sensitivity to issues of cultural identity and interaction, provides a valuable template for future projects in this area (see King's College London 2014: n.p.). The London-based Out of the Wings initiative, meanwhile, a three-year project funded by the UK's Arts and Humanities Research Council, aims to improve access to Spanish, Spanish American and Portuguese theatre to English-speaking theatre professionals, practitioners and researchers, and organizes annual festivals featuring staged readings, workshops, talks and events that showcase theatre in translation (see Out of the Wings 2019: n.p.).

Marketing translated theatre

As pointed out earlier, without an audience there can be no theatre. Yet here again, it's concerning that there is in some circles a persistent implicit suspicion of the discernment of the mainstream or mass-market audience. Such an elitist view of what constitutes theatre of artistic worth, and therefore what constitutes plays that are worthy of translation in the first place, may at worst perpetuate the myth discussed earlier that UK audiences will be unwilling to investigate theatre by unknown foreign playwrights because of their wariness of the foreign. As theatre producer Rowan Rutter points out, 'Difficult theatre isn't elitist, it's the idea of difficult that's elitist.'[3]

After all, UK consumers in other areas of the arts (or, at least, certain sub-groups of consumers) now defy previous expectations of their openness to 'the foreign'. Although admittedly starting from a disappointingly low base, sales of translated fiction in the UK by the end of the second decade of the twenty-first century were at their highest level since sales were first tracked in 2001 (see Flood 2019: n.p.). Meanwhile, subtitled TV dramas from Continental Europe and Latin America are now regular ratings successes on Channel 4's showcase for foreign-language drama, *Walter Presents*. So, if foreign books and TV series can become successful in the UK once publishers and commissioners trust their audiences more, surely the same should be true of the theatre? Has the time come, then, for mainstream UK theatres to more frequently think beyond the typical repertoire of canonical European playwrights? And should producers be introducing UK audiences more systematically to more contemporary foreign theatre and lesser-known foreign playwrights in order to satisfy the spectator's quest for a more individualized experience?

Of course, such a refocus needs to be achieved in a way that successfully reconciles more eclectic tastes with considerations of commercial viability. But without trusting audiences' preparedness to explore and experiment, there is a danger that producers will continue to seek out the comfort of familiarity rather than push the boundaries and offer audiences genuine theatrical innovations. The publishers of Stieg Larsson (over two million book sales in the UK of *The Girl with the Dragon Tattoo*) and the commissioners of the Danish-Swedish co-produced *Nordic Noir* TV drama *The Bridge* (BBC4's highest ever rating drama series up until 2019) prove that taking risks and achieving commercial success are not as mutually exclusive as some in the theatrical system might think.

Having said this, it is also naïve, and even dangerous, to assume that *theatre in translation* is a discrete genre that requires a discrete marketing approach if it is to appeal to audiences. To give an extreme example, translated plays by lesser-known foreign playwrights (such as those regularly staged at London's Royal Court Theatre or produced by theatre companies such as Foreign Affairs) clearly have very little in common with more mainstream foreign theatre in translation, such as, say, Herbert Kretzmer's adaptation of Claude-Michel Schönberg's and Alain Boubil's 1980 musical *Les Misérables*, which has run continuously in London since 1985, making it the world's longest-running musical (Cameron Mackintosh Overseas 2017: n.p.) and one that many British spectators may even fail to acknowledge as 'translated'.

The fact that plays in translation have more in common with works by British playwrights in their same genre than they do with one another confounds the notion that translated theatre should be viewed any differently from English-language theatre in terms of how it should be marketed to audiences. In this respect, the marketing of French playwright Florian Zeller's plays on the London stage (and indeed in theatres nationwide) offers a useful example of how translated drama appears to appeal to UK audiences more when it highlights the author's award-winning writing and critical acclaim than when it foregrounds the fact that Zeller's works are translations (even when they are translated by someone as well known in his own right as Christopher Hampton).

Perhaps of greater importance from the perspective of relevance theory is the notion implicit in the idea of *difficult* that translated theatre will fail to achieve as many poetic effects in the target culture as in the source culture, and that this will limit the affective response to and appeal of foreign theatre among target-culture audiences. The perception of ingrained ethnocentricity among mainstream British audiences is not only inaccurate but also demeaning. That's because it implies a systematic hierarchy of cultural and aesthetic sensitivity, whereby translated theatre will only appeal to spectators with a particular level of education, worldliness or discernment, and only spectators in this category will fully appreciate such theatre. Such assumptions perhaps tell us more about the holders of those views than about audiences themselves. As

Clive Scott points out in the context of poetry translation, the multilevel account of communication (which assumes that there are a number of levels on which text communication can take place) is a dangerous one.

> In the multilevel account, a really sensitive, well-trained reader will be able to capture, for example, a text's intertextual allusions, and rhythmic and acoustic nuances in a way denied to a less informed or responsive reader; but this latter will still derive benefit from the text, albeit at a different (lower) level of apprehension. This approach is a patronizing one, but, more dangerously, it is a mechanistic one: it assumes that all readers at a certain level have access to and enjoy the same experience. (2000: 5)

The same could be said of the patronizing assumptions about spectators' abilities to derive any aesthetic reward from translated theatre (however we might choose to define that reward) that still often pervade many theatre critics' reviews, and also cloud some theatre scholars' judgements about audiences. Theatre scholar Helen Freshwater's view in this respect is a sobering reminder of the need to pay greater attention to non-scholarly responses to theatre.

> There is evidence that audiences are beginning to be trusted by practitioners and by industry. But it seems that theatre scholars have yet to develop this trust. In fact, we have yet to step up to the challenge of addressing the question of what we really know about what theatre does for those who witness, watch or participate. Before we can do that, we need to challenge the mythologies and disperse some of the mystification which surround responses to theatrical performance. (2009: 74)

The fact that some agents in the theatrical system, at least, are placing increasing trust in audiences should not be a surprise given the mass of data that agents can now collect on potential spectators' likely theatrical tastes and preferences. Indeed, the tools that theatres' marketing departments now have at their disposal for actively targeting potential spectators via social media mean that marketing departments can not only more easily predict what is likely to appeal to audiences but also actively manipulate that appeal. As Ravenhill points out:

> Most of the theatres are full most of the time, which is absolutely extraordinary. That's a combination of it being a lot easier to market to people – you can target people, you can tell the people you've targeted to come along, which slightly contradicts access policies, because actually you work out who the audience is for that play and target them, but it's very effective. (in Needham 2012: n.p.)

In this respect, it would appear unfair to consider marketing as commodifying or over-commercializing theatrical works, whether translated or not. After all, without such supposed manipulation, more niche-appeal productions or productions outside major urban conurbations would not be commercially viable and would therefore never be produced in the first place. Here, it's difficult not to concur with Rutter that the notion of risky or brave theatre is all too often used as a cover-up for 'theatre that won't sell'. Because actually it's not that the stories that such theatre is telling are inherently too risky (and therefore unmarketable) – it's more that the finances are too risky.[4] So if marketing effectively enhances the appeal of translated theatre among potential spectators and thereby mitigates the financial risk to producers, it will serve to fulfil theatre's social and cultural role as well as satisfying the inevitable commercial demands placed upon it. And, yes, such theatre is more financially risky at first because producers have to build an audience for it and invite new audiences into theatre spaces (or existing audiences more frequently). But ultimately artistic and financial success should be seen as mutually enriching rather than mutually exclusive.

This plea for a more favourable view of marketing of the arts is particularly apt in a book that foregrounds the role of the audience. That's because audiences themselves are often an important marketing tool in their own right, as seen in my analyses of spectators' blogs and tweets in Chapter 7. In fact, as Heim reminds us, they may already be the most important tool of all.

> In this second decade of the twenty-first century, audience word of mouth has the most significant impact on ticket sales, far surpassing the authority of the traditional theatre critic. Word of mouth has always swayed audience opinion to some extent. With the emergence of new digital technologies we are now, however, documenting what were formerly only oral reviews and have evidence of the large, insightful repertoire of criticisms offered by the armchair critic. (2016: 174)

At the same time, we should not forget that there's also still a role for more traditional word-of-mouth audience activity, particularly among spectators bound more by a geographical than a technological cultural bond. Here, for example, expatriate communities living in the UK, who may often be another core target for translated theatre in the UK alongside the native English-speaking audience, might often be reached more effectively by word of mouth than by online activities. This has implications not only for the marketing of translated theatre but also for the involvement of such communities in co-creating and hosting theatrical events to enhance a sense of ownership. And not only in the UK's major metropolitan or cultural centres either – consider, for example, the role of the local Filipino diaspora in spearheading an original theatrical production during the 2019 Stevenage Festival of the Arts, or of the Polish community in Watford in organizing theatrical and music events at the town's Enrich Festival in the same year.

As already noted earlier in this chapter, marketing terms such as *product*, *brand* and *consumer* not only describe 'the very palpable activity of exchange that occurs between audience and the box office, audience and merchandise, and audience and concession stand' (Heim 2016: 130). They also explain the activity of exchange that occurs in the case of translated theatre between the text, the authors of that text (i.e. the source-text playwright and the translator) and the audience. And it's precisely at this interface that celebrity translators can play a significant role in the UK theatrical system, not least as potent publicity tools. That's because celebrity translators *feed* rather than *feed on* audiences' interest in translated drama. If a spectator's first exposure to classical French theatre is mediated by a translator such as McGough through a spectator's awareness of his role as presenter of a Sunday afternoon radio programme on poetry, and if that spectator is then motivated to explore other plays in this and other genres of foreign drama, then the celebrity translator surely deserves praise rather than damnation as the agency responsible for bringing a new audience into the theatre.

Ultimately, we should surely acknowledge that celebrity translation in the theatre, just like translation of any kind, fosters rather than stifles creativity, expands rather than limits cultural horizons, and invites rather than inhibits cultural interchange. To think otherwise is not only intellectual snobbery. It also fails to acknowledge how sustainable cultural shifts of any kind occur (from the bottom up), and risks a return to the age of theatre being the exclusive province of a cultural élite, which would be in nobody's interests – neither the theatrical system's nor the audience's, and most certainly not the translator's.

Call to action

This book inevitably raises as many questions as it answers about the phenomenon of celebrity translation in British theatre. In terms of the research gaps that remain for scholars, the most pressing requirement is for greater exploration of celebrity translators' works *in performance*. This would enable a more in-depth study of the influence that staging, casting and the theatre itself have on spectators' contextual associations and inferences. Here, of course, we should remember that it's not only actors who are celebrities and who therefore influence reception of the works in which they perform. Some theatres, such as, say, the National Theatre or the Royal Court in London, or the Swan in Stratford-upon-Avon, are arguably also celebrities in their own right in the way that they automatically give rise to a wealth of cognitive effects irrespective of what is happening on their stages.

Having said this, we should also bear in mind that performance in the context of the theatre no longer inevitably equates solely to the live event in situ. Plays performed in front of an audience are increasingly available to be viewed beyond the confines of the theatre itself – either live in local cinemas throughout the UK or any time after the event online. For example, a performance of the original production of Stephens's *A Doll's House* staged at the Young Vic in London in 2013 is available online (at the time of writing in 2020) at www.digitaltheatre.com to either rent or purchase. With this in mind, new analytical tools will be required in translation studies to properly evaluate translations that exist in written, performed and reproducible formats and that take account not only of issues such as the re-reading or re-viewing of a text but also of the different cognitive stimuli that might be triggered when spectators are exposed to a performance in isolation (e.g. at home in front of a device) as opposed to in a theatre. Such tools will be increasingly required as the theatrical experience itself becomes more diverse (through live streaming in venues other than theatres) and more fragmented (through watch-on-demand at home).

The ultimate analytical construct that would have enhanced this study of celebrity translators is a reliable theory of how the mind processes text in performance – or indeed how the mind processes text of any type. Yet as McConachie points out, 'Because there is no Grand Theory of the Mind in cognitive science that most would find acceptable, I can offer no grand theory of audience cognition for performance' (2008: 7). Yet having said this, we should not underestimate the advances that cognitive neuroscientists are currently making in understanding how the brain actually works. The implications of this for cognitive linguistics in general and relevance theory in particular are clearly immense, and suggest that literary, translation and theatre scholars might soon have to be prepared to reassess some of their ideas about how receivers infer communication and how cognitive stimuli interact with one another to create affective responses. It's already known, for example, that the brain enables both explicit memory (when we can make the link between how we have responded to a current stimulus, and what prior event made us respond in that way) and implicit memory (where we are unaware of why we have responded in the way that we have) (see McConachie 2008: 34–6). But to date, scientists lack a complete understanding of the interplay between these two functions – and it's this understanding that will help us to explore exactly how we process *new* stimuli. Once this breakthrough is achieved, many of my own findings and insights in this book may immediately become at best redundant and at worst entirely fallacious. Until such time, however, I trust I have at least set the scene for more research (and ideally more collaborative research between translation and theatre scholars) into the reception of translated theatre in the UK and the factors that might drive more favourable affective responses to such theatre.

Of course, conscious control of how we infer communication is probably an illusion – in the same way that we are deluded if we think we have complete control over our opinions in an era in which the communication that we receive is often already heavily manipulated. The political earthquakes of 2016 (the results of the UK's EU referendum and the US presidential election) have aroused intense interest among scholars and media commentators in the ways in which data companies exploit social media to influence public opinion and distort perceptions of 'the truth' (see O'Neill 2016; Davis 2017 and Davies 2017, to name just a few). Yet the techniques that such data companies use are essentially only more sophisticated versions of tools that advertisers (including theatres and theatre companies) have been using for years to entice audiences. In this respect, the *pull factor* of the celebrity translator could arguably also be seen as a way of manipulating an audience's cognitive context. With this in mind, then, there may well be a need for more research into the ethics of celebrity translation in the light of the advances in marketing sophistication discussed in the previous section.

I trust that future research will rectify the bias in this book towards male celebrity translators and female literal translators. It would undoubtedly be interesting to compare these celebrity translations with texts by female celebrity translators to examine the extent to which gender might influence how, why and what celebrities translate for the theatre. Examples of female celebrity translations for the British stage that would be particularly interesting to explore in this respect include poet and playwright Liz Lochhead's versions of Molière's *Tartuffe* (1986) and *Le Misanthrope* (2002, entitled *Miseryguts*), playwright, screenplay writer and translator Timberlake Wertenbaker's translations of Sophocles's *The Thebans* (1992), *Elektra* (2010) and *Antigone* (2011) and Euripedes's *Hecuba* (2001) and *Hippolytus* (2009), playwright and scriptwriter Anya Reiss's adaptations of Anton Chekhov's *The Seagull* (2012), *Three Sisters* (2014) and *Uncle Vanya* (2014) as well as Frank Wedekind's *Spring Awakening* (2014), and author Rachel Cusk's version of Euripedes's *Medea* (2015). Transgender playwright Jo Clifford's adaptation of Federico García Lorca's *The House of Bernarda Alba* (2011) would also be an extremely useful case study with regard to the impact of gender on translation.

Certainly, previous research into the role of gender on the translation process suggests that there may indeed be some ideologically rather than biologically driven differences between genders in these respects (see Von Flotow 1997 and Leonardi 2007). The overlaying of the construct of celebrity on the role of gender on translation process, and all that it implies in terms of the rationale for translating (and retranslating), the translation choices that are made and the public response to the translated product would make for a fascinating area of research. Might male or female celebrities be more assertive in imposing their own stamp on their texts, or which gender might audiences unconsciously expect to be more visible? These and many other gender-related questions will hopefully be the subject of future studies.

The gender issue might also be interesting to explore in terms of the dynamics of the collaboration between the celebrity translator and the director. Here, it might not be entirely coincidental that the directors of all three plays studied in this book were women (*A Life of Galileo* was directed by Roxana Silbert, *Tartuffe* by Gemma Bodinetz and *A Doll's House* by Carrie Cracknell). The fact that women have become more prominent as directors in British theatre since the start of the new millennium is arguably already starting to have an effect on adaptations of canonical works of drama in the UK. In particular, the new millennium has seen an emergence of a more collaborative approach in which the director plays an increasingly prominent role as co-adaptor and co-dramaturg along with the author of the play text (see Bull 2018) – a development that will hopefully go some way towards consigning Bassnett's assertion that theatre is 'a male entity' (1984: 462) to the history books. John Bull also concludes that such a new model for theatrical adaptation for performance suggests 'firstly, that questions of gender and gender imbalance will increasingly develop as a major theme in new adaptations/performances of the classics ... and secondly, that this will be reflected in changes in the texts/performances of future contemporary work' (2018: 297). Such issues surely deserve greater scholarly examination, both in themselves and as part of a broader exploration of the celebrity translator-director dynamic.

Finally, there would still appear to be considerable scope for using relevance theory more systematically, and perhaps also more critically, as a prism through which to study not only translated texts but also the process of translation itself. The only English-language academic work so far dedicated exclusively to translation and relevance theory is Ernst-August Gutt's *Translation and Relevance* (2000). While some translation scholars have championed relevance theory more convincingly (e.g. José Mateo Martinez 1998 and 2009; Jean Boase-Beier 2011 and 2020; and Pál Heltai 2008), the theory still appears to have had relatively little impact on translation studies as a discipline, and certainly nothing like the paradigm shift that it brought about in cognitive stylistics. This is in spite of the fact that it offers a highly plausible and accessible explanation for how receivers of communication infer the meaning of that communication, which is surely the notion that underpins the very concept and practice of translation.

Here, there may be useful lessons to be learned from some other European countries, notably Spain and Poland, which appear to have embraced relevance theory more widely, not least because of the way in which individual linguistics scholars have championed the theory in their institutions and more widely through their publications. Key figures here include Manuel Padilla Cruz at the University of Seville, Francisco Yus at the University of Alicante, and Ewa Wałaszewska and Agnieszka Piskorska at the University of Warsaw. This latter institution has previously also run courses on relevance theory and translation (see University of Warsaw 2017: n.p.) – something which no university in the English-speaking world has offered up to the time of writing.

It's certainly the case that there is a need for more work by translation scholars on how relevance theory might help us to better understand the role that the receiver of a translated text plays in constructing the meaning of that text – in other words, focusing on the end product of the translation process (the receiver's response) rather than on the process itself. More specifically in relation to theatre translation, this would surely promote greater interest in the effects that a translated play text has on the spectator, thereby moving the focus within the theatrical system away from more introspective musings on the creative process of theatre production or the preservation of aesthetic value for its own sake. After all, a play text with no receivers has no aesthetic value whatsoever as it cannot give rise to any poetic effects if there is no one to infer them – a notion that confounds the persistent view among some quarters that artistic and audience (i.e. commercial) considerations are mutually incompatible.

Given the notion in relevance theory that utterances (and texts) automatically create expectations of relevance among receivers, more relevance-theory-based research may also help translation scholars to better explain why texts are translated in the first place. Within the context of theatre translation, this could help scholars to theorize why certain texts are translated over and over again while others remain untranslated. This in turn could potentially lead to a shift in the repertoire of translated theatre available to audiences in the UK.

A more audience-led approach to commissioning translation might then also encourage producers to decide which foreign plays to stage in the UK based more on the affective response that those plays have met with in the source culture than on their assumed artistic and cultural merit from the commissioner's perspective – in other words, what can an audience do *with* this play, rather than what can this play do *for* an audience? Such a plea echoes literary translator Daniel Hahn's view that sales of translated fiction are growing in the UK because the emphasis is moving away from 'quite challenging, highbrow literary fiction' and publishers now seem to be taking more account of what people actually want to read (Edemariam 2018: n.p.). The parallels with Rutter's comments on elitist theatre earlier in this chapter are all too clear.

In the meantime, I trust that my insights into the role of the celebrity translator in enhancing spectators' affective response to translated plays will in some small way pave the way towards promotion of a greater variety of translated theatre in the UK – not only daring reinventions of canonical texts but also exciting interpretations of new plays by contemporary foreign playwrights that challenge, inspire and enrich audiences, and that inspire those audiences in some way to reassess their existing conceptions of the foreign and the translated. Because, as Stephens reminds us, that is precisely what theatre of any kind, translated or otherwise, should aim to achieve.

> The whole point of theatre is to make people different, to change people. Its main responsibility should be that the people who leave the theatre at the end of the night should in some small way be different people to when they came into the building at the beginning of the night. (cited in Thompson 2014: n.p.)

Notes

Chapter 1

1 While some of the more prolific celebrity translators might be only monolingual or have only a basic knowledge of any languages other than English (including the three celebrity translators featured in this book), well-known British playwrights who have adapted plays directly from the source text include Christopher Hampton (who speaks French and German), Michael Frayn (Russian) and Mike Poulton (Italian).

Chapter 4

1 Source (here and subsequent citations except where noted otherwise): interview with Gearing, 9 April 2015.
2 Source: personal email from Gearing, 19 July 2019.
3 The comments and italics here and in subsequent citations from Gearing's literal translation are Gearing's own.

Chapter 5

1 By the time of McGough's adaptation in 2008, there had been fifteen prose translations of *Tartuffe* into English: by Martin Clare (1732), H. Baker and J. Miller (eighteenth century), Thomas Constable (1898), Curtis Hidden Page (1908), Miles Malleson (1950), Haskell M. Block (1958), John Wood (1959), Renée Waldinger (1959), Simon Gray (1980), Jeffrey D. Hoeper (1997), Stanley Appelbaum (1998), David Edney (1998), Charles Jeffries and Luis Muñoz (1999), Martin Sorrell (2002), as well as one, published in 1957 by Random House in its Modern Library series, which does not give the name of the translator. There had also been twelve verse translations: by Thomas Shadwell (1669, unpublished) Matthew Medbourne (1670), John Oxenford (1853), Morris Bishop (1957), Richard Wilbur (1963), Donald Frame (1967), Christopher Hampton (1983), Liz Lochhead (1985), Mortimer Kassel (1989), Ranjit Bolt (1991, revised 2002), Maya Slater (2001) and Tim Mooney (2005). Looser adaptations still billed as *Tartuffe* that appeared before McGough's version include Freyda Thomas's adaptation (1997) set in a TV studio in Louisiana and P. K. Atre's 'Indian Tartuffe' (2006). Moreover, *Tartuffe* had also been the inspiration for a number of other plays prior to McGough's work, including Colley Kibber's *The Non-Juror* (1717) based on Medbourne's translation, Frances Sheridan's *The Dupe* (1764), Isaac Bickerstaff's *The Hypocrite* based on Cibber's adaptation (1768) and Richard Brinsley Sheridan's *The School for Scandal* (1777) (UNESCO 2020: n.p.). As if this were not already sufficient recycling of Molière's play, new versions have continued to emerge even since

McGough's adaptation was first staged in 2008 up until the time of writing (2019). As well as new 2008 translations in prose (Prudence Steiner) and verse (Constance Congdon), there was a new adaptation by Preston Lane in 2009 that relocated the work to modern-day Paris and a further adaptation in English rhyming couplets set in London in 2017 written by Andrew Hilton and Dominic Power and performed at the Tobacco Theatre in Bristol in that same year. Subsequently, there were two new UK stage productions in 2018 alone. First, Christopher Hampton and Gérald Garutti's bilingual version in blank verse opened at London's Theatre Royal Haymarket in May of that year, relocating the play to Los Angeles and recasting Tartuffe as a radical American evangelist. In September 2018, meanwhile, Anil Gupta and Richard Pinto's adaptation for the RSC at the Swan Theatre in Stratford-upon-Avon saw Tartuffe recast as Tahir Taufiq Arsuf and transposed Molière's work to Birmingham's Pakistani community. Finally, John Donnelly's version of *Tartuffe* that opened at London's National Theatre in February 2019 shifted the play's focus away from religion towards the guilt engendered by social inequality and reimagines Orgon as a wily insider trader who is as much a charlatan as Tartuffe.
2 Source (here and subsequent citations except where indicated otherwise): personal telephone conversation with McGough, 21 April 2012.
3 Throughout this chapter, I will follow the standard practice of representing lexical concepts (i.e. linguistically encoded meanings) in small capitals (e.g. BLATHERSKITE) and ad hoc concepts (i.e. occasion-specific meanings) in small capitals followed by an asterisk (BLATHERSKITE*) (see Wilson 2014: 140).

Chapter 6

1 Source (here and in the following citations): interview with Barslund, 18 June 2014.
2 Source: personal email correspondence with Stephens, 6 September 2016.

Chapter 7

1 These and subsequent tweets have been paraphrased slightly to avoid identification of the Twitter users who sent them.
2 The translator of this version of *A Doll's House* was actually one of the founders of the UK Touring Theatre, Felicity Rhys, who also played Nora in this production. This information is only revealed in an interview with Rhys that appeared in *The Oxford Times* on 2 October 2014 prior to the company's performance of the play at the Cornerstone in Didcot, Oxfordshire, on 4 October (Johnson 2014: n.p.).

Chapter 8

1 In 1997, Stephen Fry starred as Oscar Wilde in the British biographical film *Wilde*, for which he received a Golden Globe nomination as Best Actor. Nicole Kidman, meanwhile, played Virginia Woolf in the 2002 drama film *The Hours*. Based on Michael Cunningham's Pulitzer Prize-winning novel of the same name, and so not

a biographical film in the same sense as *Wilde*, *The Hours* was nominated for nine Academy Awards in 2003, and Kidman became the first Australian to win an Oscar for Best Actress.
2   Source: personal email from O'Thomas, 20 August 2018.
3   Source: discussion during the 'Brexit the Stage: What Next for British Theatre and Europe?' conference at the Victoria and Albert Museum, London on 22 April 2017.
4   Source: personal email from Rutter, 3 October 2018.

Select bibliography

Baines, R., C. Marinetti and M. Perteghella (eds), *Staging and Performing Translation: Text and Theatre Practice*, Basingstoke: Palgrave Macmillan, 2011.
Bennett, S., *Theatre Audiences: A Theory of Production and Reception*, London: Routledge, 1997.
Boase-Beier, J., *Translation and Style*, Oxon and New York: Routledge, 2020.
Clark, B., *Relevance Theory*, Cambridge: Cambridge University Press, 2013.
Heim, C., *Audience as Performer*, Oxon and New York: Routledge, 2016.
Marshall, P. D., *Celebrity and Power: Fame in Contemporary Culture*, Minneapolis: University of Minnesota Press, 1997.
McConachie, B., *Engaging Audiences: A Cognitive Approach to Spectating in the Theatre*, New York: Palgrave Macmillan, 2008.
Pilkington, A., *Poetic Effects: A Relevance Theory Perspective*, Amsterdam and Philadelphia: John Benjamin, 2000.
Sperber, D. and D. Wilson, *Relevance: Communication and Cognition*, 2nd edn, Oxford: Blackwell, 1995.

References

Aaltonen, S. (2000), *Time-Sharing on Stage: Drama Translation in Theatre and Society*, Clevedon: Multilingual Matters.
Aarseth, A. (2005), 'Ibsen and Darwin: A Reading of The Wild Duck', *Modern Drama*, 48 (1): 1–10.
Aczel, R. (2005), 'Voice', in D. Herman, M. Jahn and M. Ryan (eds), *Routledge Encyclopedia of Narrative Theory*, 634–6, Oxon and New York: Routledge.
Adam, A. (1962), *Histoire de la littérature française au XVIIe siècle, Vol. III L'apogée du siècle: Boileau, Molière*, Paris: Editions Mondiales.
Albertazzi, L., ed. (2000), *Meaning and Cognition*, Amsterdam and Philadelphia: John Benjamin.
Allen, E. (2014), 'Lost in the Book Review', *In Other Words*, 44: 26–33.
Anderman, G. (2005), *Europe on Stage*, London: Oberon.
Anthony, L. (2014), AntConc (Version 3.4.3) [computer software], Tokyo: Waseda University. Available online: http://www.antlab.sci.waseda.ac.jp/ (accessed 16 October 2015).
Archer, W. (1904), *Ibsen's Prose Dramas, Vol. 1*, London: Walter Scott.
Arts Council (2014), 'Royal Shakespeare Company'. Available online: http://www.arts council.org.uk/funding/browse-regularly-funded-organisations/npo/royal-shakespea re-company/ (accessed 19 August 2014).
Aylesworth, G. (2015), 'Postmodernism', in E. Zalta (ed.), *The Stanford Encyclopedia of Philosophy*. Available online: http://plato.stanford.edu/archives/spr2015/entries/post modernism (accessed 19 February 2016).
Baines, R., C. Marinetti and M. Perteghella, eds (2011), *Staging and Performing Translation: Text and Theatre Practice*, Basingstoke: Palgrave Macmillan.
Baker, H. and J. Miller (2000), *Tartuffe*, New York: Dover Publications.
Baker, M. (2000), 'Towards a Methodology for Investigating the Style of a Literary Translator', *Target*, 12 (2): 241–66.
Baker, M. (2006), *Translation and Conflict: A Narrative Account*, Oxon and New York: Routledge.
Baker, M. (2010), 'A Narrative Perspective on Translation in Situations of Conflict', in N. Al Zidjaly (ed.), *Building Bridges: Integrating Language, Linguistics, Literature and Translation in English Studies*, 145–58, Newcastle: Cambridge Scholars.
Bara, B. (2010), *Cognitive Pragmatics: The Mental Processes of Communication*, trans. J. Douthwaite, Cambridge, MA and London: MIT Press.
Barrett, B. (2013), '"The Biggest Risk to New Writing: Waiting for Permission": An Interview with Mark Ravenhill'. Available online: http://www.ayoungertheatre.com/the-biggest-risk-to-new-writing-waiting-for-permission-an-interview-with-mark-r avenhill/ (accessed 9 February 2014).
Barthes, R. (1977), *Image Music Text*, London: Fontana.
Barthes, R. (1979), 'Barthes on Theatre', trans. P. Mathers, *Theatre Quarterly*, 9 (33): 25–30.
Bassnett, S. (1980), *Translation Studies*, Oxon and New York: Routledge.

Bassnett, S. (1984), 'Towards a Theory of Women's Theatre,' in H. Schmid and A. van Kesteren (eds), *Semiotics of Drama and Theatre*, 445–65, Amsterdam: John Benjamin.
Bassnett, S. (1985), 'Ways through the Labyrinth: Strategies and Methods for Translating Theatre Texts', in T. Hermans (ed.), *The Manipulation of Literature*, 87–103, Beckenham: Croon Helm.
Bassnett, S. (1991), 'Translating for the Theatre: The Case Against Performability', *TTR (Traduction, Terminologie, Rédaction)*, 4 (1): 99–111.
Bassnett, S. (1998), 'Still Trapped in the Labyrinth: Further Reflections on Translation and Theatre', in S. Bassnett and A. Lefevere (eds), *Constructing Cultures: Essays on Literary Translation*, 90–108, Clevedon: Multilingual Matters.
Bassnett, S. (2011), *Reflections on Translation*, Clevedon: Multilingual Matters.
Bassnett, S. (2014), *Translation Studies*, 4th edn, Oxon and New York: Routledge.
Bassnett, S. and P. Bush, eds (2006), *The Translator As Writer*, London and New York: Continuum.
Bassnett, S. and A. Lefevere, eds (1998), *Constructing Cultures: Essays on Literary Translation*, Clevedon: Multilingual Matters.
Bellos, D. (2011), *Is That a Fish in Your Ear?*, London: Penguin.
Ben Chaim, D. (1984), *Distance in the Theatre: The Aesthetics of Audience Response*, Ann Arbor: UMI Research Press.
Bennett, S. (1997), *Theatre Audiences: A Theory of Production and Reception*, London: Routledge.
Berman, A. (2004), 'Translation and the Trials of the Foreign', trans. L. Venuti, in L. Venuti (ed.), *The Translation Studies Reader*, 2nd edn, 276–89, Oxon and New York: Routledge.
Bigliazzi, S., P. Kofler and P. Ambrosi, eds (2013), *Theatre Translation in Performance*, Oxon and New York: Routledge.
Billington, M. (2005), 'On the Shore of the Wide World – Review', *The Guardian*, 19 April 2005. Available online: https://www.theguardian.com/stage/2005/apr/19/theatre (accessed 18 September 2016).
Billington, M. (2012a), 'A Doll's House – Review', *The Guardian*, 10 July 2012. Available online: https://www.theguardian.com/stage/2012/jul/10/dolls-house-young-vic-review (accessed 18 September 2016).
Billington, M. (2012b), 'Hedda Gabbler – Review', *The Guardian*, 13 September 2012. Available online: https://www.theguardian.com/stage/2012/sep/13/hedda-gabler-review (accessed 9 January 2019).
Blakemore, D. (1992), *Understanding Utterances: Introduction to Pragmatics*, Oxon: Blackwell.
Blank, G. (2007), *Critics, Ratings and Society: The Sociology of Reviews*, Lanham and Plymouth: Rowman & Littlefield.
Boase-Beier, J. (2004), 'Saying What Someone else Meant: Style, Relevance and Translation', *International Journal of Applied Linguistics*, 14 (2): 276–87.
Boase-Beier, J. (2006), 'Loosening the Grip of the Text: Theory as an Aid to Creativity', in E. Loffredo and M. Perteghella (eds), *Translation and Creativity*, 47–56, London and New York: Continuum.
Boase-Beier, J. (2010), 'Who Needs Theory?' in A. Fawcett, K. Guadarrama García and R. Hyde Parker (eds), *Translation: Theory and Practice in Dialogue*, 25–38, London and New York: Continuum.
Boase-Beier, J. (2011), *A Critical Introduction to Translation Studies*, London and New York: Continuum.

Boase-Beier, J. (2015), *Translating the Poetry of the Holocaust*, London and New York: Bloomsbury.
Boase-Beier, J. (2020), *Translation and Style*, 2nd edn, Oxon and New York: Routledge.
Boase-Beier, J. and M. Holman (1998), *The Practices of Literary Translation: Constraints and Creativity*, Manchester: St Jerome.
Bolt, R. (1994), 'Translating Molière', *In Other Words*, (3): 17–22.
Bolt, R. (2010), *The Art of Translation*, London: Oberon.
Bolton, J. (2008), 'Introduction', in S. Stephens, *Harper Regan*, 3–24, London: Methuen Drama.
Bolton, J. (2013), 'Simon Stephens', in D. Rebellato (ed.), *Modern British Playwriting 2000–2009*, 101–24, London: Bloomsbury Methuen Drama.
Bolton, J. (2014), 'Introduction', in S. Stephens, *Blindsided*, i–x, London: Bloomsbury Methuen Drama.
Bourdieu, P. (1984), *Distinction: A Social Critique on the Judgement of Taste*, trans. R. Nice, London: Routledge.
Bradley, J. (2011), 'Not Lost in Translation', in R. Baines, C. Marinetti and M. Perteghella (eds), *Staging and Performing Translation: Text and Theatre Practice*, 187–99, Basingstoke: Palgrave Macmillan.
Brecht, B. ([1955] 1963), *Leben des Galilei*, Berlin: Suhrkamp.
Brecht, B. (1964), *Brecht on Theatre: The Development of an Aesthetic*, trans. and ed. J. Willett, London: Methuen.
Brecht, B. (1993), *Journals 1934–1955*, London: Methuen.
Brecht, B. ([1980] 1995), 'Life of Galileo', in *Collected Plays: Five*, trans. J. Willett, 1–106, London: Methuen.
Brodie, G. (2012), 'Theatrical Translation for Performance: Conflict of Interests, Conflict of Cultures', in R. Wilson and B. Maher (eds), *Words, Images and Performances in Translation*, 63–81, London and New York: Continuum.
Brodie, G. (2018), *The Translator on Stage*, London and New York: Bloomsbury
Brown, I. (2009), 'Roger McGough – That Awkward Age Review'. Available online: http://www.edinburghguide.com/festival/2009/edinburghfringe/rogermcgoughthatawkwardage-4155 (accessed 12 July 2015).
Brustein, R. (1962), *The Theatre of Revolt*, New York: Little.
Bull, J. (2018), 'Add-Aptation: Simon Stephens, Carrie Cracknell and Katie Mitchell's "Dialogues" with the Classic Cannon', *Journal of Contemporary Drama in English*, 6 (2): 280–99.
Buss, D. (2016), *Evolutionary Psychology: The New Science of the Mind*, 5th edn, Oxon and New York: Routledge.
Cameron Mackintosh Overseas (2017), 'Les Misérables: Facts and Figures'. Available online: https://www.lesmis.com/uk/history/facts-and-figures/ (accessed 20 April 2017).
Campbell, P., ed. (1996), *Analysing Performance: Issues and Interpretations*, Manchester and New York: Manchester University Press.
Caramazza, A. (1997), 'How Many Levels of Processing Are there in Lexical Access?', *Cognitive Neuropsychology*, 14 (1): 177–208.
Carston, R. (2002a), *Thoughts and Utterances: The Pragmatics of Explicit Communication*, Oxford: Blackwell.
Carston, R. (2002b), 'Linguistic Meaning, Communicated Meaning and Cognitive Pragmatics', *Mind and Language: Special Issue on Pragmatics and Cognitive Science*, 17 (1): 127–48.
Cashmore, E. (2006), *Celebrity Culture*, Oxon and New York: Routledge.

Cavendish, D. (2012), 'A Doll's House, Young Vic, Review', *The Telegraph*, 10 July 2012. Available online: http://www.telegraph.co.uk/culture/theatre/theatre-reviews/9390146/A-Dolls-House-Young-Vic-review.html (accessed 22 January 2017).

Clapp, S. (2013), 'Port – Review', *The Guardian*, 3 February 2013. Available online: https://www.theguardian.com/stage/2013/feb/03/port-lyttelton-simon-stephens-review (accessed 18 September 2016).

Clark, B. (2013), *Relevance Theory*, Cambridge: Cambridge University Press.

Clarke, A. (2011), 'A Laugh-Filled Evening with Tartuffe', *East Anglian Daily Times*, 26 October 2011. Available online: http://www.eadt.co.uk/what-s on/a_laugh_filled_evening_with_tartuffe_1_1109052 (accessed 26 October 2015).

Coelsch-Foisner, S. and H. Klein, eds (2004), *Drama Translation and Theatre Practice*, Frankfurt: Peter Lang.

Cole, T. (2012), 'Simon Cowell's Cookery Programme "Is Not a Show for Snobs"', *Radio Times*, 21 June 2012. Available online: http://www.radiotimes.com/news/2012-06-21/simon-cowells-cookery-programme-is-not-a-show-for-snobs (accessed 23 August 2014).

Cracknell, C. (2012), 'Nora, Now: A Doll's House Film for the Modern World', *The Guardian*, 17 October 2012. Available online: https://www.theguardian.com/stage/2012/oct/17/nora-dolls-house-film-modern-world (accessed 18 September 2016).

Dalley, J. and S. Hemming (2012), 'Interview with Playwright Simon Stephens'. Available online: http://podcast.ft.com/2012/06/22/interview-with-playwright-simon-stephens (accessed 17 September 2016).

Damasio, A. (1989), 'Concepts in the Brain', *Mind and Language*, 4 (1–2): 24–8.

Davies, W. (2017), 'How Statistics Lost their Power – and Why We Should Fear What Comes Next', *The Guardian*, 19 January 2017. Available online: https://www.theguardian.com/politics/2017/jan/19/crisis-of-statistics-big-data-democracy (accessed 20 April 2017).

Davis, E. (2017), *Post-Truth*, London: Little, Brown.

Dawkins, R. (2016), *The Selfish Gene, 40th Anniversary Edition*, Oxford: Oxford University Press.

De Botton, A. (2014), 'Don't Despise Celebrity Culture – The Impulse to Admire can be Precious', *The Guardian*, 31 January 2014. Available online: http://www.theguardian.com/commentisfree/2014/jan/31/dont-despise-celebrity-culture-angelina-jolie (accessed 13 February 2014).

Dodd, P. (2013), 'Mark Ravenhill Talks about Translating Bertolt Brecht's Play *A Life of Galileo*'. Available online: http://www.bbc.co.uk/programmes/p0151jgs (accessed 9 August 2014).

Dolan, J. (1988), *The Feminist Spectator as Critic*, Ann Arbor, MI: UMI Research Press.

Dolan, J. (2005), *Utopia in Performance: Finding Hope at the Theater*, Ann Arbor: Michigan University Press.

Dolan, T. (1999), *A Dictionary of Hiberno-English*, Dublin: Gill and Macmillan.

Dowden, N. (2013), 'Responding to Voltaire', Plays International 28. Available online: http://www.playsinternational.org.uk/page5.html (accessed 18 August 2014).

Durbach, E. (1994), 'A Century of Ibsen Criticism', in J. McFarlane (ed.), *The Cambridge Companion to Ibsen*, 233–51, Cambridge: Cambridge University Press.

Eagleton, T. (1990), *The Ideology of the Aesthetic*, Oxford: Blackwell.

Edemariam, A. (2018), 'The Next Elena Ferrante? The Best European Fiction Coming Your Way', *The Guardian*, 19 May 2018. Available online: https://www.theguardian.c

om/books/2018/may/19/the-next-elena-ferrante-the-best-european-fiction-coming-yo ur-way (accessed 4 September 2018).

Elam, K. (2002), *The Semiotics of Theatre and Drama*, 2nd edn, London and New York: Routledge.

English Touring Theatre (2011), 'Tartuffe, Roger McGough after Molière, Dates and Tickets'. Available online: http://www.ett.org.uk/archive/tartuffe/dates-tickets (accessed 29 December 2015).

Espasa, E. (2000), 'Performability in Translation: Speakability? Playability? Or Just Saleability?' in C. Upton (ed.), *Moving Target: Theatre Translation and Cultural Relocation*, 49–62, Manchester: St Jerome.

Evans, S. (2008), 'Tartuffe – June 2008'. Available online: http://ilovetheatre.me/2008/06 /13/tartuffe-june-2008 (accessed 26 October 2015).

Evans, V. (2011), 'Language and Cognition: The View from Cognitive Linguistics', in V. Cook and B. Bassetti (eds), *Language and Bilingual Cognition*, 69–108, London: Taylor and Francis.

Even-Zohar, I. (2004), 'The Position of Translated Literature Within the Literary Polysystem', in L. Venuti (ed.), *The Translation Studies Reader*, 2nd edn, 199–204, Oxon and New York: Routledge.

Ewbank, I. (1979), 'Ibsen and the Language of Women', in M. Jacobus (ed.), *Women Writing and Writing about Women*, 114–32, London: Croon Helm.

Ewbank, I. (1988), 'Henrik Ibsen: National Language and International Drama', in B. Hemmer and V. Ystad (eds), *Contemporary Approaches to Ibsen Vol. VI*, 57–67, Oslo: Norwegian University Press.

Ewbank, I. (1998), 'Translating Ibsen for the English Stage', *Tijdschrift voor Skandinavistiek*, 19 (1): 51–74.

Fauconnier, G. and M. Turner (2002), *The Way We Think: Conceptual Blending and the Mind's Hidden Complexities*, New York: Basic Books.

Fauskanger, K. (2013), '"Lerkefugelen" tillbaka på DNS', *Bergens Tidende*, 12 January 2013. Available online: http://www.bt.no/kultur/Lerkefuglen-tilbake-pa-DNS-2825171.html (accessed 5 September 2016).

Feay, S. (2014), 'Roger McGough: The Poet on 1960s Liverpool, Radio 4 and Improving with Age', *The Independent*, 29 November 2014. Available online: http://www.inde pendent.co.uk/arts-entertainment/books/features/roger-mcgough-the-poet-on-1960s- liverpool-radio-4-and-improving-with-age-9890997.html (accessed 12 July 2015).

Finney, G. (1989), *Women in Modern Drama: Freud, Feminism and European Theater at the Turn of the Century*, Ithaca, NY and London: Cornell University Press.

Finney, G. (1994), 'Ibsen and Feminism', in J. McFarlane (ed.), *The Cambridge Companion to Ibsen*, 89–105, Cambridge: Cambridge University Press.

Fish, S. (1980), *Is There a Text in This Class? The Authority of Interpretive Communities*, Cambridge, MA: Harvard University Press.

Flood, A. (2019), 'Translated Fiction Enjoys Sales Boom as UK Readers Flock to European Authors', *The Guardian*, 6 March 2019. Available online: https://www.theguardian.com/ books/2019/mar/06/translated-fiction-enjoys-sales-boom-as-uk-readers-flock-to-euro pean-authors (accessed 5 June 2019).

Foreign Affairs (2017), 'The Company – Who We Are and Our Work'. Available online: http://www.foreignaffairs.org.uk/about (accessed 14 April 2017).

Foucault, M. (1977), 'What Is an Author?' trans. D. Bouchard and S. Simon, in D. Bouchard (ed.), *Language, Counter-Memory, Practice*, 124–7, Ithaca: Cornell University Press.

Freshwater, H. (2009), *Theatre and Audience*, London: Palgrave Macmillan.
Furlong, A. (2007), 'A Modest Proposal: Linguistics and Literary Studies', *Canadian Journal of Applied Linguistics*, 10 (3): 325–47.
Furlong, A. (2008), 'You Can't Put Your Foot in the Same River Once: Relevance Stylistics and Rereading', in G. Watson (ed.), *The State of Stylistics: PALA Papers*, 283–302, Amsterdam and New York: Rodopi.
Furniss, T. and M. Bath (2007), *Reading Poetry: An Introduction*, 2nd edn, Harlow: Pearson.
Gardner, L. (2014), 'Blindsided – Review', *The Guardian*, 31 January 2014. Available online: https://www.theguardian.com/stage/2014/jan/31/blindsided-review?CMP=Share_iOSApp_Other (accessed 18 September 2016).
Garton, J. (1994), 'The Middle Plays', in J. McFarlane (ed.), *The Cambridge Companion to Ibsen*, 106–25, Cambridge: Cambridge University Press.
Garton, J. (2004), 'Translating Ibsen: From Page to Page – to Stage', in S. Coelsch-Foisner and H. Klein (eds), *Drama Translation and Theatre Practice*, 89–98, Frankfurt: Peter Lang.
Garton, J. (2014), 'A New Ibsen for Penguin Classics', in B. J. Epstein (ed.), *True North: Translation in the Nordic Countries*, 168–80, Newcastle: Cambridge Scholars.
Gaston Hall, H. (1960), *Molière: Tartuffe*, London: Edward Arnold.
Gauntlett, D. (2007), *Creative Explorations: New Approaches to Identities and Audiences*, Oxon and New York: Routledge.
Gearing, D. (2005), *A Life of Galileo*, unpublished literal translation.
Gearing, D. (2014), 'Deborah Gearing: Playwright'. Available online: http://deborahgearing-playwright.moonfruit.com (accessed 9 February 2014).
Gebauer, G. and C. Wulf (1995), *Mimesis*, trans. D. Renau, Berkeley and Los Angeles, CA: University of California Press.
Geeraerts, D. and H. Cuyckens, eds (2010), *The Oxford Handbook of Cognitive Linguistics*, Oxford: Oxford University Press.
Genette, G. (1997), *Paratexts: Thresholds of interpretation*, trans. J. E. Lewin, Cambridge: Cambridge University Press.
Godin, S. (2011), *Linchpin: Are You Indispensable?* New York: Penguin.
Gonzalez-Marquez, M., I. Mittelberg, S. Coulson and M. Spivey, eds (2007), *Methods in Cognitive Linguistics*, Amsterdam: John Benjamin.
Gregory, W. (2009), 'Claim the Limelight: Theatre Translators, Take Centre Stage!', *The Linguist*, 48 (5): 8–9.
Griggs, Y. (2016), *The Bloomsbury Introduction to Adaptation Studies*, London and New York: Bloomsbury.
Guest, D. (2011), 'Review: Tartuffe', *West Sussex County Times*, 19 October 2011. Available online: http://www.wscountytimes.co.uk/what-s-on/entertainments/review-tartuffe-theatre-royal-brighton-until-saturday-october-22-1-3164751 (accessed 26 October 2015).
Gutt, E. (2000), *Translation and Relevance: Cognition and Context*, Manchester: St Jerome.
Hadley, J. and M. Akashi (2015), 'Translation and Celebrity: The Translation Strategies of Haruki Murakami and their Implications for the Visibility Paradigm', *Perspectives: Studies in Translation Theories and Practice*, 23 (3): 458–74.
Hampe, B., ed. (2005), *From Perception to Meaning: Image Schemas in Cognitive Linguistics*, Berlin: Walter de Gruyter.
Hampton, C. (2011), 'Interview with Christopher Hampton', in R. Baines, C. Marinetti and M. Perteghella (eds), *Staging and Performing Translation: Text and Theatre Practice*, 173–86, Basingstoke: Palgrave Macmillan.

Hare, D. (2016), 'How I Learned to Love Adaptation', *The Guardian*, 23 January 2016. Available online: https://www.theguardian.com/stage/2016/jan/23/david-hare-adaptations-the-master-builder-chekhov-old-vic (accessed 3 September 2016).
Haydon, A. (2014), 'European Theatre Is Still Foreign to Us', *The Guardian*, 14 May 2014. Available online: https://www.theguardian.com/stage/theatreblog/2014/may/14/uk-theatre-european-plays-in-translation (accessed 15 April 2017).
Hayman, R. (1983), *Brecht: A Biography*, London: Weidenfeld and Nicolson.
Head, D., ed. (2006), *The Cambridge Guide to Literature in English*, Cambridge: Cambridge University Press.
Heaney, S. (1999), *Beowulf*, London: Faber and Faber.
Heim, C. (2016), *Audience as Performer*, Oxon and New York: Routledge.
Heltai, P. (2008), 'The Performance of Relevance Theory in Translation Studies', in E. Walaszewska, M. Kisielewska-Krysiuk, A. Korzeniowska and M. Grzegorzewska (eds), *Relevant Worlds: Current Perspectives on Language, Translation and Relevance Theory*, 156–70, Newcastle: Cambridge Scholars.
Hemmer, B. (1994), 'Ibsen and the Realistic Problem Drama', in J. McFarlane (ed.), *The Cambridge Companion to Ibsen*, 68–88, Cambridge: Cambridge University Press.
Hermans, T. (1996), 'The Translator's Voice in Translated Narrative', *Target*, 8 (1): 23–48.
Hermans, T. (2007), *The Conference of the Tongues*, Manchester: St Jerome.
Hickling, A. (2010), 'The Cherry Orchard – Review', *The Guardian*, 22 October 2010. Available online: http://www.theguardian.com/culture/2010/oct/22/the-cherry-orchard-review (accessed 25 October 2014).
Hodgson, B. (2011), '17th-Century French Comedy Proves a Hit for Roger McGough', *The Journal*, 27 September 2011. Available online: http://www.thejournal.co.uk/culture/arts/17th-century-french-comedy-proves-hit-4424280 (accessed 26 October 2015).
Home Office (2015), 'Controlling or Coercive Behaviour in an Intimate or Family Relationship: Statutory Guidance Framework'. Available online: https://www.gov.uk/government/uploads/system/uploads/attachment_data/file/ 482528/Controlling_or_coercive_behaviour_-_statutory_guidance.pdf (accessed 19 October 2016).
Hutcheon, L. (2006), *A Theory of Adaptation*, Oxon and New York: Routledge.
Hutcheon, L. with S. O'Flynn (2013), *A Theory of Adaptation*, 2nd edn, Oxon and New York: Routledge.
Hutton, D. (2014), 'Interview: Mark Ravenhill'. Available online: http://dan-hutton.co.uk/2014/07/31/interview-mark-ravenhill (accessed 9 August 2014).
Ibsen, H. ([1879] 2013), *Et dukkehjem*, Milton Keynes: JiaHu.
Innes, C. (2011), 'Simon Stephens', in M. Middeke, P. Schnierer and A. Sierz (eds), *The Methuen Drama Guide to Contemporary British Playwrights*, 445–64, London: Methuen Drama.
Jakobson, R. (1960), 'Closing Statement: Linguistics and Poetics', in T. Sebeok (ed.), *Style in Language*, 350–77, Cambridge, MA: MIT Press.
Jakobson, R. (1968), 'Poetry of Grammar and Grammar of Poetry', *Lingua* 21: 597–609.
Johnson, A. (2014), 'Henrick [sic] Ibsen's "A Doll's House" to be performed at Cornerstone in Didcot', *The Oxford Times*, 2 October 2014. Available online: http://www.oxfordtimes.co.uk/news/11510264.Ibsen_at_his_best_in__A_Doll_s_House (accessed 21 January 2017).
Johnston, D., ed. (1996), *Stages of Translation*, Bath: Absolute Classics.
Johnston, D. (2013), 'Professing Translation: The Acts-in-Between', *Target*, 25 (3): 365–84.

Jones, C. (2008), 'Tartuffe, Liverpool Playhouse', *Liverpool Echo*, 15 May 2008. Available online: http://www.liverpoolecho.co.uk/whats-on/film-tv/tartuffe-liverpool-playhouse-3486182 (accessed 26 October 2015).

Jones, C. (2011), 'Review: Tartuffe at the Liverpool Playhouse', *Liverpool Echo*, 14 September 2011. Available online: http://www.liverpoolecho.co.uk/news/liverpool-news/review-tartuffe-liverpool-playhouse-3365156 (accessed 26 October 2015).

Jones, F. (2011), *Poetry Translating as Expert Action*, Amsterdam and Philadelphia: John Benjamin.

Kahneman, D. (2011), *Thinking, Fast and Slow*, London: Penguin.

Keenan, M. (2013), *Child Sexual Abuse and the Catholic Church: Gender, Power and Organizational Culture*, Oxon and New York: Oxford University Press.

Kiebuzinska, C. (2001), *Intertextual Loops in Modern Drama*, Cranbury, NJ and London: Associated University Presses.

King's College London (2014), 'Translation Plays'. Available online: https://www.kcl.ac.uk/Cultural/-/Projects/Translation-Plays.aspx (accessed 20 April 2017).

Kjørup, F. (2008), 'Grammetrics and Cognitive Semantics: Metaphorical and Force Dynamic Aspects of Verse-Syntax Counterpoint', *Cognitive Semiotics* 2: 83–101.

Knapp, S. and W. Michaels (1985), 'Against Theory', in W. Thomas Mitchell (ed.), *Against Theory: Literary Studies and the New Pragmatism*, 11–30, Chicago and London: University of Chicago Press.

Kotler, P. and K. Keller (2016), *Marketing Management*, 15th edn, Harlow: Pearson.

Krebs, K. (2012), 'Translation and Adaptation – Two Sides of an Ideological Coin?' in L. Raw (ed.), *Translation, Adaptation and Transformation*, 42–53, London: Continuum.

Krebs, K., ed. (2014), *Translation and Adaptation in Theatre and Film*, Oxon and New York: Routledge.

Laera, M., ed. (2014), *Theatre and Adaptation: Return, Rewrite, Repeat*, London: Bloomsbury Methuen Drama.

Lane, D. (2010), *Contemporary British Drama*, Edinburgh: Edinburgh University Press.

Lawson, M. (2006), 'Alienation Effect', *The Guardian*, 14 July 2006. Available online: http://www.theguardian.com/commentisfree/2006/jul/14/arts.theatre (accessed 9 February 2014).

Lawson, M. (2014), 'The Master Linguist: The Problem with Translating Ibsen', *The Guardian*, 29 October 2014. Available online: https://www.theguardian.com/stage/2014/oct/29/the-master-linguist-the-problem-with-translating-ibsen (accessed 15 April 2017).

Leech, G. (1969), *A Linguistic Guide to English Poetry*, London: Longman.

Leech, G. (1983), *Principles of Pragmatics*, London: Longman.

Lefevere, A. (1992), *Translation, Rewriting, and the Manipulation of Literary Fame*, London and New York: Routledge.

Lefeverre, A. (2004), 'Mother Courage's Cucumbers: Text, System and Refraction in a Theory of Literature', in L. Venuti (ed.), *The Translation Studies Reader*, 2nd edn, 239–55, Oxon and New York: Routledge.

Leonardi, V., ed. (2007), *Gender and Ideology in Translation: Do Men and Women Translate Differently? A Contrastive Analysis from Italian into English*, Bern: Peter Lang.

Levelt, W., A. Roelofs and A. Meyer (1999), 'A Theory of Lexical Access in Speech Production', *Behavioral and Brain Sciences*, 22 (1): 1–75.

Logan, B. (2003), 'Whose Play Is It Anyway?', *The Guardian*, 12 March 2003. Available online: https://www.theguardian.com/stage/2003/mar/12/theatre.artsfeatures (accessed 15 April 2017).

Long, N. (2001), *Development Sociology: Actor Perspectives*, Oxon and New York: Routledge.
Luft, J. and H. Ingham (1963), 'The Johari Window, A Graphic Model of Awareness in Interpersonal Relations', in J. Luft (ed.), *An Introduction to Group Dynamics*, 10–12, Palo Alto: National Press.
MacKenzie, I. (2002), *Paradigms of Reading*, Basingstoke: Palgrave.
Malmkjær, K. (1992), 'Review – Translation and Relevance: Cognition and Context', *Mind and Language*, 7 (3): 298–309.
Marinetti, C. (2013a), 'Transnational, Multilingual and Post-Dramatic: Rethinking the Location of Translation in Contemporary Theatre', in S. Bigliazzi, P. Kofler and P. Ambrosi (eds), *Theatre Translation in Performance*, 27–37, Oxon and New York: Routledge.
Marinetti, C., ed. (2013b), 'Translation in the Theatre', *Target*, 25 (3): 307–20.
Marinetti, C. and M. Rose (2013), 'Process, Practice and Landscapes of Reception: An Ethnographic Study of Theatre Translation', *Translation Studies*, 6 (2): 166–82.
Marshall, P. D. (1997), *Celebrity and Power: Fame in Contemporary Culture*, Minneapolis: University of Minnesota Press.
Marshall, P. D. (2014), 'Persona Studies: Mapping the Proliferation of the Public Self', *Journalism* 15 (2): 153–70.
Mateo Martinez, J. (1998), 'Be Relevant (Relevance, Translation and Cross-Culture)', *Revista alcantina de estudios ingleses* (11): 171–82.
Mateo Martinez, J. (2009), 'Contrasting Relevance in Poetry Translation', *Perspectives: Studies in Translation Theory and Practice* 17 (1): 1–14.
McConachie, B. (2008), *Engaging Audiences: A Cognitive Approach to Spectating in the Theatre*, New York: Palgrave Macmillan.
McCullough, C. (1992), 'From Brecht to Brechtian: Estrangement and Appropriation', in G. Holderness (ed.), *The Politics of Theatre and Drama*, 120–33, London: Palgrave Macmillan.
McFarlane, J. (1961), 'A Doll's House: Commentary', in J. McFarlane (ed.), *The Oxford Ibsen Vol. 5*, 435–64, Oxford: Oxford University Press.
McFarlane, J. (1989), *Ibsen and Meaning: Studies, Essays and Prefaces 1953-87*, Norwich: Norvic Press.
McFarlane, J., ed. (1994), *The Cambridge Companion to Ibsen*, Cambridge: Cambridge University Press.
McGough, R. (2004), *Collected Poems*, London: Penguin.
McGough, R. (2008), *Tartuffe*, London: Methuen Drama.
McGough, R. (2012), 'Roger McGough: This Much I Know', *The Guardian*, 4 November 2012. Available online: http://www.theguardian.com/lifeandstyle/2012/nov/04/roger-mcgough-poet-this-much-i-know (accessed 9 August 2015).
McGough, R. (2013), 'How I brought Molière to the Mersey', *The Guardian*, 5 February 2013. Available online: https://www.theguardian.com/stage/2013/feb/05/roger-mcgough-moliere-mersey (accessed 27 April 2017).
McIntyre, D. (2006), *Point of View in Plays: A Cognitive Stylistic Approach to Viewpoint in Drama and Other Text-Types*, Amsterdam and Philadelphia: John Benjamin.
Meyer, M. (1967), *Ibsen: A Biography*, London: Rupert Hart-Davis.
Meyer, M. (1985), *A Doll's House*, London: Methuen.
Minsky, M. (1977), 'Frame System Theory', in P. Johnson-Laird and P. Wason (eds), *Thinking: Readings in Cognitive Science*, 355–76, Cambridge: Cambridge University Press.
Moi, T. (2006), *Henrik Ibsen and the Birth of Modernism*, Oxford: Oxford University Press.
Molière ([1669] 2003), *Le Tartuffe*, Paris: Bordas.

National Theatre (2014), 'Platform Papers: On Translation'. Available online: http://www.nationaltheatre.org.uk/discover-more/platforms/platform-papers/on-translation (accessed 21 October 2014).

Needham, A. (2012), 'Theatres Take Fewer Risks as Funding Dries Up, Warn Playwrights', *The Guardian*, 19 February 2012. Available online: https://www.theguardian.com/stage/2012/feb/19/theatre-risks-playwrights-hare-ravenhill (accessed 19 April 2017).

Needle, J. and P. Thomson (1981), Brecht, Oxford: Blackwell.

Newmark, P. (1988), *A Textbook of Translation*, London: Prentice Hall Longman.

Nida, E. (1964), *Toward a Science of Translating*, Leiden: E. J. Brill.

Ogilvy, D. (2007), *Ogilvy on Advertising*, London: Prion.

O'Neill, C. (2016), *Weapons of Math Destruction*, London: Penguin.

O'Reilly, E. (2008), 'Roger McGough'. Available online: http://literature.britishcouncil.org/roger-mcgough (accessed 12 July 2015).

O'Thomas, M. (2017), 'Humanum Ex Machina: Translation in the Post-global, Posthuman World', *Target*, 29 (2): 284–300.

Out of the Wings (2019), 'Out of the Wings Festival 2019'. Available online: https://ootwfestival.com (accessed 10 June 2019).

Oxford Dictionaries (2016), 'Oxford Living Dictionaries'. Available online: https://en.oxforddictionaries.com (accessed 16 February 2016).

Patterson, R. (2008), 'Interview: Mark Ravenhill'. Available online: http://www.musicomh.com/extra/theatre/interview-mark-ravenhill (accessed 23 August 2014).

Pavis, P. (1982), *Languages of the Stage: Essays in the Semiology of the Theatre*, New York: Performing Arts Journal Publications.

Pavis, P. (1989), 'Problems of Translation for the Stage: Interculturalism and Postmodern Theatre', in H. Scolnikov and P. Holland (eds), *The Play Out of Context: Transferring Plays from Culture to Culture*, 25–44, Cambridge: Cambridge University Press.

Pavis, P. (1992), *Theatre at the Crossroads of Culture*, trans. L. Kruger, London and New York: Routledge.

Pavis, P. (1993), 'Production and Reception in the Theatre', in J. Hilton (ed.), *New Directions in Theatre*, 25–71, London: Palgrave.

Perteghella, M. (2004a), *A Descriptive Framework for Collaboration in Theatre Translation*, PhD thesis, University of East Anglia, Norwich (unpublished).

Perteghella, M. (2004b), 'A Descriptive-Anthropological Model of Theatre Translation', in S. Coelsch-Foisner and H. Klein (eds), *Drama Translation and Theatre Practice*, 1–22, Frankfurt: Peter Lang.

Perteghella, M. (2008), 'Adaptation: "Bastard Child" or Critique? Putting Terminology Centre Stage', *Journal of Romance Studies*, 8 (3): 51–65.

Perteghella, M. and E. Loffredo, eds (2007), *Translation and Creativity*, London and New York: Continuum.

Peter, J. (2008), 'Review, Tartuffe', *The Sunday Times*, 25 May 2008. Available online (accessed via proprietary database).

Phillips, S. (2006), '"Bovvered" Wins Word of the Year Award', *The Guardian*, 12 October 2006. Available online: https://www.theguardian.com/news/blog/2006/oct/12/bovveredwinswl (accessed 2 May 2019).

Pilkington, A. (1996), 'Introduction: Relevance Theory and Literary Style', *Language and Literature* 5 (3): 157–62.

Pilkington, A. (2000), *Poetic Effects: A Relevance Theory Perspective*, Amsterdam and Philadelphia: John Benjamin.

Prince, G. (1988), *Dictionary of Narratology*, Aldershot: Scholar Press.

Raffel, B. (1988), *The Art of Translating Poetry*, Pennsylvania University Park: Pennsylvania State University Press.

Rappaport, H. (2001), 'Lost in Translation: The Too-Often Unsung Work of the Literal Translator', *The Author* (112): 176–7.

Ravenhill, M. (2001), *Plays: 1*, London: Methuen.

Ravenhill, M. (2005), 'Theatres Must Stop Producing so Many New Plays and Focus More on the Classics', *The Guardian*, 17 October 2005. Available online: http://www.theguardian.com/stage/2005/oct/17/theatre1 (accessed 9 February 2014).

Ravenhill, M. (2006), *The Cut and Product*, London: Methuen.

Ravenhill, M. (2007), 'The Fight over Funding Is About Much More than the Olympics. It's Art v Sport: The Showdown', *The Guardian*, 30 April 2007. Available online: https://www.theguardian.com/politics/2007/apr/30/olympics2012.politicsandthearts (accessed 4 February 2014).

Ravenhill, M. (2008), *Plays: 2*, London: Methuen Drama.

Ravenhill, M. (2009), 'Foreword', in D. Rebellato, *Theatre and Globalization*, ix–xiv, Basingstoke: Palgrave Macmillan.

Ravenhill, M. (2010), 'Let's Cut the Arts Budget', *The Guardian*, 25 July 2012. Available online: http://www.theguardian.com/commentisfree/2010/jul/25/arts-funding-cuts-theatre-galleries (accessed 4 February 2014).

Ravenhill, M. (2013a), *A Life of Galileo*, London: Bloomsbury Methuen Drama.

Ravenhill, M. (2013b), *Plays 3*, London: Bloomsbury Methuen Drama.

Ravenhill, M. (2013c), 'We Need to Have a Plan B', *The Guardian*, 3 August 2013. Available online: http://www.theguardian.com/culture/2013/aug/03/mark-ravenhill-edinburgh-festival-speech-full-text (accessed 4 February 2014).

Raw, L., ed. (2012), *Translation, Adaptation and Transformation*, London: Continuum.

Rebellato, D. (2001), 'Introduction', in M. Ravenhill, *Plays: 1*, ix–xx, London: Methuen.

Rebellato, D. (2005), 'Simon Stephens', *Contemporary Theatre Review* 15 (1): 174–8.

Rebellato, D. (2010), 'Simon Stephens', in D. Kennedy (ed.), *The Oxford Companion to Theatre and Performance*, 574, Oxford: Oxford University Press.

Recanati, F. (2000), 'Does Linguistic Communication Rest on Inference?', *Mind and Language* 17 (1–2): 105–26.

Redmond, S. (2014), *Celebrity and the Media*, Basingstoke: Palgrave Macmillan.

Rees, J. (2012), 'Q & A: Playwright Simon Stephens'. Available online: http://www.theartsdesk.com/theatre/theartsdesk-qa-playwright-simon-stephens?page=0,3 (accessed 17 September 2016).

Reiß, K. and H. Vermeer (1984), *Grundlegung einer allgemeinen Translationstheorie*, Tübingen: Niemeyer.

Research Councils UK (2016), 'Translation, Adaptation, Otherness: "Foreignisation" in Theatre Practice'. Available online: http://gtr.rcuk.ac.uk/projects?ref=AH/N005740/1 (accessed 14 April 2017).

Roelofs, A., A. Meyer and W. Levelt (1998), 'A Case for the Lemma/Lexeme Distinction in Models of Speaking: Comment on Caramazza and Miozzo (1997)', *Cognition* (69): 219–30.

Rojek, C. (2001), *Celebrity*, London: Reaktion.

Rokem, F. (1997), 'Slapping Women: Ibsen's Nora, Strindberg's Julie and Freud's Dora', in L. Hope Lefkovitz (ed.), *Textual Bodies: Changing Boundaries of Literary Representation*, 221–45, New York: State University of New York Press.

Royal Court Theatre (2014), 'International Playwrights' Programme'. Available online: http://www.royalcourttheatre.com/playwriting/international-playwriting/international-play-development (accessed 21 October 2014).

Royal Shakespeare Company (2017), 'Snow in Midsummer'. Available online: https://ww w.rsc.org.uk/snow-in-midsummer/about-the-play (accessed 14 April 2017).

Rustin, S. (2013), 'Why a Doll's House by Henrik Ibsen Is More Relevant than Ever', *The Guardian*, 10 August 2013. Available online: https://www.theguardian.com/stage/2013/ aug/10/dolls-house-henrik-ibsen-relevant (accessed 18 September 2016).

Schank, R. and R. Abelson (1977), 'Scripts, Plans and Knowledge', in P. Johnson-Laird and P. Wason (eds), *Thinking: Readings in Cognitive Science*, 421–32, Cambridge: Cambridge University Press.

Schleiermacher, F. (1977), *Hermeneutics: The Handwritten Manuscripts*, trans. J. Duke and J. Forstman, ed. H. Kimmerle, Missoula: Scholars Press.

Schleiermacher, F. (2004), 'On the Different Methods of Translating', trans. S. Bernofsky, in L. Venuti (ed.), *The Translation Studies Reader*, 2nd edn, 43–63, Oxon and New York: Routledge.

Schmid, H.-J., ed. (2012), *Cognitive Pragmatics*, Berlin and Boston: Walter de Gruyter.

Scott, C. (1986), *A Question of Syllables: Essays in Nineteenth-Century French Verse*, Cambridge: Cambridge University Press.

Scott, C. (1997), 'Translating Rhythm', *Translation and Literature* 6 (1): 31–47.

Scott, C. (2000), *Translating Baudelaire*, Exeter: University of Exeter Press.

Scott, C. (2011), 'Free Verse and the Translation of Rhythm', *Thinking Verse* 1: 67–101.

Scott, V. (2000), *Molière: A Theatrical Life*, Cambridge: Cambridge University Press.

Sembhy, R. (2013), 'The Price Is Right for Waitrose', *Sunday Express*, 26 May 2013. Available online: http://www.express.co.uk/finance/personalfinance/402688/The-price -is-right-for-Waitrose (accessed 23 August 2014).

Short, M. (1989), 'Discourse Analysis and the Analysis of Drama', in R. Carter and P. Simpson (eds), *Language, Discourse and Literature: An Introductory Reader in Discourse*, 137–68, London: Unwin Hyman.

Short, M. (1996), *Exploring the Language of Poems, Plays and Prose*, Harlow: Longman.

Shuttleworth, M. and M. Cowie (2014), *Dictionary of Translation Studies*, Oxon and New York: Routledge.

Sierz, A. (2000), *In-Yer-Face Theatre: British Drama Today*, London: Faber and Faber.

Sierz, A. (2001a), *In-Yer-Face Theatre: British Drama Today*, London: Faber and Faber.

Sierz, A. (2001b), 'Interview with Mark Ravenhill'. Available online: http://www.inyerface theatre.com/archive8.html (accessed 18 August 2014).

Sierz, A. (2008), 'New Writing in Britain: How Do We Define the Contemporary?' Available online: http://theatrefutures.org.uk/sidcup_papers/2008/12/17/new-writing -in-britain-how-do-we-define-the-contemporary (accessed 18 August 2014).

Singh, A. (2015), 'Mark Haddon – Don't Use Curious Incident… as an Autism "Textbook"', *The Telegraph*, 8 June 2015. Available online: http://www.telegraph.co.u k/culture/culturenews/9311242/Mark-Haddon-dont-use-Curious-Incident...-as-an-autism-textbook.html (accessed 20 January 2017).

Smidt, K. (2000), *Ibsen Translated*, Oslo: Solum Forlag.

Smith, R. (2011), 'Review: Tartuffe, Richmond Theatre'. Available online: https://lovethe atre21.wordpress.com/2011/10/05/review-tartuffe-richmond-theatre (accessed 26 October 2015).

Snell-Hornby, M. (1984), 'Sprechbare Sprache, Spielbarer Text. Zur Problematik der Bühnenübersetzung', in R. Watts and U. Weidmann (eds), *Modes of Interpretation. Essays Presented to Ernst Leisi on the Occasion of His 65th Birthday*, 101–16, Tübigen: Narr.

Snell-Hornby, M. (2007), 'Theatre and Opera Translation', in P. Kuhiwczak and K. Littau (eds), *A Companion to Translation Studies*, 106–19, Clevedon: Multilingual Matters.

Solska, A. (2012), 'The Relevance-Based Model of Context in Processing Puns', *Research in Language*, 10 (4): 387–404.
Sperber, D. and D. Wilson (1995), *Relevance: Communication and Cognition*, 2nd edn, Oxford: Blackwell.
Squiers, A. (2014), *An Introduction to the Social and Political Philosophy of Bertolt Brecht: Revolution and Aesthetics*, Amsterdam and New York: Rodopi.
Stephens, S. (2005), *Plays: 1*, London: Methuen Drama.
Stephens, S. (2009), *Plays: 2*, London: Methuen Drama.
Stephens, S. (2011), *Plays: 3*, London: Bloomsbury Methuen Drama.
Stephens, S. (2012a), 'Simon Stephens Talks on His New Play Three Kingdoms', *The Standard*, 3 May 2012 Available online: http://www.standard.co.uk/goingout/theatre/interview-simon-stephens-talks-on-his-new-play-three-kingdoms-7707198.html (accessed 17 September 2016).
Stephens, S. (2012b), *A Doll's House*, London: Bloomsbury Methuen Drama.
Stephens, S. (2013a), 'Simon Stephens: Stockport State of Mind', *The Guardian*, 23 January 2013. Available online: https://www.theguardian.com/stage/2013/jan/23/simon-stephens-port (accessed 18 September 2016).
Stephens, S. (2013b), *Port*, London: Bloomsbury Methuen Drama.
Stephens, S. (2014a), *Blindsided*, London: Bloomsbury Methuen Drama.
Stephens, S. (2014b), 'Q & A with Simon Stephens', *The Economist*, 4 April 2014. Available online: http://www.economist.com/blogs/prospero/2014/04/qa-simon-stephens (accessed 17 September 2016).
Stephens, S. (2014c), 'Interview with Andrew Haydon'. Available online: http://postcardsgods.blogspot.co.uk/2014/07/full-text-simon-stephens.html (accessed 30 August 2016).
Stephens, S. (2014d), 'Simon Stephens: Why My Cherry Orchard Is a Failure', *The Guardian*, 16 October 2014. Available online: https://www.theguardian.com/stage/2014/oct/16/the-cherry-orchard-chekhov-simon-stephens-katie-mitchell (accessed 17 September 2016).
Stephens, S. (2015), *Song from Far Away*, London: Bloomsbury Methuen Drama.
Stephens, S. (2016), *A Working Diary*, London: Bloomsbury Methuen Drama.
Stockwell, P. (2002), *Cognitive Poetics: An Introduction*, London: Routledge.
Stockwell, P. (2013), 'The Positioned Reader', *Language and Literature*, 22 (3): 263–77.
Suleiman, S. and I. Crosman, eds (1980), *The Reader in the Text: Essays on Audience and Interpretation*, Princeton: Princeton University Press.
Taylor, P. (2009), 'Writers' Archives: A Sad State of Affairs', *The Independent*, 31 December 2009. Available online: http://www.independent.co.uk/arts-entertainment/books/features/writers-archives-a-sad-estate-of-affairs-1853561.html (accessed 4 April 2015).
Taylor, T. and M. Toolan (1984), 'Recent Trends in Stylistics', *Journal of Literary Semantics*, 13 (1): 57–79.
Templeton, J. (1989), 'The Doll House Backlash: Criticism, Feminism and Ibsen', *PMLA*, 104 (1): 28–40.
Templeton, J. (1997), *Ibsen's Women*, Cambridge: Cambridge University Press.
Thompson, J. (2014), 'Fear and Loathing in Late Capitalism: An Interview with Simon Stephens'. Available online: http://thequietus.com/articles/15091-simon-stephens-birdland-theatre-interview (accessed 17 September 2016).
Time Out (2011), 'Tartuffe', 26 September 2011. Available online: http://www.timeout.com/london/theatre/tartuffe-2 (accessed 26 October 2015).
Törnqvist, E. (1995), *Ibsen: A Doll's House*, Cambridge: Cambridge University Press.

Toury, G. (1980), *In Search of a Theory of Translation*, Tel Aviv: Porter Institute for Poetics and Semiotics.

Toury, G. (1995), *Descriptive Translation Studies and Beyond*, Amsterdam and Philadelphia: John Benjamin.

Toury, G. (2004), 'The Nature and Role of Norms in Translation', in L. Venuti (ed.), *The Translation Studies Reader*, 2nd edn, 205–18, Oxon and New York: Routledge.

Trueman, M. (2013), 'Theatre's Women of Substance', *The Guardian*, 14 November 2013. Available online: https://www.theguardian.com/stage/2013/nov/14/theatre-women-great-stage-roles (accessed 12 January 2017).

Tsur, R. (2008), *Toward a Theory of Cognitive Poetics*, 2nd edn, Eastbourne: Sussex Academic Press.

Tulloch, J. (2005), *Shakespeare and Chekhov in Production and Reception: Theatrical Events and Their Audiences*, Iowa City: University of Iowa Press.

Turner, C. (2006), 'Life of Galileo: Between Contemplation and the Command to Participate', in P. Thomson and G. Sacks (eds), *The Cambridge Companion to Brecht*, 2nd edn, 143–59, Cambridge: Cambridge University Press.

Turner, G. (2013), *Understanding Celebrity*, 2nd edn, London: Sage.

Turner, J. (2014), *Philology: The Forgotten Origins of the Modern Humanities*, Princeton and Oxon: Princeton University Press.

TVTropes (2015), 'Gratuitous Iambic Pentameter'. Available online: http://tvtropes.org/pmwiki/pmwiki.php/Main/GratuitousIambic Pentameter (accessed 29 December 2015).

Tymoczko, M. (2003), 'Ideology and the Position of the Translator: In What Sense Is a Translator "In-Between"?' in M. Calzada Pérez (ed.), *Apropos of Ideology: Translation Studies on Ideology – Ideologies in Translation Studies*, 181–201, Manchester: St Jerome.

Tyson, L. (2015), *Critical Theory Today*, 3rd edn, Oxon and New York: Routledge.

Tyulenev, S. (2013), 'Social Systems and Translation', in Y. Gambier and L. van Doorslaer (eds), *Handbook of Translation Studies*, 160–6, Amsterdam: John Benjamins.

UK Touring Company (2014), 'A Doll's House – Henrik Ibsen'. Available online: http://www.uktouringtheatre.co.uk/a-dolls-house-2014/4583785837 (accessed 21 January 2017).

UNESCO (2001), 'Memory of the World – Henrik Ibsen: A Doll's House'. Available online: http://www.unesco.org/new/en/communication-and-information/flagship-project-activities/memory-of-the-world/register/full-list-of-registered-heritage/registered-heritage-page-4/henrik-ibsen-a-dolls-house (accessed 22 November 2016).

UNESCO (2020), 'Index Translationum'. Available online: http://www.unesco.org/xtrans (accessed 18 February 2020).

University of Warsaw (2017), 'Relevance Theory and Translation'. Available online: http://informatorects.uw.edu.pl/en/courses/view?prz_kod=3301-JS1804 (accessed 29 April 2017).

Unwin, S. (2005), *A Guide to the Plays of Bertolt Brecht*, London: Methuen.

Upton, C., ed. (2000), *Moving Target: Theatre Translation and Cultural Relocation*, Manchester: St Jerome.

Venuti, L. (1998), *The Scandals of Translation*, London and New York: Routledge.

Venuti, L. (2004), 'How to Read a Translation'. Available online: http://wordswithoutborders.org/article/how-to-read-a-translation (accessed 30 March 2016).

Venuti, L. (2008), *The Translator's Invisibility: A History of Translation*, 2nd edn, London and New York: Routledge.

Venuti, L. (2013a), *Translation Changes Everything: Theory and Practice*, London and New York: Routledge.

Venuti, L. (2013b), 'Translating Jacopone da Todi: Archaic Poetries and Modern Audiences', in E. Allen and S. Bernofsky (eds), *In Translation: Translators on their Work and What It Means*, 187–208, New York and Chichester: Columbia University Press.

Verdonk, P. (2002), *Stylistics*, Oxford: Oxford University Press.

Vermeer, H. (1970), 'Generative Transformationsgrammatik, Sprachvergleich und Sprachtypologie', *Zeitschrift für Phonetik*, (23): 385–404.

Vermeer, H. (1978), 'Ein Rahmen für eine allgemeine Translationstheorie', *Lebende Sprachen*, 23 (3): 99–102.

Vermeer, H. (2004), 'Skopos and Commission in Translational Action', in L. Venuti (ed.), *The Translation Studies Reader*, 2nd edn, 227–38, Oxon and New York: Routledge.

Von Flotow, L. (1997), *Translation and Gender: Translation in the 'Era of Feminism'*, Manchester: St Jerome.

Wadsworth, P. (1987), *Molière and the Italian Theatrical Tradition*, Birmingham: Summa Publications.

Wales, K. (2011), *A Dictionary of Stylistics*, 3rd edn, Harlow: Longman.

Walker, L. (2008), 'Tartuffe, Playhouse, Liverpool', *The Independent*, 20 May 2008. Available online: http://www.independent.co.uk/arts-entertainment/theatre-dance/reviews/tartuffe-playhouse-liverpool-830947.html (accessed 10 August 2015).

Wardle, I. (1992), *Theatre Criticism*, London: Faber and Faber.

Wellek, R. (1963), *Concepts of Criticism*, New Haven and London: Yale University Press.

White, J. (1996), *Brecht: 'Leben des Galilei'*, London: Grant and Cutler.

Willett, J. and R. Mannheim (1995), 'Introduction', in B. Brecht, *Brecht Collected Plays: Five*, vi–xxviiii, London: Methuen.

Williams, R. (1977), *Marxism and Literature*, Oxford: Oxford University Press.

Wilson, D. (2014), 'Relevance Theory'. Available online: https://www.ucl.ac.uk/pals/research/linguistics/publications/wpl/14papers/Wilson_UCLWPL_2014.pdf (accessed 18 February 2016).

Wilson, D. and D. Sperber (2002), 'Truthfulness and Relevance', *Mind*, 111 (443): 583–632.

Wilson, D. and D. Sperber (2004), 'Relevance Theory', in L. Horn and G. Ward (eds), *The Handbook of Pragmatics*, 607–32, Oxford: Blackwell.

Wilson, D. and D. Sperber (2012), *Meaning and Relevance*, Cambridge: Cambridge University Press.

Wimsatt, W. and Beardsley M. (1954), 'The Intentional Fallacy', in W. Wimsatt (ed.), *The Verbal Icon: Studies in the Meaning of Poetry*, 3–20, Lexington: University of Kentucky Press.

Wizisla, E. (2009), *Walter Benjamin and Bertolt Brecht: The Story of a Friendship*, New Haven: Yale University Press.

Wolf, A. (2011), 'Inferential Meaning in Drama Translation: The Role of Implicature in the Staging Process of Anoulih's Antigone', in R. Baines, C. Marinetti and M. Perteghella (eds), *Staging and Performing Translation*, 87–104, Basingstoke: Palgrave Macmillan.

Wonfor, S. (2012), 'Interview: Olivier Award-winning playwright Simon Stephens', *The Journal*, 29 October 2012. Available online: http://www.thejournal.co.uk/culture/arts/interview-olivier-award-winning-playwright-simon-4402848 (accessed 17 September 2016).

Wootton, D. (2006), 'David Wootton Asks – Apart from Brecht – Why Has Our Culture Failed to Turn Galileo into a Hero?' Available online: http://www.socialaffairsunit.org.uk/blog/archives/001221.php (accessed 4 April 2015).

Worrall, N. (1994), 'Commentary', in H. Ibsen, *A Doll's House*, xix–xlix, London: Methuen Drama.

Wright, B. (2003), *Roger McGough: The Poetics of Accessibility*, PhD thesis, Anglia Polytechnic University, Cambridge (unpublished).

Wright, C. (2016), *Literary Translation*, Oxon and New York: Routledge.

Wright, C. and M. Freely (2017), '"Translators Are the Jazz Musicians of the Literary World": Translating Pamuk, Literary Translation Networks and the Changing Face of the Profession', *The Translator*, 23 (1): 97–105.

Young, H. (2011), 'Roger McGough Adds His Poetic Sparkle to English Touring Theatre's Tartuffe'. Available online: http://magazine.brighton.co.uk/Theatre-and-Comedy/Coming-Up/Roger-McGough-Adds-His-Poetic-Sparkle-To-English-Touring-Theatres-Tartuffe/30_66_3471 (accessed 26 October 2015).

Young Vic (2012), 'Your Reviews: A Doll's House'. Available online: http://www.youngvic.org/yourreviews/a-dolls-house (accessed 21 January 2017).

YouTube (2011), 'Tartuffe – Gemma and Roger'. Available online: https://www.youtube.com/watch?v=vfXO_invFJ8 (accessed 20 August 2015).

Zatlin, P. (2005), *Theatrical Translation and Film Adaptation: A Practitioner's View*, Clevedon: Multilingual Matters.

Index

Aaltonen, Sirkku   13, 18, 23
   and time-sharing   24
acculturation   17–18
Aczel, Richard   7
adaptation
   adaptations as original texts   26
   adaptation studies   18, 25–7
   as recontextualization   27
   vs. translation   5, 6, 25, 27, 29, 187
ad hoc concept   92, 93, 96
alexandrine   88, 105
alienation effect   28, 70
Allen, Esther   168
anachronism in translation   102–4, 169
Anderman, Gunilla   1, 17, 26, 121, 122
AntConc   167
Archer, William   122, 139
audience as performer   173, 178, 188, 192
audience research
   ethnography   163, 173, 177
   face-to-face research   162–3, 173, 177
   limitations of   162–3, 173, 177
   scholarly approaches   162
   using demographic data   163
   using Twitter posts (tweets)   174–8
Auftrag   15
authorial intent   41

Baines, Roger, Cristina Marinetti and
      Manuela Perteghella   18, 24
Baker, Mona   8, 183
   private, shared and public
      narratives   165, 173
Barrett, Billy   60, 70
Barslund, Charlotte   56, 123–5
Barthes, Roland
   on death of the author   41, 90
   on polyphonic system of
      information   178
Bassnett, Susan   1, 19, 20–2, 25, 179, 186
   and Andre Lefevere   189
   and Peter Bush   187

Bellos, David   45
Bennett, Susan   28, 30, 162, 178, 179
Berman, Antoine   96–7, 131
Bigliazzi, Silvia, Peter Kofler and Paola
      Ambrosi   2, 18, 19
Billington, Michael   139, 149, 175
Birmingham Repertory   55, 56, 59, 164
blogs   164–73
Boase-Beier, Jean   8, 32, 130, 187
   implied author   32
   relevance theory   35, 62–3, 195
   responsibilities of the translator   45, 46
   translation as a conceptual blend   168
   usefulness of theories of
      translation   11
Bodinetz, Gemma   89, 91, 171, 182, 195
Bolt, Ranjit   89, 90, 105–6, 168, 186
Bolton, Jacqueline   126–7, 143, 145,
      148–9, 152–3, 158
brand
   brand capital   186
   definition   184–5
   and voice   184–6
Brecht, Bertolt
   at Birmingham Rep   59
   episches Theater   28
   estate   54, 60–1, 116
   Leben des Galilei
      American version   53–4
      authorial motivations   52–5
      Berlin version   54
      Danish version   52–3
      politics   51, 53, 62
      reception of texts in
         performance   27–9, 52–3, 60,
         127, 130, 170
      religion   53, 54, 62, 67–9, 71–2, 77
      science   53–5, 76–8, 79–83
      textual examples   64, 66–7, 70–1,
         75, 78–9
      translations prior to
         Ravenhill's   55–7, 61

The Threepenny Opera 59
Verfremdungseffekt 28, 70
Brodie, Geraldine 1, 2, 18, 24, 25, 186, 188
Bull, John 126, 138-9, 144, 179, 195

Carston, Robyn 36, 62, 93
Cashmore, Ellis 3
celebrity
    celebrity culture 3, 4, 17, 30, 184-6
    celebrity studies 3, 18
    definition 1, 3-4
celebrity translation. *See also* complementarity; encyclopaedic entries; voice
    and acculturation 18, 23
    and aesthetics 18, 26, 159, 177, 180, 196
    and artistic freedom 5, 116
    and audiences 16, 23, 26, 30, 44, 48, 181-3, 189-93
    celebration of 19, 21, 22, 23, 49, 192-3
    celebrity translator motivations 5, 44, 49 (*see also* McGough, Roger, *Tartuffe*; Ravenhill, Mark, *A Life of Galileo*; Stephens, Simon, *A Doll's House*)
    commissioning 1, 5, 13-16, 20, 21 (*see also* McGough, Roger, *Tartuffe*; Ravenhill, Mark, *A Life of Galileo*; Stephens, Simon, *A Doll's House*)
    definition 3-6
    dynamic between celebrity translator and director 27, 195
    dynamic between source-text playwright and celebrity translator 25-6, 46, 51, 182
    as editing 5
    examples 4, 5, 38-40
    financial considerations 20-1, 24, 26
    and gender 194-5
    genre in its own right 115
    history 1
    ideological implications 6, 22-3, 27, 184-6

    in Japan 4
    as marketing tool 5, 13, 21, 23, 183, 192 (*see also* McGough, Roger, and marketability)
    negative associations 183
    in poetry 5
    power and status 4, 18, 21-2, 47, 116, 183, 186
    and truth 33, 46
Chekhov, Anton 5, 38-9, 56, 126, 195
    The Cherry Orchard 126
    The Seagull 5, 126, 195
Clark, Billy 34, 36, 51, 70
Clifford, Jo 195
Coelsch-Foisner, Sabine and Hoger Klein 18
cognitive context
    definition 93
    external influences on 130, 164, 165, 193
    individual *vs.* collective 32, 37, 130, 161, 163, 179-80
    measurement in practice 161-2
cognitive effects. *See also* relevance theory
    battle for 82
    blend of 40, 69
    breadth of 32, 40, 69, 83, 169, 173, 176, 193
    vs. contextual effects 37
    contrasting 142, 159
    definition 33
    and echoic reception 172
    intensity of 40, 169, 173, 176
    and literary texts 34-5, 36, 48, 63
    order of 64, 128-9
    positive 33-5, 39, 60, 63, 83, 172, 182
    shared 36, 83
    triggers for 96, 99-100, 108, 112-13, 118, 170, 172
cognitive filters 38-40, 75
cognitive linguistics 31, 193
cognitive neuroscience 31, 192-3
cognitive poetics 30, 31-2
cognitive state 1, 43-4, 45-6, 74, 183
collaboration
    between scholars 193
    in theatrical productions 159, 176, 188, 195
    in translation 22, 29

common aesthetic effect
  and relevance theory   37, 130, 180
  in a social mediatised world   179–80
complementarity
  between Ravenhill and Brecht   51, 69, 74, 83–4, 164, 181
  between McGough and Molière   89, 90, 104, 115–16, 181
  between Stephens and Ibsen   127–9, 181
conceptual blending   40, 129. *See also* Boase-Beier, Jean
  three-dimensional   168
conceptual meaning   62, 63
contextual associations
  and communicative intentions   63, 75, 95, 103
  cumulative effect   33, 36, 130–1, 142, 185
  dominance of pre-existing   140, 162–3, 181
  potential for similarities among spectators   32, 36, 48–9, 140, 180
  triggers   31, 40, 60, 128–9, 142, 172, 193
contextual assumptions   2, 32, 46, 48, 86, 97
  about celebrity translators   92–3
  accessibility   95
contextual effects   37–8. *See also* relevance theory
  vs. cognitive effects   37
corpus research   165–73
Cracknell, Carrie   121, 127, 176, 178, 195
Cusk, Rachel   195

Darwin, Charles   158
deconstruction   19
Delgado, Maria   187
Derrida, Jacques   19
domestication   16–18, 24, 29, 72, 114, 132, 187
Duke of York's Theatre   174

Edgar, David   55, 56, 57
encyclopaedic entries
  activation of   95–6, 97–8, 107–8, 113, 167

  and celebrity translation   86, 92–6, 116
  cumulative effect of   100, 172
  definition   92
  vs. logical and lexical entries   92
enjambment   108–9
Enrich Festival   192
episches Theater   28
epitext   152
equivalence
  of emotional response   27, 84
  of meaning   11, 26, 29, 83
Espasa, Eva   22
Evans, Vyvyan   32, 48
Even-Zohar, Itamar   12, 91
Ewbank, Inga-Stina   120, 122, 159
Eyre, Richard, 5
explicatures   36, 42, 62–6
  definition   36, 62
  weak explicatures   63

faithfulness. *See* equivalence
Farrell, Joseph   187
fast and slow thinking   130
Fauconnier, Gilles and Mark Turner   31, 40, 129
fingerprinting   8, 185
Finney, Gail   118, 120, 121, 138
Fish, Stanley   41, 43, 44
Fletcher, Nick   175, 176
Foreign Affairs   184, 190
foreignization   17–18, 23, 24, 29, 187
formalism   31, 33
Fosse, Jon   126, 127
  I Am the Wind   126
  on reception of *A Doll's House* in Norway   138
Frankcom, Sarah   153
Freely, Maureen   184
Freshwater, Helen   191
Friel, Brian   175
Furlong, Anne   35, 129–30
  role of intention in literary texts   42, 43, 45, 48
  spontaneous and non-spontaneous interpretations   130
Furniss, Tom and Michael Bath   105

Gardner, Lyn   145
Garton, Janet   118, 120, 121

gaslighting 149–50
Gaston Hall, Hugh 86, 87, 109, 113
Gauntlett, David 162
Gearing, Deborah 72, 77, 81, 123, 187
  career 55–8
  commission to translate Leben des
    Galilei 54, 55–7, 59
  examples of literal translation of *Leben
    des Galilei* 64, 67, 71, 75, 79
  Rosalind: A Question of Life 56
Gebauer, Gunter and Christoph Wulf 88
gender and celebrity translation 194–5
Genette, Gérard 152
Grice, Paul 33, 35–6
  conversational implicature 35
  and pragmatic interpretation 42, 62
Griggs, Yvonne 91
Gutt, Ernst-August 35, 45, 47, 195

Haddon, Mark 156
Hahn, Daniel 196
Hampton, Christopher 1, 5, 89, 186, 190
Hare, David 5, 55, 61, 186
Head, Dominic 80
Heaney, Seamus 5, 82
Heim, Caroline 173, 178, 188, 192
Hemmer, Bjørn 119
Hermans, Theo 8, 22, 142
hourglass concept 37–8
Hutcheon, Linda 18, 25
Hutton, Dan 59

iambic pentameter 105–6
Ibsen, Henrik
  and characterization 119
  critical acclaim 118, 119
  Et dukkehjem
    authorial motivations 119–23
    critical response 117, 118, 138
    feminism 118, 120, 138
    Nora 119, 121, 128, 131, 138–9,
      146, 148, 153
    patriarchy 148
    plot 117–18
    problem or critical realism 119
    scholarly perspectives 119–21
    sexual tension in 123–4
    socialism 121
    social upheaval 119, 145
    textual examples 133, 135–7, 144,
      147, 151, 154–5
    title 153
    translations and adaptations
      of 117, 119, 120
    truthfulness in 119, 134, 138, 144
    UNESCO recognition 118
    use of extended metaphors 131–2,
      148, 159
    vidunderlig (miraculous) 122,
      131–2
  gengangere (*Ghosts*) 5, 119, 121, 122,
    123, 146, 152
  Hedda Gabler 121, 146, 175
    reception in English-speaking
      world 119, 138
    style (sprogtone) 121–3, 159
    in translation 121, 159
    use of Dano-Norwegian 121, 132,
      148, 153
implicatures. *See also* Grice, Paul
  and communicative intentions 42, 48
  definition 36, 62
  vs. explicatures 62–6
  higher-order implicatures 131
  and literary texts 129–30
  weak implicatures 46, 62, 63, 83–4
    chains of weak implicatures 129–34
implied author 32, 35
implied reader 55, 72
indirect translation. *See* literal translation
inference 34, 64, 92–3. *See also* relevance
  theory, ostensive-inferential
  communication
  inferential equivalence 69
  inferred author 33, 43, 46, 90
  intended *vs.* unintended 132
informed reader 44
intention
  authorial intent 41
  communal interpretation of 41,
    48–9
  intentional fallacy 41, 48
  intentionless meaning 42
  interpretation of communicative
    intention 44, 45, 48–9
  and relevance theory 41–5, 48
intertextual coherence 15
in-yer-face theatre 58, 84, 126

Jakobson, Roman   106
Johari Window   42
Johnston, David   16, 21, 25, 32, 47, 60–1
Jones, Francis   22

Kahneman, Daniel   130
Knapp, Steve and Walter Benn Michaels   42
Krebs, Katja   18, 26
Kretzmer, Herbert   190

Laera, Margherita   18, 184
Lan, David   127
Lane, David   126
language-body   19, 24
Lawson, Mark   61
Leech, Geoffrey   31, 108
Lefevere, André   12. *See also under* Bassnett, Susan
  and refractions   37
literal translation. *See also* voice
  commissioning   13–14, 20 (*see also under* Barslund, Charlotte; Gearing, Deborah)
  as a literary work in its own right   187
  and machine translation   188
  as neutral translation   23
  as part of a two stage translation process   1, 20–1, 24, 187
  rethinking the role of the literary translator   186–9
  status of literal translators   57, 124, 186–7
literary departments   13–15, 17
literary system   12, 13
Liverpool Everyman   88, 89
Liverpool Playhouse   88, 89
Lochhead, Liz   89, 110, 168, 194
Luft, Joseph and Harry Ingham   42

McConachie, Bruce   30, 129, 162, 179, 194
McDiarmid, Ian   9
McFarlane, James   118, 120, 122, 146, 152, 153
McGough, Roger. *See also* Bodinetz, Gemma
  background   88–9, 112
  'The Bee's Knees'   99

career   88–9
familiarity of voice   86, 89, 91, 98–9, 102, 171 (*see also* under McGough, Roger, *Tartuffe*)
'First Day at School'   109
'The Lesson'   109
'Let Me Die a Youngman's Death'   109
Lily the Pink   88
and marketability   89, 91, 182, 192–3
other Molière translations   89
Poetry Please presenter   89, 114, 192–3
'Prayer to Saint Grobianus'   94
Tartuffe
  and allegiance to Molière   89, 90, 104
  anachronism   102–4, 169
  characterization of Dorine   110
  characterization of *Tartuffe*   97–8, 106
  commission to translate   85, 89, 91
  enjambment   108–9
  irony   91, 114–15
  McGough's voice in   94–5, 98–9, 101–4, 107–8, 109–14, 169–73, 181
  motivations for translating   88–92
  neologism   95, 110–11, 170
  performances in UK   165
  puns   100–2, 170, 172
  religious references   97–100
  repeated exoticization   112–15
  and reviews and blogs   165–73
  self-referentiality in   114
  sociolects and idiolects   109–12
  textual examples   93, 98, 101, 103, 106, 108, 110, 112, 113–14, 170
  and underlying network of signification   96–100
  and verse   88, 90, 104–9, 106–8, 169, 171
  on translation   86, 89, 90, 114–15
machine translation   188
McIntyre, Dan   24, 32
MacKenzie, Ian   34, 43, 93, 129–30
Malmkjær, Kirstin   45

Marinetti, Cristina, 1, 2, 12, 18, 24.
    See also Baines, Roger, Cristina
    Marinetti and Manuela
    Perteghella
  and Margaret Rose   173
marketing. *See also* celebrity translation
  audience as marketing tool   173,
    178, 192
  as commodification   183, 191
  of translated theatre   3, 24, 83–4, 180,
    182–4, 189–93
  word-of-mouth   172, 192
Marshall, P. David   3, 4, 18
Marx, Eleanor   119, 121
meaning. *See also* relevance theory;
    visualization of layers of
    interpretation
  authorial *vs.* readerly   23, 25
  conceptual   62, 63
  definitive   48
  fixed   47
  intended *vs.* interpreted   30, 42, 45,
    48, 93
  intentionless meaning   42
  and layers of interpretation   62, 63
  linguistically encoded (literal)   62,
    63, 69
  location of meaning   28, 30, 43, 45,
    47–8
  pragmatic dimension of   92–3
meme   158
Meyer, Michael   118, 119, 120, 121,
    138, 144
mind map   93
Moi, Toril   118, 119–20, 139
Molière
  career as playwright   85
  comedy   87, 88
  controversy   86–7
  L'École des femmes   86
  religion   86–7, 97, 113
  social vulgarity   109–10
  Tartuffe
    authorial motivations   86–8
    Bendinelli affair   87, 103–4
    faux dévot   87
    plot   85
    reception   85, 86
    religion   86–7, 97, 113
    as social comedy   87, 88, 97, 111
  textual examples   97, 100, 101,
    103, 106, 108, 110, 111
  translations   85, 199 n. 5(1)
  writing in verse   88, 105–6
monolingualism in UK   6, 187
Morahan, Hattie   174, 175–7
motivations for celebrity translation   44–5,
    51, 58–62, 88–92
multilevel account of
    communication   191

National Theatre   12, 193
  and translation policy   14
Needle, Jan and Peter Thomson   80
neologism   95, 110–11, 170
Newmark, Peter   44
Nida, Eugene   33, 47
Nordic Noir   190
norms   13–14, 123

Old Vic Theatre   175
O'Neill   194
O'Thomas, Mark   188
Out of the Wings   189

Padilla Cruz, Manuel   196
pantomime   87, 104, 111, 114
Patterson, Richard   73
Pavis, Patrice
  context of production and
    reception   130, 177
  hourglass concept   37–8
  verbo-corps (language body)   19, 24
performability   1, 20–2, 23, 29
performativity   1, 24
persona studies   4
Perteghella, Manuela   1, 18, 27, 186,
    187–8. *See also* Baines, Roger,
    Cristina Marinetti and Manuela
    Perteghella
  and Eugenia Loffredo   187
Pilkington, Adrian   35, 40, 63, 104–5, 107
Piskorska, Agnieszka   196
play texts
  analysis   2, 29–30, 31, 48–9,
    178–80, 185
  vs. stage versions   28–30, 41, 62–3,
    178–80
  translation   1–3, 6, 12, 14–18, 21, 23,
    27, 196

poetic effects
    and audiences   109, 196
    vs. cognitive effects   142
    explanation   36, 130
    intensity of   159
    reward of   107, 159, 185
    in source culture vs. target
        culture   190
Poetry Please   89, 114, 192–3
Poetry translation   5, 22, 29, 105, 191
point of view   7
polysystems   23, 29, 91. *See also* systems
positionality   22, 27
pragmatic dimension of meaning   92–3
Prince, Gerald   7
proposition expressed   62
puns   100–2, 170, 172

Raffel, Burton   22
Ravenhill, Mark
    and adaptation   55, 56–7, 59, 60
    Candide   6, 59, 70
    career as playwright   58, 60
    The Cut   73
    The Experiment   58
    Faust is Dead   58
    gay playwright label   60
    Handbag   58, 80
    A Life of Galileo
        and audience types   163–4
        Brecht estate   54, 60–1
        commission to translate   59
        commodification in market-
            dominated society   73, 80–2
        funding of the arts   76
        motivations for translating   51,
            58–62
        performances in UK   59
        political and social ennui   70–5
        queering up a text   59–60, 69
        Ravenhill's voice in   51–2, 59–60,
            66–83, 181
        religion   67–9
        textual examples   67, 71, 76, 79
        truth in the postmodern
            world   77–8
    on marketing of theatre   191
    The Mother   59
    Mother Clap's Molly House   58, 69–70
    Over There   58
    Product   73
    RSC residency   58, 59
    Shoot/Get Treasure/Repeat   58, 73
    Shopping and Fucking   58, 62, 69,
        77, 80
    Some Explicit Polaroids   58, 77
    Ten Plagues   58
    translations of Ravenhill's plays   62
    Vicious   69
Reader-response theory   8, 43. *See also*
    under translation, theories of
Rebellato, Dan
    on Mark Ravenhill   58, 76, 77
    on Simon Stephens   126, 140, 146
Recanati, François   42
reception
    adaptation   26
    Brecht   27–9
    of celebrity translation   1–4, 14, 19,
        23, 30, 38, 43, 162, 182–3
    of communication   48
    and distinctive voice   82, 109
    epitexts   152
    influence of reviews and blogs   164–73
    refractions   37
    of stimuli   38
    of texts in performance   9, 23–5,
        29–30, 35, 36, 131, 162, 164
        vs. written text   178–80
    and theatre translation studies   23–5,
        26, 29–30
reception theory   19
Redmond, Sean   3, 4
refractions   37
Reiss, Anya   5, 194–5
Reiß, Katharina   14
    and Vermeer   14–15, 44
relevance
    definition   33
    expectations   131
    maximum vs. optimal relevance   34
    principles of relevance   34
    relevance-guided comprehension
        heuristic   34, 60
relevance theory. *See also under* cognitive;
        encyclopaedic entries;
        explicatures; implicatures
    cognitive neuroscience   48–9, 63
    contextual effects   37–8
        vs. cognitive effects   37

contrasting cognitive effects 142
echoic use of language 70, 172
explanation 32–5
group response effect 36–7, 180
intention 35, 41–5, 48, 127
irony 114–15
for literature 34–5
meaning 40, 45–8
ostensive-inferential communication 34, 51, 66
and positive cognitive effects 33, 38, 46, 172
and puns 100–2
and translation 33, 35, 45, 195–6
and truthfulness 33, 42–3, 46
retranslation 12, 14–15, 21, 23, 24
reviews and blogs 164–73
revoicing 15
Reza, Yasmina 6
ripple effect 163
Rojek, Chris 18
Rokem, Freddie 119
Rowan, Dominic 175, 176
Royal Court Theatre 126, 188, 190, 193
and translation policy 13
Royal Exchange Theatre 145
Royal Shakespeare Company 9, 58, 59, 61, 183–4, 187
Rutter, Rowan 189, 191–2, 196

salience balance 47, 83
Schleiermacher, Friedrich 44, 115
Schönberg, Claude-Michel and Alain Boubil
    Les Misérables 190
Scott, Clive 105
    multilevel account of communication 191
Scott, Virginia 86
search engine optimization 166
Sharp, Lesley 143
Short, Mick 7
    character-character level of discourse 132
    fingerprinting 8, 185
Shuttleworth, Mark and Moira Cowie 12
Sierz, Alex 58, 60, 70, 126
signification, underlying network of 96–100, 131
Silbert, Roxanna 195

skopos 14–16, 29
and the literal translator 16, 187
Snell-Hornby, Mary 19
Solska, Agnieszka 100
Sperber, Dan and Deirdre Wilson. *See* relevance; relevance theory
spontaneous *vs.* post-rationalized communication 36, 174
Squiers, Anthony 28
Stephens, Simon
    on authorial voice 178
    Birdland 126
    Blindsided 126, 144–6, 152
    Bluebird 126, 157
    career 125–6
    Carmen Disruption 126
    on character and narrative development 126–7
    The Cherry Orchard 126
    on collaboration in the theatre 188
    Country Music 140, 150
    The Curious Incident of the Dog in the Night-Time 125–6, 156–7
    A Doll's House (*see also* Cracknell, Carrie)
        alcoholism 150–2
        allegiance to Ibsen 127–8
        atomization of society 128
        commission to translate 127
        cues of Englishness 123, 132–3
        emotionally damaged characters 134, 146–52
        motivations for translating 125–9
        Nora 127, 128–9, 132, 134–46, 148–9, 153
        performances in UK 174
        search for home 134, 152–8
        social media responses 174–8
        Stephens's voice in 118, 131, 132, 134, 142, 150, 158–9, 178, 181
        textual examples 133, 135–7, 144, 147, 151, 154–5, 157
        Torvald 146–52
        truthfulness 144
        use of language 148–9, 159
    female characters in other works 129, 134, 139–46
    Harper Regan 140, 142–4, 152, 157
    Herons 140, 150, 157

I Am the Wind   126
Marine Parade   144, 152
Motortown   126, 150, 152
Obsession   126
One Minute   140
On the Shore of the Wide World   125, 144, 149, 150, 152
Pornography   126, 149
Port   140-2, 152
Punk Rock   126, 144, 150, 152
The Seagull   5, 126
Song from Far Away   157
on theatre audiences   197
Three Kingdoms   150
The Threepenny Opera   126
on translation and adaptation   126, 127, 186
translations of Stephens's work   126
Wastwater   150
Stevenage Festival of the Arts   192
Stevens, Sophie   189
Stockwell, Peter   23, 31
Stoppard, Tom   38-40, 59
style. *See also* voice
    authorial style   7, 121-3, 130, 167
    stylistic devices   36, 63, 123, 130
Swan Theatre   193
systems   12-13
systems theory   16

Templeton, Joan   118, 120-1, 138, 139
Text world theory
Thatcherism   128, 145
theatre reviews   164-73
theatre translation studies
    and collaborative translation   23, 29
    cross-disciplinary approach   19, 189
    history   18-25
    and ideology   22-3, 27
    and new types of theatrical experience   193
    and reception   23-5, 26, 29-30
    and relationship between written text and performance   19-20, 24, 29, 193
theatrical system   25, 59, 60, 61, 91
    definition   13
    literal translators in   124, 186, 187
    and translation   24, 27, 29, 47, 181, 183

thematic tropes   130
time-sharing   24
Törnqvist, Egil   118, 131, 132, 139, 153
Toury, Gideon   13-14, 33, 123
translated theatre in the UK
    acculturation   17-18
    audience response   30, 182, 184, 187, 188, 189
    collaboration   187-8
    elitism   189, 193
    ethics   23, 80, 186-7, 194
    ethnocentricity   23, 183, 187, 190
    marketing   3, 24, 83-4, 180, 182-4, 189-93
    repertoire of   12, 16, 190, 196-7
    retranslation   12, 14-15, 21, 23, 24, 196
    taking risks   12-13, 182, 190, 192
    vs. translated fiction and TV in the UK   189-90, 196
    translation practices   1, 13-14, 20-1, 24, 186-9
translation, theories of. *See also* theatre translation studies
    vs. reader-response theories   29
    usefulness   11, 18, 29
Tsur, Reuven   23, 31
Tulloch, John   30, 162, 173
Turner, Cathy   53
Turner, Graeme   3, 18
Twitter posts (tweets)   174-8
two-stage translation   1, 20-1, 24, 187
Tymoczko, Maria   22, 27, 47

UK Touring Theatre   175
underlying network of signification   96-100, 131
Unwin, Stephen   5, 53
Upton, Carole-Anne   18, 186

Venuti, Lawrence. *See also* visibility
    anachronism   102
    domestication and foreignization   16-18
    ethnocentricity   23
    exoticization   112
    first rule for reading translations   168
    illusion of transparency   16

verbo-corps 19, 24
Verdonk, Peter 52
Verfremdungseffekt 28, 70
Vermeer, Hans 14–15, 44
visibility
   of celebrity translators 17–18, 29
   textual *vs.* contextual visibility 33
   of translation 16–17, 24, 185–6, 188
visualization of layers of interpretation 64
voice
   associations with actor's voices 9, 159, 176, 178
   as construct of a text 8
   definitions 6–9, 184–6
   narrative voice 7
   and point of view 7
   and style 7, 46, 168, 184–6
   of literal translator 9, 16, 56–7, 124–5, 178
   revoicing 15
   of spectator 174–8, 179
   translation as blend of voices 185–6
voice of the celebrity translator 8, 15, 23, 26, 36, 171–2, 181
   and comedic devices 104–15, 168, 169–73
   conscious celebrity voice 52, 66–75, 91
   and cumulative associations 8, 48–9, 134, 159
   external influences on inference of 164–73
   fluidity of 102
   and linguistic peculiarities 115–16, 134
   and specific ad hoc concepts 96–104
   unconscious celebrity voice 52, 66, 75–83

Wałaszewska, Ewa
Wales, Katie 7
Walter Presents 189
weak implicatures. *See* implicatures
Wertenbaker, Timberlake 194
White, John 52, 53
Wilbur, Richard 89, 90, 110, 168
Willett, John and Ralph Mannheim 54
Wimsatt, William and Monroe Beardsley 41, 48
Wizisla, Erdmut 53
Wolf, Alain 36
word cloud 167
word of mouth 172, 192
Worrall, Non 120
Wright, Chantal 184, 187

Young Vic 118, 145, 156, 174–7, 193
Yus, Francisco 196

Zatlin, Phyllis 18, 187, 188–9
Zeller, Florian 190

www.ingramcontent.com/pod-product-compliance
Lightning Source LLC
Chambersburg PA
CBHW072150290426
44111CB00012B/2022